Essential Grammar in Use

A self-study reference and practice book for elementary students of English

with answers

THIRD EDITION

Raymond Murphy

CAMBRIDGE UNIVERSITY PRESS
www.cambridge.org

CAMBRIDGE UNIVERSITY PRESS
Cambridge, New York, Melbourne, Madrid, Cape Town,
Singapore, São Paulo, Delhi, Tokyo, Mexico City

Cambridge University Press
The Edinburgh Building, Cambridge CB2 8RU, UK

www.cambridge.org
Information on this title: www.cambridge.org/9780521675802

First published 1990
Second edition 1997
Third edition 2007
13th printing 2012

Printed in the United Kingdom at the University Press, Cambridge

A catalogue record for this publication is available from the British Library

ISBN 978-0-521-67580-2 Edition with answers
ISBN 978-0-521-67581-9 Edition without answers
ISBN 978-0-521-67543-7 Edition with answers and CD-ROM
ISBN 978-0-521-67544-4 CD-ROM for Windows (single user)
ISBN 978-0-521-67545-1 Network CD-ROM (30 users)
ISBN 978-3-12-539538-1 Klett edition with CD-ROM
ISBN 978-3-12-539536-7 Klett Edition

Contents

IF YOU ARE NOT SURE WHICH UNITS TO STUDY, USE THE **STUDY GUIDE** ON PAGE 271

IF YOU ARE NOT SURE WHICH UNITS TO STUDY, USE THE **STUDY GUIDE** ON PAGE 271.

A and the

Determiners and pronouns

Adjectives and adverbs

Word order

Conjunctions and clauses

IF YOU ARE NOT SURE WHICH UNITS TO STUDY, USE THE **STUDY GUIDE** ON PAGE 271.

IF YOU ARE NOT SURE WHICH UNITS TO STUDY, USE THE **STUDY GUIDE** ON PAGE 271.

Thanks

For their help in producing this third edition of Essential Grammar in Use, I would like to thank Liz Driscoll, Jessica Roberts and Alison Sharpe. I would also like to thank the teachers and reviewers from various countries who provided me with feedback on the previous edition.

Illustrations by Kate Charlesworth, Richard Deverell, Gillian Martin, Roger Penwill, Lisa Smith, Ian West and Simon Williams

Design by Kamae Design

To the student (working without a teacher)

This is a grammar book for elementary students of English. There are 115 units in the book and each unit is about a different point of English grammar. There is a list of units at the beginning of the book (*Contents*).

Do not study all the units in order from beginning to end. It is better to choose the units that you *need* to do. For example, if you have a problem with the present perfect (*I have been, he has done* etc.), study Units 15–20.

Use the *Contents* or the *Index* (at the back of the book) to find the unit (or units) that you need.

Contents

Index

If you are not sure which units you need to study, use the *Study guide* at the back of the book.

IF YOU ARE NOT SURE WHICH IS RIGHT	STUDY UNIT
1.14 Please be quiet. ……… **A** I working. **B** I work. **C** I'm working. **D** I'm work.	8, 23
1.15 Tom ……… a shower every morning. **A** has **B** having **C** is having **D** have	8, 58
1.16 What ……… at the weekend? **A** do you usually **B** are you usually doing **C** are you usually do **D** do you usually do **E** you do usually	8, 23
1.17 Sarah isn't feeling well. ……… a headache. **A** She have **B** She have got **C** She has **D** She's got	9, 58
1.18 Tracey and Jeff ……… any children. **A** don't have **B** doesn't have **C** no have **D** haven't got **E** hasn't got	9, 58
Past	
2.1 The weather ……… last week. **A** is good **B** was good **C** were good **D** good **E** had good	10
2.2 Why ……… late this morning? **A** you was B did you **C** was you **D** you were **E** were you	10
2.3 Terry ……… in a bank from 1996 to 2003. **A** work **B** working **C** works **D** worked **E** was work	11
2.4 Caroline ……… to the cinema three times last week. **A** go **B** went **C** goes **D** got **E** was	11
2.5 I ……… television yesterday. **A** didn't watch **B** didn't watched **C** wasn't watched **D** don't watch **E** didn't watching	12, 23
2.6 'How ………?' 'I don't know. I didn't see it.' **A** happened the accident **B** did happen the accident **C** does the accident happen **D** did the accident happen **E** the accident happened	12
2.7 What ……… at 11.30 yesterday? **A** were you doing **B** was you doing **C** you were doing **D** were you do **E** you was doing	13
2.8 Jack was reading a book when the phone ……… . **A** ringing **B** ring **C** rang **D** was ringing **E** was ring	14
2.9 I saw Lucy and Steve this morning. They ……… at the bus stop. **A** waiting **B** waited **C** were waiting **D** was waiting **E** were waited	14
Present perfect	
3.1 'Where's Rebecca?' '……… to bed.' **A** She is gone **B** She has gone **C** She goes **D** She have gone **E** She's gone	15
3.2 'Are Diane and Paul here?' 'No, they ……….' **A** don't arrive yet **B** have already arrived **C** haven't already arrived **D** haven't arrived yet	16

IF YOU ARE NOT SURE WHICH IS RIGHT	STUDY UNIT
3.3 My sister ……… by plane. **A** has never travel **B** has never travelled **C** is never travelled **D** has never been travelled **E** have never travelled	17, 23
3.4 ……… that woman before, but I can't remember where. **A** I see **B** I seen **C** I've saw **D** I've seen **E** I've seeing	17, 23
3.5 'How long ……… married?' 'Since 1998.' **A** you are **B** you have been **C** has you been **D** are you **E** have you been	18
3.6 'Do you know Lisa?' 'Yes, ……… her for a long time.' **A** I knew **B** I've known **C** I know **D** I am knowing	18
3.7 Richard has been in Canada ……… . **A** for six months **B** since six months **C** six months ago **D** in six months	19, 104
3.8 'When did Tom go out?' '………' **A** For ten minutes. **B** Since ten minutes. **C** Ten minutes ago. **D** In ten minutes.	19
3.9 We ……… a holiday last year. **A** don't have **B** haven't had **C** hasn't had **D** didn't have **E** didn't had	20
3.10 Where ……… on Sunday afternoon? I couldn't find you. **A** you were **B** you have been **C** was you **D** have you been **E** were you	20
Passive	
4.1 This house ……… 100 years ago. **A** is built **B** is building **C** was building **D** was built **E** built	21, 23
4.2 We ……… to the party last week. **A** didn't invite **B** didn't invited **C** weren't invited **D** wasn't invited **E** haven't been invited	21, 23
4.3 'Where ……… born?' 'In Cairo.' **A** you are **B** you were **C** was you **D** are you **E** were you	21
4.4 My car is at the garage. It ……… . **A** is being repaired **B** is repairing **C** have been repaired **D** repaired **E** repairs	22
4.5 I can't find my keys. I think ……… . **A** they've been stolen **B** they are stolen **C** they've stolen **D** they're being stolen	22
Verb forms	
5.1 It ………, so we didn't need an umbrella. **A** wasn't rained **B** wasn't rain **C** didn't raining **D** wasn't raining	23
5.2 Somebody ……… this window. **A** has broke **B** has broken **C** has breaked **D** has break	24

Study guide (pages 271–282)

Each unit is two pages. The information is on the left-hand page and the exercises are on the right:

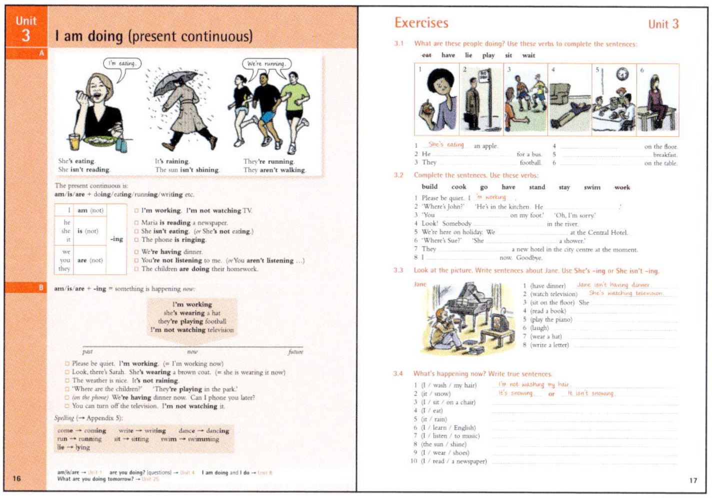

Information

Exercises

Study the left-hand page (information), and then do the exercises on the right-hand page.

Use the Key to check your answers. The Key is on pages 283–309.

Study the left-hand page again if necessary.

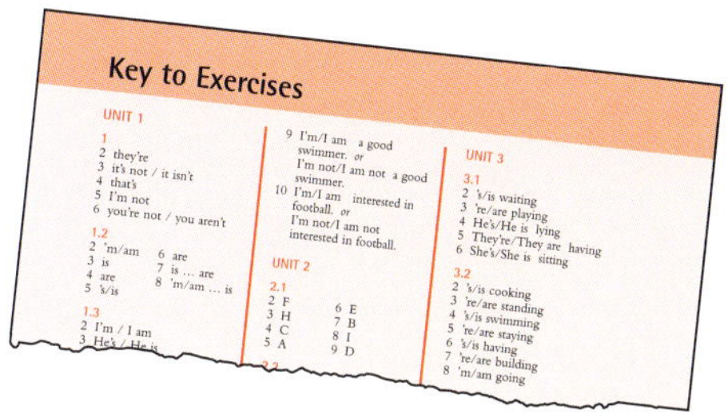

Don't forget the seven *Appendices* at the back of the book (pages 243–251). These will give you information about active and passive forms, irregular verbs, short forms, spelling and phrasal verbs.

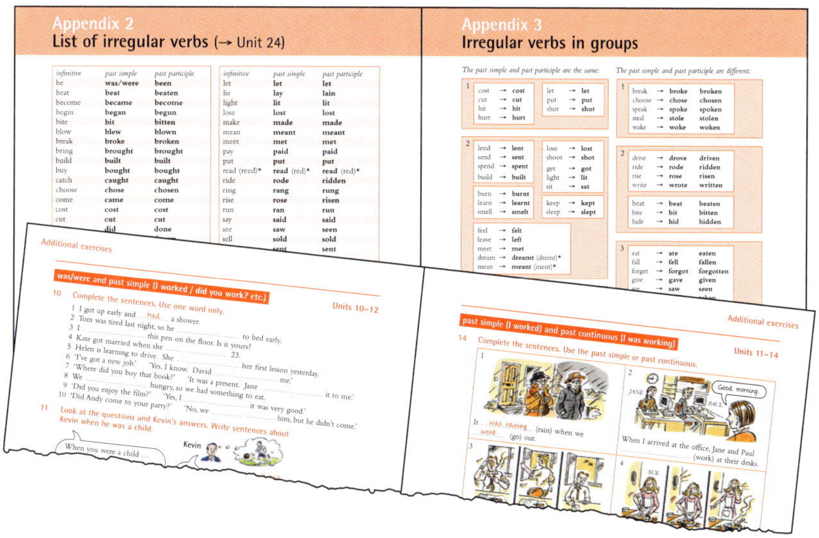

There are also *Additional exercises* at the back of the book (pages 252–270). There is a list of these exercises on page 252.

CD Rom

You can buy this book with or without a CD Rom. On the CD Rom there are more exercises on all the units, and these are different from the exercises in the book. There are also more than 600 test questions.

To the teacher

The most important features of this book are:

- It is a grammar book. It does not deal with other aspects of the language.
- It is for elementary learners. It does not cover areas of grammar which are not normally taught at elementary level.
- It is a reference book with exercises. It is not a course book and is not organised progressively.
- It is addressed to learners and intended for self-study.

Organisation of the book

There are 115 units in the book, each one focusing on a particular area of grammar. The material is organised in grammatical categories, such as tenses, questions and articles. Units are *not* ordered according to difficulty, and should therefore be selected and used in the order appropriate for the learner(s). The book should *not* be worked through from beginning to end. The units are listed in the *Contents* and there is a comprehensive *Index* at the end of the book.

Each unit has the same format consisting of two facing pages. The grammar point is presented and explained on the left-hand page and the corresponding exercises are on the right. There are seven *Appendices* (pages 243–251) dealing with active and passive forms, irregular verbs, short forms (contractions), spelling and phrasal verbs. It might be useful for teachers to draw students' attention to these.

At the back of the book there is a set of *Additional exercises* (pages 252–270). These exercises provide 'mixed' practice bringing together grammar points from a number of different units (especially those concerning verb forms). There are 35 exercises in this section and there is a full list on page 252.

Also at the back of the book there is a *Study guide* to help students decide which units to study – see page 271.

Finally, there is a *Key* (pages 283–309) for students to check their answers to all the exercises in the book. An edition without the *Study guide* and *Key* is available for teachers who would prefer it for their students.

Level

The book is for elementary learners, i.e. learners with very little English, but not for complete beginners. It is intended mainly for elementary students who are beyond the early stages of a beginners' course. It could also be used by low-intermediate learners whose grammar is weaker than other aspects of their English or who have problems with particular areas of basic grammar.

The explanations are addressed to the elementary learner and are therefore as simple and as short as possible. The vocabulary used in the examples and exercises has also been restricted so that the book can be used at this level.

Using the book

The book can be used by students working alone (see *To the student*) or as supplementary course material. In either case the book can serve as an elementary grammar book.

When used as course material, the book can be used for immediate consolidation or for later revision or remedial work. It might be used by the whole class or by individual students needing extra help and practice.

In some cases it may be desirable to use the left-hand pages (presentation and explanation) in class, but it should be noted that these have been written for individual study and reference. In most cases, it would probably be better for teachers to present the grammar point in their preferred way with the exercises being done for homework. The left-hand page is then available for later reference by the student.

Some teachers may prefer to keep the book for revision and remedial work. In this case, individual students or groups of students can be directed to the appropriate units for self-study and practice.

CD Rom

The book is sold with or without a CD Rom. This contains further exercises on all the units in the book, as well as a bank of more than 600 test questions from which users can select to compile their own tests. The CD Rom is also available separately.

Essential Grammar in Use *Third Edition*

This is a new edition of *Essential Grammar in Use*. The differences between this edition and the second edition are:

- The book has been redesigned with new colour illustrations.
- There is one new unit (Unit 35) and some reorganisation, so that most units have different numbers from the previous edition.
- There are many (usually minor) revisions to the explanations, examples and exercises.
- There are two new pages of *Additional exercises* (pages 252–270).
- There is a new *Study guide* at the back of the book to help users decide which units to study.
- There is a new CD Rom with further exercises to accompany the book.

Unit 1 am/is/are

A

B

positive

I	**am**	(I**'m**)
he she it	**is**	(he**'s**) (she**'s**) (it**'s**)
we you they	**are**	(we**'re**) (you**'re**) (they**'re**)

short form

negative

I	**am not**	(I**'m not**)
he she it	**is not**	(he**'s not** *or* he **isn't**) (she**'s not** *or* she **isn't**) (it**'s not** *or* it **isn't**)
we you they	**are not**	(we**'re not** *or* we **aren't**) (you**'re not** *or* you **aren't**) (they**'re not** *or* they **aren't**)

short forms

- ☐ I**'m** cold. Can you close the window, please?
- ☐ I**'m** 32 years old. My sister **is** 29.
- ☐ Steve **is** ill. He**'s** in bed.
- ☐ My brother **is** afraid of dogs.
- ☐ It**'s** ten o'clock. You**'re** late again.
- ☐ Ann and I **are** good friends.
- ☐ Your keys **are** on the table.

- ☐ I**'m** tired, but I**'m not** hungry.
- ☐ Tom **isn't** interested in politics. He**'s** interested in music.
- ☐ Jane **isn't** a teacher. She**'s** a student.
- ☐ Those people **aren't** English. They**'re** Australian.
- ☐ It**'s** sunny today, but it **isn't** warm.

C

that**'s** = that **is**   there**'s** = there **is**   here**'s** = here **is**

- ☐ Thank you. That**'s** very kind of you.
- ☐ Look! There**'s** Chris.
- ☐ 'Here**'s** your key.' 'Thank you.'

am/is/are (questions) → Unit 2   there is/are → Unit 37   a/an → Unit 65   short forms → Appendix 4

1.1 Write the short form (she's / we aren't etc.).

1 she is ......she's......
2 they are ....
3 it is not ....
4 that is ....
5 I am not ....
6 you are not ....

1.2 Write am, is or are.

1 The weather ....is.... nice today.
2 I .... not rich.
3 This bag .... heavy.
4 These bags .... heavy.
5 Look! There .... Carol.
6 My brother and I .... good tennis players.
7 Emily .... at home. Her children .... at school.
8 I .... a taxi driver. My sister .... a nurse.

1.3 Complete the sentences.

1 Steve is ill. ....He's.... in bed.
2 I'm not hungry, but .... thirsty.
3 Mr Thomas is a very old man. .... 98.
4 These chairs aren't beautiful, but .... comfortable.
5 The weather is nice today. .... warm and sunny.
6 '.................. late.' 'No, I'm not. I'm early!'
7 Catherine isn't at home. .... at work.
8 '.................. your coat.' 'Oh, thank you very much.'

1.4 Look at Lisa's sentences in 1A. Now write sentences about yourself.

1 (name?) My ....
2 (from?) I ....
3 (age?) I ....
4 (job?) I ....
5 (favourite colour or colours?) My ....
6 (interested in ... ?) I ....

1.5 Write sentences for the pictures. Use:

afraid **angry** **cold** **hot** **hungry** ~~**thirsty**~~

1 ....She's thirsty....
2 They ....
3 He ....
4 ....
5 ....
6 ....

1.6 Write true sentences, positive or negative. Use is/isn't or are/aren't.

1 (it / hot today) ....It isn't hot today.... **or** ....It's hot today....
2 (it / windy today) It ....
3 (my hands / cold) My ....
4 (Brazil / a very big country) ....
5 (diamonds / cheap) ....
6 (Toronto / in the US) ....

Write true sentences, positive or negative. Use I'm / I'm not.

7 (tired) ....I'm tired.... **or** ....I'm not tired....
8 (hungry) I ....
9 (a good swimmer) ....
10 (interested in football) ....

→ Additional exercise 1 (page 252)

Unit 2

am/is/are (questions)

A

positive		*question*	
I	**am**	**am**	I?
he she it	**is**	**is**	he? she?
we you they	**are**	**are**	we? you? they?

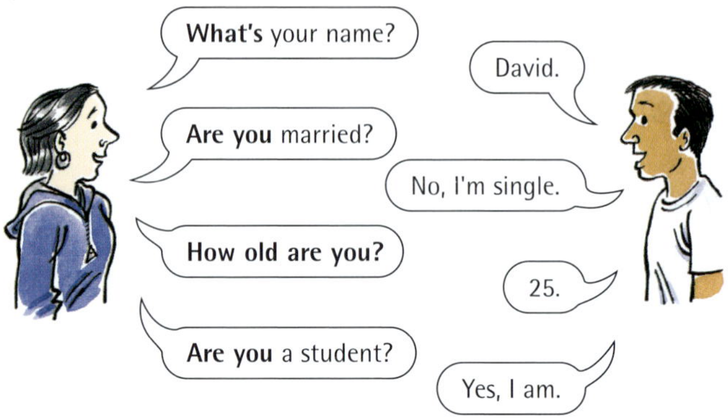

- 'Am I late?' 'No, **you're** on time.'
- '**Is your mother** at home?' 'No, **she's** out.'
- '**Are your parents** at home?' 'No, **they're** out.'
- '**Is it** cold in your room?' 'Yes, a little.'
- **Your shoes are** nice. **Are they** new?

We say:

- **Is she** at home? / **Is your mother** at home? (*not* Is at home your mother?)
- **Are they** new? / **Are your shoes** new? (*not* Are new your shoes?)

B

Where … ? / What … ? / Who … ? / How … ? / Why … ?

- **Where is** your mother? Is she at home?
- '**Where are** you from?' 'Canada.'
- '**What colour is** your car?' 'It's red.'
- '**How old is** Joe?' 'He's 24.'
- **How are** your parents? Are they well?
- These postcards are nice. **How much are** they?
- This hotel isn't very good. **Why is** it so expensive?

what**'s** = what **is**   who**'s** = who **is**   how**'s** = how **is**   where**'s** = where **is**

- **What's** the time?
- **Where's** Lucy?
- **Who's** that man?
- **How's** your father?

C

Short answers

Yes,	I	**am.**
	he she it	**is.**
	we you they	**are.**

No,	I**'m**	**not.**
	he**'s** she**'s** it**'s**	
	we**'re** you**'re** they**'re**	

or

No,	he she it	**isn't.**
	we you they	**aren't.**

- '**Are you** tired?' '**Yes, I am.**'
- '**Are you** hungry?' '**No, I'm not**, but I'm thirsty.'
- '**Is your friend** English?' '**Yes, he is.**'
- '**Are** these **your keys**?' '**Yes, they are.**'
- '**That's** my seat.' '**No, it isn't.**'

am/is/are → Unit 1   questions → Unit 44   what/which/how → Unit 47

2.1 Find the right answers for the questions.

1 Where's the camera?	A London.	1 G
2 Is your car blue?	B No, I'm not.	2 .....
3 Is Linda from London?	C Yes, you are.	3 .....
4 Am I late?	D My sister.	4 .....
5 Where's Ann from?	E Black.	5 .....
6 What colour is your bag?	F No, it's black.	6 .....
7 Are you hungry?	G In your bag.	7 .....
8 How is George?	H No, she's American.	8 .....
9 Who's that woman?	I Very well.	9 .....

2.2 Make questions with these words.

1 (is / at home / your mother) Is your mother at home ?
2 (your parents / are / well) Are your parents well ?
3 (interesting / is / your job) ..... ?
4 (the shops / are / open today) ..... ?
5 (from / where / you / are) ..... ?
6 (interested in sport / you / are) ..... ?
7 (is / near here / the post office) ..... ?
8 (at school / are / your children) ..... ?
9 (you / are / late / why) ..... ?

2.3 Complete the questions. Use What ... / Who ... / Where ... / How ... .

1 ..... How are your parents? — They're very well.
2 ..... the bus stop? — At the end of the street.
3 ..... your children? — Five, six and ten.
4 ..... these oranges? — £1.50 a kilo.
5 ..... your favourite sport? — Skiing.
6 ..... the man in this photograph? — That's my father.
7 ..... your new shoes? — Black.

2.4 Write the questions.

PAUL

1 (name?) What's your name? — Paul.
2 (American?) ..... — No, I'm Australian.
3 (how old?) ..... — I'm 30.
4 (a teacher?) ..... — No, I'm a lawyer.
5 (married?) ..... — Yes, I am.
6 (wife a lawyer?) ..... — No, she's a designer.
7 (from?) ..... — She's Italian.
8 (her name?) ..... — Anna.
9 (how old?) ..... — She's 27.

2.5 Write short answers (Yes, I am. / No, he isn't. etc.).

1 Are you married? No, I'm not.
2 Are you thirsty? .....
3 Is it cold today? .....
4 Are your hands cold? .....
5 Is it dark now? .....
6 Are you a teacher? .....

→ Additional exercises 1–2 (pages 252–53)

I am doing (present continuous)

A

She**'s eating**.
She **isn't reading**.

It**'s raining**.
The sun **isn't shining**.

They**'re running**.
They **aren't walking**.

The present continuous is:
am/is/are + do**ing**/eat**ing**/runn**ing**/writ**ing** etc.

I	**am** (not)	**-ing**
he she it	**is** (not)	
we you they	**are** (not)	

- I**'m working**. I**'m not watching** TV.
- Maria **is reading** a newspaper.
- She **isn't eating**. (*or* She**'s not** eat**ing**.)
- The phone **is ringing**.
- We**'re having** dinner.
- You**'re not listening** to me. (*or* You **aren't listening** ...)
- The children **are doing** their homework.

B

am/is/are + **-ing** = something is happening *now:*

I'm working
she**'s wearing** a hat
they**'re playing** football
I'm not watching television

past — *now* — *future*

- Please be quiet. **I'm working**. (= I'm working now)
- Look, there's Sarah. She**'s wearing** a brown coat. (= she is wearing it now)
- The weather is nice. It**'s not raining**.
- 'Where are the children?' 'They**'re playing** in the park.'
- *(on the phone)* We**'re having** dinner now. Can I phone you later?
- You can turn off the television. **I'm not watching** it.

Spelling (→ Appendix 5):

com**e** → com**ing** writ**e** → writ**ing** danc**e** → danc**ing**
r**un** → ru**nn**ing s**it** → si**tt**ing sw**im** → swi**mm**ing
lie → l**y**ing

am/is/are → Unit 1 are you doing? (questions) → Unit 4 I am doing and I do → Unit 8
What are you doing tomorrow? → Unit 25

Exercises

3.1 What are these people doing? Use these verbs to complete the sentences:

~~eat~~ have lie play sit wait

1 She's eating an apple.
2 He .... for a bus.
3 They .... football.
4 .... on the floor.
5 .... breakfast.
6 .... on the table.

3.2 Complete the sentences. Use these verbs:

build cook go have stand stay swim ~~work~~

1 Please be quiet. I 'm working .
2 'Where's John?' 'He's in the kitchen. He ....'
3 'You .... on my foot.' 'Oh, I'm sorry.'
4 Look! Somebody .... in the river.
5 We're here on holiday. We .... at the Central Hotel.
6 'Where's Sue?' 'She .... a shower.'
7 They .... a new hotel in the city centre at the moment.
8 I .... now. Goodbye.

3.3 Look at the picture. Write sentences about Jane. Use **She's -ing** or **She isn't -ing**.

Jane

1 (have dinner) Jane isn't having dinner.
2 (watch television) She's watching television.
3 (sit on the floor) She ....
4 (read a book) ....
5 (play the piano) ....
6 (laugh) ....
7 (wear a hat) ....
8 (write a letter) ....

3.4 What's happening now? Write true sentences.

1 (I / wash / my hair) I'm not washing my hair.
2 (it / snow) It's snowing. **or** It isn't snowing.
3 (I / sit / on a chair) ....
4 (I / eat) ....
5 (it / rain) ....
6 (I / learn / English) ....
7 (I / listen / to music) ....
8 (the sun / shine) ....
9 (I / wear / shoes) ....
10 (I / read / a newspaper) ....

Unit 4

are you doing? (present continuous questions)

A

positive

I	**am**	**doing** **working** **going** **staying** etc.
he she it	**is**	
we you they	**are**	

question

am	I	**doing?** **working?** **going?** **staying?** etc.
is	he she it	
are	we you they	

- ☐ '**Are** you **feeling** OK?' 'Yes, I'm fine, thanks.'
- ☐ '**Is** it **raining**?' 'Yes, take an umbrella.'
- ☐ Why **are** you **wearing** a coat? It's not cold.
- ☐ 'What**'s** Paul **doing**?' 'He**'s reading** the newspaper.'
- ☐ 'What **are** the children **doing**?' 'They**'re watching** television.'
- ☐ Look, there's Emily! Where**'s** she **going**?
- ☐ Who **are** you **waiting** for? **Are** you **waiting** for Sue?

B

Study the word order:

is/are + *subject* + **-ing**

	Is	he	**working** today?
	Is	Paul	**working** today? (*not* Is working Paul today?)
Where	**are**	they	**going**?
Where	**are**	those people	**going**? (*not* Where are going those people?)

C

Short answers

Yes,	I	**am**.
	he she it	**is**.
	we you they	**are**.

No,	I**'m**	**not**.
	he**'s** she**'s** it**'s**	
	we**'re** you**'re** they**'re**	

or

No,	he she it	**isn't**.
	we you they	**aren't**.

- ☐ '**Are** you **going** now?' '**Yes, I am.**'
- ☐ '**Is** Paul **working** today?' '**Yes, he is.**'
- ☐ '**Is** it **raining**?' '**No, it isn't.**'
- ☐ '**Are** your friends **staying** at a hotel?' '**No, they aren't.** They're staying with me.'

I am doing → Unit 3 What are you doing tomorrow? → Unit 25 questions → Units 44–47

4.1 Look at the pictures and write the questions.

4.2 Look at the pictures and complete the questions. Use:

cry eat go laugh look at ~~read~~

4.3 Make questions from these words. Put the words in the right order.

1 (is / working / Paul / today) Is Paul working today?
2 (what / the children / are / doing) What are the children doing?
3 (you / are / listening / to me) ?
4 (where / your friends / are / going) ?
5 (are / watching / your parents / television) ?
6 (what / Jessica / is / cooking) ?
7 (why / you / are / looking / at me) ?
8 (is / coming / the bus) ?

4.4 Write short answers (Yes, I am. / No, he isn't. etc.).

1 Are you watching TV? No, I'm not.
2 Are you wearing a watch? ...
3 Are you eating something? ...
4 Is it raining? ...
5 Are you sitting on the floor? ...
6 Are you feeling well? ...

→ Additional exercise 3 (page 253)

Unit 5

I do/work/like etc. (present simple)

A

They're looking at their books.
They **read** a lot.

He's eating an ice-cream.
He **likes** ice-cream.

They **read** / he **likes** / I **work** etc. = the *present simple:*

I/we/you/they	**read**	**like**	**work**	**live**	**watch**	**do**	**have**
he/she/it	**reads**	**likes**	**works**	**lives**	**watches**	**does**	**has**

Remember:
he works / **she** lives / **it** rains etc.

- **I work** in a shop. **My brother works** in a bank. (*not* My brother work)
- **Lucy lives** in London. **Her parents live** in Scotland.
- **It rains** a lot in winter.

I **have** → he/she/it **has**:

- **John has** a shower every day.

Spelling (→ Appendix 5):

-es after **-s** / **-sh** / **-ch**:	pass → pass**es**	fini**sh** → finish**es**	wat**ch** → watch**es**
-y → **-ies**:	stud**y** → stud**ies**	tr**y** → tr**ies**	
also:	do → do**es**	go → go**es**	

B

We use the present simple for things that are true in general, or for things that happen sometimes or all the time:

- I **like** big cities.
- Your English is good. You **speak** very well.
- Tim **works** very hard. He **starts** at 7.30 and **finishes** at 8 o'clock in the evening.
- The earth **goes** round the sun.
- We **do** a lot of different things in our free time.
- It **costs** a lot of money to build a hospital.

C

always/never/often/usually/sometimes + present simple

- Sue **always gets** to work early. (*not* Sue gets always)
- I **never eat** breakfast. (*not* I eat never)
- We **often go** away at weekends.
- Mark **usually plays** football on Sundays.
- I **sometimes walk** to work, but not very often.

I don't ... (negative) → Unit 6 **Do you** ... ? (questions) → Unit 7 **I am doing** and **I do** → Unit 8
always/usually/often etc. (word order) → Unit 94

5.1 Write these verbs with -s or -es.

1 (read) she *reads* ....
2 (think) he ....
3 (fly) it ....
4 (dance) he ....
5 (have) she ....
6 (finish) it ....

5.2 Complete the sentences about the people in the pictures. Use:

eat go live ~~play~~ play sleep

1 *He plays* the piano.
2 They .... in a very big house.
3 .... a lot of fruit.
4 .... tennis.
5 .... to the cinema a lot.
6 .... seven hours a night.

5.3 Complete the sentences. Use:

boil close cost cost like like meet open ~~speak~~ teach wash

1 Maria *speaks* four languages.
2 The shops in the city centre usually .... at 9 o'clock in the morning.
3 The City Museum .... at 5 o'clock in the evening.
4 Tina is a teacher. She .... mathematics to young children.
5 My job is very interesting. I .... a lot of people.
6 Peter's car is always dirty. He never .... it.
7 Food is expensive. It .... a lot of money.
8 Shoes are expensive. They .... a lot of money.
9 Water .... at 100 degrees Celsius.
10 Julia and I are good friends. I .... her and she .... me.

5.4 Write sentences from these words. Use the right form of the verb (arrive or arrives etc.).

1 (always / early / Sue / arrive) *Sue always arrives early.*
2 (to the cinema / never / I / go) I ....
3 (work / Martina / hard / always) ....
4 (like / chocolate / children / usually) ....
5 (Julia / parties / enjoy / always) ....
6 (often / people's names / I / forget) ....
7 (television / Tim / watch / never) ....
8 (usually / dinner / we / have / at 7.30) ....
9 (Jenny / always / nice clothes / wear) ....

5.5 Write sentences about yourself. Use always/never/often/usually/sometimes.

1 (watch TV in the evening) *I usually watch TV in the evening.*
2 (read in bed) I ....
3 (get up before 7 o'clock) ....
4 (go to work/school by bus) ....
5 (drink coffee in the morning) ....

Unit 6

I don't ... (present simple negative)

A

The present simple negative is **don't/doesn't** + *verb:*

She **doesn't drink** coffee.

He **doesn't like** his job.

positive

I we you they	**work** **like** **do** **have**
he she it	**works** **likes** **does** **has**

negative

I we you they	**don't** (**do not**)	**work** **like** **do** **have**
he she it	**doesn't** (**does not**)	

- ☐ I **drink** coffee, but I **don't drink** tea.
- ☐ Sue **drinks** tea, but she **doesn't drink** coffee.
- ☐ You **don't work** very hard.
- ☐ We **don't watch** television very often.
- ☐ The weather is usually nice. It **doesn't rain** very often.
- ☐ Gary and Nicole **don't know** many people.

B

Remember:

I/we/you/they	**don't** ...
he/she/it	**doesn't** ...

- ☐ **I don't** like football.
- ☐ **He doesn't** like football.

- ☐ **I don't** like Fred and **Fred doesn't** like me. (*not* Fred don't like)
- ☐ **My car doesn't** use much petrol. (*not* My car don't use)
- ☐ Sometimes he is late, but **it doesn't** happen very often.

C

We use **don't/doesn't** + *infinitive* (don't **like** / doesn't **speak** / doesn't **do** etc.):

- ☐ I **don't like** washing the car. I **don't do** it very often.
- ☐ Sarah **speaks** Spanish, but she **doesn't speak** Italian. (*not* doesn't speaks)
- ☐ Bill **doesn't do** his job very well. (*not* Bill doesn't his job)
- ☐ Paula **doesn't** usually **have** breakfast. (*not* doesn't ... has)

I do/work/like etc. (present simple) → **Unit 5** **Do you ... ?** (present simple questions) → **Unit 7**

Exercises

6.1 Write the negative.

1 I play the piano very well. — I don't play the piano very well.
2 Jane plays the piano very well. — Jane ...
3 They know my phone number. — They ...
4 We work very hard. — ...
5 He has a bath every day. — ...
6 You do the same thing every day. — ...

6.2 Study the information and write sentences with **like**.

	BEN AND SOPHIE	KATE	YOU
1 classical music?	yes	no	?
2 boxing?	no	yes	
3 horror films?	yes	no	

1 Ben and Sophie like classical music.
Kate ...
I ... classical music.

2 Ben and Sophie ...
Kate ...
I ...

3 ...
...
...

6.3 Write about yourself. Use:

I never ... or **I often ...** or **I don't ... very often.**

1 (watch TV) I don't watch TV very often. **or** I never watch TV. **or** I often watch TV.
2 (go to the theatre) ...
3 (ride a bicycle) ...
4 (eat in restaurants) ...
5 (travel by train) ...

6.4 Complete the sentences. All of them are negative. Use **don't/doesn't** + these verbs:

cost **go** **know** ~~**read**~~ **see** **use** **wear**

1 I buy a newspaper every day, but sometimes I don't read it.
2 Paul has a car, but he ... it very often.
3 Paul and his friends like films, but they ... to the cinema very often.
4 Amanda is married, but she ... a ring.
5 I ... much about politics. I'm not interested in it.
6 The Regent Hotel isn't expensive. It ... much to stay there.
7 Brian lives very near us, but we ... him very often.

6.5 Put the verb into the correct form, positive or negative.

1 Margaret speaks four languages – English, French, German and Spanish. (speak)
2 I don't like my job. It's very boring. (like)
3 'Where's Martin?' 'I'm sorry. I ... .' (know)
4 Sue is a very quiet person. She ... very much. (talk)
5 Andy ... a lot of tea. It's his favourite drink. (drink)
6 It's not true! I ... it! (believe)
7 That's a very beautiful picture. I ... it very much. (like)
8 Mark is a vegetarian. He ... meat. (eat)

Do you ... ? (present simple questions)

A

We use **do/does** in present simple questions:

positive

I we you they	**work** **like** **do** **have**
he she it	**works** **likes** **does** **has**

question

do	I we you they	**work?** **like?** **do?** **have?**
does	he she it	

B

Study the word order:

do/does + *subject* + *infinitive*

	Do	you	**work**	on Sundays?
	Do	your friends	**live**	near here?
	Does	Chris	**play**	tennis?
Where	**do**	your parents	**live?**	
How often	**do**	you	**wash**	your hair?
What	**does**	this word	**mean?**	
How much	**does**	it	**cost**	to fly to Rome?

Questions with **always/usually/often**:

	Do	you	**always**	**have**	breakfast?
	Does	Chris	**often**	**phone**	you?
What	**do**	you	**usually**	**do**	at weekends?

What do you **do**? = What's your job?

- '**What do** you **do**?' 'I work in a bank.'

C

Remember:

do I/we/you/they ... **does** he/she/it ...

- **Do they** like music?
- **Does he** like music?

D

Short answers

Yes,	I/we/you/they **do**.
	he/she/it **does**.

No,	I/we/you/they **don't**.
	he/she/it **doesn't**.

- '**Do you** play tennis?' '**No, I don't.**'
- '**Do your parents** speak English?' '**Yes, they do.**'
- '**Does Gary** work hard?' '**Yes, he does.**'
- '**Does your sister** live in London.' '**No, she doesn't.**'

I do/work/like etc. → Unit 5   I don't ... (negative) → Unit 6   questions → Units 44–47

7.1 Write questions with Do ... ? and Does ... ?

1 I like chocolate. How about you? Do you like chocolate ?
2 I play tennis. How about you? .... you .... ?
3 You live near here. How about Lucy? .... Lucy .... ?
4 Tom plays tennis. How about his friends? .... ?
5 You speak English. How about your brother? .... ?
6 I do yoga every morning. How about you? .... ?
7 Sue often goes away. How about Paul? .... ?
8 I want to be famous. How about you? .... ?
9 You work hard. How about Anna? .... ?

7.2 Make questions from these words + do/does. Put the words in the right order.

1 (where / live / your parents) Where do your parents live ?
2 (you / early / always / get up) Do you always get up early ?
3 (how often / TV / you / watch) .... ?
4 (you / want / what / for dinner) .... ?
5 (like / you / football) .... ?
6 (your brother / like / football) .... ?
7 (what / you / do / in your free time) .... ?
8 (your sister / work / where) .... ?
9 (to the cinema / often / you / go) .... ?
10 (what / mean / this word) .... ?
11 (often / snow / it / here) .... ?
12 (go / usually / to bed / what time / you)
.... ?
13 (how much / to phone New York / it / cost)
.... ?
14 (you / for breakfast / have / usually / what)
.... ?

7.3 Complete the questions. Use these verbs:

~~do~~ do enjoy go like start teach work

1	What do you do ?	I work in a bookshop.
2	.... it?	It's OK.
3	What time .... in the morning?	At 9 o'clock.
4	.... on Saturdays?	Sometimes.
5	How .... to work?	Usually by bus.
6	And your husband. What .... ?	He's a teacher.
7	What .... ?	Science.
8	.... his job?	Yes, he loves it.

7.4 Write short answers (Yes, he does. / No, I don't. etc.).

1 Do you watch TV a lot? No, I don't. **or** Yes, I do.
2 Do you live in a big city? ....
3 Do you often ride a bicycle? ....
4 Does it rain a lot where you live? ....
5 Do you play the piano? ....

→ Additional exercises 4–7 (pages 253–54)

Unit 8

I am doing (present continuous) and **I do** (present simple)

A

Jack is watching television.
He is *not* playing the guitar.

But Jack has a guitar.
He often plays it and he plays very well.

Jack **plays** the guitar,
but he **is not playing** the guitar now.

Is he playing the guitar?	**No, he isn't.**	*(present continuous)*
Does he play the guitar?	**Yes, he does.**	*(present simple)*

B

Present continuous (**I am doing**) = now, at the time of speaking:

I'm doing

past — *now* — *future*

- ☐ Please be quiet. **I'm** work**ing**. (*not* I work)
- ☐ Tom **is** hav**ing** a shower at the moment. (*not* Tom has)
- ☐ Take an umbrella with you. It**'s** rain**ing**.
- ☐ You can turn off the television. **I'm** not watch**ing** it.
- ☐ Why are you under the table? What **are** you do**ing**?

C

Present simple (**I do**) = in general, all the time or sometimes:

I do

past — *now* — *future*

- ☐ I **work** every day from 9 o'clock to 5.30.
- ☐ Tom **has** a shower every morning.
- ☐ It **rains** a lot in winter.
- ☐ I **don't watch** television very often.
- ☐ What **do** you usually **do** at the weekend?

D

We do *not* use these verbs in the present continuous (**I am -ing**):

like	**love**	**want**	**know**	**understand**	**remember**	**depend**
prefer	**hate**	**need**	**mean**	**believe**	**forget**	

Use only the present simple with these verbs (I **want** / **do you like?** etc.):

- ☐ I'm tired. I **want** to go home. (*not* I'm wanting)
- ☐ '**Do** you **know** that girl?' 'Yes, but I **don't remember** her name.'
- ☐ I **don't understand**. What **do** you **mean**?

present continuous → Units 3–4 present simple → Units 5–7 present for the future → Unit 25

8.1 Answer the questions about the pictures.

1

Does he take photographs? Yes, he does.
Is he taking a photograph? No, he isn't.
What is he doing?
He's having a bath.

2

Is she driving a bus? ....
Does she drive a bus? ....
What is she doing?
....

3

Does he clean windows? ....
Is he cleaning a window? ....
What is he doing?
....

4

Are they teaching? ....
Do they teach? ....
What do they do?
....

8.2 Complete the sentences with am/is/are or do/don't/does/doesn't.

1 Excuse me, do you speak English?
2 'Where's Kate?' 'I .... know.'
3 What's funny? Why .... you laughing?
4 'What .... your sister do?' 'She's a dentist.'
5 It .... raining. I .... want to go out in the rain.
6 'Where .... you come from?' 'Canada.'
7 How much .... it cost to send a letter to Canada?
8 Steve is a good tennis player, but he .... play very often.

8.3 Put the verb in the present continuous (I am doing) or the present simple (I do).

1 Excuse me, do you speak (you/speak) English?
2 'Where's Tom?' 'He's having (he/have) a shower.'
3 I don't watch (I/not/watch) television very often.
4 Listen! Somebody .... (sing).
5 Sandra is tired. .... (she/want) to go home now.
6 How often .... (you/read) a newspaper?
7 'Excuse me, but .... (you/sit) in my place.' 'Oh, I'm sorry.'
8 I'm sorry, ... (I/not/understand). Can you speak more slowly?
9 It's late. .... (I/go) home now. .... (you/come) with me?
10 What time .... (your father / finish) work every day?
11 You can turn off the radio. .... (I/not/listen) to it.
12 'Where's Paul?' 'In the kitchen. .... (he/cook) something.'
13 Martin .... (not/usually/drive) to work. He .... (usually/walk).
14 Sue .... (not/like) coffee. .... (she/prefer) tea.

I have ... and I've got ...

A

You can say **I have** or **I've got**, **he has** or **he's got**:

I we you they	**have**	*or*	I we you they	**have got**	(I**'ve got**) (we**'ve got**) (you**'ve got**) (they**'ve got**)
he she it	**has**	*or*	he she it	**has got**	(he**'s got**) (she**'s got**) (it**'s got**)

short form

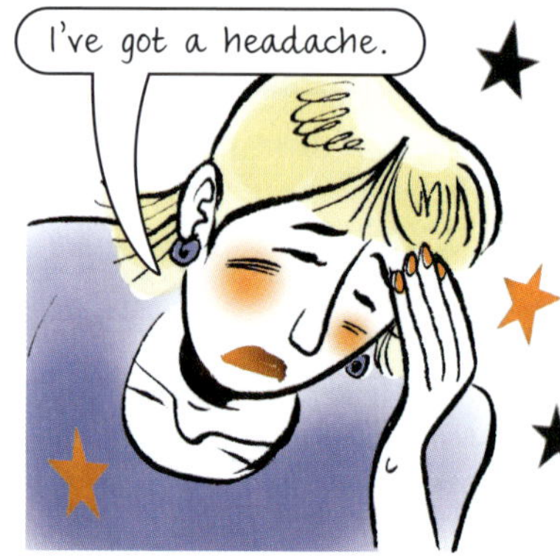

- I **have** blue eyes. *or* I**'ve got** blue eyes.
- Tim **has** two sisters. *or* Tim **has got** two sisters.
- Our car **has** four doors. *or* Our car **has got** four doors.
- Sarah isn't feeling well. She **has** a headache. *or* She**'s got** a headache.
- They like animals. They **have** a horse, three dogs and six cats. *or* They**'ve got** a horse …

B

I **haven't got** / **have** you **got**? etc.

negative

I we you they	**have not** (**haven't**)	**got**
he she it	**has not** (**hasn't**)	

question

have	I we you they	**got?**
has	he she it	

short answers

Yes, No,	I we you they	**have**. **haven't**.
Yes, No,	he she it	**has**. **hasn't**.

- I**'ve got** a motorbike, but I **haven't got** a car.
- Tracey and Jeff **haven't got** any children.
- It's a nice house, but it **hasn't got** a garden.
- '**Have** you **got** a camera?' 'No, I **haven't**.'
- 'What **have** you **got** in your bag?' 'Nothing. It's empty.'
- '**Has** Helen **got** a car?' 'Yes, she **has**.'
- What kind of car **has** she **got**?

C

I **don't have** / **do** you **have**? etc.

In negatives and questions you can also use **do/does** … :

- They **don't have** any children. (= They **haven't got** any children.)
- It's a nice house, but it **doesn't have** a garden. (= it **hasn't got** a garden)
- **Does** Helen **have** a car? (= **Has** Helen **got** a car?)
- What **do** you **have** in your bag? (= What **have** you **got** in your bag?)

had / didn't have (past) → Units 11–12 have breakfast / have a shower etc. → Unit 58 some/any → Unit 76

9.1 Write the short form with **got** (**we've got** / **he hasn't got** etc.).

1 we have got *we've got*
2 he has got ....
3 they have got ....
4 she has not got ....
5 it has got ....
6 I have not got ....

9.2 Read the questions and answers. Then write sentences about Mark.

	Question	Mark	
1	Have you got a car?	No.	1 *He hasn't got a car.*
2	Have you got a computer?	Yes.	2 He ....
3	Have you got a dog?	No.	3 ....
4	Have you got a mobile phone?	No.	4 ....
5	Have you got a watch?	Yes.	5 ....
6	Have you got any brothers or sisters?	Yes, two brothers and a sister.	6 ....

Mark

What about you? Write sentences with **I've got** or **I haven't got**.

7 (a computer) ....
8 (a dog) ....
9 (a bike) ....
10 (brothers/sisters) ....

9.3 Write these sentences with **got** (**I've got** / **have you got** etc.). The meaning is the same.

1 They have two children. *They've got two children.*
2 She doesn't have a key. *She hasn't got a key.*
3 He has a new job. ....
4 They don't have much money. ....
5 Do you have an umbrella? ....
6 We have a lot of work to do. ....
7 I don't have your phone number. ....
8 Does your father have a car? ....
9 How much money do we have? ....

9.4 Write **have got** (**'ve got**), **has got** (**'s got**), **haven't got** or **hasn't got**.

1 Sarah *hasn't got* a car. She goes everywhere by bicycle.
2 They like animals. They *'ve got* three dogs and two cats.
3 Charles isn't happy. He .... a lot of problems.
4 They don't read much. They .... many books.
5 'What's wrong?' 'I .... something in my eye.'
6 'Where's my pen?' 'I don't know. I .... it.'
7 Julia wants to go to the concert, but she .... a ticket.

9.5 Complete the sentences. Use **have/has got** or **haven't/hasn't got** with:

a lot of friends **four wheels** **~~a headache~~** **six legs**
~~a garden~~ **much time** **a key**

1 I'm not feeling well. I *'ve got a headache.*
2 It's a nice house, but it *hasn't got a garden.*
3 Most cars ....
4 Everybody likes Tom. He ....
5 I can't open the door. I ....
6 An insect ....
7 We must hurry. We ....

→ Additional exercises 5–7 (page 254)

Unit 10 was/were

A

last night *now*

Now Robert **is** at work.

At midnight last night he **wasn't** at work.

He **was** in bed.
He **was** asleep.

am/is (present) → **was** (past):

- I **am** tired. (now) — I **was** tired **last night**.
- Where **is** Kate? (now) — Where **was** Kate **yesterday**?
- The weather **is** good today. — The weather **was** good **last week**.

are (present) → **were** (past):

- You **are** late. (now) — You **were** late **yesterday**.
- They **aren't** here. (now) — They **weren't** here **last Sunday**.

B

positive

I he she it	**was**
we you they	**were**

negative

I he she it	**was not** **(wasn't)**
we you they	**were not** **(weren't)**

question

was	I? he? she? it?
were	we? you? they?

- Last year Rachel **was** 22, so she **is** 23 now.
- When I **was** a child, I **was** afraid of dogs.
- We **were** hungry after the journey, but we **weren't** tired.
- The hotel **was** comfortable, but it **wasn't** expensive.

- **Was** the weather nice when you **were** on holiday?
- Your shoes are nice. **Were** they expensive?
- Why **were** you late this morning?

C

Short answers

Yes,	I/he/she/it **was**.
	we/you/they **were**.

No,	I/he/she/it **wasn't**.
	we/you/they **weren't**.

- '**Were you** late?' '**No, I wasn't.**'
- '**Was Ted** at work yesterday?' '**Yes, he was.**'
- '**Were Sue and Steve** at the party?' '**No, they weren't.**'

am/is/are → Units 1–2 I was doing → Unit 13

Exercises

10.1 Where were these people at 3 o'clock yesterday afternoon?

1 Gary was in bed.
2 Jack and Kate ....
3 Sue ....
4 ....
5 ....
6 And you? I ....

10.2 Write am/is/are (present) or was/were (past).

1 Last year she was 22, so she is 23 now.
2 Today the weather .... nice, but yesterday it .... very cold.
3 I .... hungry. Can I have something to eat?
4 I feel fine this morning, but I .... very tired last night.
5 Where .... you at 11 o'clock last Friday morning?
6 Don't buy those shoes. They .... very expensive.
7 I like your new jacket. .... it expensive?
8 This time last year I .... in Paris.
9 'Where .... the children?' 'I don't know. They .... here a few minutes ago.'

10.3 Write was/were or wasn't/weren't.

1 We weren't happy with the hotel. Our room was very small and it wasn't clean.
2 Mark .... at work last week because he .... ill. He's better now.
3 Yesterday .... a public holiday, so the banks .... closed. They're open today.
4 '........ Kate and Bill at the party?' 'Kate .... there, but Bill ....'
5 'Where are my keys?' 'I don't know. They .... on the table, but they're not there now.'
6 You .... at home last night. Where .... you?

10.4 Write questions from these words + was/were. Put the words in the right order.

1 (late / you / this morning / why?)
Why were you late this morning? → The traffic was bad.
2 (difficult / your exam?)
.... → No, it was easy.
3 (last week / where / Sue and Chris?)
.... → They were on holiday.
4 (your new camera / how much?)
.... → Sixty pounds.
5 (angry / you / yesterday / why?)
.... → Because you were late.
6 (nice / the weather / last week?)
.... → Yes, it was beautiful.

Unit 11

worked/got/went etc. (past simple)

A

They **watch** television every evening. *(present simple)*

They **watched** television yesterday evening. *(past simple)*

watched is the *past simple:*

I/we/you/they he/she/it	**watched**

B

The past simple is often **-ed** (*regular verbs*). For example:

work → **worked** dance → **danced**
clean → **cleaned** stay → **stayed**
start → **started** need → **needed**

- I clean my teeth every morning. This morning I **cleaned** my teeth.
- Terry **worked** in a bank from 1996 to 2003.
- Yesterday it **rained** all morning. It **stopped** at lunchtime.
- We **enjoyed** the party last night. We **danced** a lot and **talked** to a lot of people. The party **finished** at midnight.

Spelling (→ Appendix 5):

tr**y** → tri**ed** stud**y** → studi**ed** cop**y** → copi**ed**
st**op** → sto**pped** pl**an** → pla**nned**

C

Some verbs are *irregular* (= not regular). The past simple is *not* **-ed**. Here are some important irregular verbs (see also Appendix 2–3):

begin →	**began**	fall →	**fell**	leave →	**left**	sell →	**sold**
break	**broke**	find	**found**	lose	**lost**	sit	**sat**
bring	**brought**	fly	**flew**	make	**made**	sleep	**slept**
build	**built**	forget	**forgot**	meet	**met**	speak	**spoke**
buy	**bought**	get	**got**	pay	**paid**	stand	**stood**
catch	**caught**	give	**gave**	put	**put**	take	**took**
come	**came**	go	**went**	read	**read** (red)*	tell	**told**
do	**did**	have	**had**	ring	**rang**	think	**thought**
drink	**drank**	hear	**heard**	say	**said**	win	**won**
eat	**ate**	know	**knew**	see	**saw**	write	**wrote**

* *pronounced 'red'*

- I usually get up early, but this morning I **got** up at 9 o'clock.
- We **did** a lot of work yesterday.
- Caroline **went** to the cinema three times last week.
- James **came** into the room, **took** off his coat and **sat** down.

was/were → Unit 10 I didn't / Did you ... ? (negative and questions) → Unit 12 ago → Unit 19

11.1 Complete the sentences. Use a verb from the box.

~~clean~~ die enjoy finish happen open rain start stay want

1 I ……cleaned…… my teeth three times yesterday.
2 It was hot in the room, so I …………… the window.
3 The film was very long. It …………… at 7.15 and …………… at 10 o'clock.
4 When I was a child, I …………… to be a doctor.
5 The accident …………… last Sunday afternoon.
6 It's a nice day today, but yesterday it …………… all day.
7 We …………… our holiday last year. We …………… at a very nice place.
8 Anna's grandfather …………… when he was 90 years old.

11.2 Write the past simple of these verbs.

1 get ……got……	4 pay ……………	7 go ……………	10 know ……………
2 see ……………	5 visit ……………	8 think ……………	11 put ……………
3 play ……………	6 buy ……………	9 copy ……………	12 speak ……………

11.3 Read about Lisa's journey to Madrid. Put the verbs in the correct form.

Last Tuesday Lisa (1) ……flew…… from London to Madrid. She (2) …………… up at 6 o'clock in the morning and (3) …………… a cup of coffee. At 6.30 she (4) …………… home and (5) …………… to the airport. When she (6) …………… there, she (7) …………… the car, (8) …………… to the airport building, and (9) …………… in. Then she (10) …………… breakfast at a café and (11) …………… for her flight. The plane (12) …………… on time and (13) …………… in Madrid two hours later. Finally she (14) …………… a taxi from the airport to her hotel in the centre of Madrid.

fly, get
have
leave, drive
get, park, walk
check, have
wait, depart
arrive, take

11.4 Write sentences about the past (yesterday / last week etc.).

1 James always goes to work by car. Yesterday ……he went to work by car.……
2 Rachel often loses her keys. She …………… last week.
3 Kate meets her friends every evening. She …………… yesterday evening.
4 I usually buy two newspapers every day. Yesterday I ……………
5 We often go to the cinema at weekends. Last Sunday we ……………
6 I eat an orange every day. Yesterday I ……………
7 Tom always has a shower in the morning. This morning he ……………
8 Our friends often come to see us. They …………… last Friday.

11.5 Write sentences about what you did yesterday.

1 ……I went to the theatre.……
2 ……………
3 ……………
4 ……………
5 ……………
6 ……………

→ Additional exercise 10 (page 256)

Unit 12 I didn't ... Did you ... ? (past simple negative and questions)

A

We use **did** in past simple negatives and questions:

infinitive	*positive*		*negative*			*question*		
play	I	**played**	I	**did not (didn't)**	play	**did**	I	play?
start	we	**started**	we		start		we	start?
watch	you	**watched**	you		watch		you	watch?
have	they	**had**	they		have		they	have?
see	he	**saw**	he		see		he	see?
do	she	**did**	she		do		she	do?
go	it	**went**	it		go		it	go?

B

do/does *(present)* → **did** *(past):*

- I **don't** watch television very often.
  I **didn't** watch television **yesterday**.
- **Does** she often go away?
  Did she go away **last week**?

C

We use **did/didn't** + *infinitive* (**watch/play/go** etc.):

I **watched**	*but*	I **didn't watch**	(*not* I didn't watched)
they **went**		**did** they **go**?	(*not* did they went?)
he **had**		he **didn't have**	
you **did**		**did** you **do**?	

- I **played** tennis yesterday, but I **didn't win**.
- '**Did** you **do** the shopping?' 'No, I **didn't have** time.'
- We **went** to the cinema, but we **didn't enjoy** the film.

D

Study the word order in questions:

	did +	*subject* +	*infinitive*	
	Did	your sister	**phone**	you?
What	**did**	you	**do**	last night?
How	**did**	the accident	**happen**?	
Where	**did**	your parents	**go**	for their holiday?

E

Short answers

Yes,	I/we/you/they he/she/it	**did**.

No,	I/we/you/they he/she/it	**didn't**.

- '**Did you** see Joe yesterday?' '**No, I didn't.**'
- '**Did it** rain on Sunday?' '**Yes, it did.**'
- '**Did Helen** come to the party?' '**No, she didn't.**'
- '**Did your parents** have a good holiday?' '**Yes, they did.**'

worked/got/went etc. (past simple) → **Unit 11**

Exercises

12.1 Complete these sentences with the verb in the negative.

1 I saw Barbara, but I ....didn't see.... Jane.
2 They worked on Monday, but they .... on Tuesday.
3 We went to the post office, but we .... to the bank.
4 She had a pen, but she .... any paper.
5 Jack did French at school, but he .... German.

12.2 Write questions with Did ... ?

1 I watched TV last night. How about you? ....Did you watch TV last night.... ?
2 I enjoyed the party. How about you? .... ?
3 I had a good holiday. How about you? .... ?
4 I finished work early. How about you? .... ?
5 I slept well last night. How about you? .... ?

12.3 What did you do yesterday? Write positive or negative sentences.

1 (watch TV) ....I watched TV.... **or** ....I didn't watch TV....
2 (get up before 7 o'clock) I ....
3 (have a shower) ....
4 (buy a magazine) ....
5 (eat meat) ....
6 (go to bed before 10.30) ....

12.4 Write B's questions. Use:

arrive cost go go to bed late happen have a nice time ~~stay~~ win

1 A: We went to New York last month. B: Where ....did you stay.... ? A: With some friends.	5 A: We came home by taxi. B: How much .... ? A: Ten pounds.
2 A: I was late for the meeting. B: What time .... ? A: Half past nine.	6 A: I'm tired this morning. B: .... ? A: No, but I didn't sleep very well.
3 A: I played tennis this afternoon. B: .... ? A: No, I lost.	7 A: We went to the beach yesterday. B: .... ? A: Yes, it was great.
4 A: I had a nice holiday. B: Good. Where .... ? A: To the mountains.	8 A: The window is broken. B: How .... ? A: I don't know.

12.5 Put the verb in the correct form – positive, negative or question.

1 We went to the cinema, but the film wasn't very good. We ....didn't enjoy.... it. (enjoy)
2 Tim .... some new clothes yesterday – two shirts, a jacket and a pullover. (buy)
3 '.................... yesterday?' 'No, it was a nice day.' (rain)
4 We were tired, so we .... long at the party. (stay)
5 It was very warm in the room, so I .... a window. (open)
6 'Did you phone Chris this morning?' 'No, I .... time.' (have)
7 'I cut my hand this morning.' 'How .... that?' (do)
8 'Why weren't you at the meeting yesterday?' 'I .... about it.' (know)

→ Additional exercises 10–13 (page 256)

I was doing (past continuous)

A

It is 6 o'clock now.
Paul **is** at home.
He **is watching** television.

At 4 o'clock he **wasn't** at home.
He **was** at the sports club.

He **was swimming** in the pool.
He **wasn't watching** television.

3.30 → 4.00 → 4.15

3.30: he started swimming
4.00: he **was swimming**
4.15: he finished swimming

B

was/were + -ing is the *past continuous:*

positive

I / he / she / it	**was**	**doing** / **watching** / **playing** / **swimming** / **living** etc.
we / you / they	**were**	

negative

I / he / she / it	**was not** (**wasn't**)	**doing** / **watching** / **playing** / **swimming** / **living** etc.
we / you / they	**were not** (**weren't**)	

question

was	I / he / she / it	**doing?** / **watching?** / **playing?** / **swimming?** / **living?** etc.
were	we / you / they	

- What **were** you **doing** at 11.30 yesterday? **Were** you **working**?
- 'What did he say?' 'I don't know. I **wasn't listening**.'
- It **was raining**, so we didn't go out.
- In 2001 we **were living** in Canada.
- Today she's wearing a skirt, but yesterday she **was wearing** trousers.
- I woke up early yesterday. It was a beautiful morning. The sun **was shining** and the birds **were singing**.

Spelling (**live** → **living** / **run** → **running** / **lie** → **lying** etc.) → Appendix 5

C

am/is/are + -ing *(present)* → **was/were + -ing** *(past):*

present
- **I'm working** (now).
- It **isn't raining** (now).
- What **are** you **doing** (now)?

past
- I **was working** at 10.30 last night.
- It **wasn't raining** when we went out.
- What **were** you **doing** at three o'clock?

was/were → Unit 10 **I was doing** and **I did** (past continuous and simple) → Unit 14

13.1 Look at the pictures. Where were these people at 3 o'clock yesterday afternoon? And what were they doing? Write two sentences for each picture.

1	2	3	4	5
RACHEL	*JACK KATE*	*TIM*	*TRACEY*	*MR AND MRS HALL*
at home watch TV	at the cinema watch a film	in his car drive	at the station wait for a train	in the park walk

1 *Rachel was at home. She was watching TV.*
2 Jack and Kate .... They ....
3 Tim ....
4 ....
5 ....
6 And you? I ....

13.2 Sarah did a lot of things yesterday morning. Look at the pictures and complete the sentences.

1 At 8.45 *she was washing her car.*
2 At 10.45 she ....
3 At 8 o'clock ....
4 At 12.10 ....
5 At 7.15 ....
6 At 9.30 ....

13.3 Complete the questions. Use **was/were -ing**. Use **what/where/why** if necessary.

1 (you/live) *Where were you living* in 1999?	In London.
2 (you/do) .... at 2 o'clock?	I was asleep.
3 (it/rain) .... when you got up?	No, it was sunny.
4 (Sue/drive) .... so fast?	Because she was late.
5 (Tim/wear) .... a suit yesterday?	No, a T-shirt and jeans.

13.4 Look at the picture. You saw Joe in the street yesterday afternoon. What was he doing? Write positive or negative sentences.

Joe

1 (wear / a jacket) *He wasn't wearing a jacket.*
2 (carry / a bag) ....
3 (go / to the dentist) ....
4 (eat / an ice-cream) ....
5 (carry / an umbrella) ....
6 (go / home) ....
7 (wear / a hat) ....
8 (ride / a bicycle) ....

Unit 14 I was doing (past continuous) and I did (past simple)

A

Jack was reading a book. | The phone rang. | He stopped reading. | He answered the phone.

What **happened**? The phone **rang**. *(past simple)*

What **was** Jack **doing** when the phone rang?
He **was reading** a book. } *(past continuous)*

What **did** he **do** when the phone rang?
He **stopped** reading and **answered** the phone. } *(past simple)*

Jack began reading *before* the phone rang.
So *when* the phone rang, he **was reading**.

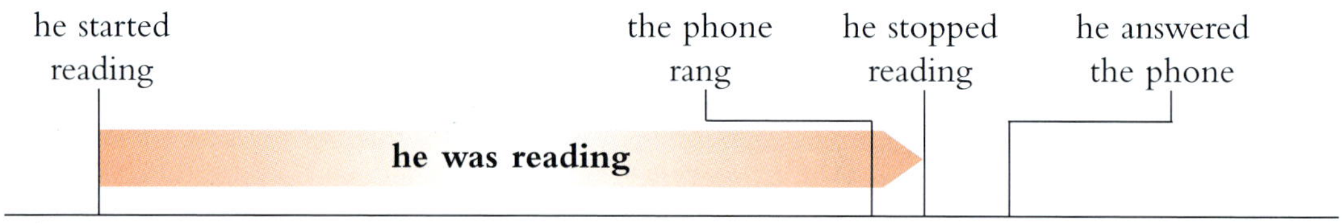

B

past simple

- A: What **did** you **do** yesterday morning?
  B: We **played** tennis. (from 10 to 11.30)

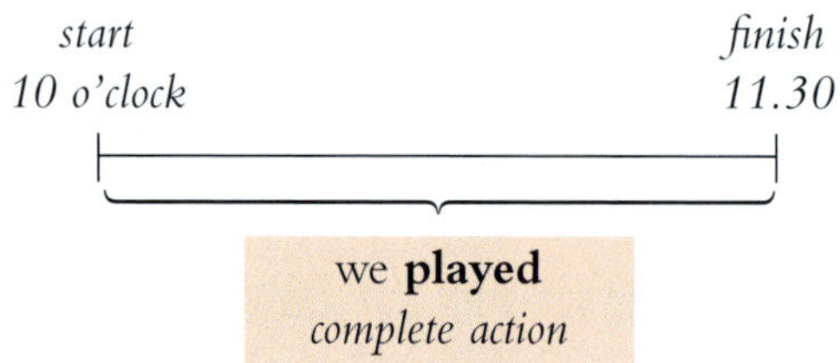

- Jack **read** a book yesterday. (= from beginning to end)
- **Did** you **watch** the film on television last night?
- It **didn't rain** while we were on holiday.

past continuous

- A: What **were** you **doing** at 10.30?
  B: We **were playing** tennis.

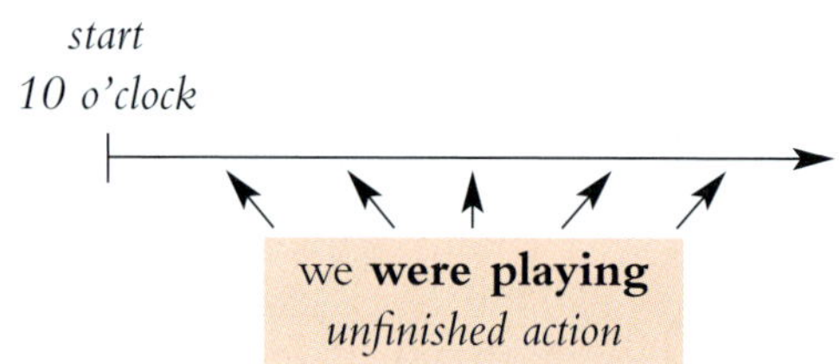

- Jack **was reading** a book when the phone rang.
- **Were** you **watching** television when I phoned you?
- It **wasn't raining** when I got up.

- I **started** work at 9 o'clock and **finished** at 4.30. At 2.30 **I was working**.
- It **was raining** when we **went** out. (= it started raining *before* we went out)
- I **saw** Lucy and Steve this morning. They **were waiting** at the bus stop.
- Kelly **fell** asleep while she **was reading**.

I did (past simple) → Units 11–12 **I was doing** (past continuous) → Unit 13 **while** → Unit 105

14.1 Look at the pictures. Put the verbs in the correct form, past continuous or past simple.

1 

Lucy ....broke.... (break) her arm last week. It .... (happen) when she .... (paint) her room. She .... (fall) off the ladder.

2 

The train .... (arrive) at the station and Paula .... (get) off. Two friends of hers, Jon and Rachel, ... (wait) to meet her.

3 

Yesterday Sue .... (walk) along the road when she .... (meet) James. He .... (go) to the station to catch a train and he .... (carry) a bag. They .... (stop) to talk for a few minutes.

14.2 Put the verb into the past continuous or past simple.

1 A: What ....were you doing.... (you/do) when the phone ....rang.... (ring)?
B: I ....was watching.... (watch) television.

2 A: Was Jane busy when you went to see her?
B: Yes, she .... (study).

3 A: What time .... (the post / arrive) this morning?
B: It .... (come) while I .... (have) breakfast.

4 A: Was Tracey at work today?
B: No, she .... (not/go) to work. She was ill.

5 A: How fast .... (you/drive) when the police .... (stop) you?
B: I'm not sure, but I .... (not/drive) very fast.

6 A: .... (your team / win) the football match yesterday?
B: The weather was very bad, so we .... (not/play).

7 A: How .... (you/break) the window?
B: We .... (play) football. I .... (kick) the ball and it .... (hit) the window.

8 A: .... (you/see) Jenny last night?
B: Yes, she .... (wear) a very nice jacket.

9 A: What .... (you/do) at 2 o'clock this morning?
B: I was asleep.

10 A: I .... (lose) my key last night.
B: How .... (you/get) into your room?
A: I .... (climb) in through a window.

→ Additional exercises 14–15 (pages 257–58)

Unit 15

I have done (present perfect 1)

A

His shoes are dirty.

He is cleaning his shoes.

He **has cleaned** his shoes. (= his shoes are clean *now*)

They are at home.

They are going out.

They **have gone** out. (= they are not at home *now*)

B

has cleaned / **have gone** etc. is the *present perfect* (**have** + *past participle*):

I we you they	**have** ('**ve**) **have not** (**haven't**)	**cleaned** **finished** **started** **lost** **done** **been** **gone**
he she it	**has** ('**s**) **has not** (**hasn't**)	

↑ *past participle*

have	I we you they	**cleaned?** **finished?** **started?**	*regular verbs*
has	he she it	**lost?** **done?** **been?** **gone?**	*irregular verbs*

Regular verbs The past participle is **-ed** (the same as the past simple):

clean → I have clean**ed**   finish → we have finish**ed**   start → she has start**ed**

Irregular verbs The past participle is not **-ed**.
Sometimes the past simple and past participle are the same:

buy → I **bought** / I have **bought**   have → he **had** / he has **had**

Sometimes the past simple and past participle are different:

break → I **broke** / I have **broken**   see → you **saw** / you have **seen**
fall → it **fell** / it has **fallen**   go → they **went** / they have **gone**

C

We use the present perfect for *an action in the past* with a result *now:*

- ☐ **I've lost** my passport. (= I can't find my passport *now*)
- ☐ 'Where's Rebecca?' 'She**'s gone** to bed.' (= she is in bed *now*)
- ☐ We**'ve bought** a new car. (= we have a new car *now*)
- ☐ It's Rachel's birthday tomorrow and I **haven't bought** her a present. (= I don't have a present for her *now*)
- ☐ 'Bob is away on holiday.' 'Oh, where **has** he **gone**?' (= where is he *now*?)
- ☐ Can I take this newspaper? **Have** you **finished** with it? (= do you need it *now*?)

present perfect → Units 16–19   present perfect and past simple → Unit 20   irregular verbs → Unit 24, Appendix 2–3

15.1 Look at the pictures. What has happened? Choose from the box.

go to bed	~~clean his shoes~~	stop raining
close the door	fall down	have a shower

before → *now*

1 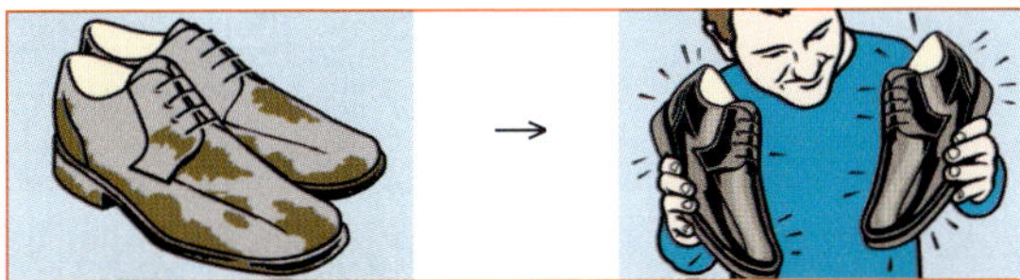
He has cleaned his shoes.

2 
She ....

3 
They ....

4 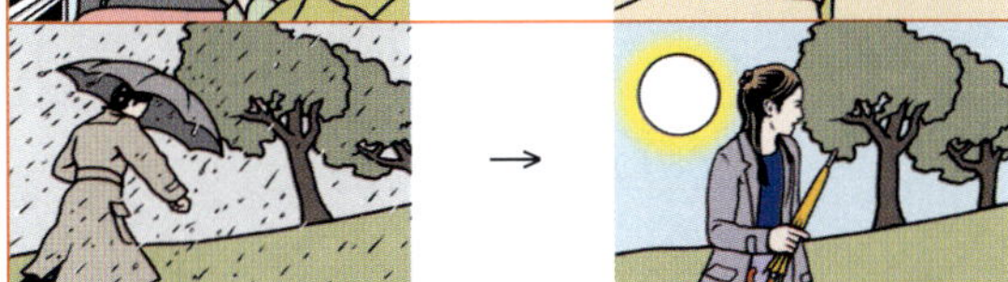
It ....

5 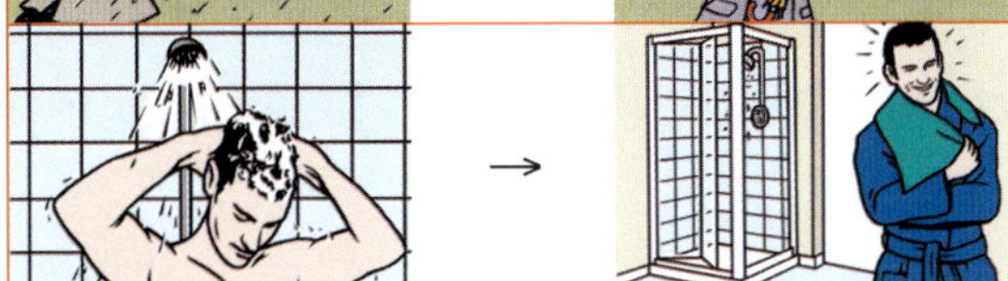
He ....

6 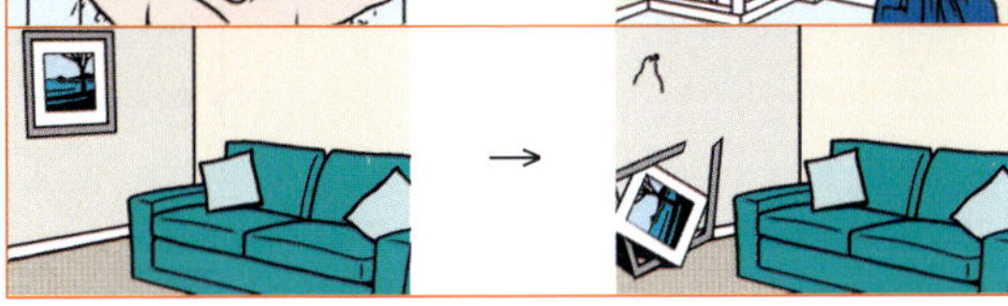
The ....

15.2 Complete the sentences with a verb from the box.

break	buy	decide	~~finish~~	forget	go	go
invite	read	see	not/see	take	tell	not/tell

1 'Can I have a look at your newspaper?' 'Yes, I 've finished with it.'
2 I .... some new shoes. Do you want to see them?
3 'Where is Liz?' 'She's not here. She .... out.'
4 I'm looking for Paula. .... you .... her?
5 Look! Somebody .... that window.
6 'Does Lisa know that you're going away?' 'Yes, I .... her.'
7 I can't find my umbrella. Somebody .... it.
8 'Where are my glasses?' 'I don't know. I .... them.'
9 I'm looking for Sarah. Where .... she .... ?
10 I know that woman, but I .... her name.
11 Sue is having a party tonight. She .... a lot of people.
12 What are you going to do? .... you .... ?
13 A: Does Bill know about the meeting tomorrow?
B: I don't think so. I .... him.
14 'Do you want this magazine?' 'No, I .... it, thanks.'

Unit 16 I've just ... I've already ... I haven't ... yet (present perfect 2)

A I've just ...

just = a short time ago

- A: Are Diane and Paul here?
  B: Yes, they**'ve just arrived**.
- A: Are you hungry?
  B: No, I**'ve just had** dinner.
- A: Is Tom here?
  B: No, I'm afraid he**'s just gone**.
  (= he **has** just gone)

They **have just arrived**.

B I've already ...

already = before you expected / before I expected

- A: What time are Diane and Paul coming?
  B: They**'ve already arrived**.
  (= before you expected)
- It's only 9 o'clock and Anna **has already gone** to bed. (= before I expected)
- A: Jon, this is Emma.
  B: Yes, I know. We**'ve already met**.

C I haven't ... yet / Have you ... yet?

yet = until now
We use **yet** in negative sentences and questions. **Yet** is usually at the end.

yet in negative sentences (**I haven't ... yet**)

- A: Are Diane and Paul here?
  B: No, they **haven't arrived yet**.
  (but B expects Diane and Paul to arrive soon)
- A: Does James know that you're going away?
  B: No, I **haven't told** him **yet**.
  (but B is going to tell him soon)
- Silvia has bought a new dress, but she **hasn't worn** it **yet**.

The film **hasn't started yet**.

yet in questions (**Have you ... yet?**)

- A: **Have** Diane and Paul **arrived yet**?
  B: No, not yet. We're still waiting for them.
- A: **Has** Nicole **started** her new job **yet**?
  B: No, she starts next week.
- A: This is my new dress.
  B: Oh, it's nice. **Have** you **worn** it **yet**?

present perfect → Units 15, 17–20 word order → Unit 94 **still**, **yet** and **already** → Unit 95

16.1 Write a sentence with **just** for each picture.

1 They've just arrived.
2 He ....
3 They ....
4 The race ....

16.2 Complete the sentences. Use **already** + present perfect.

1 What time is Paul arriving? — He's already arrived.
2 Do your friends want to see the film? — No, they .... it.
3 Don't forget to phone Tom. — I ....
4 When is Martin going away? — He ....
5 Do you want to read the newspaper? — I ....
6 When does Sarah start her new job? — She ....

16.3 Write a sentence with **just** (**They've just ... / She's just ...** etc.) or a negative sentence with **yet** (**They haven't ... yet / She hasn't ... yet** etc.).

1 *a few minutes ago* — *now*

(she / go / out)
She hasn't gone out yet.

2 *a few minutes ago* — *now*

(the bus / go)
The bus ....

3 *a few minutes ago* — *now*

(the train / leave)
....

4 *a few minutes ago* — *now*

(he / open / it)
....

5 *a few minutes ago* — *now*

(they / finish / their dinner)
....

6 *a few minutes ago* — *now*

(it / stop / raining)
....

16.4 Write questions with **yet**.

1 Your friend has got a new job. Perhaps she has started it. You ask her:
Have you started your new job yet?
2 Your friend has some new neighbours. Perhaps he has met them. You ask him:
.... you ....
3 Your friend must pay her phone bill. Perhaps she has paid it. You ask her:
....
4 Tom was trying to sell his car. Perhaps he has sold it. You ask a friend about Tom:
....

Unit 17 Have you ever ... ? (present perfect 3)

A

We use the *present perfect* (**have been** / **have had** / **have played** etc.) when we talk about a time from the past until now – for example, a person's life:

Have you ever been to Japan?

——— *time from the past until now* ———

past *now*

- ☐ '**Have** you **been** to France?' 'No, I **haven't**.'
- ☐ **I've been** to Canada, but I **haven't been** to the United States.
- ☐ Mary is an interesting person. She **has had** many different jobs and **has lived** in many places.
- ☐ **I've seen** that woman before, but I can't remember where.
- ☐ How many times **has** Brazil **won** the World Cup?
- ☐ '**Have** you **read** this book?' 'Yes, **I've read** it twice.' (**twice** = two times)

B

present perfect + **ever** (in questions) and **never**:

- ☐ '**Has** Ann **ever been** to Australia?' 'Yes, once.' (**once** = one time)
- ☐ '**Have** you **ever played** golf?' 'Yes, I play a lot.'
- ☐ My sister **has never travelled** by plane.
- ☐ **I've never ridden** a horse.
- ☐ 'Who is that man?' 'I don't know. **I've never seen** him before.'

C

gone and **been**

Bill **has gone** to Spain.
(= he is in Spain *now*)

two weeks later

Bill **has been** to Spain.
(= he went to Spain, but now he is back)

Compare:

- ☐ I can't find Susan. Where **has** she **gone**? (= where is she now?)
- ☐ Oh, hello Susan! I was looking for you. Where **have** you **been**?

present perfect → Units 15–16, 18 present perfect and past simple → Unit 20

Exercises

17.1 You are asking Helen questions beginning Have you ever ... ? Write the questions.

Helen

1 (London?)	Have you ever been to London?	No, never.
2 (play / golf?)	Have you ever played golf?	Yes, many times.
3 (Australia?)	Have	Yes, once.
4 (lose / your passport?)	....	No, never.
5 (fly / in a helicopter?)	....	Yes, a few times.
6 (win / a race?)	....	No, never.
7 (New York?)	....	Yes, twice.
8 (drive / a bus?)	....	No, never.
9 (break / your leg?)	....	Yes, once.

17.2 Write sentences about Helen. (Look at her answers in Exercise 17.1.)

1 (New York) She's been to New York twice.
2 (Australia) She ....
3 (win / a race) ....
4 (fly / in a helicopter) ....

Now write about yourself. How often have you done these things?

5 (New York) I ....
6 (play / tennis) ....
7 (drive / a lorry) ....
8 (be / late for work or school) ....

17.3 Mary is 65 years old. She has had an interesting life. What has she done?

Mary

~~have~~	be
do	write
travel	meet

all over the world	a lot of interesting things
~~many different jobs~~	a lot of interesting people
ten books	married three times

1 She has had many different jobs.
2 She ....
3 ....
4 ....
5 ....
6 ....

17.4 Write gone or been.

1 Bill is on holiday at the moment. He's gone to Spain.
2 'Where's Jane?' 'She's not here. I think she's .... to the bank.'
3 Hello, Sue. Where have you .... ? Have you .... to the bank?
4 'Have you ever .... to Mexico?' 'No, never.'
5 My parents aren't at home at the moment. They've .... out.
6 There's a new restaurant in town. Have you .... to it?
7 Rebecca knows Paris well. She's .... there many times.
8 Helen was here earlier, but I think she's .... now.

→ Additional exercises 16, 18 (pages 258–59, 260)

Unit 18

How long have you ... ? (present perfect 4)

A

Jane is on holiday in Ireland.
She is there now.

She arrived in Ireland on Monday.
Today is Thursday.

How long **has she been** in Ireland?

She **has been** in Ireland { **since Monday**. / **for three days**. }

Compare **is** and **has been**:

She **is** in Ireland **now**. — **is** = *present*

She **has been** in Ireland { **since Monday**. / **for three days**. } — **has been** = *present perfect*

Monday → *now* / *Thursday*

B

Compare:

present simple	*present perfect simple* (**have been** / **have lived** / **have known** etc.)
Dan and Kate **are** married.	They **have been** married **for five years**. (*not* They are married for five years.)
Are you married?	**How long have** you **been** married? (*not* How long are you married?)
Do you **know** Lisa?	**How long have** you **known** her? (*not* How long do you know her?)
I **know** Lisa.	**I've known** her **for a long time**. (*not* I know her for ...)
Vicky **lives** in London.	**How long has** she **lived** in London? She **has lived** there **all her life**.
I **have** a car.	**How long have** you **had** your car? **I've had** it **since April**.

present continuous	*present perfect continuous* (**have been** + **-ing**)
I'm learning German.	**How long have** you **been learning** German? (*not* How long are you learning German?) **I've been learning** German **for two years**.
David **is watching** TV.	**How long has** he **been watching** TV? He**'s been** (= He **has been**) **watching** TV **since 5 o'clock**.
It**'s raining**.	It**'s been** (= It **has been**) **raining all day**.

for and since → Units 19, 104

18.1 Complete these sentences.

1 Jane is in Ireland. She *has been* in Ireland since Monday.
2 I know Lisa. I *have known* her for a long time.
3 Sarah and Andy are married. They .... married since 1999.
4 Brian is ill. He .... ill for the last few days.
5 We live in Scott Road. We .... there for a long time.
6 Catherine works in a bank. She .... in a bank for five years.
7 Alan has a headache. He .... a headache since he got up this morning.
8 I'm learning English. I .... English for six months.

18.2 Make questions with How long ... ?

1 Jane is on holiday. — *How long has she been on holiday* ?
2 Scott and Judy are in Brazil. — How long .... ?
3 I know Amy. — How long .... you .... ?
4 Diana is learning Italian. — .... ?
5 My brother lives in Canada. — .... ?
6 I'm a teacher. — .... ?
7 It is raining. — .... ?

18.3

Look at the pictures and complete the sentences with:

for ten minutes	all day	all her life
~~for ten years~~	since he was 20	since Sunday

1 *They have been married for ten years.*
2 She ....
3 They ....
4 The sun ....
5 She ....
6 He ....

18.4 Which is right?

1 Mark ~~lives~~ / has lived in Canada since April. (has lived *is right*)
2 Jane and I are friends. I know / I've known her very well.
3 Jane and I are friends. I know / I've known her for a long time.
4 A: Sorry I'm late. How long are you waiting/ have you been waiting?
B: Not long. Only five minutes.
5 Martin works / has worked in a hotel now. He likes his job a lot.
6 Ruth is reading the newspaper. She is reading / She has been reading it for two hours.
7 'How long do you live / have you lived in this house?' 'About ten years.'
8 'Is that a new coat?' 'No, I have / I've had this coat for a long time.'
9 Tom is / has been in Spain at the moment. He is / He has been there for the last three days.

Unit 19 for since ago

A for and since

We use **for** and **since** to say *how long*:

- Jane is in Ireland. She **has been** there { **for three days**. / **since Monday**. }

We use **for** + a period of time (**three days** / **two years** etc.):

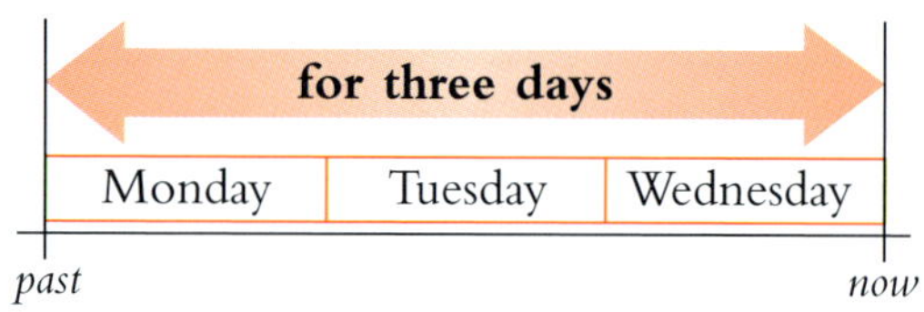

for	
three days	ten minutes
an hour	two hours
a week	four weeks
a month	six months
five years	a long time

- Richard has been in Canada **for six months**. (*not* since six months)
- We've been waiting **for two hours**. (*not* since two hours)
- I've lived in London **for a long time**.

We use **since** + the start of the period (**Monday** / **9 o'clock** etc.):

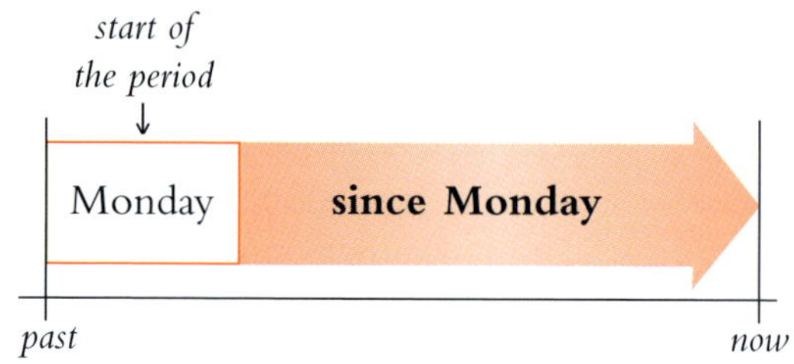

since	
Monday	Wednesday
9 o'clock	12.30
24 July	Christmas
January	I was ten years old
1985	we arrived

- Richard has been in Canada **since January**. (= from January to now)
- We've been waiting **since 9 o'clock**. (= from 9 o'clock to now)
- I've lived in London **since I was ten years old**.

B ago

ago = before now:

- Susan started her new job **three weeks ago**. (= three weeks before now)
- 'When did Tom go out?' '**Ten minutes ago**.' (= ten minutes before now)
- I had dinner **an hour ago**.
- Life was very different **a hundred years ago**.

We use **ago** with the *past* (**started**/**did**/**had**/**was** etc.).

Compare **ago** and **for**:

- **When did** Jane **arrive** in Ireland?
  She **arrived** in Ireland **three days ago**.
- **How long has** she **been** in Ireland?
  She **has been** in Ireland **for three days**.

present perfect + **for/since** → Unit 18 **from/until/since/for** → Unit 104 **for** and **during** → Unit 105

Exercises

19.1 Write for or since.

1 Jane has been in Ireland ....*since*.... Monday.
2 Jane has been in Ireland ....*for*.... three days.
3 My aunt has lived in Australia .... 15 years.
4 Jennifer is in her office. She has been there .... 7 o'clock.
5 India has been an independent country .... 1947.
6 The bus is late. We've been waiting .... 20 minutes.
7 Nobody lives in those houses. They have been empty .... many years.
8 Michael has been ill .... a long time. He has been in hospital .... October.

19.2 Answer these questions. Use ago.

1 When was your last meal? ....*Three hours ago.*....
2 When was the last time you were ill? ....
3 When did you last go to the cinema? ....
4 When was the last time you were in a car? ....
5 When was the last time you went on holiday? ....

19.3 Complete the sentences. Use for or ago with these words.

1 Jane arrived in Ireland ....*three days ago.*.... (three days)
2 Jane has been in Ireland ....*for three days.*.... (three days)
3 Lynn and Mark have been married .... (20 years)
4 Lynn and Mark got married .... (20 years)
5 Dan arrived .... (an hour)
6 I bought these shoes .... (a few days)
7 Silvia has been learning English .... (six months)
8 Have you known Lisa .... ? (a long time)

19.4 Complete the sentences with for or since.

1 (Jane is in Ireland – she arrived there three days ago)
....*Jane has been in Ireland for three days.*....
2 (Jack is here – he arrived on Tuesday)
Jack has ....
3 (It's raining – it started an hour ago)
It's been ....
4 (I know Sue – I first met her in 2002)
I've ....
5 (Claire and Matthew are married – they got married six months ago)
Claire and Matthew have ....
6 (Liz is studying medicine at university – she started three years ago)
Liz has ....
7 (David plays the piano – he started when he was seven years old)
David has ....

19.5 Write sentences about yourself. Begin your sentences with:

I've lived ... I've been ... I've been learning ... I've known ... I've had ...

1 ....*I've lived in this town for three years.*....
2 ....
3 ....
4 ....
5 ....

→ Additional exercises 16–18 (pages 258–60)

Unit 20

I have done (present perfect) and I did (past)

A

With a *finished time* (**yesterday** / **last week** etc.), we use the past (**arrived/saw/was** etc.):

past + *finished time*

We **arrived**	yesterday. last week. at 3 o'clock. in 2002. six months ago.

Do *not* use the present perfect (**have arrived** / **have done** / **have been** etc.) with a finished time:

- I **saw** Paula **yesterday**. (*not* I have seen)
- Where **were** you **on Sunday afternoon?** (*not* Where have you been)
- We **didn't have** a holiday **last year**. (*not* We haven't had)
- 'What **did** you **do last night**?' 'I **stayed** at home.'
- William Shakespeare **lived from 1564 to 1616**. He **was** a writer. He **wrote** many plays and poems.

Use the past to ask **When … ?** or **What time … ?**:

- **When did** you **buy** your computer? (*not* When have you bought?)
- **What time did** Andy **go** out? (*not* What time has Andy gone out)

B

Compare:

present perfect

- I **have lost** my key. (= I can't find it *now*)
- Ben **has gone** home. (= he isn't here *now*)
- **Have** you **seen** Kate? (= where is she *now*?)

- **Have** you **ever been** to Spain? (= in your life, until *now*)
- My friend is a writer. He **has written** many books.
- The letter **hasn't arrived** yet.
- We**'ve lived** in Singapore for six years. (= we live there *now*)

past

- I **lost** my key **last week**.
- Ben **went** home **ten minutes ago**.
- **Did** you **see** Kate **on Saturday**?

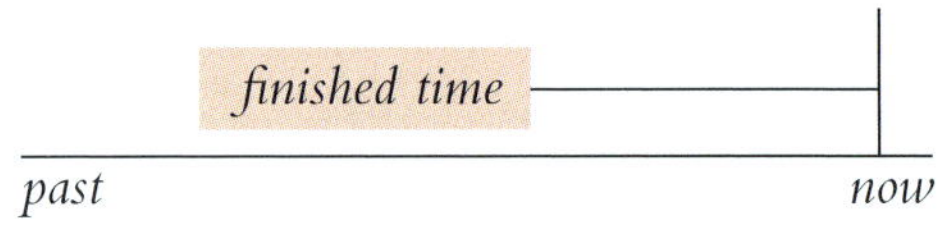

- **Did** you **go** to Spain **last year**?
- Shakespeare **wrote** many plays and poems.
- The letter **didn't arrive yesterday**.
- We **lived** in Glasgow for six years, but now we live in Singapore.

past simple → Units 11–12 present perfect → Units 15–18

Exercises

20.1 Complete the answers to the questions.

1	Have you seen Kate?	Yes, I saw her five minutes ago.
2	Have you started your new job?	Yes, I .... last week.
3	Have your friends arrived?	Yes, they .... at 5 o'clock.
4	Has Sarah gone away?	Yes, ... on Friday.
5	Have you worn your new suit?	Yes, ... yesterday.

20.2 Are these sentences OK? Correct the verbs that are wrong. (The verbs are underlined.)

1 I've lost my key. I can't find it. ... OK
2 Have you seen Kate yesterday? ... Did you see
3 I've finished my work at 2 o'clock. ....
4 I'm ready now. I've finished my work. ....
5 What time have you finished your work? ....
6 Sue isn't here. She's gone out. ....
7 Steve's grandmother has died two years ago. ....
8 Where have you been last night? ....

20.3 Put the verb in the present perfect or past.

1 My friend is a writer. He has written (write) many books.
2 We didn't have (not/have) a holiday last year.
3 I .... (play) tennis yesterday afternoon.
4 What time .... (you/go) to bed last night?
5 .... (you/ever/meet) a famous person?
6 The weather .... (not/be) very good yesterday.
7 Kathy travels a lot. She .... (visit) many countries.
8 I .... (switch) off the light before going out this morning.
9 I live in New York now, but I .... (live) in Mexico for many years.
10 'What's Canada like? Is it beautiful?' 'I don't know. I .... (not/be) there.'

20.4 Put the verb in the present perfect or past.

1 A: Have you ever been (you/ever/be) to Florida?
B: Yes, we went (go) there on holiday two years ago.
A: .... (you/have) a good time?
B: Yes, it .... (be) great.

2 A: Where's Alan? .... (you/see) him?
B: Yes, he .... (go) out a few minutes ago.
A: And Rachel?
B: I don't know. I .... (not/see) her.

3 Rose works in a factory. She .... (work) there for six months. Before that she .... (be) a waitress in a restaurant. She .... (work) there for two years, but she .... (not/enjoy) it very much.

4 A: Do you know Martin's sister?
B: I .... (see) her a few times, but I .... (never/speak) to her. .... (you/ever/speak) to her?
A: Yes. I .... (meet) her at a party last week. She's very nice.

→ Additional exercises 19–23, 29–31 (pages 260–62, 265–67)

Unit 21 is done was done (passive 1)

A

The office **is cleaned** every day.

The office **was cleaned** yesterday.

Compare active and passive:

Somebody **cleans** the office every day. *(active)*

The office **is cleaned** every day. *(passive)*

Somebody **cleaned** the office yesterday. *(active)*

The office **was cleaned** yesterday. *(passive)*

B

The passive is:

				past participle
present simple *past simple*	**am/is/are** **was/were**	(not)	+	**cleaned** **done** **invented** **built** **injured** **taken** etc.

The past participle of regular verbs is **-ed** (clean**ed**/damag**ed** etc.).
For a list of irregular past participles (**done/built/taken** etc.), see Appendix 2–3.

- Butter **is made** from milk.
- Oranges **are imported** into Britain.
- How often **are** these rooms **cleaned**?
- I **am** never **invited** to parties.

- This house **was built** 100 years ago.
- These houses **were built** 100 years ago.
- When **was** the telephone **invented**?
- We **weren't invited** to the party last week.
- '**Was** anybody **injured** in the accident?' 'Yes, two people **were taken** to hospital.'

C

was/were born

- I **was born** in Berlin in 1989. (*not* I am born)
- 'Where **were** you **born**?' 'In Cairo.'

D

passive + **by** ...

- The telephone was invented **by Alexander Bell** in 1876. (= Alexander Bell invented it)
- I was bitten **by a dog** a few days ago.
- Do you like these paintings? They were painted **by a friend of mine**.

is being done / has been done → Unit 22 irregular verbs → Unit 24, Appendix 2–3 **by** → Unit 111
active and passive → Appendix 1

21.1 Write sentences from these words. Some of the sentences are questions. Sentences 1–7 are present.

1 (the office / clean / every day) *The office is cleaned every day.*
2 (these rooms / clean / every day?) *Are these rooms cleaned every day?*
3 (glass / make / from sand) Glass ....
4 (stamps / sell / in a post office) ....
5 (this room / not / use / very often) ....
6 (we / allow / to park here?) ....
7 (how / this word / pronounce?) ....

Sentences 8–15 are past.

8 (the office / clean / yesterday) *The office was cleaned yesterday.*
9 (the house / paint / last month) The house ....
10 (my phone / steal / a few days ago) ....
11 (three people / injure / in the accident) ....
12 (when / this bridge / build?) ....
13 (I / not / wake up / by the noise) ....
14 (how / these windows / break?) ....
15 (you / invite / to Jon's party last week?)
....

21.2 These sentences are not correct. Correct them.

1 This house built 100 years ago. *This house was built*
2 Football plays in most countries of the world. ....
3 Why did the letter send to the wrong address? ....
4 A garage is a place where cars repair. ....
5 Where are you born? ....
6 How many languages are speaking in Switzerland? ....
7 Somebody broke into our house, but nothing stolen. ....
8 When was invented the bicycle? ....

21.3 Complete the sentences. Use the passive (present or past) of these verbs:

~~**clean**~~ **damage** **find** **give** **invite** **make** **make** **show** **steal** ~~**take**~~

1 The room *is cleaned* every day.
2 I saw an accident yesterday. Two people *were taken* to hospital.
3 Paper .... from wood.
4 There was a fire at the hotel last week. Two of the rooms ....
5 'Where did you get this picture?' 'It .... to me by a friend of mine.'
6 Many American programmes .... on British television.
7 'Did Jim and Sue go to the wedding?' 'No. They ...., but they didn't go.'
8 'How old is this film?' 'It .... in 1965.'
9 My car .... last week, but the next day it .... by the police.

21.4 Where were they born?

1 (Ian / Edinburgh) *Ian was born in Edinburgh.*
2 (Sally / Manchester) Sally ....
3 (her parents / Ireland) Her ....
4 (you / ???) I ....
5 (your mother / ???) ....

Unit 22 is being done / has been done (passive 2)

A

is/are being … *(present continuous passive)*

Somebody **is painting** the door . *(active)*

The door **is being painted**. *(passive)*

- ☐ My car is at the garage. It **is being repaired**. (= somebody is repairing it)
- ☐ Some new houses **are being built** opposite the park. (= somebody is building them)

Compare the present continuous and present simple:

- ☐ The office **is being cleaned** at the moment. *(continuous)*
  The office **is cleaned** every day. *(simple)*
- ☐ In Britain football matches **are** often **played** at the weekend, but no matches **are being played** next weekend.

For the present continuous and present simple, see Units 8 and 25.

B

has/have been … *(present perfect passive)*

before *now*

Somebody **has painted** the door . *(active)*

The door **has been painted**. *(passive)*

- ☐ My key **has been stolen**. (= somebody has stolen it)
- ☐ My keys **have been stolen**. (= somebody has stolen them)
- ☐ I'm not going to the party. I **haven't been invited**. (= nobody has invited me)
- ☐ **Has** this shirt **been washed**? (= has somebody washed it?)

Compare the present perfect and past simple:

- ☐ The room isn't dirty any more. It **has been cleaned**. *(present perfect)*
  The room **was cleaned** yesterday. *(past simple)*
- ☐ I can't find my keys. I think they**'ve been stolen**. *(present perfect)*
  My keys **were stolen** last week. *(past simple)*

For the present perfect and past simple, see Unit 20.

is done / was done → Unit 21 active and passive → Appendix 1

Exercises

22.1 What's happening?

1 The car is being repaired.
2 A bridge ……
3 The windows ……
4 The grass ……

22.2 Look at the pictures. What is happening or what has happened? Use the present continuous (is/are being ...) or the present perfect (has/have been ...).

1 (the office / clean) The office is being cleaned.
2 (the shirts / iron) The shirts have been ironed.
3 (the window / break) The window ……
4 (the roof / repair) The roof ……
5 (the car / damage) ……
6 (the houses / knock / down) ……
7 (the trees / cut / down) ……
8 (they / invite / to a party) ……

22.3 Complete the sentences. (Study Unit 21 before you do this exercise.)

1 I can't use my office at the moment. It is being painted (paint).
2 We didn't go to the party. We weren't invited (not/invite).
3 The washing machine was broken, but it's OK now. It …… (repair).
4 The washing machine …… (repair) yesterday afternoon.
5 A factory is a place where things …… (make).
6 How old are these houses? When …… (they/build)?
7 A: …… (the computer / use) at the moment?
B: Yes, Steve is using it.
8 I've never seen these flowers before. What …… (they/call)?
9 My sunglasses …… (steal) at the beach yesterday.
10 The bridge is closed at the moment. It …… (damage) last week and it …… (not/repair) yet.

→ Additional exercises 24–27 (pages 263–64)

be/have/do in present and past tenses

A

be (= **am**/**is**/**are**/**was**/**were**) + **-ing** (**cleaning**/**working** etc.)

am/**is**/**are** + -ing *(present continuous)* → Units 3–4 and 25	☐ Please be quiet. I'**m working**. ☐ It **isn't raining** at the moment. ☐ What **are** you **doing** this evening?
was/**were** + -ing *(past continuous)* → Unit 13	☐ I **was working** when she arrived. ☐ It **wasn't raining**, so we didn't need an umbrella. ☐ What **were** you **doing** at 3 o'clock?

B

be + *past participle* (**cleaned**/**made**/**eaten** etc.)

am/**is**/**are** + *past participle* *(passive present simple)* → Unit 21	☐ **I'm** never **invited** to parties. ☐ Butter **is made** from milk. ☐ These offices **aren't cleaned** every day.
was/**were** + *past participle* *(passive past simple)* → Unit 21	☐ The office **was cleaned** yesterday. ☐ These houses **were built** 100 years ago. ☐ How **was** the window **broken**? ☐ Where **were** you **born**?

C

have/**has** + *past participle* (**cleaned**/**lost**/**eaten**/**been** etc.)

have/**has** + *past participle* *(present perfect)* → Units 15–18	☐ **I've cleaned** my room. ☐ Tom **has lost** his passport. ☐ Kate **hasn't been** to Canada. ☐ Where **have** Paul and Nicole **gone**?

D

do/**does**/**did** + *infinitive* (**clean**/**like**/**eat**/**go** etc.)

do/**does** + *infinitive* *(present simple negative and questions)* → Units 6–7	☐ I like coffee, but I **don't like** tea. ☐ Chris **doesn't go** out very often. ☐ What **do** you usually **do** at weekends? ☐ **Does** Silvia **live** alone?
did + *infinitive* *(past simple negative and questions)* → Unit 12	☐ I **didn't watch** TV yesterday. ☐ It **didn't rain** last week. ☐ What time **did** Paul and Nicole **go** out?

irregular verbs → **Unit 24, Appendix 2–3**

Exercises

23.1 Write is/are or do/does.

1 ...Do... you work in the evenings?
2 Where ...are... they going?
3 Why .... you looking at me?
4 .... Bill live near you?
5 .... you like cooking?
6 .... the sun shining?
7 What time .... the shops close?
8 .... Maria working today?
9 What .... this word mean?
10 .... you feeling all right?

23.2 Write am not/isn't/aren't or don't/doesn't. All these sentences are negative.

1 Tom ...doesn't... work at weekends.
2 I'm very tired. I .... want to go out this evening.
3 I'm very tired. I .... going out this evening.
4 Gary .... working this week. He's on holiday.
5 My parents are usually at home. They .... go out very often.
6 Nicole has travelled a lot, but she .... speak any foreign languages.
7 You can turn off the television. I .... watching it.
8 Liz has invited us to her party next week, but we .... going.

23.3 Write was/were/did/have/has.

1 Where ...were... your shoes made?
2 .... you go out last night?
3 What .... you doing at 10.30?
4 Where .... your mother born?
5 .... Barbara gone home?
6 What time .... she go?
7 When .... these houses built?
8 .... Steve arrived yet?
9 Why .... you go home early?
10 How long .... they been married?

23.4 Write is/are/was/were/have/has.

1 Joe ...has... lost his passport.
2 This bridge .... built ten years ago.
3 .... you finished your work yet?
4 This town is always clean. The streets .... cleaned every day.
5 Where .... you born?
6 I .... just made some coffee. Would you like some?
7 Glass .... made from sand.
8 This is a very old photograph. It .... taken a long time ago.
9 David .... bought a new car.

23.5 Complete the sentences. Choose from the box and put the verb into the correct form.

damage	~~rain~~	enjoy	~~go~~	pronounce	eat
listen	use	open	go	understand	

1 I'm going to take an umbrella with me. It's ...raining... .
2 Why are you so tired? Did you ...go... to bed late last night?
3 Where are the chocolates? Have you .... them all?
4 How is your new job? Are you .... it?
5 My car was badly .... in the accident, but I was OK.
6 Chris has got a car, but she doesn't .... it very often.
7 Mary isn't at home. She has .... away for a few days.
8 I don't .... the problem. Can you explain it again?
9 Martin is in his room. He's .... to music.
10 I don't know how to say this word. How is it .... ?
11 How do you .... this window? Can you show me?

Unit 24

Regular and irregular verbs

A

Regular verbs

The *past simple* and *past participle* of regular verbs is **-ed**:

clean → clean**ed** live → liv**ed** paint → paint**ed** study → studi**ed**

Past simple (→ Unit 11)

- □ I **cleaned** my room yesterday.
- □ Charlie **studied** engineering at university.

Past participle

have/has + *past participle* (present perfect → Units 15–18):

- □ I **have cleaned** my room.
- □ Tina **has lived** in London for ten years.

be (**is**/**are**/**were**/**has been** etc.) + *past participle* (passive → Units 21–22):

- □ These rooms **are cleaned** every day.
- □ My car **has been repaired**.

B

Irregular verbs

The past simple and past participle of irregular verbs do *not* end in **-ed**:

	make	break	cut
past simple	**made**	**broke**	**cut**
past participle	**made**	**broken**	**cut**

Sometimes the past simple and past participle are the same. For example:

	make	find	buy	cut
past simple } *past participle*	**made**	**found**	**bought**	**cut**

- □ I **made** a cake yesterday. *(past simple)*
- □ I **have made** some coffee. *(past participle – present perfect)*
- □ Butter **is made** from milk. *(past participle – passive present)*

Sometimes the past simple and past participle are different. For example:

	break	know	begin	go
past simple	**broke**	**knew**	**began**	**went**
past participle	**broken**	**known**	**begun**	**gone**

- □ Somebody **broke** this window last night. *(past simple)*
- □ Somebody **has broken** this window. *(past participle – present perfect)*
- □ This window **was broken** last night. *(past participle – passive past)*

irregular verbs → Appendix 2–3 spelling (regular verbs) → Appendix 5

24.1 Write the past simple / past participle of these verbs. (The past simple and past participle are the same for all the verbs in this exercise.)

1 make	made	6 enjoy	....	11 hear	....
2 cut	cut	7 buy	....	12 put	....
3 get	....	8 sit	....	13 catch	....
4 bring	....	9 leave	....	14 watch	....
5 pay	....	10 happen	....	15 understand	....

24.2 Write the past simple and past participle of these verbs.

1 break	broke	broken	8 come	....	....
2 begin	....	....	9 know	....	....
3 eat	....	....	10 take	....	....
4 drink	....	....	11 go	....	....
5 drive	....	....	12 give	....	....
6 speak	....	....	13 throw	....	....
7 write	....	....	14 forget	....	....

24.3 Put the verb in the right form.

1 I washed my hands because they were dirty. (wash)
2 Somebody has broken this window. (break)
3 I feel good. I .... very well last night. (sleep)
4 We .... a really good film yesterday. (see)
5 It .... a lot while we were on holiday. (rain)
6 I've .... my bag. (lose) Have you .... it? (see)
7 Rosa's bicycle was .... last week. (steal)
8 I .... to bed early because I was tired. (go)
9 Have you .... your work yet? (finish)
10 The shopping centre was .... about 20 years ago. (build)
11 Anna .... to drive when she was 18. (learn)
12 I've never .... a horse. (ride)
13 Julia is a good friend of mine. I've .... her for a long time. (know)
14 Yesterday I .... and .... my leg. (fall / hurt)
15 My brother .... in the London Marathon last year. Have you ever .... in a marathon? (run / run)

24.4 Complete these sentences. Choose from the box and put the verb into the correct form.

cost	drive	fly	~~make~~	meet	sell
speak	swim	tell	think	wake up	win

1 I have made some coffee. Would you like some?
2 Have you .... John about your new job?
3 We played basketball on Sunday. We didn't play very well, but we .... the game.
4 I know Gary, but I've never .... his wife.
5 We were .... by loud music in the middle of the night.
6 Stephanie jumped into the river and .... to the other side.
7 'Did you like the film?' 'Yes, I .... it was very good.'
8 Many different languages are .... in the Philippines.
9 Our holiday .... a lot of money because we stayed in an expensive hotel.
10 Have you ever .... a very fast car?
11 All the tickets for the concert were .... very quickly.
12 A bird .... in through the open window while we were having our dinner.

Unit 25

What are you doing tomorrow?

A

They **are playing** tennis (**now**).

today is Sunday

He **is playing** tennis **tomorrow**.

We use **am/is/are** + **-ing** *(present continuous)* for something happening now:

- 'Where are Sue and Amanda?' 'They**'re playing** tennis in the park.'
- Please be quiet. **I'm working**.

We also use **am/is/are** + **-ing** for the *future* (tomorrow / next week etc.):

- Andrew **is playing** tennis tomorrow.
- **I'm** not **working** next week.

B

I am doing something tomorrow = I have arranged to do it, I have a plan to do it:

- Sophie **is going** to the dentist on Friday. (= she has an appointment with the dentist)
- We**'re having** a party next weekend.
- **Are** you **meeting** your friends tonight?
- What **are** you **doing** tomorrow evening?
- **I'm** not **going** out tonight. **I'm staying** at home.

You can also say '**I'm going to** do something' (→ Unit 26).

C

Be careful! Do not use the *present simple* (**I stay** / **do you go** etc.) to say what somebody has arranged to do:

- **I'm staying** at home this evening. (*not* I stay)
- **Are** you **going** out tonight? (*not* Do you go)
- Lisa **isn't coming** to the party next week. (*not* Lisa doesn't come)

But we use the present simple for timetables, programmes, trains, buses etc. :

- The train **arrives** at 7.30.
- What time **does** the film **finish**?

Compare:

present continuous (usually for people)	*present simple* (for timetables, programmes etc.)
I'm going to a concert tomorrow.	The concert **starts** at 7.30.
What time **are** you **leaving**?	What time **does** your train **leave**?

present continuous → Units 3–4 present simple → Units 5–7 **I'm going to ...** → Unit 26

Exercises

25.1 Look at the pictures. What are these people doing next Friday?

1 ....*Andrew is playing tennis on Friday.*..........
2 Richard .... to the cinema.
3 Rachel ....
4 .... lunch with Ken.
5 ....

25.2 Write questions. All the sentences are future.

1 (you / go / out / tonight?) ....*Are you going out tonight?*..........
2 (you / work / next week?) ....
3 (what / you / do / tomorrow evening?) ....
4 (what time / your friends / come?) ....
5 (when / Liz / go / on holiday?) ....

25.3 Write sentences about yourself. What are you doing in the next few days?

1 ....*I'm staying at home tonight.*..........
2 ....*I'm going to the theatre on Monday.*..........
3 ....
4 ....
5 ....
6 ....

25.4 Put the verb in the present continuous (he is leaving etc.) or present simple (the train leaves etc.).

1 '..........*Are you going*.......... (you/go) out tonight?' 'No, I'm too tired.'
2 ....*We're going*.......... (we/go) to a concert tonight. ....*It starts*.......... (it/start) at 7.30.
3 Do you know about Sally? .... (she/get) married next month!
4 A: My parents .... (go) on holiday next week.
B: Oh, that's nice. Where .... (they/go)?
5 Silvia is doing an English course at the moment. The course .... (finish) on Friday.
6 There's a party tomorrow night, but .... (I/not/go).
7 .... (I/go) out with some friends tonight. Why don't you come too? .... (we/meet) outside the Royal Hotel at 8 o'clock.
8 A: How .... (you/get) home after the party tomorrow? By taxi?
B: No, I can go by bus. The last bus .... (leave) at midnight.
9 A: Do you want to go to the cinema tonight?
B: Yes, what time .... (the film / begin)?
10 A: What .... (you/do) tomorrow afternoon?
B: .... (I/work).

I'm going to ...

A

I'm going to do something

She **is going to watch** TV this evening.

We use **am/is/are going to** ... for the *future:*

I	**am**	(not) **going to**	do ...
he/she/it	**is**		drink ...
we/you/they	**are**		watch ...

am	I	**going to**	buy ... ?
is	he/she/it		eat ... ?
are	we/you/they		wear ... ?

B

I am going to do something = I have decided to do it, my intention is to do it:

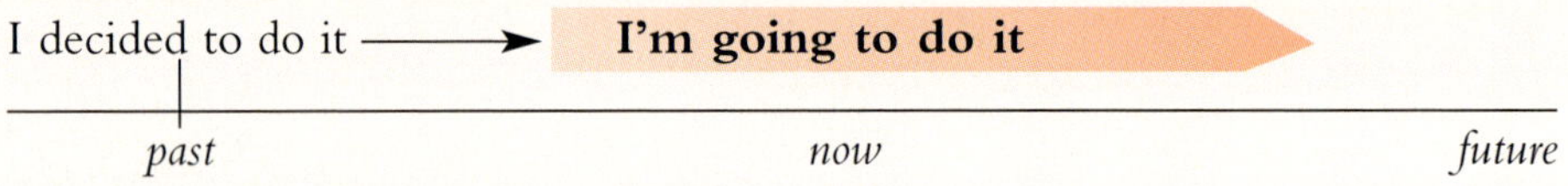

- **I'm going to buy** some books tomorrow.
- Sarah **is going to sell** her car.
- **I'm not going to have** breakfast this morning. I'm not hungry.
- What **are** you **going to wear** to the wedding next week?
- 'Your hands are dirty.' 'Yes, I know. **I'm going to wash** them.'
- **Are** you **going to invite** Martin to your party?

We also use the present continuous (**I am doing**) for the future, usually for arrangements (→ Unit 25):

- I **am playing** tennis with Julia tomorrow.

C

Something **is going to happen**

Something **is going to happen** = we can see *now* that it is sure to happen:

- Look at the sky! It**'s going to rain**.
  (black clouds *now* → rain)
- Oh dear! It's 9 o'clock and I'm not ready.
  I'm going to be late.
  (9 o'clock *now* and not ready → late)

present for the future → **Unit 25** will → **Units 27–28**

Exercises

26.1 What are these people saying?

26.2 Complete the sentences. Use going to + these verbs:

do eat give lie down stay walk ~~wash~~ watch ~~wear~~

1 My hands are dirty. *I'm going to wash* them.
2 What *are you going to wear* to the party tonight?
3 It's a nice day. I don't want to take the bus. I ....
4 Steve is going to London next week. He .... with some friends.
5 I'm hungry. I .... this sandwich.
6 It's Sharon's birthday next week. We .... her a present.
7 Sue says she's feeling very tired. She .... for an hour.
8 There's a good film on Channel 6 tonight. .... you .... it?
9 What .... Rachel .... when she leaves school?

26.3 Look at the pictures. What is going to happen?

1 *It's going to rain.*
2 The shelf ....
3 The car ....
4 He ....

26.4 What are you going to do today or tomorrow? Write three sentences.

1 I'm ....
2 ....
3 ....

Unit 27 will/shall 1

A

SARAH

Sarah goes to work every day. She is always there from 8.30 until 4.30.

It is 11 o'clock now. Sarah **is** at work.

At 11 o'clock yesterday, she **was** at work.

At 11 o'clock tomorrow, she **will be** at work.

will + *infinitive* (**will be** / **will win** / **will come** etc.):

I/we/you/they he/she/it	**will** (**'ll**) **will not** (**won't**)	**be** **win** **eat** **come** etc.

will	I/we/you/they he/she/it	**be?** **win?** **eat?** **come?** etc.

'll = **will**: **I'll** (I will) / you**'ll** / she**'ll** etc.
won't = **will not**: I **won't** (= I will not) / you **won't** / she **won't** etc.

B

We use **will** for the *future* (tomorrow / next week etc.):

- Sue travels a lot. Today she is in Madrid. Tomorrow she**'ll be** in Rome. Next week she**'ll be** in Tokyo.
- You can call me this evening. **I'll be** at home.
- Leave the old bread in the garden. The birds **will eat** it.
- We**'ll** probably **go** out this evening.
- **Will** you **be** at home this evening?

- I **won't be** here tomorrow. (= I will not be here)
- Don't drink coffee before you go to bed. You **won't sleep**.

We often say **I think** ... **will** ... :

- **I think** Kelly **will pass** the exam.
- **I don't think** it **will rain** this afternoon.
- **Do you think** the exam **will be** difficult?

C

We do *not* use **will** for things we have already arranged or decided to do (→ Units 25–26):

- We**'re going** to the cinema on Saturday. Do you want to come with us? (*not* We will go)
- **I'm** not **working** tomorrow. (*not* I won't work)
- **Are** you **going to do** the exam? (*not* Will you do)

D

shall

You can say **I shall** (= I will) and **we shall** (= we will):

- **I shall be** late tomorrow. *or* **I will** (**I'll**) **be** late tomorrow.
- I think **we shall win**. *or* I think **we will** (**we'll**) **win**.

But *do not* use **shall** with **you/they/he/she/it**:

- **Tom will** be late. (*not* Tom shall be)

What are you doing tomorrow? → Unit 25 I'm going to ... → Unit 26 will/shall 2 → Unit 28

Exercises

27.1 Helen is travelling in Europe. Complete the sentences with she was, she's or she'll be.

1 Yesterday ..... she was ..... in Paris.
2 Tomorrow .... in Amsterdam.
3 Last week .... in Barcelona.
4 Next week .... in London.
5 At the moment .... in Brussels.
6 Three days ago .... in Munich.
7 At the end of her trip .... very tired.

27.2 Where will you be? Write sentences about yourself. Use:

I'll be ... or **I'll probably be ...** or **I don't know where I'll be**.

1 (at 10 o'clock tomorrow) ..... I'll probably be on the beach. .....
2 (one hour from now) ....
3 (at midnight tonight) ....
4 (at 3 o'clock tomorrow afternoon) ....
5 (two years from now) ....

27.3 Put in will ('ll) or won't.

1 Don't drink coffee before you go to bed. You ..... won't ..... sleep.
2 'Are you ready yet?' 'Not yet. I .... be ready in five minutes.'
3 I'm going away for a few days. I'm leaving tonight, so I .... be at home tomorrow.
4 It .... rain, so you don't need to take an umbrella.
5 A: I don't feel very well this evening.
B: Well, go to bed early and you .... feel better in the morning.
6 It's Bill's birthday next Monday. He .... be 25.
7 I'm sorry I was late this morning. It .... happen again.

27.4 Write sentences with I think ... or I don't think ... .

1 (Kelly will pass the exam) ..... I think Kelly will pass the exam. .....
2 (Kelly won't pass the exam) ..... I don't think Kelly will pass the exam. .....
3 (we'll win the game) I ....
4 (I won't be here tomorrow) ....
5 (Sue will like her present) ....
6 (they won't get married) ....
7 (you won't enjoy the film) ....

27.5 Which is right? (Study Unit 25 before you do this exercise.)

1 ~~We'll go~~ / We're going to the theatre tonight. We've got tickets. (We're going *is right*)
2 'What will you do / are you doing tomorrow evening?' 'Nothing. I'm free.'
3 They'll go / They're going away tomorrow morning. Their train is at 8.40.
4 I'm sure your aunt will lend / is lending us some money. She's very rich.
5 'Why are you putting on your coat?' 'I'll go / I'm going out.'
6 Do you think Claire will phone / is phoning us tonight?
7 Steve can't meet us on Saturday. He'll work / He's working.
8 Will you / Shall you be at home tomorrow evening?
9 A: What are your plans for the weekend?
B: Some friends will come / are coming to stay with us.

will/shall 2

A

You can use **I'll** ... (**I will**) when you offer something or decide to do something:

- 'My bag is very heavy.' **'I'll carry** it for you.'
- **'I'll phone** you tomorrow, OK?' 'OK, bye.'

We often say **I think I'll** ... / **I don't think I'll** ... when we decide to do something:

- I'm tired. **I think I'll go** to bed early tonight.
- It's a nice day. **I think I'll sit** outside.
- It's raining. **I don't think I'll go** out.

Do *not* use the present simple (**I go** / **I phone** etc.) in sentences like these:

- **I'll phone** you tomorrow, OK? (*not* I phone you)
- I think **I'll go** to bed early. (*not* I go to bed)

B

Do *not* use **I'll** ... for something you decided before (→ Units 25–26):

- **I'm working** tomorrow. (*not* I'll work)
- There's a good film on TV tonight. **I'm going to watch** it. (*not* I'll watch)
- What **are** you **doing** at the weekend? (*not* What will you do)

C

Shall I ... ? Shall we ... ?

Shall I / **Shall we** ... **?** = Do you think this is a good thing to do? Do you think this is a good idea?

- It's very warm in this room. **Shall I open** the window?
- '**Shall I phone** you this evening?' 'Yes, please.'
- I'm going to a party tonight. What **shall I wear**?

- It's a nice day. **Shall we go** for a walk?
- Where **shall we go** for our holidays this year?
- 'Let's go out this evening.' 'OK, what time **shall we meet**?'

What are you doing tomorrow? → Unit 25 I'm going to ... → Unit 26 will/shall 1 → Unit 27
Let's → Units 35, 53

28.1 Complete the sentences. Use I'll (I will) + these verbs:

~~carry~~ do eat send show sit stay

1 My bag is very heavy. — I'll carry .... it for you.
2 Enjoy your holiday. — Thank you. .... you a postcard.
3 I don't want this banana. — Well, I'm hungry. .... it.
4 Do you want a chair? — No, it's OK. .... on the floor.
5 Did you phone Jenny? — Oh no, I forgot. .... it now.
6 Are you coming with me? — No, I don't think so. .... here.
7 How do you use this camera? — Give it to me and .... you.

28.2 Complete the sentences. Use I think I'll ... or I don't think I'll ... + these verbs:

buy buy ~~go~~ have play

1 It's cold today. I don't think I'll go .... out.
2 I'm hungry. I .... something to eat.
3 I feel very tired. .... tennis.
4 I like this hat. .... it.
5 This camera is too expensive. .... it.

28.3 Which is right?

1 ~~I phone~~ / I'll phone you tomorrow, OK? (I'll phone *is right*)
2 I haven't done the shopping yet. I do / I'll do it later.
3 I like sport. I watch / I'll watch a lot of sport on TV.
4 I need some exercise. I think I go / I'll go for a walk.
5 Gerry is going to buy / will buy a new car. He told me last week.
6 'This letter is for Rose.' 'OK. I give / I'll give / I'm going to give it to her.'
7 A: Are you doing / Will you do anything this evening?
B: Yes, I'm going / I'll go out with some friends.
8 I can't go out with you tomorrow night. I work / I'm working / I'll work.

28.4 Write sentences with Shall I ... ? Choose from the two boxes.

make	turn off
~~open~~	turn on

some sandwiches	the television
the light	~~the window~~

1 It's very warm in this room. — Shall I open the window?
2 This programme isn't very good. — ....
3 I'm hungry. — ....
4 It's dark in this room. — ....

28.5 Write sentences with Shall we ... ? Choose from the two boxes.

what	where
~~what time~~	who

buy	invite
go	~~meet~~

1 Let's go out tonight. — OK, what time shall we meet?
2 Let's have a holiday. — OK, ...
3 Let's spend some money. — OK, ...
4 Let's have a party. — OK, ...

→ Additional exercises 28–31 (pages 264–67)

Unit 29

might

A

He **might go** to New York.
(= it is possible that he will go to New York)

It **might rain**.
(= it is possible that it will rain)

might + *infinitive* (**might go** / **might be** / **might rain** etc.):

I/we/you/they he/she/it	**might** (not)	**be** **go** **play** **come** etc.

B

I might = it is possible that I will:

- I **might go** to the cinema this evening, but I'm not sure. (= it is possible that I will go)
- A: When is Rebecca going to phone you?
  B: I don't know. She **might phone** this afternoon.
- Take an umbrella with you. It **might rain**.
- Buy a lottery ticket. You **might be** lucky. (= perhaps you will be lucky)
- 'Are you going out tonight?' **'I might.'** (= I might go out)

Study the difference:

- **I'm playing** tennis tomorrow. *(sure)*
  I **might play** tennis tomorrow. *(possible)*
- Rebecca **is going to phone** later. *(sure)*
  Rebecca **might phone** later. *(possible)*

C

I might not = it is possible that I will not:

- I **might not go** to work tomorrow. (= it is possible that I will not go)
- Sue **might not come** to the party. (= it is possible that she will not come)

D

may

You can use **may** in the same way. **I may** = **I might**:

- I **may go** to the cinema this evening. (= I might go)
- Sue **may not come** to the party. (= Sue might not come)

May I ... **?** = Is it OK to ... ? / Can I ... ?:

- **May I** ask a question? (= is it OK to ask / can I ask?)
- '**May I** sit here?' 'Yes, of course.'

will → Units 27–28 can → Unit 30

Exercises

29.1 Write sentences with **might**.

1 (it's possible that I'll go to the cinema) I might go to the cinema.
2 (it's possible that I'll see you tomorrow) I ……………………
3 (it's possible that Sarah will forget to phone) ……………………
4 (it's possible that it will snow today) ……………………
5 (it's possible that I'll be late tonight) ……………………

Write sentences with **might not**.

6 (it's possible that Mark will not be here next week) ……………………
7 (it's possible that I won't have time to go out) ……………………

29.2 Somebody is asking you about your plans. You have some ideas, but you are not sure. Choose from the list and write sentences with **I might**.

fish **go away** **~~Italy~~** **Monday** **a new car** **taxi**

1 Where are you going for your holidays? — I'm not sure. I might go to Italy.
2 What are you doing at the weekend? — I don't know. I ……………………
3 When will you see Kate again? — I'm not sure. ……………………
4 What are you going to have for dinner? — I don't know. ……………………
5 How are you going to get home tonight? — I'm not sure. ……………………
6 I hear you won some money. What are you going to do with it? — I haven't decided yet. ……………………

29.3 You ask Bill questions about his plans for tomorrow. Sometimes he is sure, but usually he is not sure.

1 Are you playing tennis tomorrow? — Yes, in the afternoon.
2 Are you going out tomorrow evening? — Possibly.
3 Are you going to get up early? — Perhaps.
4 Are you working tomorrow? — No, I'm not.
5 Will you be at home tomorrow morning? — Maybe.
6 Are you going to watch television? — I might.
7 Are you going out in the afternoon? — Yes, I am.
8 Are you going shopping? — Perhaps.

Bill

Now write about Bill. Use **might** where necessary.

1 He's playing tennis tomorrow afternoon.
2 He might go out tomorrow evening.
3 He ……………………
4 ……………………
5 ……………………
6 ……………………
7 ……………………
8 ……………………

29.4 Write three things that you *might* do tomorrow.

1 ……………………
2 ……………………
3 ……………………

can and could

A

He **can play** the piano.

can + *infinitive* (**can do** / **can play** / **can come** etc.):

I/we/you/they he/she/it	**can** **can't** (**cannot**)	**do** **play** **see** **come** etc.

can	I/we/you/they he/she/it	**do?** **play?** **see?** **come?** etc.

B

I can do something = I *know how* to do it, or *it is possible* for me to do it:

- I **can play** the piano. My brother **can play** the piano too.
- Sarah **can speak** Italian, but she **can't speak** Spanish.
- '**Can** you **swim**?' 'Yes, but I'm not a very good swimmer.'
- '**Can** you **change** twenty pounds?' 'I'm sorry, I **can't**.'
- I'm having a party next week, but Paul and Rachel **can't come**.

C

For the past (yesterday / last week etc.), we use **could/couldn't**:

- When I was young, I **could run** very fast.
- Before Maria came to Britain, she **couldn't understand** much English. Now she **can understand** everything.
- I was tired last night, but I **couldn't sleep**.
- I had a party last week, but Paul and Rachel **couldn't come**.

D

Can you ... ? Could you ... ? Can I ... ? Could I ... ?

We use **Can you ... ?** or **Could you ... ?** when we ask people to do things:

- **Can you** open the door, please? *or* **Could you** open the door, please?
- **Can you** wait a moment, please? *or* **Could you** wait ... ?

We use **Can I have ... ?** or **Could I have ... ?** to ask for something:

- *(in a shop)* **Can I have** these postcards, please? *or* **Could I have** ... ?

Can I ... ? or **Could I ... ?** = is it OK to do something?:

- Tom, **can I** borrow your umbrella? *or* Tom, **could I** borrow your umbrella?
- *(on the phone)* Hello, **can I** speak to Gary, please? *or* ... **could I** speak ... ?

May I ... ? → Unit 29

30.1 Ask Steve if he can do these things:

1 Can you swim?
2 ....
3 ....
4 ....
5 ....
6 ....

Can you do these things? Write sentences about yourself. Use I can or I can't.

7 I ....
8 ....
9 ....
10 ....
11 ....
12 ....

30.2 Complete these sentences. Use **can** or **can't** + one of these verbs:

~~**come**~~ **find** **hear** **see** **speak**

1 I'm sorry, but we can't come to your party next Saturday.
2 I like this hotel room. You .... the mountains from the window.
3 You are speaking very quietly. I .... you.
4 Have you seen my bag? I .... it.
5 Catherine got the job because she .... five languages.

30.3 Complete these sentences. Use **can't** or **couldn't** + one of these verbs:

decide **eat** **find** **go** **go** ~~**sleep**~~

1 I was tired, but I couldn't sleep .
2 I wasn't hungry yesterday. I .... my dinner.
3 Kate doesn't know what to do. She ....
4 I wanted to speak to Martin yesterday, but I .... him.
5 James .... to the concert next Saturday. He has to work.
6 Paula .... to the meeting last week. She was ill.

30.4 What do you say in these situations? Use **can** or **could**.

Unit 31

must mustn't don't need to

A

must + *infinitive* (**must do** / **must work** etc.):

I/we/you/they he/she/it	**must**	**do** **go** **see** **eat** etc.

B

I must (do something) = I need to do it:

- I'm very hungry. I **must eat** something.
- It's a fantastic film. You **must see** it.
- The windows are very dirty. We **must clean** them.

For the past (yesterday / last week etc.), we use **had to** … (*not* must):

- I was very hungry. I **had to eat** something. (*not* I must eat)
- We **had to walk** home last night. There were no buses. (*not* We must walk)

C

mustn't (= must not)

I mustn't (do something) = it is necessary *not* to do it, it is the wrong thing to do:

- I **must hurry**. I **mustn't be** late.
- I **mustn't forget** to phone Jane.
  (= I **must remember** to phone her)
- Be happy! You **mustn't be** sad. (= don't be sad)
- You **mustn't touch** the pictures.
  (= don't touch the pictures)

D

don't need to

I don't need (to do something) = it is not necessary:

- I **don't need to go** yet. I can stay a little longer.
- You **don't need to shout**. I can hear you OK.

You can also say **don't have to** … :

- I **don't have to go** yet. I can stay a little longer.

Compare **don't need to** and **mustn't**:

- You **don't need to** go. You can stay here if you want.
- You **mustn't** go. You must stay here.

I have to … → Unit 33

Exercises

31.1 Complete the sentences. Use must + these verbs:

be ~~**eat**~~ **go** **learn** **meet** **wash** **win**

1 I'm very hungry. I ...must eat... something.
2 Marilyn is a very interesting person. You .... her.
3 My hands are dirty. I .... them.
4 You .... to drive. It will be very useful.
5 I .... to the post office. I need some stamps.
6 The game tomorrow is very important for us. We ....
7 You can't always have things immediately. You .... patient.

31.2 Write I must or I had to.

1 ...I had to... walk home last night. There were no buses.
2 It's late. .... go now.
3 I don't usually work on Saturdays, but last Saturday .... work.
4 .... get up early tomorrow. I've got a lot to do.
5 I went to London by train last week. The train was full and .... stand all the way.
6 I was nearly late for my appointment this morning. .... run to get there on time.
7 I forgot to phone David yesterday. .... phone him later today.

31.3 Complete the sentences. Use mustn't or don't need to + one of these verbs:

forget ~~**go**~~ **hurry** **lose** **phone** **wait**

1 I ...don't need to go... home yet. I can stay a little longer.
2 We have a lot of time. We ....
3 Keep these papers in a safe place. You .... them.
4 I'm not ready yet, but you .... for me. You can go now and I'll come later.
5 We .... to turn off the lights before we leave.
6 I must contact David, but I .... him – I can send him an email.

31.4 Find the sentences with the same meaning.

1 We can leave the meeting early.	A We must stay until the end.	1 ...E...
2 We must leave the meeting early.	B We couldn't stay until the end.	2 ....
3 We mustn't leave the meeting early.	C We can't stay until the end.	3 ....
4 We had to leave the meeting early.	D We can stay until the end.	4 ....
5 We don't need to leave the meeting early.	E We don't need to stay until the end.	5 ....

31.5 Write must / mustn't / had to / don't need to.

1 You ...don't need to... go. You can stay here if you want.
2 It's a fantastic film. You ...must... see it.
3 The restaurant won't be busy tonight. We .... reserve a table.
4 I was very busy last week. I .... work every evening.
5 I want to know what happened. You .... tell me.
6 You .... tell Sue what happened. I don't want her to know.
7 I .... hurry or I'll be late.
8 'Why were you so late?' 'I .... wait half an hour for a bus.'
9 We .... decide now. We can decide later.
10 It's Lisa's birthday next week. I .... forget to buy her a present.

Unit 32

should

A

should + *infinitive*
(**should do** / **should watch** etc.):

I/we/you/they he/she/it	**should** **shouldn't**	**do** **stop** **go** **watch** etc.

B

You **should** do something = it is a good thing to do, it is the right thing to do:

- Tom doesn't study enough. He **should study** harder.
- It's a good film. You **should go** and see it.
- When you play tennis, you **should** always **watch** the ball.

C

You **shouldn't** do something = it is not a good thing to do.
Shouldn't = should not:

- Tom **shouldn't go** to bed so late.
- You watch TV all the time. You **shouldn't watch** TV so much.

D

We often say **I think** ... **should** ...

I think ... **should** ... :

- **I think** Lisa **should buy** some new clothes.
  (= I think it is a good idea.)
- It's late. **I think** I **should go** home now.
- A: Shall I buy this coat?
  B: Yes, I **think** you **should**.

I don't think ... **should** ... :

- **I don't think** you **should work** so hard.
  (= I don't think it is a good idea.)
- **I don't think** we **should go** yet. It's too early.

Do you think ... **should** ... ?:

- **Do you think** I **should buy** this hat?
- What time **do you think** we **should go** home?

E

Must is stronger than **should**:

- It's a **good** film. You **should** go and see it.
- It's a **fantastic** film. You **must** go and see it.

F

Another way to say **should** is **ought to**:

- It's a good film. You **ought to go** and see it. (= you should go)
- I think Lisa **ought to buy** some new clothes. (= Lisa should buy)

shall → Units 27–28 must → Unit 31

Exercises

32.1 Complete the sentences. Use you should + these verbs:

eat go take visit ~~watch~~ wear

1 When you play tennis, *you should watch* the ball.
2 It's late and you're very tired. .... to bed.
3 .... plenty of fruit and vegetables.
4 If you have time, ... the Science Museum. It's very interesting.
5 When you're driving, ... a seat belt.
6 It's too far to walk from here to the station. .... a taxi.

32.2 Write about the people in the pictures. Use He/She shouldn't ... so ... .

1 *She shouldn't watch TV so much.*
2 He ....
3 .... hard.
4 ....

32.3 You are not sure what to do, so you ask a friend. Write questions with Do you think I should ... ?

1 You are in a shop. You are trying on a jacket. (buy?)
You ask your friend: *Do you think I should buy this jacket?*
2 You can't drive. (learn?)
You ask your friend: Do you think ....
3 You don't like your job. (get another job?)
You ask your friend: ....
4 You are going to have a party. (invite Gary?)
You ask your friend: ....

32.4 Write sentences with I think ... should ... and I don't think ... should ... .

1 We have to get up early tomorrow. (go home now) *I think we should go home now.*
2 That coat is too big for you. (buy it) *I don't think you should buy it.*
3 You don't need your car. (sell it) ....
4 Karen needs a rest. (have a holiday) ....
5 Sally and Dan are too young. (get married) ....
6 You're not well this morning. (go to work) ....
7 James isn't well today. (go to the doctor) ....
8 The hotel is too expensive for us. (stay there) ....

32.5 What do <u>you</u> think? Write sentences with should.

1 I think *everybody should learn another language.*
2 I think everybody ....
3 I think ....
4 I don't think ....
5 I think I should ....

Unit 33

I have to ...

A

I have to do something = it is necessary for me to do it, I am obliged to do it

I/we/you/they	**have**	**to do** **to work** **to go** **to wear** etc.
he/she/it	**has**	

- I'll be late for work tomorrow. I **have to go** to the dentist.
- Jane starts work at 7 o'clock, so she **has to get** up at 6.
- You **have to pass** a test before you can get a driving licence.

B

The past (yesterday / last week etc.) is **had to** ... :

- I was late for work yesterday. I **had to go** to the dentist.
- We **had to walk** home last night. There were no buses.

C

In questions and negatives we use **do/does** (present) and **did** (past):

present

do	I/we/you/they	**have to** ... ?
does	he/she/it	

I/we/you/they	**don't**	**have to** ...
he/she/it	**doesn't**	

past

did	I/we/you/they he/she/it	**have to** ... ?

I/we/you/they he/she/it	**didn't have to** ...

- What time **do you have to go** to the dentist tomorrow?
- **Does** Jane **have to work** on Sundays?
- Why **did** they **have to leave** the party early?

I **don't have to** (do something) = it is not necessary to do it:

- I'm not working tomorrow, so I **don't have to get** up early.
- Ian **doesn't have to work** very hard. He's got an easy job.
- We **didn't have to wait** very long for the bus – it came in a few minutes.

D

must and **have to**

You can use **must** or **have to** when you say what *you* think is necessary, when you give *your* opinion:

- It's a fantastic film. You **must** see it. *or* You **have to** see it.

When you are *not* giving your personal opinion, use **have to** (*not* **must**). Compare:

- Jane won't be at work this afternoon. She **has to** go to the doctor.
  (this is not my personal opinion – it is a fact)
- Jane isn't well. She doesn't want to go to the doctor, but I told her she **must** go.
  (this is my personal opinion)

must / mustn't / don't need to → Unit 31

33.1 Complete the sentences. Use **have to** or **has to** + these verbs:

do hit read speak travel ~~wear~~

1 My eyes are not very good. I *have to wear* glasses.
2 At the end of the course all the students .... a test.
3 Sarah is studying literature. She .... a lot of books.
4 Albert doesn't understand much English. You .... very slowly to him.
5 Kate is not often at home. She .... a lot in her job.
6 In tennis you .... the ball over the net.

33.2 Complete the sentences. Use **have to** or **had to** + these verbs:

answer buy change go ~~walk~~

1 We *had to walk* home last night. There were no buses.
2 It's late. I .... now. I'll see you tomorrow.
3 I went to the supermarket after work yesterday. I .... some food.
4 This train doesn't go all the way to London. You .... at Bristol.
5 We did an exam yesterday. We .... six questions out of ten.

33.3 Complete the questions. Some are present and some are past.

1 I have to get up early tomorrow. — What time *do you have to get up* ?
2 George had to wait a long time. — How long .... ?
3 Liz has to go somewhere. — Where .... ?
4 We had to pay a lot of money. — How much .... ?
5 I have to do some work. — What exactly .... ?

33.4 Write sentences with **don't/doesn't/didn't have to ...** .

1 Why are you going out? You *don't have to go out.*
2 Why is Sue waiting? She ....
3 Why did you get up early? You ....
4 Why is Paul working so hard? He ....
5 Why do you want to leave now? We ....

33.5 Which is correct? Sometimes **must** and **have to** are both correct. Sometimes only one is correct.

1 It's a fantastic film. You must see / have to see it. *(both are correct)*
2 Julia won't be at work this afternoon. She ~~must go~~ / has to go to the doctor. (has to go *is correct)*
3 You can't park your car here for nothing. You must pay / have to pay.
4 I didn't have any money with me last night, so I must borrow / had to borrow some.
5 I eat too much chocolate. I really must stop / have to stop.
6 Paul is in a hurry. He must meet / has to meet somebody in five minutes.
7 What's wrong? You must tell / have to tell me. I want to help you.

33.6 Write some things that you (or your friends or family) have to do or had to do.

1 (every day) *I have to travel ten miles every day.*
2 (every day) ....
3 (yesterday) ....
4 (tomorrow) ....

Unit 34

Would you like ... ? I'd like ...

A

Would you like ... ? = Do you want ... ?

We use **Would you like ... ?** to offer things:

- A: **Would you like** some coffee?
  B: No, thank you.
- A: **Would you like** a chocolate?
  B: Yes, please.
- A: What **would you like**, tea or coffee?
  B: Tea, please.

We use **Would you like to ... ?** to invite somebody:

- **Would you like to go** for a walk?
- A: **Would you like to have** dinner with us on Sunday?
  B: Yes, **I'd love to.** (= I would love to have dinner with you)
- What **would you like to do** this evening?

B

I'd like ... is a polite way to say 'I want'. **I'd** like = **I would** like:

- I'm thirsty. **I'd like** a drink.
- *(in a tourist office)* **I'd like** some information about hotels, please.
- I'm feeling tired. **I'd like to stay** at home this evening.

C

Would you like ... ? and **Do you like ... ?**

Would you like ... ? / I'd like ...

Would you like some tea? = Do you want some tea?

- A: **Would you like** to go to the cinema tonight?
  (= do you want to go *tonight*?)
  B: Yes, I'd love to.
- **I'd like** an orange, please.
  (= can I have an orange?)
- What **would you like** to do next weekend?

Do you like ... ? / I like ...

Do you like tea? = Do you think tea is nice?

- A: **Do you like** going to the cinema? *(in general)*
  B: Yes, I go to the cinema a lot.
- **I like** oranges. *(in general)*
- What **do you like** to do at weekends?

like to do and like -ing → Unit 52   I would do something if ... → Unit 100

Exercises

34.1 What are the people in the pictures saying? Use Would you like ... ?

34.2 What do you say to Sue in these situations? Use Would you like to ... ?

1 You want to go to the cinema tonight. Perhaps Sue will go with you. (go)
You say: *Would you like to go to the cinema tonight?*

2 You want to play tennis tomorrow. Perhaps Sue will play too. (play)
You say: ....

3 You have an extra ticket for a concert next week. Perhaps Sue will come. (come)
You say: ....

4 It's raining and Sue is going out. She hasn't got an umbrella, but you have one. (borrow)
You say: ....

34.3 Which is right?

1 '~~Do you like~~ / Would you like a chocolate?' 'Yes, please.' (Would you like *is right*)
2 'Do you like / Would you like bananas?' 'Yes, I love them.'
3 'Do you like / Would you like an ice-cream?' 'No, thank you.'
4 'What do you like / would you like to drink?' 'A glass of water, please.'
5 'Do you like / Would you like to go out for a walk?' 'Not now. Perhaps later.'
6 I like / I'd like tomatoes, but I don't eat them very often.
7 What time do you like / would you like to have dinner this evening?
8 'Do you like / Would you like something to eat?' 'No, thanks. I'm not hungry.'
9 'Do you like / Would you like your new job?' 'Yes, I'm enjoying it.'
10 I'm tired. I like / I'd like to go to sleep now.
11 'I like / I'd like a sandwich, please.' 'Sure. What kind of sandwich?'
12 'What kind of music do you like / would you like?' 'All kinds.'

Unit 35

Do this! Don't do that! Let's do this!

A

We use **come/look/go/wait/do/be** etc. when we tell somebody to do something:

- '**Come** here and **look** at this!' 'What is it?'
- I don't want to talk to you. **Go** away!
- I'm not ready yet. Please **wait** for me.
- Please **be** quiet. I'm working.

also

- Bye! **Have** a good holiday! / **Have** a nice time! / **Have** a good flight! / **Have** fun!
  (= I hope you have a good holiday etc.)
- '**Have** a chocolate.' 'Oh, thanks.'
  (= would you like a chocolate?)

B

We use **don't** ... when we tell somebody not to do something:

- Be careful! **Don't fall**.
- Please **don't go**. Stay here with me.
- Be here on time. **Don't be** late.

C

You can say **Let's** ... when you want people to do things with you. **Let's** = Let us.

- It's a nice day. **Let's go** out.
  (= *you and I* can go out)
- Come on! **Let's dance**.
  (= *you and I* can dance)
- Are you ready? **Let's go**.
- **Let's have** fish for dinner tonight.
- A: Shall we go out tonight?
  B: No, I'm tired. **Let's stay** at home.

The negative is **Let's not** ... :

- It's cold. **Let's not** go out. Let's stay at home.
- **Let's not** have fish for dinner tonight. Let's have chicken.

Or you can say **Don't let's** ... :

- It's cold. **Don't let's** go out. Let's stay at home.

shall we ... ? → Unit 28

Exercises

35.1 Look at the pictures. What are the people saying? Some sentences are positive (**buy/come** etc.) and some are negative (**don't buy / don't come** etc.). Use these verbs:

be buy ~~come~~ ~~drink~~ drop forget have sit sleep smile

35.2 Complete the sentences. Use **let's** with:

~~go for a swim~~ go to a restaurant take a taxi wait a little watch TV

1 Would you like to play tennis?	No, let's go for a swim .
2 Do you want to walk home?	No, ...
3 Shall I put a CD on?	No, ...
4 Shall we have dinner at home?	No, ...
5 Would you like to go now?	No, ...

35.3 Answer with **No, don't ...** or **No, let's not ...** .

1 Shall I wait for you?	No, don't wait for me.
2 Shall we go home now?	No, let's not go home yet.
3 Shall we go out?	....
4 Do you want me to close the window?	....
5 Shall I phone you tonight?	....
6 Do you think we should wait for Andy?	....
7 Do you want me to turn on the light?	....
8 Shall we go by bus?	....

Unit 36

I used to ...

A

DAVE a few years ago *DAVE today*

Dave **used to work** in a factory. Now he **works** in a supermarket.

Dave **used to work** in a factory = he worked in a factory before, but he doesn't work there now:

he **used to** work	he works
past	*now*

B

You can say **I used to work** ... / **she used to have** ... / **they used to be** ... etc. :

I/you/we/they he/she/it	**used to**	**be** **work** **have** **play** etc.

- When I was a child, I **used to like** chocolate.
- I **used to read** a lot of books, but I don't read much these days.
- Liz has got short hair now, but it **used to be** very long.
- They **used to live** in the same street as us, so we **used to see** them a lot. But we don't see them very often these days.
- Helen **used to have** a piano, but she sold it a few years ago.

The negative is **I didn't use to** ... :

- When I was a child, I **didn't use to like** tomatoes.

The question is **did you use to** ... ?:

- Where **did** you **use to live** before you came here?

C

We use **used to** ... only for the past. You cannot say 'I use to ...' for the present:

- I **used to play** tennis. These days I **play** golf. (*not* I use to play golf)
- We usually **get** up early. (*not* We use to get up early)

by → Units 21, 63, 109 at/on → Units 103, 106–107 preposition + -ing → Unit 112

36.1 Look at the pictures. Complete the sentences with **used to** ... .

1 

She used to have long hair.

2 

He .... football.

3 

.... a taxi driver.

4 

.... in the country.

5 

....

6 

This building ....

36.2 Karen works very hard and has very little free time. A few years ago, things were different.

Karen a few years ago 

Do you do any sport?	Yes, I swim every day and I play volleyball.
Do you go out much?	Yes, most evenings.
Do you play a musical instrument?	Yes, the guitar.
Do you like reading?	Yes, I read a lot.
Do you travel much?	Yes, I go away two or three times a year.

Karen now

Write sentences about Karen with **used to** ... .

1 She used to swim every day.
2 She ....
3 ....
4 ....
5 ....
6 ....

36.3 Complete these sentences. Use **used to** or the present simple (**I play / he lives** etc.).

1 I used to play tennis. I stopped playing a few years ago.
2 'Do you do any sport?' 'Yes, I play basketball.'
3 'Have you got a car?' 'No, I .... one, but I sold it.'
4 George .... a waiter. Now he's the manager of a hotel.
5 'Do you go to work by car?' 'Sometimes, but most days I .... by train.'
6 When I was a child, I never .... meat, but I eat it now.
7 Mary loves watching TV. She .... TV every evening.
8 We .... near the airport, but we moved to the city centre a few years ago.
9 Normally I start work at 7 o'clock, so I .... up very early.
10 What games .... you .... when you were a child?

there is there are

A

There's a man on the roof.

There's a train at 10.30.

There are seven days in a week.

singular

there is ...	(**there's**)
is there ... ?	
there is not ...	(**there isn't** *or* **there's not**)

- **There's** a big tree in the garden.
- **There's** nothing on TV tonight.
- A: Have you got any money?
  B: Yes, **there's** some in my bag.
- A: Excuse me, **is there** a hotel near here?
  B: Yes, **there is**. / No, **there isn't**.
- We can't go skiing. **There isn't** any snow.

plural

there are ...	
are there ... ?	
there are not ...	(**there aren't**)

- **There are** some big trees in the garden.
- **There are** a lot of accidents on this road.
- A: **Are there** any restaurants near here?
  B: Yes, **there are**. / No, **there aren't**.
- This restaurant is very quiet. **There aren't** many people here.
- How many players **are there** in a football team?
- **There are** 11 players in a football team.

B

there is and **it is**

there is

There's a book on the table.
(*not* It's a book on the table.)

it is

I like this book. **It's** interesting.
(**It** = this book)

Compare:

- 'What's **that noise**?' '**It**'s a train.' (**It** = that noise)
  There's a train at 10.30. **It**'s a fast train. (**It** = the 10.30 train)
- **There's** a lot of salt in this soup.
  I don't like **this soup**. **It**'s too salty. (**It** = this soup)

there was / were / has been etc. → Unit 38 it and there → Unit 39 some and any → Unit 76

Exercises

37.1 Kentham is a small town. Look at the information in the box and write sentences about Kentham with **There is/are** or **There isn't/aren't**.

1	a castle?	No
2	any restaurants?	Yes (a lot)
3	a hospital?	Yes
4	a swimming pool?	No
5	any cinemas?	Yes (two)
6	a university?	No
7	any big hotels?	No

1 There isn't a castle.
2 There are a lot of restaurants.
3 ……
4 ……
5 ……
6 ……
7 ……

37.2 Write sentences about your town (or a town that you know). Use **There is/are** or **There isn't/aren't**.

1 There are a few restaurants.
2 There's a big park.
3 ……
4 ……
5 ……
6 ……

37.3 Write **there is / there isn't / is there** or **there are / there aren't / are there**.

1 Kentham isn't an old town. There aren't any old buildings.
2 Look! …… a photograph of your brother in the newspaper!
3 'Excuse me, …… a bank near here?' 'Yes, at the end of the street.'
4 …… five people in my family: my parents, my two sisters and me.
5 'How many students …… in the class?' 'Twenty.'
6 The road is usually very quiet. …… much traffic.
7 …… a bus from the city centre to the airport?' 'Yes, every 20 minutes.'
8 …… any problems?' 'No, everything is OK.'
9 …… nowhere to sit down. …… any chairs.

37.4 Write sentences with **There are ...** . Choose from the boxes.

~~seven~~	twenty-six
eight	thirty
fifteen	fifty

letters	~~days~~
players	days
planets	states

September	the solar system
the USA	~~a week~~
a rugby team	the English alphabet

1 There are seven days in a week.
2 ……
3 ……
4 ……
5 ……
6 ……

37.5 Write **there's / is there** or **it's / is it**.

1 'There's a train at 10.30.' 'Is it a fast train?'
2 I'm not going to buy this shirt. …… too expensive.
3 'What's wrong?' '…… something in my eye.'
4 …… a red car outside your house. …… yours?
5 '…… anything good on TV tonight?' 'Yes, …… a film at 8.15.'
6 'What's that building?' '…… a school.'
7 '…… a restaurant in this hotel?' 'No, I'm afraid not.'

Unit 38 there was/were there has/have been there will be

A there was / there were *(past)*

There is a train every hour.

The time now is 11.15.
There was a train at 11 o'clock.

Compare:

there is/are *(present)*

- **There is** a good film on TV tonight.
- We are staying at a very big hotel. **There are** 550 rooms.
- **Are there** any phone messages for me this morning?
- I'm hungry, but **there isn't** anything to eat.

there was/were *(past)*

- **There was** a good film on TV last night.
- We stayed at a very big hotel. **There were** 550 rooms.
- **Were there** any phone messages for me yesterday?
- I was hungry when I got home, but **there wasn't** anything to eat.

B there has been / there have been *(present perfect)*

- Look! **There's been** an accident.
  (**there's been** = there **has** been)
- This road is very dangerous. **There have been** many accidents.

Compare **there was** *(past)*:

- **There was** an accident **last night**.
  (*not* There has been an accident last night.)

For past simple and present perfect, see Unit 20.

C there will be

- Do you think **there will be** a lot of people at the party on Saturday?
- The manager of the company is leaving, so **there will be** a new manager soon.
- I'm going away tomorrow. I'll do my packing today because **there won't be** time tomorrow.
  (**there won't be** = there **will not** be)

was/were → Unit 10 has/have been → Units 15–18 will → Unit 27 there is/are → Unit 37
there and it → Units 37, 39 some and any → Unit 76

Exercises

38.1 Look at the two pictures. Now the room is empty, but what was in the room last week? Choose from the box and write sentences with There was ... or There were ... .

an armchair	a carpet	some flowers	a sofa
some books	~~a clock~~	three pictures	a small table

1 *There was a clock* .... on the wall near the window.
2 .... on the floor.
3 .... on the wall near the door.
4 .... in the middle of the room.
5 .... on the table.
6 .... on the shelves.
7 .... in the corner near the door.
8 .... opposite the armchair.

38.2 Write there was / there wasn't / was there or there were / there weren't / were there.

1 I was hungry, but *there wasn't* anything to eat.
2 *Were there* any phone messages for me yesterday?
3 I opened the envelope, but it was empty. .... nothing in it.
4 'We stayed at a very nice hotel.' 'Really? .... a swimming pool?'
5 'Did you buy any eggs?' 'No, ... any in the shop.'
6 The wallet was empty. .... any money in it.
7 '........ many people at the meeting?' 'No, very few.'
8 We didn't visit the museum. .... enough time.
9 I'm sorry I'm late. .... a lot of traffic.
10 Twenty years ago .... many tourists here. Now there are a lot.

38.3 Write there + is / are / was / were / has been / have been / will be.

1 *There was* a good film on TV last night.
2 .... 24 hours in a day.
3 .... a party at the club last Friday, but I didn't go.
4 'Where can I buy a newspaper?' '........ a shop at the end of the street.'
5 'Why are those policemen outside the bank?' '........ a robbery.'
6 When we arrived at the theatre, ... a long queue outside.
7 When you arrive tomorrow, ... somebody at the station to meet you.
8 Ten years ago .... 500 children at the school. Now .... more than a thousand.
9 Last week I went back to the town where I was born. It's very different now. .... a lot of changes.
10 I think everything will be OK. I don't think .... any problems.

Unit 39

It ...

A

We use **it** for time/day/distance/weather:

time

- ☐ What time is **it**?
- ☐ **It**'s half past ten.
- ☐ **It**'s late.
- ☐ **It**'s time to go home.

day

- ☐ What day is **it**?
- ☐ **It**'s Thursday.
- ☐ **It**'s 16 March.
- ☐ **It** was my birthday yesterday.

distance

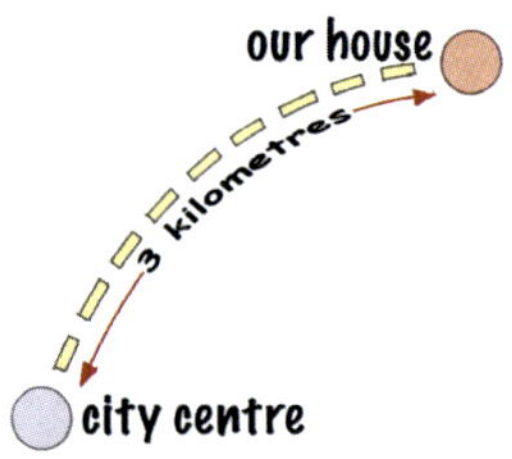

- ☐ **It**'s three kilometres from our house to the city centre.
- ☐ How far is **it** from New York to Los Angeles?
- ☐ **It**'s a long way from here to the station.
- ☐ We can walk home. **It** isn't far.

We use **far** in questions (**is it far**?) and negatives (**it isn't far**). In positive sentences, we use **a long way** (**it's a long way**).

weather

- ☐ **It**'s raining. **It** isn't raining. Is **it** snowing?
- ☐ **It** rains a lot here. **It** didn't rain yesterday.
  Does **it** snow very often?
- ☐ **It**'s warm/hot/cold/fine/cloudy/windy/sunny/foggy/dark etc.
- ☐ **It**'s a nice day today.

Compare **it** and **there**:

- ☐ **It rains** a lot in winter.
  There is **a lot of rain** in winter.
- ☐ **It** was very **windy**.
  There was **a strong wind** yesterday.

B

It's nice to ... etc.

It's	easy / difficult / impossible / dangerous / safe expensive / interesting / nice / wonderful / terrible etc.	**to** ...

- ☐ **It**'s nice **to see you again**.
- ☐ **It**'s impossible **to understand her**.
- ☐ **It** wasn't easy **to find your house**.

C

Don't forget **it**:

- ☐ **It**'s raining again. (*not* Is raining again)
- ☐ Is **it** true that you're going away? (*not* Is true that ...)

there is → Unit 37

39.1 Write about the weather in the pictures. Use **It's ...** .

1 It's raining.
2 ....
3 ....
4 ....
5 ....
6 ....

39.2 Write **it is (it's)** or **is it**.

1 What time is it ?
2 We must go now. .... very late.
3 .... true that Bill can fly a helicopter?
4 'What day .... today? Tuesday?' 'No, ... Wednesday.'
5 .... ten kilometres from the airport to the city centre.
6 .... possible to phone you at your office?
7 'Do you want to walk to the hotel?' 'I don't know. How far .... ?'
8 .... Lisa's birthday today. She's 27.
9 I don't believe it! .... impossible.

39.3 Write questions with **How far ... ?**

1 (here / the station) How far is it from here to the station?
2 (the hotel / the beach) How ....
3 (New York / Washington) ....
4 (your house / the airport) ....

39.4 Write **it** or **there**.

1 The weather isn't so nice today. It 's cloudy.
2 There was a strong wind yesterday.
3 .... 's hot in this room. Open a window.
4 .... was a nice day yesterday. .... was warm and sunny.
5 .... was a storm last night. Did you hear it?
6 I was afraid because .... was very dark.
7 .... 's often cold here, but .... isn't much rain.
8 .... 's a long way from here to the nearest shop.

39.5 Complete the sentences. Choose from the boxes.

it's — easy, ~~difficult~~, impossible, dangerous, nice, interesting

to — work in this office, visit different places, see you again, ~~get up early~~, go out alone, make friends

1 If you go to bed late, it's difficult to get up early in the morning.
2 Hello, Jane. .... How are you?
3 .... There is too much noise.
4 Everybody is very nice at work. ....
5 I like travelling. ....
6 Some cities are not safe. .... at night.

Unit 40

I am, I don't etc.

A

She isn't tired, but **he is**.
(**he is** = he is tired)

He likes tea, but **she doesn't**.
(**she doesn't** = she doesn't like tea)

In these examples, it is not necessary to repeat some words ('he is *tired*', 'she doesn't *like tea*').

You can use these verbs in the same way:

am/is/are
was/were
have/has
do/does/did
can
will
might
must

- I haven't got a car, but my sister **has**. (= my sister has got a car)
- A: Please help me.
  B: I'm sorry. I **can't**. (= I can't help you)
- A: Are you tired?
  B: I **was**, but I'**m not** now. (= I was tired, but I'm not tired now)
- A: Do you think Jane will phone this evening?
  B: She **might**. (= she might phone)
- A: Are you going now?
  B: Yes, I'm afraid I **must**. (= I must go)

You *cannot* use **'m/'s/'ve** etc. (*short forms*) in this way. You must use **am/is/have** etc. :
- She isn't tired, but he **is**. (*not* … but he's)

But you *can* use **isn't** / **haven't** / **won't** etc. (*negative* short forms):
- My sister has got a car, but I **haven't**.
- 'Are you and Jane working tomorrow?' 'I am, but Jane **isn't**.'

B

You can use **I am** / **I'm not** etc. after **Yes** and **No**:
- 'Are you tired?' 'Yes, I **am**. / No, I'**m not**.'
- 'Will Alan be here tomorrow?' 'Yes, he **will**. / No, he **won't**.'
- 'Is there a bus to the airport?' 'Yes, there **is**. / No, there **isn't**.'

C

We use **do/does** for the *present simple* (→ Units 6–7):
- I don't like hot weather, but Sue **does**. (= Sue likes hot weather)
- Sue works hard, but I **don't**. (= I don't work hard)
- 'Do you enjoy your work?' 'Yes, I **do**.'

We use **did** for the *past simple* (→ Unit 12):
- A: Did you and Chris enjoy the film?
  B: I **did**, but Chris **didn't**. (= I enjoyed it, but Chris didn't enjoy it)
- 'I had a good time.' 'I **did** too.' (= I enjoyed it too)
- 'Did it rain yesterday?' 'No, it **didn't**.'

have you? / don't you? etc. → Unit 41   **so am I / neither do I** etc. → Unit 42

Exercises

40.1 Complete these sentences. Use only one verb (is/have/can etc.) each time.

1 Kate wasn't hungry, but we *were* .
2 I'm not married, but my brother ....
3 Bill can't help you, but I ....
4 I haven't seen the film, but Tom ....
5 Karen won't be here, but Chris ....
6 You weren't late, but I ....

40.2 Complete these sentences with a negative verb (isn't/haven't/can't etc.).

1 My sister can play the piano, but I *can't* .
2 Sam is working today, but I ....
3 I was working, but my friends ....
4 Mark has been to China, but I ....
5 I'm ready to go, but Tom ....
6 I've got a key, but Sally ....

40.3 Complete these sentences with do/does/did or don't/doesn't/didn't.

1 I don't like hot weather, but Sue *does* .
2 Sue likes hot weather, but I *don't* .
3 My mother wears glasses, but my father ....
4 You don't know Paul very well, but I ....
5 I didn't enjoy the party, but my friends ....
6 I don't watch TV much, but Peter ....
7 Kate lives in London, but her parents ....
8 You had breakfast this morning, but I ....

40.4 Complete the sentences. Write about yourself and other people.

1 I didn't *go out last night, but my friends did.*
2 I like ...., but ....
3 I don't ...., but ....
4 I'm ....
5 I haven't ....

40.5 Put in a verb, positive or negative.

1 'Are you tired?' 'I *was* earlier, but I'm not now.'
2 Steve is happy today, but he .... yesterday.
3 The post office isn't open yet, but the shops ....
4 I haven't got a telescope, but I know somebody who ....
5 I would like to help you, but I'm afraid I ....
6 I don't usually go to work by car, but I .... yesterday.
7 A: Have you ever been to the United States?
B: No, but Sandra .... She went there on holiday last year.
8 'Do you and Chris watch TV a lot?' 'I .... , but Chris doesn't.'
9 I've been invited to Sam's wedding, but Kate ....
10 'Do you think Sarah will pass her driving test?' 'Yes, I'm sure she ....'
11 'Are you going out tonight?' 'I .... I don't know for sure.'

40.6 Answer these questions about yourself. Use Yes, I have. / No, I'm not. etc.

1 Are you American? *No, I'm not.*
2 Have you got a car? ....
3 Do you feel OK? ....
4 Is it snowing? ....
5 Are you hungry? ....
6 Do you like classical music? ....
7 Will you be in Paris tomorrow? ....
8 Have you ever broken your arm? ....
9 Did you buy anything yesterday? ....
10 Were you asleep at 3 a.m.? ....

Unit 41

Have you? Are you? Don't you? etc.

A

You can say **have you?** / **is it?** / **can't he?** etc. to show that you are interested or surprised:

- '**You're** late.' 'Oh, **am I?** I'm sorry.'
- '**I was** ill last week.' '**Were you?** I didn't know that.'
- '**It's** raining again.' '**Is it?** It was sunny ten minutes ago.'
- '**There's** a letter for you.' '**Is there?** Where is it?'
- '**Bill can't** drive.' '**Can't he?** I didn't know that.'
- '**I'm not** hungry.' '**Aren't you?** I am.'
- '**Sue isn't** at work today.' '**Isn't she?** Is she ill?'

Use **do/does** for the *present simple*, and **did** for the *past simple:*

- '**I speak** four languages.' '**Do you?** Which ones?'
- '**Tim doesn't** eat meat.' '**Doesn't he?** Does he eat fish?'
- '**Nicole got** married last week.' '**Did she?** Really?'

B

Question tags

You can use **have you?** / **is it?** / **can't she?** etc. at the end of a sentence.

These 'mini-questions' are *question tags*.

positive sentence → *negative* question tag

It's a beautiful day,	**isn't it?**	Yes, it's perfect.
Sally lives in London,	**doesn't she?**	Yes, that's right.
You closed the window,	**didn't you?**	Yes, I think so.
Those shoes are nice,	**aren't they?**	Yes, very nice.
Tom will be here soon,	**won't he?**	Yes, probably.

negative sentence → *positive* question tag

That isn't your car,	**is it?**	No, it's my mother's.
You haven't met my mother,	**have you?**	No, I haven't.
Sally doesn't go out much,	**does she?**	No, she doesn't.
You won't be late,	**will you?**	No, I'm never late.

I am / I don't etc. → Unit 40

Exercises

41.1 Answer with Do you? / Doesn't she? / Did they? etc.

1	I speak four languages.	*Do you*? Which ones?
2	I work in a bank.	........? I work in a bank too.
3	I didn't go to work yesterday.	........? Were you ill?
4	Jane doesn't like me.	........? Why not?
5	You look tired.	........? I feel fine.
6	Kate phoned me last night.	........? What did she say?

41.2 Answer with Have you? / Haven't you? / Did she? / Didn't she? etc.

1	I've bought a new car.	*Have you*? What make is it?
2	Tim doesn't eat meat.	*Doesn't he*? Does he eat fish?
3	I've lost my key.	........? When did you last have it?
4	Sue can't drive.	........? She should learn.
5	I was born in Italy.	........? I didn't know that.
6	I didn't sleep well last night.	........? Was the bed uncomfortable?
7	There's a film on TV tonight.	........? Are you going to watch it?
8	I'm not happy.	........? Why not?
9	I saw Paula last week.	........? How is she?
10	Maria works in a factory.	........? What kind of factory?
11	I won't be here next week.	........? Where will you be?
12	The clock isn't working.	........? It was working yesterday.

41.3 Complete these sentences with a question tag (isn't it? / haven't you? etc.).

1	It's a beautiful day, *isn't it*?	Yes, it's perfect.
2	These flowers are nice, ...?	Yes, what are they?
3	Jane was at the party, ...?	Yes, but I didn't speak to her.
4	You've been to Paris, ...?	Yes, many times.
5	You speak German, ...?	Yes, but not very well.
6	Martin looks tired, ...?	Yes, he works very hard.
7	You'll help me, ...?	Yes, of course I will.

41.4 Complete these sentences with a question tag, positive (is it? / do you? etc.) or negative (isn't it? / don't you? etc.).

1	You haven't got a car, *have you*?	No, I can't drive.
2	You aren't tired, ...?	No, I feel fine.
3	Lisa is a very nice person, ...?	Yes, everybody likes her.
4	You can play the piano, ...?	Yes, but I'm not very good.
5	You don't know Mike's sister, ...?	No, I've never met her.
6	Sarah went to university, ...?	Yes, she studied psychology.
7	The film wasn't very good, ...?	No, it was terrible.
8	Anna lives near you, ...?	That's right. In the same street.
9	You won't tell anybody what I said, ...?	No, of course not.

too/either so am I / neither do I etc.

A too and either

We use **too** and **either** at the end of a sentence.

We use **too** after a *positive* verb:

- A: I'm happy.
  B: **I'm** happy **too**.
- A: I enjoyed the film.
  B: I **enjoyed** it **too**.
- Jane is a doctor. Her husband **is** a doctor **too**.

We use **either** after *a negative* verb:

- A: I'm not happy.
  B: **I'm not** happy **either**.
  (*not* I'm not … too)
- A: I can't cook.
  B: I **can't either**. (*not* I can't too)
- Bill doesn't watch TV. He **doesn't** read newspapers **either**.

B so am I / neither do I etc.

so neither	**am/is/are** … **was/were** … **do/does** … **did** … **have/has** … **can** … **will** … **would** …

so am I = I am too
so have I = I have too (etc.):

- A: **I'm** working.
  B: **So am I.** (= I'm working too)
- A: **I was** late for work today.
  B: **So was Sam.** (= Sam was late too)
- A: **I work** in a bank.
  B: **So do I.**
- A: **We went** to the cinema last night.
  B: Did you? **So did we.**
- A: **I'd** like to go to Australia.
  B: **So would I.**

neither am I = I'm not either
neither can I = I can't either (etc.):

- A: **I haven't** got a key.
  B: **Neither have I.** (= I haven't either)
- A: **Kate can't** cook.
  B: **Neither can Tom.**
  (= Tom can't either)
- A: **I won't** (= will not) be here tomorrow.
  B: **Neither will I.**
- A: **I never go** to the cinema.
  B: **Neither do I.**

You can also use **Nor** (= Neither):

- A: I'm not married.
  B: **Nor am I.** *or* **Neither am I.**

Remember: So **am I** (*not* So I am), Neither **have I** (*not* Neither I have).

I am / I don't etc. → **Unit 40**

42.1 Write too or either.

1	I'm happy.	I'm happy too .
2	I'm not hungry.	I'm not hungry ....
3	I'm going out.	I'm going out ....
4	It rained on Saturday.	It rained on Sunday ....
5	Jenny can't drive a car.	She can't ride a bicycle ....
6	I don't like shopping.	I don't like shopping ....
7	Emma's mother is a teacher.	Her father is a teacher ....

42.2 Answer with So … I (So am I / So do I / So can I etc.).

1	I went to bed late last night.	So did I.
2	I'm thirsty.	....
3	I've just had dinner.	....
4	I need a holiday.	....
5	I'll be late tomorrow.	....
6	I was very tired this morning.	....

Answer with Neither … I.

7	I can't go to the party.	....
8	I didn't phone Alex last night.	....
9	I haven't got any money.	....
10	I'm not going out tomorrow.	....
11	I don't know what to do.	....

42.3 You are talking to Maria. Write sentences about yourself. Where possible, use So … I or Neither … I. Look at these examples carefully:

Maria

I'm tired today. — You can answer: So am I. or I'm not.

I don't work hard. — You can answer: Neither do I. or I do.

	Maria	You
1	I'm learning English.	....
2	I can ride a bicycle.	....
3	I'm not American.	....
4	I like cooking.	....
5	I don't like cold weather.	....
6	I slept well last night.	....
7	I've never been to Scotland.	....
8	I don't use my phone much.	....
9	I'm going out tomorrow evening.	....
10	I haven't got a headache.	....
11	I didn't watch TV last night.	....
12	I go to the cinema a lot.	....

Unit 43

isn't, haven't, don't etc. (negatives)

A

We use **not** (**n't**) in negative sentences:

positive → *negative*

am	**am not** (**'m not**)	□ I'**m not** tired.
is	**is not** (**isn't** *or* **'s not**)	□ It **isn't** (*or* It'**s not**) raining.
are	**are not** (**aren't** *or* **'re not**)	□ They **aren't** (*or* They'**re not**) here.
was	**was not** (**wasn't**)	□ Julian **wasn't** hungry.
were	**were not** (**weren't**)	□ The shops **weren't** open.
have	**have not** (**haven't**)	□ I **haven't** finished my work.
has	**has not** (**hasn't**)	□ Sue **hasn't** got a car.
will	**will not** (**won't**)	□ We **won't** be here tomorrow.
can	**cannot** (**can't**)	□ George **can't** drive.
could	**could not** (**couldn't**)	□ I **couldn't** sleep last night.
must	**must not** (**mustn't**)	□ I **mustn't** forget to phone Jane.
should	**should not** (**shouldn't**)	□ You **shouldn't** work so hard.
would	**would not** (**wouldn't**)	□ I **wouldn't** like to be an actor.

B

don't/doesn't/didn't

present simple negative	I/we/you/they	**do not** (**don't**)	**work/live/go** etc.
	he/she/it	**does not** (**doesn't**)	
past simple negative	I/they/he/she etc.	**did not** (**didn't**)	

positive	→	*negative*
I **want** to go out.	→	I **don't want** to go out.
They **work** hard.	→	They **don't work** hard.
Liz **plays** the guitar.	→	Liz **doesn't play** the guitar.
My father **likes** his job.	→	My father **doesn't like** his job.
I **got** up early this morning.	→	I **didn't get** up early this morning.
They **worked** hard yesterday.	→	They **didn't work** hard yesterday.
We **played** tennis.	→	We **didn't play** tennis.
Diane **had** dinner with us.	→	Diane **didn't have** dinner with us.

Don't ...

Look!	→	**Don't look!**
Wait for me.	→	**Don't wait** for me.

Sometimes **do** is the main verb (**don't do** / **doesn't do** / **didn't do**):

Do something!	→	**Don't do** anything!
Sue **does** a lot at weekends.	→	Sue **doesn't do** much at weekends.
I **did** what you said.	→	I **didn't do** what you said.

present simple negative → Unit 6 past simple negative → Unit 12 **don't look / don't wait** etc. → Unit 35
Why isn't/don't ... ? → Unit 44

Exercises

43.1 Make these sentences negative.

1 He's gone away. *He hasn't gone away.*
2 They're married. ....
3 I've had dinner. ....
4 It's cold today. ....
5 We'll be late. ....
6 You should go. ....

43.2 Make these sentences negative. Use **don't/doesn't/didn't.**

1 She saw me. *She didn't see me.*
2 I like cheese. ....
3 They understood. ....
4 He lives here. ....
5 Go away! ....
6 I did the shopping. ....

43.3 Make these sentences negative.

1 She can swim. *She can't swim.*
2 They've arrived. ....
3 I went to the bank. ....
4 He speaks German. ....
5 We were angry. ....
6 He'll be pleased. ....
7 Phone me tonight. ....
8 It rained yesterday. ....
9 I could hear them. ....
10 I believe you. ....

43.4 Complete these sentences with a negative verb (isn't/haven't/don't etc.).

1 They aren't rich. They *haven't* got much money.
2 'Would you like something to eat?' 'No, thank you. I .... hungry.'
3 I .... find my glasses. Have you seen them?
4 Steve .... use email much. He prefers to talk on the phone.
5 We can walk to the station from here. It .... very far.
6 'Where's Jane?' 'I .... know. I .... seen her today.'
7 Be careful! .... fall!
8 We went to the cinema last night. I .... like the film very much.
9 I've been to Japan many times, but I .... been to Korea.
10 Julia .... be here tomorrow. She's going away.
11 'Who broke that window?' 'Not me. I .... do it.'
12 We didn't see what happened. We .... looking at the time.
13 Lisa bought a new coat a few days ago, but she .... worn it yet.
14 You .... drive so fast. It's dangerous.

43.5 You ask Gary some questions. He answers 'Yes' or 'No'. Write sentences about Gary, positive or negative.

Gary

You

You	Gary		
Are you married?	No.	1	*He isn't married.*
Do you live in London?	Yes.	2	*He lives in London.*
Were you born in London?	No.	3	....
Do you like London?	No.	4	....
Would you like to live in the country?	Yes.	5	....
Can you drive?	Yes.	6	....
Have you got a car?	No.	7	....
Do you read newspapers?	No.	8	....
Are you interested in politics?	No.	9	....
Do you watch TV most evenings?	Yes.	10	....
Did you watch TV last night?	No.	11	....
Did you go out last night?	Yes.	12	....

Unit 44

is it ... ? have you ... ? do they ... ? etc. (questions 1)

A

positive	**you**	**are**	**You are** eating.	
question	**are**	**you**	**Are you** eating?	What **are you** eating?

In questions, the first verb (**is**/**are**/**have** etc.) is before the subject:

positive subject + verb			*question* verb + subject	
I	**am** late.	→	**Am**	**I** late?
That seat	**is** free.	→	**Is**	**that seat** free?
She	**was** angry.	→	Why **was**	**she** angry?
David	**has** gone.	→	Where **has**	**David** gone?
You	**have** got a car.	→	**Have**	**you** got a car?
They	**will** be here soon.	→	When **will**	**they** be here?
Paula	**can** swim.	→	**Can**	**Paula** swim?

Remember: the subject is after the first verb.

- Where **has David** gone? (*not* Where has gone David?)
- **Are those people** waiting for something? (*not* Are waiting ... ?)
- When **was the telephone** invented? (*not* When was invented ... ?)

B

do ... ? / does ... ? / did ... ?

present simple questions	**do**	I/we/you/they	**work**/**live**/**go** etc. ... ?
	does	he/she/it	
past simple questions	**did**	I/they/he/she etc.	

positive		*question*
They **work** hard.	→	**Do** they **work** hard?
You **watch** television.	→	How often **do** you **watch** television?
Chris **works** hard.	→	**Does** Chris **work** hard?
She **gets up** early.	→	What time **does** she **get** up?
They **worked** hard.	→	**Did** they **work** hard?
You **had** dinner.	→	What **did** you **have** for dinner?
She **got** up early.	→	What time **did** she **get** up?

Sometimes **do** is the main verb (do you **do** / did he **do** etc.):

- What **do** you usually **do** at weekends?
- 'What **does** your brother **do**?' 'He works in a bank.'
- 'I broke my finger last week.' 'How **did** you **do** that?' (*not* How did you that?)

C

Why isn't ... ? / Why don't ... ? etc. (**Why** + *negative*):

- Where's John? **Why isn't he** here? (*not* Why he isn't here?)
- **Why can't Paula** come to the meeting tomorrow? (*not* Why Paula can't ... ?)
- **Why didn't you** phone me last night?

present simple questions → **Unit 7** past simple questions → **Unit 12** questions 2–3 → **Units 45–46**
what/which/how → **Units 47–48**

Exercises

44.1 Write questions.

1 I can swim. (and you?) Can you swim?
2 I work hard. (and Jack?) Does Jack work hard?
3 I was late this morning. (and you?) ……
4 I've got a key. (and Kate?) ……
5 I'll be here tomorrow. (and you?) ……
6 I'm going out this evening. (and Paul?) ……
7 I like my job. (and you?) ……
8 I live near here. (and Nicole?) ……
9 I enjoyed the film. (and you?) ……
10 I had a good holiday. (and you?) ……

44.2 You are talking to a friend about driving. Write the full questions.

You

	You	Friend
1	(have / a car?) Have you got a car?	Yes, I have.
2	(use / a lot?) …… it ……	Yes, nearly every day.
3	(use / yesterday?) ……	Yes, to go to work.
4	(enjoy driving?) ……	Not very much.
5	(a good driver?) ……	I think I am.
6	(ever / have / an accident?) ……	No, never.

44.3 Make questions with these words. Put the words in the right order.

1 (has / gone / where / David?) Where has David gone?
2 (working / Rachel / is / today?) Is Rachel working today?
3 (the children / what / are / doing?) What ……
4 (made / is / how / cheese?) ……
5 (to the party / coming / is / your sister?) ……
6 (you / the truth / tell / don't / why?) ……
7 (your guests / have / yet / arrived?) ……
8 (leave / what time / your train / does?) ……
9 (to work / Emily / why / go / didn't?) ……
10 (your car / in the accident / was / damaged?)
……

44.4 Complete the questions.

1	I want to go out.	Where do you want to go?
2	Kate and Paul aren't going to the party.	Why aren't they going?
3	I'm reading.	What ……
4	Sue went to bed early.	What time ……
5	My parents are going on holiday.	When ……
6	I saw Tom a few days ago.	Where ……
7	I can't come to the party.	Why ……
8	Tina has gone away.	Where ……
9	I need some money.	How much ……
10	Angela doesn't like me.	Why ……
11	It rains sometimes.	How often ……
12	I did the shopping.	When ……

Unit 45

Who saw you? Who did you see? (questions 2)

A

Silvia saw Paul.

Who **saw** Paul?
Silvia. (Silvia saw him.)

Who **did** Silvia **see**?
Paul. (She saw Paul.)

Silvia saw Paul

subject: Somebody saw Paul. → Who saw Paul?
Silvia. (Silvia saw him.)

who is the *subject*
Paul is the *object*

object: Silvia saw somebody. → Who did Silvia see?
Paul. (She saw Paul.)

who is the *object*
Silvia is the *subject*

B

In these questions, **who/what** is the *subject:*

- **Who lives** in this house? (= somebody lives in it – who?)
  (*not* Who does live?)
- **What happened**? (= something happened – what?)
  (*not* What did happen?)
- **What's happening**? (What's = What **is**)
- **Who's got** my key? (Who's = Who **has**)

In these questions, **who/what** is the *object:*

- Who did **you** meet yesterday? (= **you** met somebody – who?)
- What did **Paul** say? (= **Paul** said something – what?)
- Who are **you** phoning?
- What was **Silvia** wearing?

Compare:

- George likes oranges. → **Who likes** oranges? – George.
  What does George like? – Oranges.
- Jane won a new car. → **Who won** a new car? – Jane.
  What did Jane win? – A new car.

C

Use **who** for people (somebody). Use **what** for things, ideas etc. (something):

- **Who** is your favourite **singer**?
- **What** is your favourite **song**?

questions → Units 44, 46 what/which/how → Unit 47

Exercises

45.1 Make questions with who or what. In these questions, who/what is the subject.

1 Somebody broke the window.	Who broke the window?
2 Something fell off the shelf.	What ....
3 Somebody wants to see you.	.... me?
4 Somebody took my umbrella.	....
5 Something made me ill.	....
6 Somebody is coming.	....

45.2 Make questions with who or what (subject or object).

1 I bought something.	What did you buy?
2 Somebody lives in this house.	Who lives in this house?
3 I phoned somebody.	....
4 Something happened last night.	....
5 Somebody knows the answer.	....
6 Somebody did the washing-up.	....
7 Jane did something.	....
8 Something woke me up.	....
9 Somebody saw the accident.	....
10 I saw somebody.	....
11 Somebody has got my pen.	....
12 This word means something.	....

45.3 You want the missing information (XXXXX). Write questions with who or what.

1 I lost **XXXXX** yesterday, but fortunately **XXXXX** found it and gave it back to me.	What did you lose? Who found it?
2 **XXXXX** phoned me last night. She wanted **XXXXX**.	Who .... What ....
3 I needed some advice, so I asked **XXXXX**. He said **XXXXX**.	....
4 I hear that **XXXXX** got married last week. **XXXXX** told me.	....
5 I met **XXXXX** on my way home this evening. She told me **XXXXX**.	....
6 Steve and I played tennis yesterday. **XXXXX** won. After the game we **XXXXX**.	....
7 It was my birthday last week and I had some presents. **XXXXX** gave me a book and Catherine gave me **XXXXX**.	....

Unit 46 Who is she talking to? What is it like? (questions 3)

A

Julia is talking to somebody.

Who is she talking **to**?

In questions beginning **Who** … ? / **What** … ? / **Where** … ? / **Which** … ?, prepositions (**to**/**from**/**with** etc.) usually go at the end:

- '**Where** are you **from**?' 'I'm from Thailand.'
- 'Jack was afraid.' '**What** was he afraid **of**?'
- '**Who** do these books belong **to**?' 'They're mine.'
- 'Tom's father is in hospital.' '**Which hospital** is he **in**?'
- 'Kate is going on holiday.' '**Who with**?' / '**Who** is she going **with**?'
- 'Can we talk?' 'Sure. **What** do you want to talk **about**?'

B

What's it like? / **What are they like?** etc.

What**'s** it like? = What **is** it like?

What's it like? = tell me something about it – is it good or bad, big or small, old or new (etc.)?

When we say '**What is it like?**', **like** is a *preposition*. It is not the verb **like** ('**Do** you **like** your new house?' etc.).

- A: There's a new restaurant in our street.
  B: **What's** it **like**? Is it good?
  A: I don't know. I haven't eaten there yet.
- A: **What's** your new teacher **like**?
  B: She's very good. We learn a lot.
- A: I met Nicole's parents yesterday.
  B: Did you? **What** are they **like**?
  A: They're very nice.
- A: Did you have a good holiday? **What** was the weather **like**?
  B: It was lovely. It was sunny every day.

questions → Units 44–45 what/which/how → Unit 47 prepositions → Units 103–113

46.1 You want the missing information (XXXXX). Write questions with **who** or **what**.

1. The letter is from **XXXXX**. — *Who is the letter from?*
2. I'm looking for a **XXXXX**. — What .... you ....
3. I went to the cinema with **XXXXX**. — ....
4. The film was about **XXXXX**. — ....
5. I gave the money to **XXXXX**. — ....
6. The book was written by **XXXXX**. — ....

46.2 Write questions about the people in the pictures. Use these verbs + a preposition:

go **listen** **look** ~~**talk**~~ **talk** **wait**

1. *Who is she talking to?*
2. What ....
3. Which restaurant ....
4. What ....
5. What ....
6. Which bus ....

46.3 Write questions beginning **Which ... ?**

1. Tom's father is in hospital. — *Which hospital is he in?*
2. We stayed at a hotel. — .... you ....
3. Jack plays for a football team. — ....
4. I went to school in this town. — ....

46.4 You want some information about another country. You ask somebody who has been there. Ask questions with **What is/are ... like?**

1. (the roads) *What are the roads like?*
2. (the food) ....
3. (the people) ....
4. (the weather) ....

46.5 Ask questions with **What was/were ... like?**

1. Your friend has just come back from holiday. Ask about the weather.
   What was the weather like?
2. Your friend has just come back from the cinema. Ask about the film.
   ....
3. Your friend has just finished an English course. Ask about the lessons.
   ....
4. Your friend has just come back from holiday. Ask about the hotel.
   ....

Unit 47 What ... ? Which ... ? How ... ? (questions 4)

A

What + *noun* (**What colour** ... **?** / **What kind** ... **?** etc.)

- **What colour** is your car?
- **What colour** are your eyes?
- **What size** is this shirt?
- **What make** is your TV set?
- **What time** is it?
- **What day** is it today?
- **What kind** of job do you want? (*or* **What type** of job ... ? / **What sort** of job ... ?)

What without a noun:

- **What's** your favourite colour?
- **What** do you want to do tonight?

B

Which + *noun* (things or people):

- **Which train** did you catch – the 9.50 or the 10.30?
- **Which doctor** did you see – Doctor Ellis, Doctor Gray or Doctor Hill?

We use **which** without a noun for things, not people:

- **Which** is bigger – Canada or Australia?

We use **who** for people (without a noun):

- **Who** is taller – Joe or Gary? (*not* Which is taller?)

C

What or **which**?

We use **which** when we are thinking about a small number of possibilities (perhaps 2, 3 or 4):

- We can go this way or that way.
  Which way shall we go?
- There are four umbrellas here.
  Which is yours?

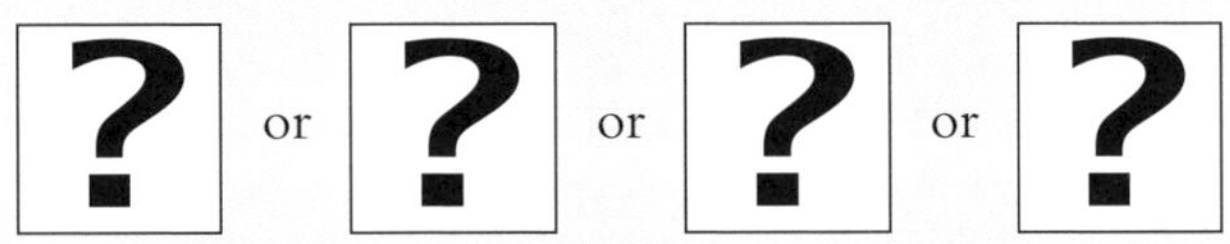

WHICH?

What is more general:

- **What's** the capital of Argentina? (of all the cities in Argentina)
- **What sort** of music do you like? (of all kinds of music)

Compare:

- **What colour** are his eyes? (*not* Which colour?)
  Which colour do you prefer, **pink or yellow**?
- **What** is the longest river in the world?
  Which is the longest river – **the Mississippi, the Amazon or the Nile**?

D

How ... ?

- '**How** was the party last night?' 'It was great.'
- '**How** do you usually go to work?' 'By bus.'

You can use **how** + *adjective/adverb* (**how tall** / **how old** / **how often** etc.):

'**How**	**tall** are you?' 'I'm 1 metre 70.'
	big is the house?' 'Not very big.'
	old is your mother?' 'She's 45.'
	far is it from here to the airport?' 'Five kilometres.'
	often do you use your car?' 'Every day.'
	long have they been married?' 'Ten years.'
	much was the meal?' 'Thirty pounds.'

questions → Units 44–46 How long does it take ... ? → Unit 48 which one(s) → Unit 75

47.1 Write questions with what.

1 I've got a new TV set. — (make?) *What make is it?*
2 I want a job. — (kind?) *What kind of job do you want?*
3 I've got a new sweater. — (colour?) What ....
4 I got up early this morning. — (time?) .... get up?
5 I like music. — (type?) ....
6 I want to buy a car. — (kind?) ....

47.2 Complete the questions. Use Which ... ?

47.3 Write what/which/who.

1 *What* is that man's name?
2 *Which* way shall we go? Left or right?
3 You can have tea or coffee. .... do you prefer?
4 '........................ day is it today?' 'Friday.'
5 This is a nice office. .... desk is yours?
6 .... is your favourite sport?
7 .... is more expensive, meat or fish?
8 .... is older, Liz or Steve?
9 .... kind of camera have you got?
10 A: I've got three cameras.
B: .... camera do you use most?
11 .... nationality are you?

47.4 Complete the questions with How + adjective or adverb (high/long etc.).

1 *How high* is Mount Everest? — Nearly 9000 metres.
2 .... is it to the station? — It's about two kilometres from here.
3 .... is Helen? — She's 26.
4 .... do the buses run? — Every ten minutes.
5 .... is the water in the pool? — Two metres.
6 .... have you lived here? — Nearly three years.

47.5 Write questions with How ... ?

1 Are you 1 metre 70? 1.75? 1.80? *How tall are you?*
2 Is this box one kilogram? Two? Three? ....
3 Are you 20 years old? 22? 25? ....
4 Did you spend £20? £30? £50? ....
5 Do you watch TV every day? Once a week? Never?
....
6 Is it 1000 miles from Paris to Moscow? 1500? 2000?
....

Unit 48

How long does it take ... ?

A

How long does it take from ... to ... ?

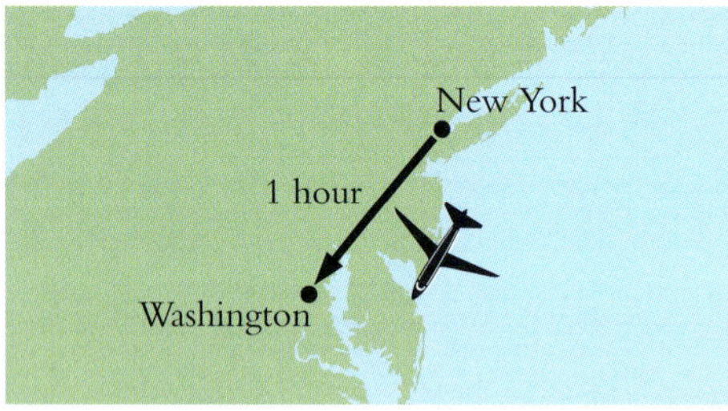

How long **does it take** by plane from New York to Washington?

It takes an hour.

- How long **does it take** by train from London to Manchester?
- **It takes** two hours by train from London to Manchester.
- How long **does it take** by car from your house to the station?
- **It takes** ten minutes by car from my house to the station.

B

How long does it take to do something?

<table>
<tr><td>How long</td><td>does
did
will</td><td>it take to ... ?</td></tr>
</table>

<table>
<tr><td rowspan="2">It</td><td colspan="2">takes
took
will take</td><td>a week
a long time
three hours</td><td rowspan="2">to ...</td></tr>
<tr><td>doesn't
didn't
won't</td><td>take</td><td>long</td></tr>
</table>

- How long **does it take to cross** the Atlantic by ship?
- 'I came by train.' 'Did you? How long **did it take** (**to get** here)?'
- How long **will it take to get** from here to the hotel?

- **It takes** a long time **to learn** a language.
- **It doesn't take** long **to cook** an omelette.
- **It won't take** long to fix the computer.

C

How long does it take you to do something?

I started reading the book on Monday.
I finished it on Wednesday evening.

It **took me** three days **to read** it.

How long	**does** **did** **will**	**it take**	you Tom them	**to** ... ?

It	**takes** **took** **will take**	me Tom them	a week a long time three hours	**to** ...

- How long **will it take me to learn** to drive?
- **It takes Tom** 20 minutes **to get** to work in the morning.
- **It took us** an hour to do the shopping.
- **Did it take you** a long time **to find** a job?
- **It will take me** an hour **to cook** dinner.

Exercises

48.1 Look at the pictures and write questions with **How long ... ?**

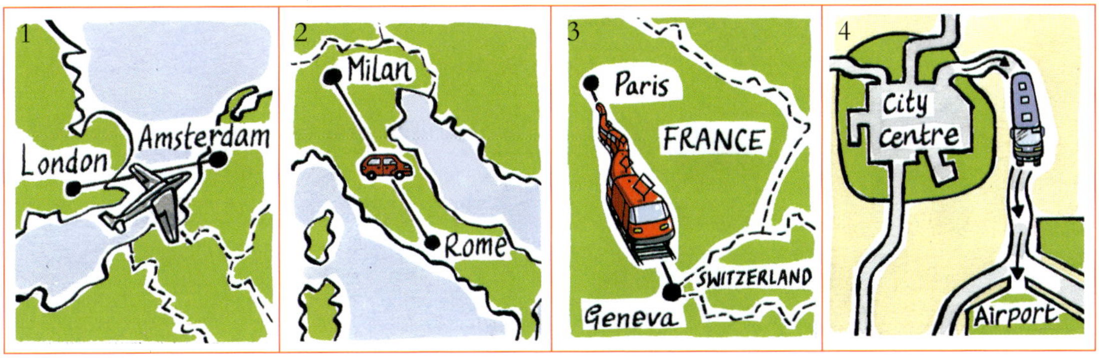

1 *How long does it take by plane from London to Amsterdam?*
2 ...
3 ...
4 ...

48.2 How long does it take to do these things? Write full sentences.

1 fly from your city/country to London
It takes two hours to fly from Madrid to London.
2 fly from your city/country to New York
...
3 study to be a doctor in your country
...
4 walk from your home to the nearest shop
...
5 get from your home to the nearest airport
...

48.3 Write questions with **How long did it take ... ?**

1 (Jane found a job.) *How long did it take her to find a job?*
2 (I walked to the station.) ... you ...
3 (Tom painted the bathroom.) ...
4 (I learnt to ski.) ...
5 (They repaired the computer.) ...

48.4 Read the situations and write sentences with **It took ... .**

1 I read a book last week. I started reading it on Monday. I finished it three days later.
It took me three days to read the book.
2 We walked home last night. We left at 10 o'clock and we arrived home at 10.20.
...
3 I learnt to drive last year. I had my first driving lesson in January. I passed my driving test six months later.
...
4 Mark drove to London yesterday. He left home at 7 o'clock and got to London at 10.
...
5 Lisa began looking for a job a long time ago. She got a job last week.
...
6 *Write a sentence about yourself.*
...

Unit 49

Do you know where ... ? I don't know what ... etc.

A

We say: Where **is** **Paula**?

but **Do you know** where **Paula** **is**?
(*not* Do you know where is Paula?)

In the same way we say:

I know / I don't know / Can you tell me } where **Paula is**.

Compare:

	but			
Who **are those people**?		**Do you know** / **Can you tell me**	who **those people are**	?
How old **is Nicole**?			how old **Nicole is**	
What time **is it**?			what time **it is**	
Where **can I** go?			where **I can** go	
How much **is this camera**?		**I know** / **I don't know** / **I don't remember**	how much **this camera is**	.
When **are you** going away?			when **you're** going away	
Where **have they** gone?			where **they have** gone	
What **was Kate** wearing?			what **Kate was** wearing	

B

Questions with **do/does/did** (*present simple* and *past simple*)

Where **does he live**?

but **Do you know** where **he lives**? (*not* Do you know where does he live?)

Compare:

	but			
How **do aeroplanes** fly?		**Do you know**	how **aeroplanes fly**	?
What **does Jane** want?		**I don't know**	what **Jane wants**	.
Why **did she** go home?		**I don't remember**	why **she went** home	
Where **did I** put the key?		**I know**	where **I put** the key	

C

Questions beginning **Is** ... **?** / **Do** ... **?** / **Can** ... **?** etc. (yes/no questions)

Compare:

	but				
Is Jack at home?		**Do you know**	**if** *or* **whether**	**Jack is** at home	?
Have they got a car?				**they've got** a car	
Can Brian swim?				**Brian can** swim	
Do they live near here?		**I don't know**		**they live** near here	.
Did anybody see you?				**anybody saw** you	

You can use **if** *or* **whether** in these sentences:

- Do you know **if** they've got a car? *or* Do you know **whether** they've got a car?
- I don't know **if** anybody saw me. *or* I don't know **whether** anybody saw me.

by → Units 21, 63, 109 at/on → Units 103, 106–107 preposition + -ing → Unit 112

Exercises

49.1 Answer these questions with **I don't know where/when/why ... etc.**

1	Have your friends gone home?	(where) *I don't know where they've gone.*
2	Is Kate in her office?	(where) I don't know ....
3	Is the castle very old?	(how old) ....
4	Will Paul be here soon?	(when) ....
5	Was he angry because I was late?	(why) ....
6	Has Sally lived here a long time?	(how long) ....

49.2 Complete the sentences.

1 (How do aeroplanes fly?) Do you know *how aeroplanes fly* ?
2 (Where does Susan work?) I don't know ....
3 (What did Peter say?) Do you remember .... ?
4 (Why did he go home early?) I don't know ....
5 (What time does the meeting begin?) Do you know .... ?
6 (How did the accident happen?) I don't remember ....

49.3 Which is right?

1 Do you know what time ~~is it~~ / it is? (Do you know what time it is? *is right*)
2 Why are you / you are going away?
3 I don't know where are they / they are going.
4 Can you tell me where is the museum / the museum is?
5 Where do you want / you want to go for your holidays?
6 Do you know what do elephants eat / elephants eat?
7 I don't know how far is it / it is from the hotel to the station.

49.4 Write questions with **Do you know if ... ?**

1 (Have they got a car?) *Do you know if they've got a car?*
2 (Are they married?) Do you know ....
3 (Does Sue know Bill?) ....
4 (Will Gary be here tomorrow?) ....
5 (Did he pass his exam?) ....

49.5 Write questions beginning **Do you know ... ?**

1 (What does Laura want?) *Do you know what Laura wants?*
2 (Where is Paula?) Do ....
3 (Is she working today?) ....
4 (What time does she start work?) ....
5 (Are the shops open tomorrow?) ....
6 (Where do Sarah and Tim live?) ....
7 (Did they go to Jane's party?) ....

49.6 Use your own ideas to complete these sentences.

1 Do you know why *the bus was late* ?
2 Do you know what time .... ?
3 Excuse me, can you tell me where .... ?
4 I don't know what ....
5 Do you know if .... ?
6 Do you know how much .... ?

Unit 50

She said that ...   He told me that ...

A

Last week you went to a party. A lot of your friends were there. Here are some things they said to you:

Today you meet Paul. You tell him about the party. You tell Paul what your friends said:

DIANE

am / **is** → **was**

- Diane said that **she was** enjoying her new job.
- She said that **her father wasn't** well.

SARAH

TIM

are → **were**

- Sarah and Tim said that **they were** going to buy a house.

PETER

have / **has** → **had**

- Peter said that **he had** to leave early.
- He said that **his sister had** gone to Australia.

KATE

can → **could**

- Kate said that **she couldn't** find a job.

STEVE

will → **would**

- Steve said that **he would** phone me.

RACHEL

do / **does** → **did**

- Rachel said that **she didn't** like her job.
- She said that **her son didn't** like school.

MIKE *YOU*

look → **looked**
feel → **felt**
etc. → etc.
(present) *(past)*

- Mike said that **I looked** tired.
- I said that **I felt** fine.

B

say and **tell**

say (→ **said**)

- He **said** that he was tired. (*not* He said me)
- What did she **say to** you? (*not* say you)

We say **he said to me**, **I said to Ann** etc.
but not 'he said me', 'I said Ann'.

tell (→ **told**)

- He **told me** that he was tired. (*not* He told that)
- What did she **tell you**? (*not* tell to you)

We say **he told me**, **I told Ann** etc.
but not 'he told to me', 'I told to Ann'.

C

You can say:

- He said **that** he was tired. *or* He said he was tired. (*without* that)
- Kate told me **that** she couldn't find a job. *or* Kate told me she couldn't find a job.

I told you to ... → Unit 53

Exercises

50.1 Read what these people say and write sentences with He/She/They said (that) ... .

1 

He said he had lost his watch.

2 

....

3 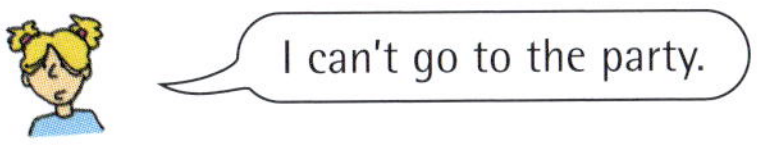

....

4 

....

5 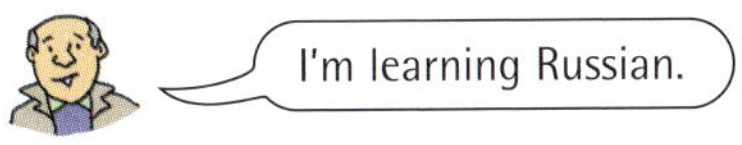

....

6 

....

7 

....

8 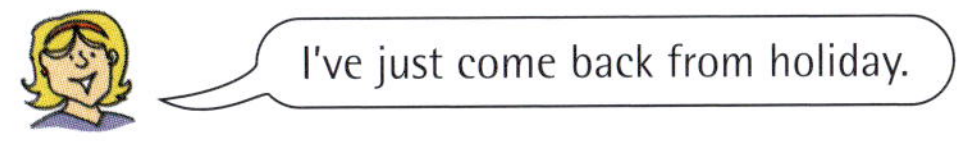

....

9 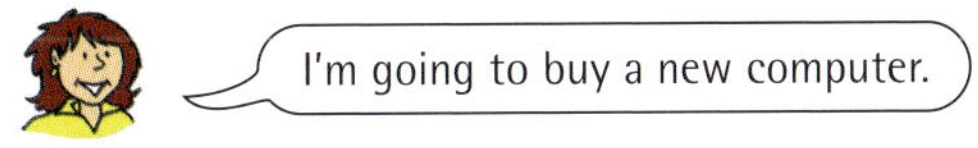

....

10 

....

50.2 Use the pictures to complete the sentences.

1 I met Diane last week. She said she was enjoying her new job.
2 Emma didn't want anything to eat. She said ....
3 I wanted to borrow Mike's ladder, but he said ....
4 Hannah was invited to the party, but she said ....
5 Susan told me she didn't want the picture. She said ....
6 Martin has just gone away on holiday. He said ....
7 I was looking for Robert. Nicole said ....
8 'Why did David stay at home?' 'He said ....'
9 'Has Mary gone out?' 'I think so. She said ....'

50.3 Write say/said or tell/told.

1 He said he was tired.
2 What did she tell you?
3 Anna .... she didn't like Peter.
4 Jack .... me that you were ill.
5 Please don't .... Dan what happened.
6 Did Lucy .... she would be late?
7 The woman .... she was a reporter.
8 The woman .... us she was a reporter.
9 They asked me a lot of questions, but I didn't .... them anything.
10 They asked me a lot of questions, but I didn't .... anything.

work/working go/going do/doing

A work/go/be etc. *(infinitive)*

We use the infinitive with **will/can/must** etc. :

will	□ Anna **will be** here soon.	→ Units 27–28
shall	□ **Shall** I **open** the window?	
might	□ I **might phone** you later.	→ Unit 29
may	□ **May** I **sit** here?	
can	□ I **can't meet** you tomorrow.	→ Unit 30
could	□ **Could** you **pass** the salt, please?	
must	□ It's late. I **must go** now.	→ Unit 31
should	□ You **shouldn't work** so hard.	→ Unit 32
would	□ **Would** you **like** some coffee?	→ Unit 34

We use the infinitive with **do/does/did**:

do/does *(present simple)*	□ **Do** you **work**? □ They **don't work** very hard. □ Helen **doesn't know** many people. □ How much **does** it **cost**?	→ Units 6–7
did *(past simple)*	□ What time **did** the train **leave**? □ We **didn't sleep** well.	→ Unit 12

B to work / to go / to be etc. (to + *infinitive*)

(I'm) **going to** ...	□ **I'm going to play** tennis tomorrow. □ What **are** you **going to do**?	→ Unit 26
(I) **have to** ...	□ I **have to go** now. □ Everybody **has to eat**.	→ Unit 33
(I) **want to** ...	□ Do you **want to go** out? □ They don't **want to come** with us.	→ Unit 52
(I) **would like to** ...	□ **I'd like to talk** to you. □ **Would** you **like to go** out?	→ Unit 34
(I) **used to** ...	□ Dave **used to work** in a factory.	→ Unit 36

C working/going/playing etc.

am/is/are + -ing *(present continuous)*	□ Please be quiet. **I'm working**. □ Tom **isn't working** today. □ What time **are** you **going** out?	→ Units 3–4, 8, 25
was/were+ -ing *(past continuous)*	□ It **was raining**, so we didn't go out. □ What **were** you **doing** when the phone rang?	→ Units 13–14

verbs + **to** ... and **-ing** (**I want to do** / **I enjoy doing**) → Unit 52 go + **-ing** → Unit 55

Exercises

51.1 Complete the sentences. Write: ... phone Paul or ... to phone Paul.

1 I'll phone Paul .
2 I'm going to phone Paul .
3 Can you .... Paul?
4 Shall I .... ?
5 I'd like ....
6 Do you have .... ?
7 You should ....
8 I want ....
9 I might ....
10 You must ....

51.2 Complete the sentences with a verb from the box. Sometimes you need the infinitive (work/go etc.) and sometimes you need -ing (working/going etc.).

do/doing	get/getting	~~sleep/sleeping~~	watch/watching
eat/eating	go/going	stay/staying	wear/wearing
fly/flying	listen/listening	wait/waiting	~~work/working~~

1 Please be quiet. I'm working .
2 I feel tired today. I didn't sleep very well last night.
3 What time do you usually .... up in the morning?
4 'Where are you .... ?' 'To the bank.'
5 Did you .... television last night?
6 Look at that plane! It's .... very low.
7 You can turn off the radio. I'm not .... to it.
8 They didn't .... anything because they weren't hungry.
9 My friends were .... for me when I arrived.
10 'Does Susan always .... glasses?' 'No, only for reading.'
11 'What are you .... tonight?' 'I'm .... at home.'

51.3 Put the verb in the correct form. Choose from:

the infinitive (work/go etc.) or
to ... (to work / to go etc.) or
-ing (working/going etc.)

1 Shall I open the window? (open)
2 It's late. I have to go now. (go)
3 Amanda isn't working this week. She's on holiday. (work)
4 I'm tired. I don't want .... out. (go)
5 It might .... , so take an umbrella with you. (rain)
6 What time do you have .... tomorrow morning? (leave)
7 I'm sorry I can't .... you. (help)
8 My brother is a student. He's .... physics. (study)
9 Would you like .... on a trip round the world? (go)
10 When you saw Maria, what was she .... ? (wear)
11 When you go to London, where are you going .... ? (stay)
12 I'm hungry. I must .... something to eat. (have)
13 'Where's Gary?' 'He's .... a bath.' (have)
14 I used .... a car, but I sold it last year. (have)
15 He spoke very quietly. I couldn't .... him. (hear)
16 You don't look well. I don't think you should .... to work today. (go)
17 I don't know what he said. I wasn't .... to him. (listen)
18 I'm sorry I'm late. I had .... a phone call. (make)
19 I want .... what happened. (know) You must .... me. (tell)
20 May I .... your phone? (use)

Unit 52

to ... (I want to do) and -ing (I enjoy doing)

A

verbs + **to** ... (**I want to do**)

want	**plan**	**decide**	**try**	
hope	**expect**	**offer**	**forget**	+ **to** ... (**to do** / **to work** / **to be** etc.)
need	**promise**	**refuse**	**learn**	

- □ What do you **want to do** this evening?
- □ It's not very late. We don't **need to go** home yet.
- □ Tina has **decided to sell** her car.
- □ You **forgot to switch** off the light when you went out.
- □ My brother is **learning to drive**.
- □ I **tried to read** my book, but I was too tired.

B

verbs + **-ing** (**I enjoy doing**)

enjoy	**stop**	**suggest**	+ **-ing** (**doing** / **working** / **being** etc.)
mind	**finish**		

- □ I **enjoy dancing**. (*not* enjoy to dance)
- □ I don't **mind getting** up early.
- □ Has it **stopped raining**?
- □ Sonia **suggested going** to the cinema.

C

verbs + **-ing** *or* **to** ...

like	**love**	**start**	**continue**	+ **-ing** (**doing** etc.) *or* **to** ... (**to do** etc.)
prefer	**hate**	**begin**		

- □ Do you **like getting** up early? *or* Do you **like to get** up early?
- □ I **prefer travelling** by car. *or* I **prefer to travel** by car.
- □ Anna **loves dancing**. *or* Anna **loves to dance**.
- □ I **hate being** late. *or* I **hate to be** late.
- □ It **started raining**. *or* It **started to rain**.

D

would like to ... etc.

would like	**would** love	+ **to** ... (**to do** / **to work** / **to be** etc.)
would prefer	**would** hate	

- □ Julia **would like to meet** you.
- □ **I'd love to go** to Australia. (**I'd** = I **would**)
- □ '**Would** you **like to sit** down?' 'No, **I'd prefer to stand**, thank you.'
- □ I like this city very much. I **wouldn't like to move**.
- □ **I'd hate to lose** my address book.

would like → Unit 34 I want you to ... → Unit 53 go + -ing → Unit 55 preposition + -ing → Unit 112

Exercises

52.1 Put the verb in the right form, *to* ... or *-ing*.

1 I enjoy ...dancing... . (dance)
2 What do you want ...to do... tonight? (do)
3 Bye! I hope .... you again soon. (see)
4 I learnt .... when I was five years old. (swim)
5 Have you finished .... the kitchen? (clean)
6 Where's Anna? I need .... her something. (ask)
7 Do you enjoy .... other countries? (visit)
8 The weather was nice, so I suggested .... for a walk by the river. (go)
9 Where's Bill? He promised .... here on time. (be)
10 I'm not in a hurry. I don't mind .... (wait)
11 What have you decided .... ? (do)
12 Gary was very angry and refused .... to me. (speak)
13 I'm tired. I want .... to bed. (go)
14 I was very upset and started .... (cry)
15 I'm trying .... (work) Please stop .... (talk)

52.2 Complete the sentences using *to* ... or *-ing*. Use these verbs:

~~go~~ go help lose rain read see send wait watch

1 'Have you ever been to Australia?' 'No, but I'd love ...to go... .'
2 Jane had a lot to do, so I offered .... her.
3 I'm surprised that you're here. I didn't expect .... you.
4 Nicole has a lot of books. She enjoys ....
5 This ring was my grandmother's. I'd hate .... it.
6 Don't forget .... us a postcard when you're on holiday.
7 I'm not going out until it stops ....
8 What shall we do this afternoon? Would you like .... to the beach?
9 When I'm tired in the evenings, I like .... television.
10 'Shall we go now?' 'No, I'd prefer .... a few minutes.'

52.3 Complete the answers to the questions.

1	Do you usually get up early ?	Yes, I like ...to get up early... .
2	Do you ever go to museums?	Yes, I enjoy ....
3	Would you like to go to a museum now?	No, I'm hungry. I'd prefer .... to a restaurant.
4	Do you often write letters?	No, I don't like ....
5	Have you ever been to New York?	No, but I'd love .... one day.
6	Do you often travel by train?	Yes, I enjoy ....
7	Shall we walk home or take a taxi?	I don't mind ...., but a taxi would be quicker.

52.4 Complete these sentences. Write about yourself. Use *to* ... or *-ing*.

1 I enjoy ....
2 I don't like ....
3 If it's a nice day tomorrow, I'd like ....
4 When I'm on holiday, I like ....
5 I don't mind ...., but ....
6 I wouldn't like ....

→ Additional exercise 32 (page 268)

I want you to ... I told you to ...

A

I want you to …

The woman **wants to go**.

The man **doesn't want** the woman **to go**. He **wants** her **to stay**.

We say:

I want	**you** **somebody** **Sarah**	**to do** something

- □ I **want you to be** happy. (*not* I want that you are happy)
- □ They didn't **want anybody to know** their secret.
- □ Do you **want me to lend** you some money?

We use **would like** in the same way:

- □ **Would** you **like me to lend** you some money?

B

We also use this structure (*verb* + somebody + **to** …) with:

ask
tell
advise
expect
persuade
teach

	verb +	somebody +	**to** …	
Sue	**asked**	a friend	**to lend**	her some money.
I	**told**	you	**to be**	careful.
What do you	**advise**	me	**to do**?	
I didn't	**expect**	them	**to be**	here.
We	**persuaded**	Gary	**to come**	with us.
I	**am teaching**	my brother	**to swim**.	

C

I told you **to** … / **I told** you **not to** …

→ Jane **told** me **to wait** for her.

→ Paul **told** Sue **not to wait** for him.

D

make and **let**

After **make** and **let**, we do *not* use **to**:

- □ He's very funny. He **makes** me **laugh**. (*not* makes me to laugh)
- □ At school our teacher **made** us **work** very hard.
- □ Sue **let** me **use** her computer because mine wasn't working. (*not* let me to use)

You can say **Let's** … (= **Let us**) when you want people to do things with you:

- □ Come on! **Let's dance**.
- □ 'Do you want to go out tonight?' 'No, I'm tired. **Let's stay** at home.'

Let's ... → Unit 35 He told me that ... → Unit 50

Exercises

53.1 Write sentences beginning I want you ... / I don't want you ... / Do you want me ... ?

1 (you must come with me) I want you to come with me.
2 (listen carefully) I want ……
3 (please don't be angry) I don't ……
4 (shall I wait for you?) Do you ……
5 (don't phone me tonight) ……
6 (you must meet Sarah) ……

53.2 Look at the pictures and complete the sentences.

1 Dan persuaded me to go to the cinema.
2 I wanted to get to the station. A woman told ……
3 Brian wasn't well. I advised ……
4 Linda had a lot of luggage. She asked ……
5 I was too busy to talk to Tom. I told ……
6 I wanted to make a phone call. Paul let ……
7 Sue is going to phone later. I told ……
8 Ann's mother taught ……

53.3 Complete these sentences with the verbs in the list. Sometimes to is necessary (to go / to wait etc.); sometimes to is not necessary (go/wait etc.).

arrive borrow get ~~go~~ go make repeat tell think wait

1 Please stay here. I don't want you to go yet.
2 I didn't hear what she said, so I asked her …… it.
3 'Shall we begin?' 'No, let's …… a few minutes.'
4 Are they already here? I expected them …… much later.
5 Kevin's parents didn't want him …… married.
6 I want to stay here. You can't make me …… with you.
7 'Is that your bicycle?' 'No, it's John's. He let me …… it.'
8 Rachel can't come to the party. She told me …… you.
9 Would you like a drink? Would you like me …… some coffee?
10 'Kate doesn't like me.' 'What makes you …… that?'

Unit 54

I went to the shop to ...

A

Paula wanted a newspaper, so she went to the shop.

Why did she go to the shop?
To get a newspaper.

She went to the shop **to get** a newspaper.

to ... (**to get** / **to see** etc.) tells us *why* a person does something:

- 'Why are you going out?' '**To get** some bread.'
- Catherine went to the station **to meet** her friend.
- Sue turned on the television **to watch** the news.
- I'd like to go to Spain **to learn** Spanish.

money/time to (do something):

- We need some **money to buy** food.
- I haven't got **time to watch** television.

B

to ... and **for** ...

to + *verb* (**to get** / **to see** etc.)	**for** + *noun* (**for a newspaper** / **for food** etc.)
I went to the shop **to get** a newspaper. (*not* for get)	I went to the shop **for a newspaper**.
They're going to Brazil **to see** their friends.	They're going to Brazil **for a holiday**.
We need some money **to buy** food.	We need some money **for food**.

C

wait for ... :

- Please **wait for** me.
- Are you **waiting for** the bus?

wait to (do something):

- Hurry up! I'm **waiting to go**.
- Are you **waiting to see** the doctor?

wait for (somebody/something) **to** ... :

- I can't go out yet. I'm **waiting for John to phone**.
- Are you **waiting for the doctor to come**?

go to ... and **go for** ... → Unit 55 **something to eat** / **nothing to do** etc. → Unit 79
enough + to/for ... → Unit 91 **too + to/for** ... → Unit 92

Exercises

54.1 Write sentences beginning I went to ... . Choose from the boxes.

the café the chemist	~~the post office~~ the supermarket	+	buy some food get some medicine	~~get some stamps~~ meet a friend

1 I went to the post office to get some stamps.
2 I went ...
3 ...
4 ...

54.2 Complete the sentences. Choose from the box.

to get some fresh air to open this door	to read the newspaper to see who it was	to wake him up ~~to watch the news~~

1 I turned on the television to watch the news .
2 Alice sat down in an armchair ... .
3 Do I need a key ... ?
4 I went for a walk by the river ... .
5 I knocked on the door of David's room ... .
6 The doorbell rang, so I looked out of the window ... .

54.3 Use your own ideas to finish these sentences. Use to ... .

1 I went to the shop to get a newspaper .
2 I'm very busy. I haven't got time ... .
3 I phoned Ann ... .
4 I'm going out ... .
5 I borrowed some money ... .

54.4 Write to or for.

1 I went out to get some bread.
2 We went to a restaurant ... have dinner.
3 Robert wants to go to university ... study economics.
4 I'm going to London ... an interview next week.
5 I'm going to London ... visit some friends of mine.
6 Have you got time ... a cup of coffee?
7 I got up late this morning. I didn't have time ... wash.
8 Everybody needs money ... live.
9 We didn't have any money ... a taxi, so we walked home.
10 The office is very small. There's space only ... a desk and chair.
11 A: Excuse me, are you waiting ... use the phone?
B: No, I'm waiting ... somebody.

54.5 Complete these sentences. Choose from:

~~John / phone~~ **it / to arrive** **you / tell me** **the film / begin**

1 I can't go out yet. I'm waiting for John to phone .
2 I sat down in the cinema and waited ... .
3 We called an ambulance and waited ... .
4 'Do you know what to do?' 'No, I'm waiting ... .'

go to ... go on ... go for ... go -ing

A

go to ... (**go to work** / **go to London** / **go to a concert** etc.)

- ☐ What time do you usually **go to work**?
- ☐ I'm **going to China** next week.
- ☐ Sophie didn't want to **go to the concert**.
- ☐ 'Where's Tom?' 'He's **gone to bed**.'
- ☐ I **went to the dentist** yesterday.

go to sleep = start to sleep:

- ☐ I was very tired and **went to sleep** quickly.

go home (without **to**)

- ☐ I'm **going home** now. (*not* going to home)

B

go on ...

go on	holiday a trip a tour an excursion a cruise strike

- ☐ We're **going on holiday** next week.
- ☐ Children often **go on school trips**.
- ☐ When we were in Scotland, we **went on a lot of excursions** to different places.
- ☐ Workers at the airport have **gone on strike**. (= they are refusing to work)

C

go for ...

go (somewhere) **for**	a walk a run a swim a drink a meal

- ☐ 'Where's Emma?' 'She's **gone for a walk**.'
- ☐ Do you **go for a run** every morning?
- ☐ The water looks nice. I'm **going for a swim**.
- ☐ I met Chris in town, so we **went for a coffee**.
- ☐ Shall we **go** out **for a meal**? I know a good restaurant.

D

go + -ing

We use **go + -ing** for many sports (**swimming** / **skiing** etc.) and also **shopping**.

I **go** he is **going** we **went** they have **gone** she wants to **go**	**shopping** **swimming** **fishing** **sailing** **skiing** **jogging** etc.

- ☐ Are you **going shopping** this afternoon?
- ☐ It's a nice day. Let's **go swimming**. (*or* Let's **go for a** swim.)
- ☐ Richard has a small boat and he often **goes sailing**.
- ☐ I **went jogging** before breakfast this morning.

55.1 Write to/on/for where necessary.

1 I'm going ...to... China next week.
2 Richard often goes ...–... sailing. *(no preposition)*
3 Sue went .... Mexico last year.
4 Would you like to go .... the cinema this evening?
5 Jack goes .... jogging every morning.
6 I'm going out .... a walk. Do you want to come?
7 I'm tired because I went .... bed very late last night.
8 Martin is going .... holiday .... Italy next week.
9 The weather was warm and the river was clean, so we went .... a swim.
10 The taxi drivers went .... strike when I was in New York.
11 I need some stamps, so I'm going .... the post office.
12 It's late. I have to go .... home now.
13 Would you like to go .... a tour of the city?
14 Shall we go out .... dinner this evening?
15 My parents are going .... a cruise this summer.

55.2 Use the pictures to complete the sentences. Use go/goes/going/went + -ing.

1 Richard has a boat. He often ...goes sailing... .
2 Last Saturday Diane went ....
3 Gary .... every day.
4 Nicole is going on holiday next month. She is ....
5 Peter is going out later. He has to ....
6 Sarah .... after work yesterday.

55.3 Complete the sentences. Use the words in the box. Use to/on/for if necessary.

~~a swim~~	holiday	Portugal	shopping	sleep
a walk	home	riding	skiing	university

1 The water looks nice. Let's go ...for a swim... .
2 After leaving school, Tina went .... where she studied psychology.
3 I'm going .... now. I have to buy a few things.
4 I was very tired last night. I sat down in an armchair and went ....
5 I wasn't enjoying the party, so I went .... early.
6 We live near the mountains. In winter we go .... most weekends.
7 Richard has got a horse. He goes .... a lot.
8 The weather is nice. Shall we go .... along the river?
9 A: Are you going .... soon?
B: Yes, next month. We're going .... We've never been there before.

Unit 56

get

A

get a letter / **get a job** etc. (**get** + *noun*) = receive/buy/find:

you **don't have** something → you **get** it → you **have** it

- 'Did you **get** my postcard?' 'Yes, I **got** it yesterday.' (= receive)
- I like your sweater. Where did you **get** it? (= buy)
- Is it difficult to **get** a job at the moment? (= find)
- *(on the phone)* 'Hello, can I speak to Lisa, please?' 'Sure. I'll **get** her.'

also **get a bus** / **a train** / **a taxi** (= take a bus/train etc.):

- 'Did you walk here?' 'No, I **got** the bus.'

B

get hungry / **get cold** / **get tired** etc. (**get** + *adjective*) = become:

you're **not hungry** → you **get hungry** → you **are hungry**

- If you don't eat, you **get hungry**.
- Drink your coffee. It**'s getting cold**.
- I'm sorry your mother is ill. I hope she **gets better** soon.
- It was raining very hard. We didn't have an umbrella, so we **got** very **wet**.

also **get married**
get dressed (= put your clothes on)
get lost (= lose your way)

- Nicole and Frank are **getting married** soon.
- I got up and **got dressed** quickly.
- We didn't have a map, so we **got lost**.

C

get to a place = arrive:

- I usually **get to work** before 8.30. (= arrive at work)
- We left London at 10 o'clock and **got to Manchester** at 12.45.

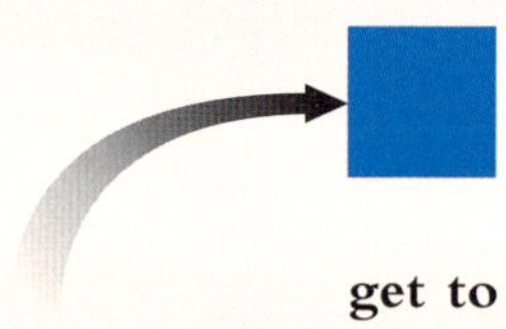

get to

get here/**there** (without **to**):

- How did you **get here**? By bus?

get home (without **to**):

- What time did you **get home** last night?

D

get in/**out**/**on**/**off**

get in (a car)

get out (**of** a car)

get on

get off

(a bus / a train / a plane)

- Kate **got in the car** and drove away. (You can also say: Kate got **into** the car and …)
- A car stopped and a man **got out**. (*but* A man got out **of the car**.)
- We **got on the bus** outside the hotel and **got off** in Church Street.

get to → Unit 108 in/out/on/off → Units 110, 114 get up → Unit 114 get on → Appendix 6

Exercises

56.1 Complete these sentences. Use **get/gets** and choose from the box.

a doctor	a lot of rain	a taxi	~~my postcard~~	the job
a good salary	a new computer	a ticket	some milk	your jacket

1 Did you ......*get my postcard*...... ? I sent it a week ago.
2 Where did you .... ? It's very nice.
3 Quick! This man is ill. We must ....
4 I don't want to walk home. Let's ....
5 Tom has an interview tomorrow. I hope he ....
6 When you go out, can you .... ?
7 'Are you going to the concert?' 'Yes, if I can ....'
8 Margaret has got a well-paid job. She ....
9 The weather is horrible here in winter. We ....
10 I'm going to .... The one I have is too slow.

56.2 Complete these sentences. Use **getting** + these words:

~~**cold**~~ **dark** **late** **married** **ready**

1 Drink your coffee. It's ......*getting cold*...... .
2 Turn on the light. It's ....
3 'I'm .... next week.' 'Really? Congratulations!'
4 'Where's Karen?' 'She's .... to go out.'
5 It's .... It's time to go home.

56.3 Complete the sentences. Use **get/gets/got** + these words:

angry **better** ~~**hungry**~~ **lost** **married** **old** **wet**

1 If you don't eat, you ......*get hungry*...... .
2 Don't go out in the rain. You'll ....
3 My brother .... last year. His wife's name is Sarah.
4 Martin is always very calm. He never ....
5 We tried to find the hotel, but we ....
6 Everybody wants to stay young, but we all ....
7 Yesterday the weather wasn't so good at first, but it .... during the day.

56.4 Write sentences with **I left ... and got to ...** .

1 home / 7.30 → work / 8.15
I left home at 7.30 and got to work at 8.15.

2 London / 10.15 → Bristol / 11.45
I left London at 10.15 and ....

3 the party / 11.15 → home / midnight
....

4 *Write a sentence about yourself.*
I left ....

56.5 Write **got in / got out of / got on / got off**.

1 Kate ......*got in*...... the car and drove away.
2 I .... the bus and walked to my house from the bus stop.
3 Isabel .... the car, shut the door and went into a shop.
4 I made a stupid mistake. I .... the wrong train.

Unit 57

do and make

A

Do is a general word for actions:

- What are you **doing** this evening? (*not* What are you making?)
- 'Shall I open the window?' 'No, it's OK. I'll **do** it.'
- Rachel's job is very boring. She **does** the same thing every day.
- I **did** a lot of things yesterday.

What do you do? = What's your job?:

- 'What do you **do**?' 'I work in a bank.'

B

Make = produce/create. For example:

She's **making** coffee. He has **made** a cake. They **make** umbrellas. It was **made** in China.

Compare **do** and **make**:

- I **did** a lot yesterday. I **cleaned** my room, I **wrote** some letters and I **made** a cake.
- A: What do you **do** in your free time? Sport? Reading? Hobbies?
  B: I **make** clothes. I **make** dresses and jackets. I also **make** toys for my children.

C

Expressions with **do**

do	an exam / a test
	a course
	homework
	housework
	somebody a favour
	an exercise

- I'm **doing my driving test** next week.
- John has just **done a training course**.
- Our children have to **do** a lot of **homework**.
- I hate **doing housework**, especially cleaning.
- Sue, could you **do me a favour**?
- I go for a run and **do exercises** every morning.

also **do the shopping** / **do the washing** / **do the washing-up** / **do the ironing** / **do the cooking** etc. :

- I **did the washing**, but I didn't **do the shopping**.

D

Expressions with **make**

make	a mistake
	an appointment
	a phone call
	a list
	a noise
	a bed

- I'm sorry, I **made a mistake**.
- I need to **make an appointment** to see the doctor.
- Excuse me, I have to **make a phone call**.
- Have you **made a shopping list**?
- It's late. Don't **make a noise**.
- Sometimes I forget to **make my bed** in the morning.

We say **make a film** *but* **take a photograph**:

- When was **this film made**? *but* When was **this photograph taken**?

do/does/did (negatives and questions) → Units 43–44 **make** somebody do something → Unit 53

Exercises

57.1 Write make/making/made or do/doing/did/done.

1 'Shall I open the window?' 'No, it's OK. I'll ....do.... it.'
2 What did you .... at the weekend? Did you go away?
3 Do you know how to .... bread?
4 Paper is .... from wood.
5 Richard didn't help me. He sat in an armchair and .... nothing.
6 'What do you .... ?' 'I'm a doctor.'
7 I asked you to clean the bathroom. Have you .... it?
8 'What do they .... in that factory?' 'Shoes.'
9 I'm .... some coffee. Would you like some?
10 Why are you angry with me? I didn't .... anything wrong.
11 'What are you .... tomorrow afternoon?' 'I'm working.'

57.2 What are these people doing?

1 ....He's making a cake....
2 They ....
3 He ....
4 ....
5 ....
6 ....
7 ....
8 ....
9 ....
10 ....

57.3 Write make or do in the correct form.

1 I hate ....doing.... housework, especially cleaning.
2 Why do you always .... the same mistake?
3 'Can you .... me a favour?' 'It depends what it is.'
4 'Have you .... your homework?' 'Not yet.'
5 I need to see the dentist, but I haven't .... an appointment.
6 I'm .... a course in photography at the moment. It's very good.
7 The last time I .... an exam was ten years ago.
8 How many phone calls did you .... yesterday?
9 When you've finished Exercise 1, you can .... Exercise 2.
10 There's something wrong with the car. The engine is .... a strange noise.
11 It was a bad mistake. It was the worst mistake I've ever ....
12 Let's .... a list of all the things we have to .... today.

Unit 58

have

A have and have got

I've got (something) or **I have** (something) = it is mine:

- **I've got** a new car. *or* I **have** a new car.
- Sue **has got** long hair. *or* Sue **has** long hair.
- **Have** they **got** any children? *or* **Do** they **have** any children?
- Tim **hasn't got** a job. *or* Tim **doesn't have** a job.
- How much time **have** you **got**? *or* How much time **do** you **have**?

also

I've got / I **have**	a headache / (a) toothache / a pain (in my leg etc.) a cold / a cough / a sore throat / a temperature / flu etc.

- **I've got** a headache. *or* I **have** a headache.
- **Have** you **got** a cold? *or* **Do** you **have** a cold?

The past is **I had** (without **got**) / **I didn't have** / **Did you have**? etc. :

- When I first met Sue, she **had** short hair.
- He **didn't have** any money because he **didn't have** a job.
- **Did** you **have** enough time to do everything you wanted?

B have breakfast / have a shower etc.

In these expressions **have** = eat/drink/take etc. You can't use 'have got'.

have	breakfast / lunch / dinner a meal / a sandwich / a pizza etc. a cup of coffee / a glass of milk etc. something to eat/drink

- 'Where's Liz?' 'She**'s having** lunch.'
- I **don't** usually **have** breakfast.
- I **had** three cups of coffee this morning.
- '**Have** a biscuit!' 'Oh, thank you.'

We also use **have** (*not* have got) in these expressions:

have	a bath / a shower a rest / a holiday / a party a nice time / a good trip / fun etc. a walk / a swim / a game (of tennis etc.) a dream / an accident a baby a look (at something)

- I **had** a shower this morning.
- We**'re having** a party next week. You must come.
- Enjoy your holiday. **Have** a nice time!
- **Did** you **have** a good time in Tokyo?
- Sandra **has** just **had** a baby.
- Can I **have** a look at your newspaper?

C

Compare:

Have got *or* **have**

- **I've got** / I **have** a new shower. It's very good.

Have (*not* **have got**)

- I **have** a shower every morning. (*not* **I've got** a shower every morning)
- A: Where's Paul?
  B: He**'s having** a shower.
  (= he's washing now)

I have / I've got → Unit 9 I've (done) (present perfect) → Units 15–18 I have to ... → Unit 33

58.1 Write the correct form of have or have got.

1 I didn't have time to do the shopping yesterday. (I / not / have)
2 'Has Lisa got (OR Does Lisa have) a car?' 'No, she can't drive.' (Lisa / have?)
3 He can't open the door. .... a key. (he / not / have)
4 .... a cold last week. He's better now. (Gary / have)
5 What's wrong? .... a headache? (you / have?)
6 We wanted to go by taxi, but .... enough money. (we / not / have)
7 Liz is very busy. .... much free time. (she / not / have)
8 .... any problems when you were on holiday? (you / have?)

58.2 What are these people doing? Choose from the list:

a bath ~~**breakfast**~~ **a cup of tea** **dinner** **a good time** **a rest**

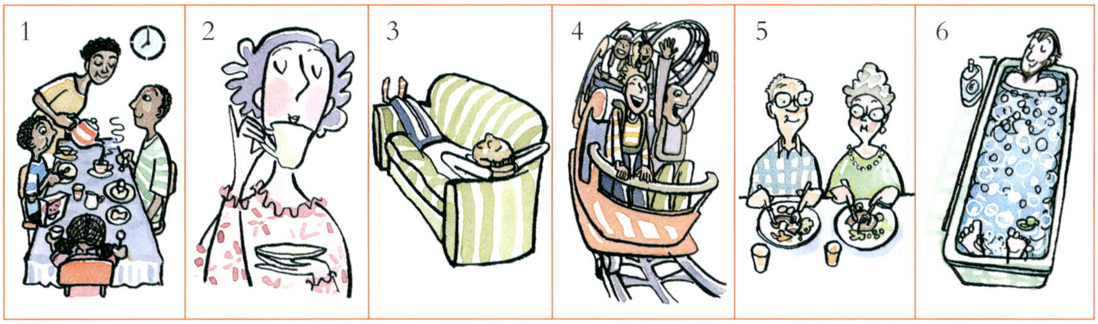

1 They're having breakfast.
2 She ....
3 He ....
4 They ....
5 ....
6 ....

58.3 What do you say in these situations? Use have.

1 Emily is going on holiday. What do you say to her before she goes?
Have a nice holiday!
2 You meet Claire at the airport. She has just got off her plane. Ask her about the flight.
Did you have a good flight?
3 Tim is going on a long trip. What do you say to him before he leaves?
....
4 It's Monday morning. You are at work. Ask Paula about her weekend.
....
5 Paul has just come home after playing tennis with a friend. Ask him about the game.
....
6 Rachel is going out this evening. What do you say to her before she goes?
....
7 Mark has just returned from holiday. Ask him about his holiday.
....

58.4 Complete the sentences. Use have/had and choose from the list.

an accident **a glass of water** **a look** **a walk** ~~**a party**~~ **something to eat**

1 We had a party a few weeks ago. We invited 50 people.
2 'Shall we .... ?' 'No, I'm not hungry.'
3 I was thirsty, so I ....
4 I like to get up early and .... before breakfast.
5 Tina is a very good driver. She has never ....
6 There's something wrong with the engine of my car. Can you .... at it?

I/me he/him they/them etc.

A

People

subject	**I**	**we**	**you**	**he**	**she**	**they**
object	**me**	**us**	**you**	**him**	**her**	**them**

subject	
I	**I** know Tom.
we	**We** know Tom.
you	**You** know Tom.
he	**He** knows Tom.
she	**She** knows Tom.
they	**They** know Tom.

	object
Tom knows **me**.	**me**
Tom knows **us**.	**us**
Tom knows **you**.	**you**
Tom knows **him**.	**him**
Tom knows **her**.	**her**
Tom knows **them**.	**them**

B

Things

subject	**it**	**they**
object	**it**	**them**

- I don't want **this book**. You can have **it**.
- I don't want **these books**. You can have **them**.
- Diane never drinks **milk**. She doesn't like **it**.
- I never go to **parties**. I don't like **them**.

C

We use **me**/**her**/**them** etc. (object) after a *preposition* (**for**/**to**/**with** etc.):

- This letter isn't **for me**. It's **for you**.
- Who is that woman? Why are you looking **at her**?
- We're going to the cinema. Do you want to come **with us**?
- Sue and Kevin are going to the cinema. Do you want to go **with them**?
- 'Where's the newspaper?' 'You're sitting **on it**.'

give it/them to … :

- I want that book. Please give **it to me**.
- Robert needs these books. Can you give **them to him**, please?

my/his/their etc. → Unit 60 Give me that book / Give it to me → Unit 96

Exercises

59.1 Complete the sentences with him/her/them.

1 I don't know those girls. Do you know ......them...... ?
2 I don't know that man. Do you know .... ?
3 I don't know those people. Do you know .... ?
4 I don't know David's wife. Do you know .... ?
5 I don't know Mr Stevens. Do you know .... ?
6 I don't know Sarah's parents. Do you know .... ?
7 I don't know the woman in the black coat. Do you know .... ?

59.2 Complete the sentences. Use I/me/you/she/her etc.

1 **I** want to see **her**, but ......she...... doesn't want to see ......me...... .
2 **They** want to see **me**, but .... don't want to see ....
3 **She** wants to see **him**, but .... doesn't want to see ....
4 **We** want to see **them**, but .... don't want to see ....
5 **He** wants to see **us**, but .... don't want to see ....
6 **They** want to see **her**, but .... doesn't want to see ....
7 **I** want to see **them**, but .... don't want to see ....
8 **You** want to see **her**, but .... doesn't want to see ....

59.3 Write sentences beginning I like ... , I don't like ... or Do you like ... ?

1 I don't eat tomatoes. ......I don't like them...... .
2 George is a very nice man. I like ....
3 This jacket isn't very nice. I don't ....
4 This is my new car. Do .... ?
5 Mrs Clark is not very friendly. I ....
6 These are my new shoes. .... ?

59.4 Complete the sentences. Use I/me/he/him etc.

1 Who is that woman? Why are you looking at ......her...... ?
2 'Do you know that man?' 'Yes, I work with ....'
3 Where are the tickets? I can't find ....
4 I can't find my keys. Where are .... ?
5 We're going out. You can come with ....
6 I've got a new computer. Do you want to see .... ?
7 Maria likes music. .... plays the piano.
8 I don't like dogs. I'm afraid of ....
9 I'm talking to you. Please listen to ....
10 Where is Anna? I want to talk to ....
11 You can have these CDs. I don't want ....
12 My brother has a new job, but .... doesn't like .... very much.

59.5 Complete the sentences.

1 I need that book. Can you ......give it to me...... ?
2 He wants the key. Can you give .... ?
3 She wants the keys. Can you .... ?
4 I want that letter. Can you .... ?
5 They want the money. Can you .... ?
6 We want the photographs. Can you .... ?

my/his/their etc.

A

I	→	**my**
we	→	**our**
you	→	**your**
he	→	**his**
she	→	**her**
they	→	**their**

I	like	**my**	house.
We	like	**our**	house.
You	like	**your**	house.
He	likes	**his**	house.
She	likes	**her**	house.
They	like	**their**	house.

it → **its**

Oxford (= **it**) is famous for **its** university.

We use **my**/**your**/**his** etc.+ *noun:*

my hands	**his** new **car**	**her parents**
our clothes	**your** best **friend**	**their room**

B

his/**her**/**their**

DONNA 	*ANDY* 	*MR AND MRS LEE* 
her car (= Donna's car) 	**his** bicycle 	**their** son 
her husband (= Donna's husband) 	**his** sister 	**their** daughter 
her children (= Donna's children) 	**his** parents 	**their** children 

C

its and **it's**

its	Oxford is famous for **its** university.
it's (= it **is**)	I like Oxford. **It's** a nice place. (= It **is** a nice place.)

mine/yours etc. → Unit 61   I/me/my/mine → Unit 62

Exercises

60.1 Complete the sentences in the same way.

1 I'm going to wash …my hands… .
2 She's going to wash …… hands.
3 We're going to wash …… .
4 He's going to wash …… .
5 They're going to wash …… .
6 Are you going to wash …… ?

60.2 Complete the sentences in the same way.

1 He …lives with his parents… .
2 They live with …… parents.
3 We …… parents.
4 Jane lives …… .
5 I …… parents.
6 John …… .
7 Do you live …… ?
8 Most children …… .

60.3 Look at the family tree, and complete the sentences with his/her/their.

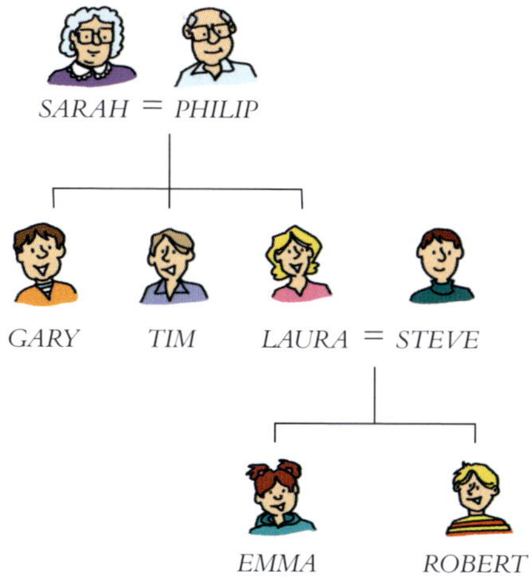

1 I saw Sarah with …her… husband, Philip.
2 I saw Laura and Steve with …… children.
3 I saw Steve with …… wife, Laura.
4 I saw Gary with …… brother, Tim.
5 I saw Laura with …… brother, Tim.
6 I saw Sarah and Philip with …… son, Tim.
7 I saw Laura with …… parents.
8 I saw Emma and Robert with …… parents.

60.4 Write my/our/your/his/her/their/its.

1 Do you like …your… job?
2 I know Mr Watson, but I don't know …… wife.
3 Alice and Tom live in London. …… son lives in Australia.
4 We're going to have a party. We're going to invite all …… friends.
5 Anna is going out with …… friends this evening.
6 I like tennis. It's …… favourite sport.
7 'Is that …… car?' 'No, I haven't got a car.'
8 I want to phone Maria. Do you know …… phone number?
9 Do you think most people are happy in …… jobs?
10 I'm going to wash …… hair before I go out.
11 This is a beautiful tree. …… leaves are a beautiful colour.
12 John has a brother and a sister. …… brother is 25, and …… sister is 21.

60.5 Complete the sentences. Use my/his/their etc. with these words:

coat **homework** **house** **husband** ~~**job**~~ **key** **name**

1 Jim doesn't enjoy …his job… . It's not very interesting.
2 I can't get in. I haven't got …… .
3 Sally is married. …… works in a bank.
4 Please take off …… and sit down.
5 'What are the children doing?' 'They're doing …… .'
6 'Do you know that man?' 'Yes, but I don't know …… .'
7 We live in Barton Street. …… is at the end on the left.

Unit 61 Whose is this? It's mine/yours/hers etc.

A

I	→	**my**	→	**mine**
we	→	**our**	→	**ours**
you	→	**your**	→	**yours**
he	→	**his**	→	**his**
she	→	**her**	→	**hers**
they	→	**their**	→	**theirs**

It's **my** money.	It's **mine**.
It's **our** money.	It's **ours**.
It's **your** money.	It's **yours**.
It's **his** money.	It's **his**.
It's **her** money.	It's **hers**.
It's **their** money.	It's **theirs**.

B

We use **my/your** etc.+ *noun* (**my hands** / **your book** etc.):

- **My hands** are cold.
- Is this **your book**?
- Helen gave me **her umbrella**.
- It's **their problem**, not **our problem**.

We use **mine/yours** etc. without a noun:

- Is this book **mine** or **yours**? (= my book or your book)
- I didn't have an umbrella, so Helen gave me **hers**. (= her umbrella)
- It's their problem, not **ours**. (= not our problem)
- We went in our car, and they went in **theirs**. (= their car)

You can use **his** with or without a noun:

- 'Is this **his camera** or **hers**?' 'It's **his**.'

C

a friend **of mine** / a friend **of his** / some friends **of yours** etc.

- I went out to meet a friend **of mine**. (*not* a friend of me)
- Tom was in the restaurant with a friend **of his**. (*not* a friend of him)
- Are those people friends **of yours**? (*not* friends of you)

D

Whose ... ?

- **Whose book** is this? (= Is it your book? his book? my book? etc.)

You can use **whose** with or without a noun:

- **Whose money** is this? / **Whose** is this? } It's mine.
- **Whose shoes** are these? / **Whose** are these? } They're John's.

my/his/their etc. → Unit 60 I/me/my/mine → Unit 62 Kate's camera / my brother's car → Unit 64

61.1 Complete the sentences with mine/yours etc.

1 It's your money. It's yours .
2 It's my bag. It's ....
3 It's our car. It's ....
4 They're her shoes. They're ....
5 It's their house. It's ....
6 They're your books. They're ....
7 They're my glasses. They're ....
8 It's his coat. It's ....

61.2 Choose the right word.

1 It's their/~~theirs~~ problem, not ~~our/~~ours. (*their and ours are right*)
2 This is a nice camera. Is it your/yours?
3 That's not my/mine umbrella. My/Mine is black.
4 Whose books are these? Your/Yours or my/mine?
5 Catherine is going out with her/hers friends this evening.
6 My/Mine room is bigger than her/hers.
7 They've got two children, but I don't know their/theirs names.
8 Can we use your washing machine? Our/Ours isn't working.

61.3 Complete these sentences. Use friend(s) of mine/yours etc.

1 I went to the cinema with a friend of mine .
2 They went on holiday with some friends of theirs .
3 She's going out with a friend ....
4 We had dinner with some ....
5 I played tennis with a ....
6 Tom is going to meet a ....
7 Do you know those people? Are they .... ?

61.4 Look at the pictures. What are the people saying?

Unit 62

I/me/my/mine

A

	I etc. (→ Unit 59)	**me** etc. (→ Unit 59)	**my** etc. (→ Unit 60)	**mine** etc. (→ Unit 61)
	**I** know Tom.	Tom knows **me**.	It's **my** car.	It's **mine**.
	**We** know Tom.	Tom knows **us**.	It's **our** car.	It's **ours**.
	**You** know Tom.	Tom knows **you**.	It's **your** car.	It's **yours**.
	**He** knows Tom.	Tom knows **him**.	It's **his** car.	It's **his**.
	**She** knows Tom.	Tom knows **her**.	It's **her** car.	It's **hers**.
	**They** know Tom.	Tom knows **them**.	It's **their** car.	It's **theirs**.

B

Study these examples:

- 'Do **you** know that man?' 'Yes, **I** know **him**, but **I** can't remember **his name**.'
- **She** was very pleased because **we** invited **her** to stay with **us** at **our house**.
- A: Where are the children? Have **you** seen them?
  B: Yes, **they** are playing with **their friends** in the park.
- That's **my pen**. Can **you** give it to **me**, please?
- 'Is this **your umbrella**?' 'No, it's **yours**.'
- **He** didn't have an umbrella, so **she** gave **him hers**. (= she gave her umbrella to him)
- **I**'m going out with a friend of **mine** this evening. (*not* a friend of me)

myself/yourself etc. → Unit 63 Give me that book / Give it to me → Unit 96

Exercises

62.1 Answer the questions in the same way.

1

Yes, I know him, but I can't remember his name .

2

Yes, I know .... , but I can't remember ....

3

Yes, I .... , but I .... names.

4

Yes, I .... , but ....

62.2 Complete the sentences in the same way.

1 We invited her to stay with us at our house .
2 He invited us to stay with .... at his house.
3 They invited me to stay with .... house.
4 I invited them to stay .... house.
5 She invited us to stay .... house.
6 Did you invite him .... house?

62.3 Complete the sentences in the same way.

1 I gave him my address, and he gave me his .
2 I gave her my address, and she gave me ....
3 He gave me his address, and I gave ....
4 We gave them .... address, and they gave ....
5 She gave him .... address, and he gave ....
6 You gave us .... address, and we gave ....
7 They gave you .... address, and you gave ....

62.4 Write him/her/yours etc.

1 Where's Amanda? Have you seen her ?
2 Where are my keys? Where did I put .... ?
3 This letter is for Bill. Can you give it to .... ?
4 We don't see .... neighbours much. They're not at home very often.
5 'I can't find my pen. Can I use .... ?' 'Yes, of course.'
6 We're going to the cinema. Why don't you come with .... ?
7 Did your sister pass .... exams?
8 Some people talk about .... jobs all the time.
9 Last night I went out for a meal with a friend of ....

Unit 63 myself/yourself/themselves etc.

A

He's looking at **himself**.

They're enjoying **themselves**.

I	→	**me**	→	**myself**
he	→	**him**	→	**himself**
she	→	**her**	→	**herself**
you	→	**you**	→	**yourself** / **yourselves**
we	→	**us**	→	**ourselves**
they	→	**them**	→	**themselves**

- **I** looked at **myself** in the mirror.
- **He** cut **himself** with a knife.
- **She** fell off her bike, but she didn't hurt **herself**.
- Please help **yourself**. *(one person)*
- Please help **yourselves**. *(two or more people)*
- We had a good holiday. **We** enjoyed **ourselves**.
- They had a nice time. **They** enjoyed **themselves**.

B

Compare:

me/him/them etc.

She is looking at **him**.
different people

- You never talk to **me**.
- I didn't pay for **them**.
- I'm sorry. Did I hurt **you**?

myself/himself/themselves etc.

He is looking at **himself**.
the same person

- Sometimes I talk to **myself**.
- They paid for **themselves**.
- Be careful. Don't hurt **yourself**.

C

by myself / **by yourself** etc. = alone:

- I went on holiday **by myself**. (= I went alone)
- 'Was she with friends?' 'No, she was **by herself**.'

D

each other

- Kate and Helen are good friends. They know **each other** well. (= Kate knows Helen / Helen knows Kate)
- Paul and I live near **each other**. (= he lives near me / I live near him)

Compare **each other** and **-selves**:

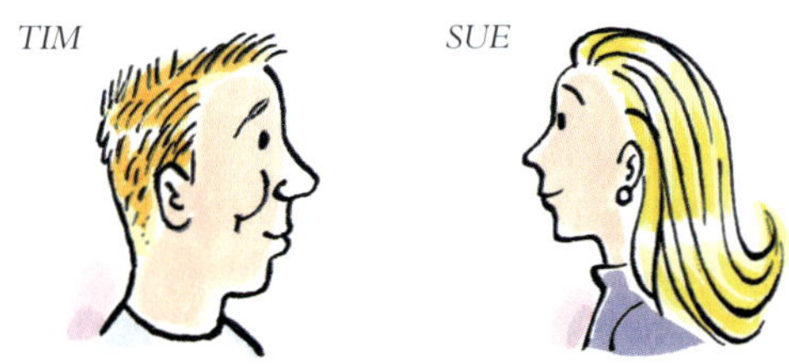

- Tim and Sue looked at **each other**. (= he looked at her, she looked at him)

- Tim and Sue looked at **themselves**. (= he looked at himself, she looked at herself)

me/him/them etc. → Unit 59

63.1 Complete the sentences with **myself/yourself** etc.

1 He looked at ...himself... in the mirror.
2 I'm not angry with you. I'm angry with ....
3 Karen had a good time in Australia. She enjoyed ....
4 My friends had a good time in Australia. They enjoyed ....
5 I picked up a very hot plate and burnt ....
6 He never thinks about other people. He only thinks about ....
7 I want to know more about you. Tell me about .... *(one person)*
8 Goodbye! Have a good trip and look after .... ! *(two people)*

63.2 Write sentences with **by myself / by yourself** etc.

1 I went on holiday alone.	I went on holiday by myself.
2 When I saw him, he was alone.	When I saw him, he ....
3 Don't go out alone.	Don't ....
4 I went to the cinema alone.	I ....
5 My sister lives alone.	My sister ....
6 Many people live alone.	Many people ....

63.3 Write sentences with **each other**.

1

They like each other.

2

They can't ....
....

3

They ....
....

4

....
....

5

....
....

6

....
....

63.4 Complete the sentences. Use:

each other or **ourselves/yourselves/themselves** or **us/you/them**

1 Paul and I live near ...each other... .
2 Who are those people? Do you know ...them... ?
3 You can help Tom, and Tom can help you. So you and Tom can help ....
4 There's food in the kitchen. If you and Chris are hungry, you can help ....
5 We didn't go to Emily's party. She didn't invite ....
6 When we go on holiday, we always enjoy ....
7 Mary and Jane were at school together, but they never see .... now.
8 Diane and I are very good friends. We've known .... for a long time.
9 'Did you see Sam and Laura at the party?' 'Yes, but I didn't speak to ....'
10 Many people talk to .... when they're alone.

-'s (Kate's camera / my brother's car etc.)

A

Kate**'s** camera
(**her** camera)

my brother**'s** car
(**his** car)

the manager**'s** office
(**his** *or* **her** office)

We normally use **-'s** for people:

- I stayed at **my sister's** house. (*not* the house of my sister)
- Have you met **Mr Black's** wife? (*not* the wife of Mr Black)
- Are you going to **James's** party?
- Paul is **a man's** name. Paula is **a woman's** name.

You can use **-'s** without a noun after it:

- Sophie's hair is longer than **Kate's**. (= Kate's hair)
- 'Whose umbrella is this?' 'It's **my mother's**.' (= my mother's umbrella)
- 'Where were you last night?' 'I was at **Paul's**.' (= Paul's house)

B

friend's and **friends'**

my **friend's** house = *one friend*
(= **his** house or **her** house)

We write **'s** after
friend/**student**/**mother** etc. *(singular)*:
my mother**'s** car *(one mother)*
my father**'s** car *(one father)*

my **friends'** house = *two or more friends*
(= **their** house)

We write **'** after
friend**s**/student**s**/parent**s** etc. *(plural)*:
my parents**'** car *(two parents)*

C

We use **of** … for things, places etc. :

- Look at the roof **of that building**. (*not* that building's roof)
- We didn't see the beginning **of the film**. (*not* the film's beginning)
- What's the name **of this village**?
- Do you know the cause **of the problem**?
- You can sit in the back **of the car**.
- Madrid is the capital **of Spain**.

mine/yours etc. → Unit 61 whose … ? → Unit 61 -'s (he's / Kate's etc.) → Appendix 4.5

Exercises

64.1 Look at the family tree. Complete the sentences about the people in the family.

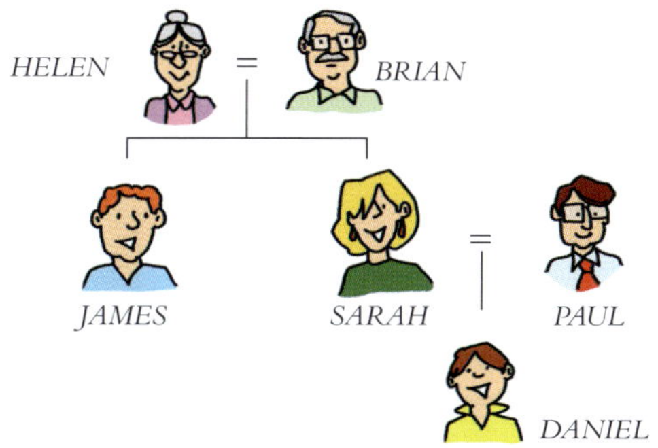

Helen and Brian are married.
They have a son, James, and a daughter, Sarah.
Sarah is married to Paul.
Sarah and Paul have a son, Daniel.

1. Brian is ...Helen's... husband.
2. Sarah is Daniel's ...mother... .
3. Helen is .... wife.
4. James is Sarah's ....
5. James is .... uncle.
6. Sarah is .... wife.
7. Helen is Daniel's ....
8. Sarah is James's ....
9. Paul is .... husband.
10. Paul is Daniel's ....
11. Daniel is .... nephew.

64.2 Look at the pictures and answer the questions. Use one word only.

1  Whose is this? ...Alice's...

2  Whose is this? ....

3  And this? ....

4  And these? ....

5  And this? ....

6  And these? ....

64.3 Are these sentences OK? Change them where necessary.

1. I stayed at the house of my sister. ...my sister's house...
2. What is the name of this village? ...OK...
3. Do you like the colour of this coat? ....
4. Do you know the phone number of Simon? ....
5. The job of my brother is very interesting. ....
6. Write your name at the top of the page. ....
7. For me, the morning is the best part of the day. ....
8. The favourite colour of Paula is blue. ....
9. When is the birthday of your mother? ....
10. The house of my parents isn't very big. ....
11. The walls of this house are very thin. ....
12. The car stopped at the end of the street. ....
13. Are you going to the party of Silvia next week? ....
14. The manager of the hotel is not here at the moment. ....

a/an ...

A

He's got **a** camera.

She's waiting for **a** taxi.

It's **a** beautiful day.

a ... = one thing or person:

- Rachel works in **a bank**. (*not* in bank)
- Can I ask **a question**? (*not* ask question)
- I haven't got **a computer**.
- There's **a woman** at the bus stop.

B

an (*not* a) before **a/e/i/o/u**:

- Do you want **an a**pple or **a b**anana?
- I'm going to buy **a h**at and **an u**mbrella.
- There was **an i**nteresting programme on TV last night.

also **an hour** (**h** is not pronounced: an ~~h~~our)
but **a university** (pronounced *yuniversity*)
a European country (pronounced *yuropean*)

another (= **an** + **other**) is one word:

- Can I have **another** cup of coffee?

C

We use **a/an** ... when we say what a thing or a person is. For example:

- The sun is **a star**.
- Football is **a game**.
- Dallas is **a city in Texas**.
- A mouse is **an animal**. It's **a small animal**.
- Joe is **a very nice person**.

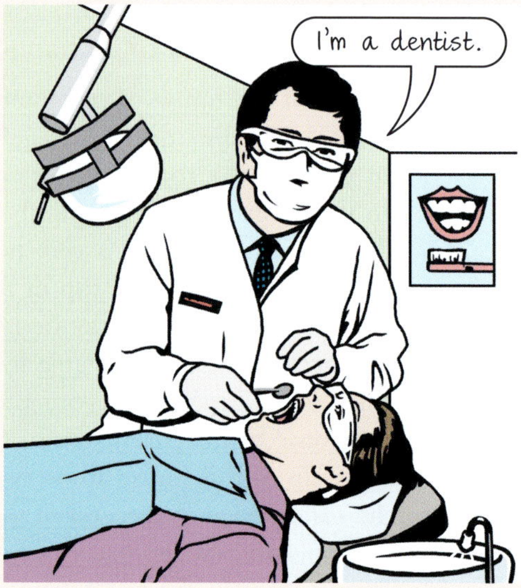

We use **a/an** ... for jobs etc. :

- A: What's your job?
  B: I'm **a dentist**. (*not* I'm dentist)
- 'What does Mark do?' 'He's **an engineer**.'
- Would you like to be **a teacher**?
- Beethoven was **a composer**.
- Picasso was **a famous painter**.
- Are you **a student**?

a car / **some money** (countable/uncountable) → Units 67–68 **a** and **the** → Unit 69

Exercises

65.1 Write a or an.

1 .....an..... old book	4 .... airport	7 .... university
2 .... window	5 .... new airport	8 .... hour
3 .... horse	6 .... organisation	9 .... economic problem

65.2 What are these things? Choose from the box.

~~bird~~	fruit	mountain	river	musical instrument
flower	game	planet	tool	vegetable

1 A duck is .....a bird..... .
2 A carrot is ....
3 Tennis is ....
4 A hammer is ....
5 Everest is ....
6 Saturn is ....
7 A banana is ....
8 The Amazon is ....
9 A rose is ....
10 A trumpet is ....

65.3 What are their jobs? Choose from the list and complete the sentences.

architect	~~dentist~~	shop assistant	photographer
electrician	nurse	taxi driver	

1 .....She's a dentist.
2 He's ....
3 She ....
4 ....
5 ....
6 ....
7 ....
8 And you? I'm ....

65.4 Write sentences. Choose from the two boxes. Use a/an where necessary.

~~I want to ask you~~	Rebecca works in
Tom never wears	Jane wants to learn
I can't ride	Mike lives in
My brother is	This evening I'm going to

+

old house	artist
party	~~question~~
bookshop	foreign language
hat	bicycle

1 .....I want to ask you a question.
2 ....
3 ....
4 ....
5 ....
6 ....
7 ....
8 ....

Unit 66

train(s) bus(es) (singular and plural)

A

The plural of a noun is usually **-s**:

singular (= one)	→	*plural* (= two or more)
a flower	→	some **flowers**
a train	→	two **trains**
one week	→	a few **weeks**
a nice place	→	some nice **places**
this student	→	these **students**

a flower

some **flowers**

Spelling (→ Appendix 5):

-s / **-sh** / **-ch** / **-x** →	**-es**	bus → bus**es**	dish → dish**es**	
		church → church**es**	box → box**es**	
	also	potato → potato**es**	tomato → tomato**es**	
-y →	**-ies**	bab**y** → bab**ies**	dictionar**y** → dictionar**ies**	
		part**y** → part**ies**		
but **-ay** / **-ey** / **-oy** →	**-ys**	d**ay** → d**ays**	monk**ey** → monk**eys**	b**oy** → b**oys**
-f / **-fe** →	**-ves**	shel**f** → shel**ves**	kni**fe** → kni**ves**	wi**fe** → wi**ves**

B

These things are plural in English:

scissors **glasses** **trousers** **jeans** **shorts** **tights** **pyjamas**

- Do you wear **glasses**?
- Where **are** the **scissors**? I need **them**.

You can also say **a pair of scissors** / **a pair of trousers** / **a pair of pyjamas** etc. :

- I need **a** new **pair of jeans**. *or* I need **some** new **jeans**. (*not* a new jeans)

C

Some plurals do *not* end in **-s**:

this **man** → these **men**	one **foot** → two **feet**	that **sheep** → those **sheep**
a **woman** → some **women**	a **tooth** → all my **teeth**	a **fish** → a lot of **fish**
a **child** → many **children**	a **mouse** → some **mice**	

also a **person** → **two people** / **some people** / **a lot of people** etc. :

- **She**'s a nice **person**.

but
- **They** are nice **people**. (*not* nice persons)

D

People is plural (= they), so we say **people are** / **people have** etc. :

- **A lot of people speak** English. (*not* speaks)
- I like **the people** here. **They are** very friendly.

Police is plural:

- **The police want** to talk to anybody who saw the accident. (*not* The police wants)

by → Units 21, 63, 109 at/on → Units 103, 106–107 preposition + -ing → Unit 112

Exercises

66.1 Write the plural.

1 flower	flowers	5 umbrella	....	9 family	....
2 boat	....	6 address	....	10 foot	....
3 woman	....	7 knife	....	11 holiday	....
4 city	....	8 sandwich	....	12 potato	....

66.2 Look at the pictures and complete the sentences.

1 There are a lot of sheep in the field.
2 Gary is cleaning his ....
3 There are three .... at the bus stop.
4 Lucy has got two ....
5 There are a lot of .... in the river.
6 The .... are falling from the tree.

66.3 Are these sentences OK? Change the sentences where necessary.

1 I'm going to buy some flowers. — OK
2 I need a new jeans. — I need a new pair of jeans. OR I need some new jeans.
3 It's a lovely park with a lot of beautiful tree. ....
4 There was a woman in the car with two mens. ....
5 Sheep eat grass. ....
6 David is married and has three childs. ....
7 Most of my friend are student. ....
8 He put on his pyjama and went to bed. ....
9 We went fishing, but we didn't catch many fish. ....
10 Do you know many persons in this town? ....
11 I like your trouser. Where did you get it? ....
12 The town centre is usually full of tourist. ....
13 I don't like mice. I'm afraid of them. ....
14 This scissor isn't very sharp. ....

66.4 Which is right? Complete the sentences.

1 It's a nice place. Many people go there on holiday. — **go** *or* **goes**?
2 Some people .... always late. — **is** *or* **are**?
3 The new city hall is not a very beautiful building. Most people .... like it. — **don't** *or* **doesn't**?
4 A lot of people .... television every day. — **watch** *or* **watches**?
5 Three people .... injured in the accident. — **was** *or* **were**?
6 How many people .... in that house? — **live** *or* **lives**?
7 .... the police know the cause of the explosion? — **Do** *or* **Does**?
8 The police .... looking for the stolen car. — **is** *or* **are**?
9 I need my glasses, but I can't find .... — **it** *or* **them**?
10 I'm going to buy .... new jeans today. — **a** *or* **some**?

Unit 67

a bottle / some water (countable/uncountable 1)

A

A noun can be *countable* or *uncountable*.

Countable nouns

For example: (a) **car** (a) **man** (a) **bottle** (a) **house** (a) **key** (an) **idea** (an) **accident**

You can use **one/two/three** (etc.) + *countable nouns* (you can count them):

one **bottle**

two **bottles**

three **men**

four **houses**

Countable nouns can be *singular* (= one) or *plural* (= two or more):

singular	**a car**	**the car**	**my car** etc.		
plural	**cars**	**two cars**	**the cars**	**some cars**	**many cars** etc.

- I've got **a car**.
- New **cars** are very expensive.
- There aren't **many cars** in the car park.

You can't use the singular (**car/bottle/key** etc.) alone. You need **a/an**:

- We can't get into the house without **a key**. (*not* without key)

B

Uncountable nouns

For example: **water** **air** **rice** **salt** **plastic** **money** **music** **tennis**

water

salt

money

music

You can't say **one/two/three** (etc.) + these things: ~~one water~~ ~~two musics~~

Uncountable nouns have only *one* form:

money the **money** my **money** some **money** much **money** etc.

- I've got **some money**.
- There isn't **much money** in the box.
- **Money** isn't everything.

You can't use **a/an** + *uncountable nouns*: ~~a~~ **money** ~~a~~ **music** ~~a~~ **water**

But you can say **a piece of** ... / **a bottle of** ... etc. + *uncountable noun:*

a bottle of water	**a carton of** milk	**a bar of** chocolate
a piece of cheese	**a bottle of** perfume	**a piece of** music
a bowl of rice	**a cup of** coffee	**a game of** tennis

a/an → Unit 65 countable/uncountable 2 → Unit 68

67.1 What are these things? Some are countable and some are uncountable. Write a/an if necessary. The names of these things are:

bucket	envelope	money	sand	toothbrush	wallet
egg	jug	~~salt~~	~~spoon~~	toothpaste	water

1 
It's salt .

2 
It's a spoon .

3 
It's ....

4 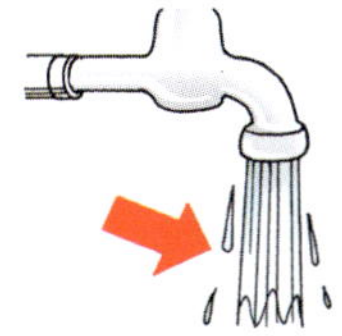
It's ....

5 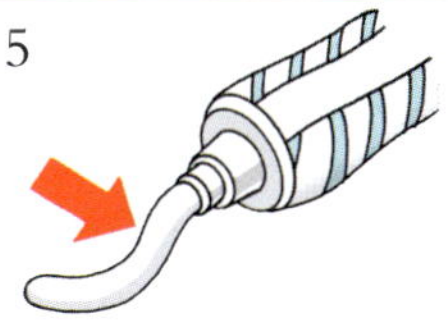
It's ....

6 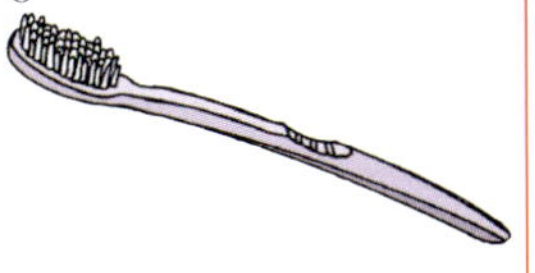
It's ....

7 
It's ....

8 
It's ....

9 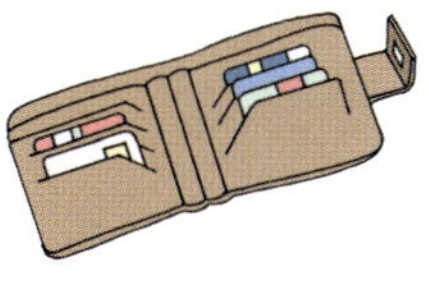
It's ....

10 
It's ....

11 
It's ....

12 
It's ....

67.2 Some of these sentences are OK, but some need a/an. Write a/an where necessary.

1 I haven't got watch. a watch
2 Do you like cheese? OK
3 I never wear hat. ....
4 Are you looking for job? ....
5 Kate doesn't eat meat. ....
6 Kate eats apple every day. ....
7 I'm going to party tonight. ....
8 Music is wonderful thing. ....
9 Jamaica is island. ....
10 I don't need key. ....
11 Everybody needs food. ....
12 I've got good idea. ....
13 Can you drive car? ....
14 Do you want cup of coffee? ....
15 I don't like coffee without milk. ....
16 Don't go out without umbrella. ....

67.3 What are these things? Write a ... of ... for each picture. Use the words in the boxes.

1 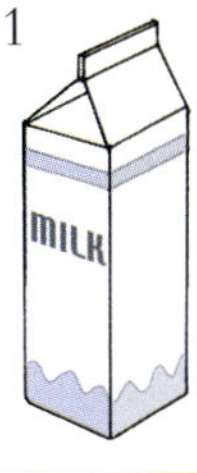

2 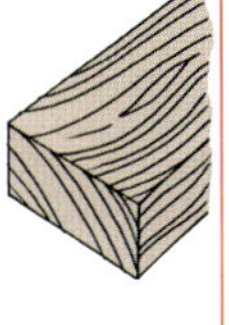

3 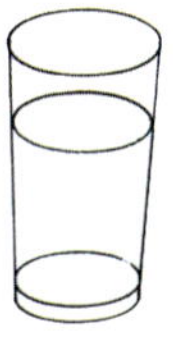

4 

5 

6 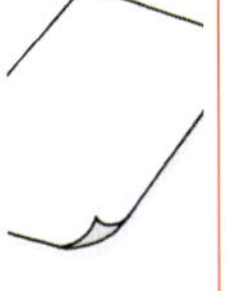

7 

8 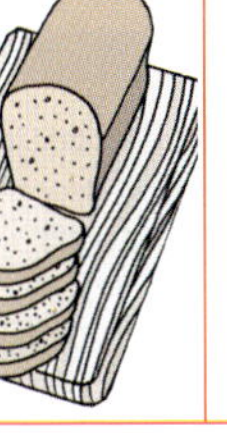

9 

bar	cup	loaf
bowl	glass	piece
~~carton~~	jar	piece

\+

bread	~~milk~~	tea
chocolate	paper	water
honey	soup	wood

1 a carton of milk
2 ....
3 ....
4 ....
5 ....
6 ....
7 ....
8 ....
9 ....

Unit 68 a cake / some cake / some cakes (countable/uncountable 2)

A

a/an and **some**

a/an + *singular countable nouns* (**car**/**apple**/**shoe** etc.):

- I need **a** new **car**.
- Would you like **an** apple?

an apple

some + *plural countable nouns* (**cars**/**apples**/**shoes** etc.):

- I need **some** new **shoes**.
- Would you like **some apples**?

some apples

some + *uncountable nouns* (**water**/**money**/**music** etc.):

- I need **some water**.
- Would you like **some cheese**? (*or* Would you like **a piece of** cheese?)

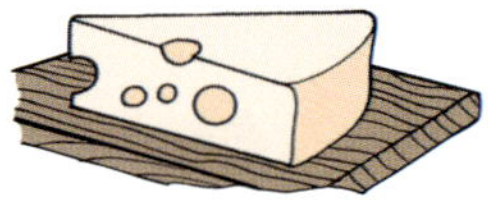

some cheese *or* **a piece of** cheese

Compare **a** and **some**:

- Nicole bought **a hat**, **some shoes** and **some perfume**.
- I read **a newspaper**, made **some phone calls**, and listened to **some music**.

B

Many nouns are sometimes countable and sometimes uncountable. For example:

a cake

some cakes

some cake *or* **a piece of cake**

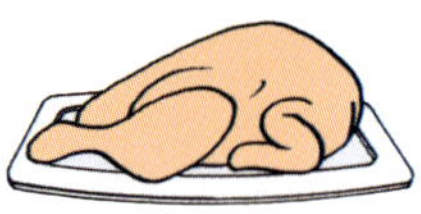

a chicken

some chickens

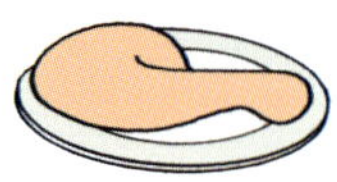

some chicken *or* **a piece of chicken**

Compare **a paper** (= a newspaper) and **some paper**:

- I want something to read. I'm going to buy **a paper**.

but - I want to make a shopping list. I need **some paper** / **a piece of paper**. (*not* a paper)

C

Be careful with:

advice **bread** **furniture** **hair** **information** **news** **weather** **work**

These nouns are usually uncountable. So you can't say **a/an** … (~~a bread~~, ~~an advice~~), and they can't be plural (~~advices~~, ~~furnitures~~ etc.).

- Can I talk to you? I need **some advice**. (*not* an advice)
- I'm going to buy **some bread**. (*not* a bread)
- They've got **some** very nice **furniture** in their house. (*not* furnitures)
- Silvia has got very long **hair**. (*not* hairs)
- I'd like **some information** about hotels in London. (*not* informations)
- Listen! I've just had **some** good **news**. (*not* a good news)
- It's nice **weather** today. (*not* a nice weather)
- 'Do you like your job?' 'Yes, but it's hard **work**.' (*not* a hard work)

We say **a job** (*but not* a work):

- I've got **a** new **job**. (*not* a new work)

countable/uncountable 1 → Unit 67 **some** and **any** → Unit 76

68.1 What did you buy? Use the pictures to write sentences (I bought ...).

1 I bought some perfume, a hat and some shoes.
2 I bought ....
3 ....
4 ....

68.2 Write sentences with Would you like a ... ? or Would you like some ... ?

1 Would you like some cheese?
2 Would you like ....?
3 Would ....?
4 ....?
5 ....?
6 ....?

68.3 Write a/an or some.

1 I read ...a... book and listened to ...some... music.
2 I need .... money. I want to buy .... food.
3 We met .... interesting people at the party.
4 I'm going to open .... window to get .... fresh air.
5 Rachel didn't eat much for lunch – only .... apple and .... bread.
6 We live in .... big house. There's .... nice garden with .... beautiful trees.
7 I'm going to make a table. First I need .... wood.
8 Listen to me carefully. I'm going to give you .... advice.
9 I want to write a letter. I need .... paper and .... pen.

68.4 Which is right?

1 I'm going to buy some new shoe/shoes. (shoes *is right*)
2 Martin has got brown eye/eyes.
3 Paula has got short black hair/hairs.
4 The tour guide gave us some information/informations about the city.
5 We're going to buy some new chair/chairs.
6 We're going to buy some new furniture/furnitures.
7 It's hard to find a work/job at the moment.
8 We had wonderful weather / a wonderful weather when we were on holiday.

a/an and the

A

a/an

There are *three* windows here.
a window = window 1 or 2 or 3

- I've got **a car**.
  (there are many cars and I've got one)
- Can I ask **a question**? (there are many questions – can I ask one?)
- Is there **a hotel** near here? (there are many hotels – is there one near here?)
- Paris is **an interesting city**. (there are many interesting cities and Paris is one)
- Lisa is **a student**.
  (there are many students and Lisa is one)

the

There is only *one* window here – **the** window.

- I'm going to clean **the car** tomorrow.
  (= my car)
- Can you repeat **the question**, please?
  (= the question that you asked)
- We enjoyed our holiday. **The hotel** was very nice. (= our hotel)
- Paris is **the capital of France**.
  (there is only one capital of France)
- Lisa is **the youngest student** in her class. (there is only one youngest student in her class)

Compare **a** and **the**:

- I bought **a jacket** and **a shirt**. **The jacket** was cheap, but **the shirt** was expensive.
  (= **the** jacket and **the** shirt **that I bought**)

B

We say **the** ... when it is clear which thing or person we mean. For example:

the door / **the ceiling** / **the floor** / **the carpet** / **the light** etc. *(of a room)*
the roof / **the garden** / **the kitchen** / **the bathroom** etc. *(of a house)*
the centre / **the station** / **the airport** / **the town hall** etc. *(of a town)*

- 'Where's Tom? 'In **the kitchen**.'
  (= the kitchen of this house or flat)
- Turn off **the light** and close **the door**.
  (= the light and the door of the room)
- Do you live far from **the centre**?
  (= the centre of your town)
- I'd like to speak to **the manager**, please.
  (= the manager of this shop etc.)

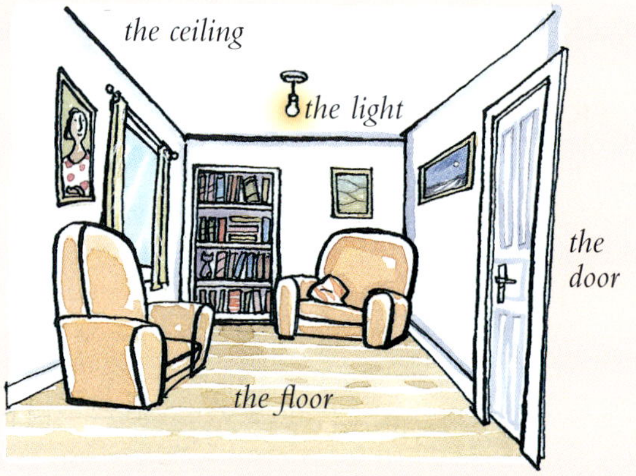

a/an → Unit 65 the → Units 70–73

Exercises

69.1 Write a/an or the.

1 We enjoyed our trip. ....The.... hotel was very nice.
2 'Can I ask ....a.... question?' 'Sure. What do you want to know?'
3 You look very tired. You need .... holiday.
4 'Where's Tom?' 'He's in .... garden.'
5 Eve is .... interesting person. You should meet her.
6 A: Excuse me, can you tell me how to get to .... city centre?
B: Yes, go straight on and then take .... next turning left.
7 A: Shall we go out for .... meal this evening?
B: Yes, that's .... good idea.
8 It's .... nice morning. Let's go for .... walk.
9 Amanda is .... student. When she finishes her studies, she wants to be .... journalist. She lives with two friends in .... apartment near .... college where she is studying. .... apartment is small, but she likes it.
10 Peter and Mary have got two children, ... boy and .... girl. .... boy is seven years old, and .... girl is three. Peter works in .... factory. Mary hasn't got .... job at the moment.

69.2 Complete the sentences. Use a or the + these words:

airport **cup** **dictionary** ~~**door**~~ **floor** **picture**

69.3 These sentences are not correct. Put in a/an or the where necessary.

1 Don't forget to turn off light when you go out. ....turn off the light....
2 Enjoy your trip, and don't forget to send me postcard. ....
3 What is name of this village? ....
4 Canada is very big country. ....
5 What is largest city in Canada? ....
6 I like this room, but I don't like colour of carpet. ....
7 'Are you OK?' 'No, I've got headache.' ....
8 We live in old house near station. ....
9 What is name of director of film we saw last night? ....

Unit 70

the ...

A

We use **the** when it is clear which thing or person we mean:

- What is **the name** of this street? (there is only one name)
- Who is **the best player** in your team? (there is only one best player)
- Can you tell me **the time**, please? (= the time *now*)
- My office is on **the first floor**. (= the first floor of the building)

Don't forget **the**:

- Do you live near **the city centre**? (*not* near city centre)
- Excuse me, where is **the nearest bank**? (*not* where is nearest ...)

B

the same ...

- We live in **the same street**. (*not* in same street)
- 'Are these two books different?' 'No, they're **the same**.' (*not* they're same)

C

We say:

the sun / the moon / the world / the sky / the sea / the country

- **The sky** is blue and **the sun** is shining.
- Do you live in a town or in **the country**?

the police / the fire brigade / the army (of a city, country etc.)

- My brother is a soldier. He's in **the army**.
- What do you think of **the police**? Do they do a good job?

the top / the end / the middle / the left etc.

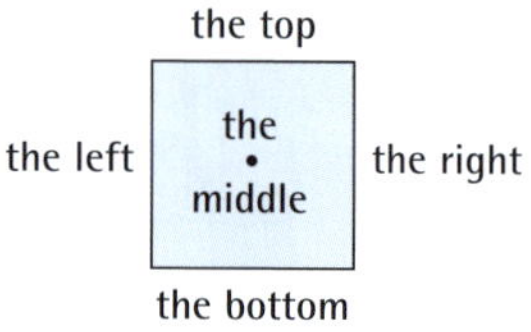

- Write your name at **the top of** the page.
- My house is at **the end of** the street.
- The table is in **the middle of** the room.
- Do you drive on **the right** or on **the left** in your country?

(play) **the piano / the guitar / the trumpet** etc. (musical instruments)

- Paula is learning to play **the piano**.

the radio

- I listen to **the radio** a lot.

the Internet

- Do you use **the Internet** much?

D

We do *not* use **the** with:

television / TV

- I watch **TV** a lot.
- What's on **television** tonight?

but Can you turn off **the television**? (= the TV set)

breakfast / lunch / dinner

- What did you have for **breakfast**? (*not* the breakfast)
- **Dinner** is ready!

next / last + week/month/year/summer/Monday etc.

- I'm not working **next week**. (*not* the next week)
- Did you have a holiday **last summer**? (*not* the last summer)

a/an and the → Unit 69 the → Units 71–73 the oldest / the most expensive etc. → Unit 90

Exercises

70.1 Put in *the* where necessary. Write 'OK' if the sentence is already correct.

1 What is name of this street? ......the name......
2 What's on television tonight? ......OK......
3 Our apartment is on second floor. ......
4 Would you like to go to moon? ......
5 Which is best hotel in this town? ......
6 What time is lunch? ......
7 How far is it to city centre? ......
8 We're going away at end of May. ......
9 What are you doing next weekend? ......
10 I didn't like her first time I met her. ......
11 I'm going out after dinner. ......
12 Internet is a good way of getting information. ......
13 My sister got married last month. ......
14 My dictionary is on top shelf on right. ......
15 We live in country about ten miles from nearest town. ......

70.2 Complete the sentences. Use *the same* + these words:

age **colour** **problem** ~~**street**~~ **time**

1 I live in North Street and you live in North Street. We live in ......the same street...... .
2 I arrived at 8.30 and you arrived at 8.30. We arrived at ....
3 Jim is 25 and Sue is 25. Jim and Sue are ....
4 My shirt is dark blue and so is my jacket. My shirt and jacket are ....
5 I've got no money and you've got no money. We've got ....

70.3 Look at the pictures and complete the sentences. Use *the* if necessary.

1 ......The sun...... is shining.
2 She's playing ....
3 They're having ....
4 He's watching ....
5 They're swimming in ....
6 Tim's name is at ...... of the list.

70.4 Complete these sentences. Choose from the list. Use *the* if necessary.

capital ~~**dinner**~~ **police** **lunch** **middle** **name** **sky** **television**

1 We had ......dinner...... at a restaurant last night.
2 We stayed at a very nice hotel, but I don't remember ....
3 ...... is very clear tonight. You can see all the stars.
4 Sometimes there are some good films on ...... late at night.
5 Somebody was trying to break into the shop, so I called ....
6 Tokyo is ...... of Japan.
7 'What did you have for ......?' 'A salad.'
8 I woke up in ...... of the night.

go to work go home go to the cinema

A

She's **at work**.

They're going **to school**.

He's **in bed**.

We say:

(go) **to work**, (be) **at work**, start **work**, finish **work**

- Bye! I'm **going to work** now. (*not* to the work)
- I **finish work** at 5 o'clock every day.

(go) **to school**, (be) **at school**, start **school**, leave **school** etc.

- What did you learn **at school** today? (*not* at the school)
- Some children don't like **school**.

(go) **to university/college**, (be) **at university/college**

- Helen wants to **go to university** when she **leaves school**.
- What did you study **at college**?

(go) **to hospital**, (be) **in hospital**

- Jack had an accident. He had to go **to hospital**.

(go) **to prison**, (be) **in prison**

- Why is he **in prison**? What did he do?

(go) **to church**, (be) **in/at church**

- David usually goes **to church** on Sundays.

(go) **to bed**, (be) **in bed**

- I'm tired. I'm **going to bed**. (*not* to the bed)
- 'Where's Jane?' 'She's **in bed**.'

(go) **home**, (be) **at home** etc.

- I'm tired. I'm **going home**. (*not* to home)
- Are you going out tonight, or are you **staying at home**?

B

We say:

(go to) **the cinema** / **the theatre** / **the bank** / **the post office** / **the station** / **the airport** / **the city centre**

- I never go to **the theatre**, but I go to **the cinema** a lot.
- 'Are you going to **the bank**?' 'No, to **the post office**.'
- The number 5 bus goes to **the airport**; the number 8 goes to **the city centre**.

(go to) **the doctor, the dentist**

- You're not well. Why don't you go to **the doctor**?
- I have to go to **the dentist** tomorrow.

the → Units 69–70, 72–73 in/at → Units 106–107 to/in/at → Unit 108 (at) home → Unit 108

71.1 Where are these people? Complete the sentences. Sometimes you need the.

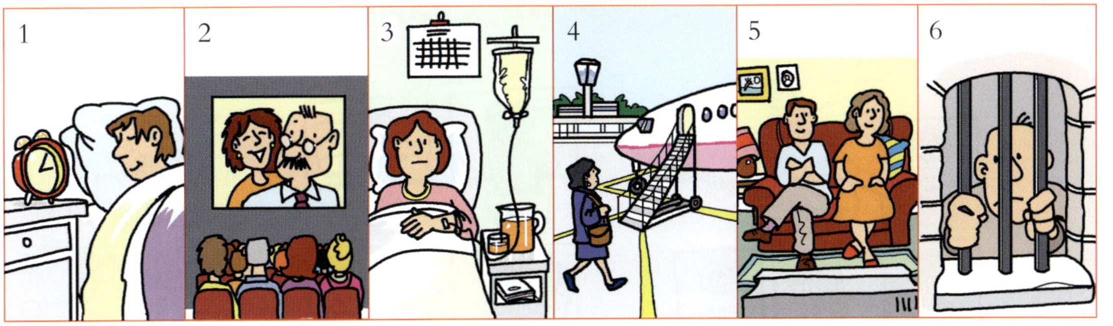

1 He's in ....bed.... .
2 They're at ....
3 She's in ....
4 She's at ....
5 They're at ....
6 He's in ....

71.2 Complete the sentences. Choose from the list. Use the if necessary.

~~bank~~ bed ~~church~~ home post office school station

1 I need to change some money. I have to go to ....the bank.... .
2 David usually goes to ....church.... on Sundays.
3 In Britain, children go to .... from the age of five.
4 There were a lot of people at .... waiting for the train.
5 I phoned you last night, but you weren't at ....
6 I'm going to .... now. Goodnight!
7 I'm going to .... to get some stamps.

71.3 Complete the sentences. Sometimes you need the.

1 If you want to catch a plane, you ....go to the airport.... .
2 If you want to see a film, you go to ....
3 If you are tired and you want to sleep, you ....
4 If you rob a bank and the police catch you, you ....
5 If you have a problem with your teeth, you ....
6 If you want to study after you leave school, you ....
7 If you are badly injured in an accident, you ....

71.4 Are these sentences OK? Correct the sentences where necessary.

1 We went to cinema last night. ....to the cinema....
2 I finish work at 5 o'clock every day. ....OK....
3 Lisa wasn't feeling well yesterday, so she went to doctor. ....
4 I wasn't feeling well this morning, so I stayed in bed. ....
5 Why is Angela always late for work? ....
6 'Where are your children?' 'They're at school.' ....
7 We have no money in bank. ....
8 When I was younger, I went to church every Sunday. ....
9 What time do you usually get home from work? ....
10 Do you live far from city centre? ....
11 'Where shall we meet?' 'At station.' ....
12 Jim is ill. He's in hospital. ....
13 Kate takes her children to school every day. ....
14 Would you like to go to university? ....
15 Would you like to go to theatre this evening? ....

I like music   I hate exams

A

Do not use **the** for general ideas:

- □ I like **music**, especially **classical music**.
  (*not* the music … the classical music)
- □ We don't eat **meat** very often. (*not* the meat)
- □ **Life** is not possible without **water**.
  (*not* The life … the water)
- □ I hate **exams**. (*not* the exams)
- □ Do you know a shop that sells **foreign newspapers**?
- □ I'm not very good at writing **letters**.

Do not use **the** for games and sports:

- □ My favourite sports are **football** and **skiing**. (*not* the football … the skiing)

Do not use **the** for languages or school subjects (**history**/**geography**/**physics**/**biology** etc.):

- □ Do you think **English** is difficult? (*not* the English)
- □ Tom's brother is studying **physics** and **chemistry**.

B

flowers or **the flowers**?

Compare:

□ **Flowers** are beautiful. (= flowers in general)	□ I love this garden. **The flowers** are beautiful. (= the flowers in this garden)
□ I don't like **cold weather**. (= cold weather in general)	□ **The weather** isn't very good today. (= the weather today)
□ We don't eat **fish** very often. (= fish in general)	□ We had a great meal last night. **The fish** was excellent. (= the fish we ate last night)
□ Are you interested in **history**? (= history in general)	□ Do you know much about **the history** of your country?

the → Units 69–71, 73

72.1 What do you think about these things?

big cities	computer games	exams	jazz	parties
chocolate	dogs	housework	museums	tennis

Choose seven of these things and write sentences with:

I like ... I don't like ... I love ... I hate ... or ... is/are all right

1 I hate exams. **or** I like exams. **or** Exams are all right. (etc.)
2 ......
3 ......
4 ......
5 ......
6 ......
7 ......
8 ......

72.2 Are you interested in these things? Write sentences with:

I'm (very) interested in ...	I know a lot about ...	I don't know much about ...
I'm not interested in ...	I know a little about ...	I don't know anything about ...

1 (history) I'm very interested in history.
2 (politics) I ......
3 (sport) ......
4 (art) ......
5 (astronomy) ......
6 (economics) ......

72.3 Which is right?

1 My favourite sport is football / ~~the football~~. (football *is right*)
2 I like this hotel. ~~Rooms~~ / The rooms are very nice. (The rooms *is right*)
3 Everybody needs friends / the friends.
4 Jane doesn't go to parties / the parties very often.
5 I went shopping this morning. Shops / The shops were very busy.
6 'Where's milk / the milk?' 'It's in the fridge.'
7 I don't like milk / the milk. I never drink it.
8 'Do you do any sports?' 'Yes, I play basketball / the basketball.'
9 'What does your brother do?' 'He sells computers / the computers.'
10 We went for a swim in the river. Water / The water was very cold.
11 I don't like swimming in cold water / the cold water.
12 Excuse me, can you pass salt / the salt, please?
13 I like this town. I like people / the people here.
14 Vegetables / The vegetables are good for you.
15 Houses / The houses in this street are all the same.
16 I can't sing this song. I don't know words / the words.
17 I enjoy taking photographs / the photographs. It's my hobby.
18 Do you want to see photographs / the photographs that I took when I was on holiday?
19 English / The English is used a lot in international business / the international business.
20 Money / The money doesn't always bring happiness / the happiness.

Unit 73

the ... (names of places)

A

Places (continents, countries, states, islands, towns etc.)

In general we do *not* use **the** with names of places:

- □ **France** is a very large country. (*not* the France)
- □ **Cairo** is the capital of **Egypt**.
- □ **Corsica** is an island in the Mediterranean.
- □ **Peru** is in **South America**.

But we use **the** in names with 'republic'/'states'/'kingdom':

the Czech **Republic**
the United **States** of America (**the** USA)
the United **Kingdom** (**the** UK)

B

the -s (plural names)

We use **the** with *plural* names of countries/islands/mountains:

the Netherlands　　**the** Canary Islands
the Philippines　　**the** Alps

C

Seas, rivers etc.

We use **the** with names of oceans/seas/rivers/canals:

the Atlantic (Ocean)　　**the** Mediterranean (Sea)　　**the** Amazon
the (River) Nile　　**the** Suez Canal　　**the** Black Sea

D

Places in towns (streets, buildings etc.)

In general we do *not* use **the** with names of streets, squares etc. :

- □ Kevin lives in **Newton Street**.
- □ Where is **Highfield Road**, please?
- □ **Times Square** is in New York.

We do not use **the** with names of airports, stations and many other important buildings:

Kennedy Airport　　**Westminster Abbey**　　**London Zoo**
Victoria Station　　**Cambridge University**　　**Edinburgh Castle**

But we use **the** with names of most hotels, museums, theatres and cinemas:

the Regent Hotel　　**the** National Theatre
the Science Museum　　**the** Odeon (cinema)

E

the … of …

We use **the** + names with … **of** … :

the Museum **of** Modern Art　　**the** University **of** California
the Great Wall **of** China　　**the** Tower **of** London

We say **the north** / **the south** / **the east** / **the west** (of ...):

- □ I've been to **the north of Italy**, but not to **the south**.

the → Units 69–72

Exercises

73.1 Answer these geography questions. Choose from the box. Use *The* if necessary.

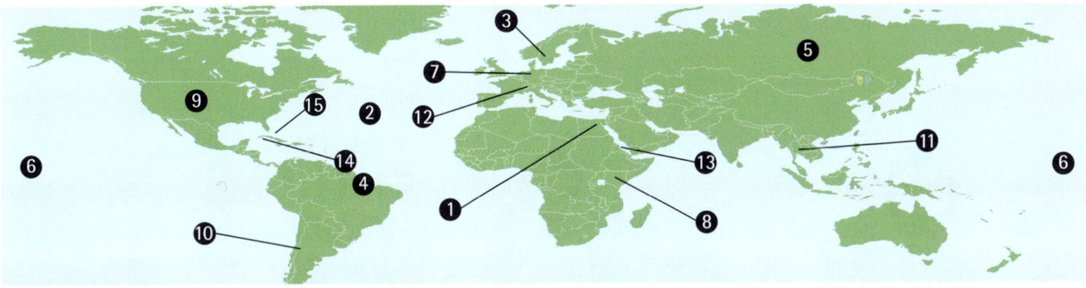

1 *Cairo* is the capital of Egypt.
2 *The Atlantic* is between Africa and America.
3 .... is a country in northern Europe.
4 .... is a river in South America.
5 .... is the largest continent in the world.
6 .... is the largest ocean.
7 .... is a river in Europe.
8 .... is a country in East Africa.
9 .... is between Canada and Mexico.
10 .... are mountains in South America.
11 .... is the capital of Thailand.
12 .... are mountains in central Europe.
13 .... is between Saudi Arabia and Africa.
14 .... is an island in the Caribbean.
15 .... are a group of islands near Florida.

Alps
Amazon
Andes
Asia
~~Atlantic~~
Bahamas
Bangkok
~~Cairo~~
Jamaica
Kenya
Pacific
Red Sea
Rhine
Sweden
United States

73.2 Write *the* where necessary. If the sentence is already correct, write OK.

1 Kevin lives in Newton Street. *OK*
2 We went to see a play at National Theatre. *at the National Theatre*
3 Have you ever been to China? ....
4 Have you ever been to Philippines? ....
5 Have you ever been to south of France? ....
6 Can you tell me where Regal Cinema is? ....
7 Can you tell me where Merrion Street is? ....
8 Can you tell me where Museum of Art is? ....
9 Europe is bigger than Australia. ....
10 Belgium is smaller than Netherlands. ....
11 Which river is longer – Mississippi or Nile? ....
12 Did you go to National Gallery when you were in London? ....
13 We stayed at Park Hotel in Hudson Road. ....
14 How far is it from Trafalgar Square to Victoria Station (*in London*)? ....
15 Rocky Mountains are in North America. ....
16 Texas is famous for oil and cowboys. ....
17 I hope to go to United States next year. ....
18 Mary comes from west of Ireland. ....
19 Alan is a student at Manchester University. ....
20 Panama Canal joins Atlantic Ocean and Pacific Ocean. ....

→ Additional exercises 33–34 (pages 269–70)

Unit 74

this/that/these/those

A

this *(singular)*

these *(plural)*

that *(singular)*

those *(plural)*

this
these

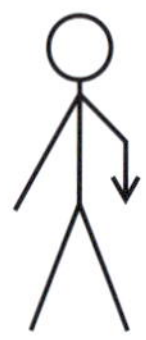

this picture
(= this picture *here*)
these flowers
(= these flowers *here*)

that
those

that picture
(= that picture *there*)
those people
(= those people *there*)

B

We use **this/that/these/those** with a noun (**this picture** / **those girls** etc.) or without a noun:

with a noun:
- □ **This hotel** is expensive, but it's very nice.
- □ Who's **that girl**?' 'I don't know.'
- □ Do you like **these shoes**? I bought them last week.
- □ **Those apples** look nice. Can I have one?

without a noun:
- □ **This** is a nice hotel, but it's very expensive.
- □ 'Excuse me, is **this** your bag?' 'Oh yes, thank you.'
- □ Who's **that**? (= Who is that person?)
- □ Which shoes do you prefer – **these** or **those**?

C

that = something that *has happened:*
- □ 'I'm sorry I forgot to phone you.' '**That**'s all right.'
- □ **That** was a really nice meal. Thank you very much.

that = what somebody *has just said:*
- □ 'You're a teacher, aren't you?' 'Yes, **that**'s right.'
- □ 'Martin has got a new job.' 'Has he? I didn't know **that**.'
- □ 'I'm going on holiday next week.' 'Oh, **that**'s nice.'

D

We use **this is** … and **is that** … **?** on the telephone:
- □ Hi Sarah, **this** is David.
  (**this** = the speaker)
- □ Is **that** Sarah?
  (**that** = the other person)

We use **this is** … to introduce people:
- □ A: Brian, **this is** Chris.
  B: Hello, Chris – nice to meet you.
  C: Hi.

this one / that one → Unit 75

Exercises

74.1 Complete the sentences. Use **this/that/these/those** + these words:

birds **house** **plates** **postcards** **seat** ~~**shoes**~~

74.2 Write questions: **Is this/that your ... ?** or **Are these/those your ... ?**

74.3 Complete the sentences with **this is** or **that's** or **that**.

1 A: I'm sorry I'm late.
B: That's all right.

2 A: I can't come to the party tomorrow.
B: Oh, ... a pity. Why not?

3 *on the phone*
SUE: Hello, Jane. .... Sue.
JANE: Oh, hi Sue. How are you?

4 A: You're lazy.
B: .... not true!

5 A: Beth plays the piano very well.
B: Does she? I didn't know ....

6 *Mark meets Paul's sister, Helen.*
PAUL: Mark, ... my sister, Helen.
MARK: Hi, Helen.

7 A: I'm sorry I was angry yesterday.
B: .... OK. Forget it!

8 A: You're a friend of Tim's, aren't you?
B: Yes, ... right.

one/ones

A

one (= **a** ...)

Would you like **one** ?

= Would you like **a chocolate** ?

one = **a/an** ... (a chocolate / an apple etc.)

- I need **a pen**. Have you got **one**? (**one** = **a pen**)
- A: Is there **a bank** near here?
  B: Yes, there's **one** at the end of this street. (**one** = **a bank**)

B

one and **ones**

one (*singular*)

Which **one**? = Which **hat**?

one = **hat/car/girl** etc.

this one / **that one**

- Which **car** is yours? **This one** or **that one**? (= this car or that car)

the one ...

- A: Which **hotel** did you stay at?
  B: **The one** opposite the station.
- I found this **key**. Is it **the one** you lost?

the ... **one**

- I don't like the black **coat**, but I like **the brown one**.
- Don't buy that **camera**. Buy **the other one**.

a/an ... **one**

- This **cup** is dirty. Can I have **a clean one**?
- That **biscuit** was nice. I'm going to have **another one**.

ones (*plural*)

Which **ones**? = Which **flowers**?

ones = **flowers/cars/girls** etc.

these/those or **these ones** / **those ones**

- Which flowers do you want? **These** or **those**? *or* **These ones** or **those ones**?

the ones ...

- A: Which **books** are yours?
  B: **The ones** on the table.
- I found these **keys**. Are they **the ones** you lost?

the ... **ones**

- I don't like the red **shoes**, but I like **the green ones**.
- Don't buy those **apples**. Buy **the other ones**.

some ... **ones**

- These **cups** are dirty. Can we have **some clean ones**?
- My **shoes** are very old. I'm going to buy **some new ones**.

which ... ? → Unit 47 another → Unit 65 this/that etc. → Unit 74

Exercises

75.1 A asks B some questions. Use the information in the box to write B's answers. Use one (not a/an ...) in the answers.

B doesn't need a car	B has just had a cup of coffee
there's a chemist in Mill Road	B is going to get a bike
~~B hasn't got a pen~~	B hasn't got an umbrella

1 A: Can you lend me a pen? B: I'm sorry, *I haven't got one* .
2 A: Would you like to have a car? B: No, I don't ....
3 A: Have you got a bike? B: No, but ....
4 A: Can you lend me an umbrella? B: I'm sorry, but ....
5 A: Would you like a cup of coffee? B: No, thank you. ....
6 A: Is there a chemist near here? B: Yes, ...

75.2 Complete the sentences. Use a/an ... one. Use the words in the list.

better big ~~clean~~ different new old

1 This cup is dirty. Can I have *a clean one* ?
2 I'm going to sell my car and buy ....
3 That's not a very good photograph, but this is ....
4 I want today's newspaper. This is ....
5 This box is too small. I need ....
6 Why do we always go to the same restaurant? Let's go to ....

75.3 A is talking to B. Use the information to complete the conversations. Use one/ones.

1 *A stayed at a hotel. It was opposite the station.* A: We stayed at a hotel. B: *Which one* ? A: *The one opposite the station.*	6 *A is looking at a picture. It's on the wall.* A: That's an interesting picture. B: .... ? A: ....
2 *A sees some shoes in a shop window. They're green.* A: I like those shoes. B: Which .... ? A: The	7 *A sees a girl in a group of people. She's tall with long hair.* A: Do you know that girl? B: .... ? A: ....
3 *A is looking at a house. It has a red door.* A: That's a nice house. B: .... ? A: .... with	8 *A is looking at some flowers in the garden. They're yellow.* A: Those flowers are beautiful. B: .... ? A: ....
4 *A is looking at some CDs. They're on the top shelf.* A: Are those your CDs? B: .... ? A:	9 *A is looking at a man in a restaurant. He has a moustache and glasses.* A: Who's that man? B: .... ? A: ....
5 *A is looking at a jacket in a shop. It's black.* A: Do you like that jacket? B: .... ? A:	10 *A took some photos at the party last week.* A: Did I show you my photos? B: .... ? A: ....

some and any

A

some

Use **some** in *positive* sentences:
- I'm going to buy **some** clothes.
- There's **some** ice in the fridge.
- We made **some** mistakes.

any

Use **any** in *negative* sentences:
- I'm **not** going to buy **any** clothes.
- There **isn't any** milk in the fridge.
- We **didn't** make **any** mistakes.

B

any and **some** in questions

In most questions (but not all) we use **any** (*not* **some**):
- Is there **any** ice in the fridge?
- Has he got **any** friends?
- Do you need **any** help?

We normally use **some** (*not* **any**) when we *offer* things (**Would you like** ... **?**):
- A: Would you like **some** coffee?
  B: Yes, please.

or when we *ask for* things (**Can I have** ... **?** etc.):
- A: Can I have **some** soup, please?
  B: Yes. Help yourself.
- A: Can you lend me **some** money?
  B: Sure. How much do you need?

C

some and **any** without a noun

- I didn't take any photographs, but Jane took **some**. (= some photographs)
- You can have some coffee, but I don't want **any**. (= any coffee)
- I've just made some coffee. Would you like **some**? (= some coffee)
- 'Where's your luggage?' 'I haven't got **any**.' (= any luggage)
- 'Are there any biscuits?' 'Yes, there are **some** in the kitchen.' (= some biscuits)

D

something / **somebody** (*or* **someone**)
- She said **something**.
- I saw **somebody** (*or* **someone**).
- Would you like **something** to eat?
- **Somebody**'s at the door.

anything / **anybody** (*or* **anyone**)
- She **didn't** say **anything**.
- I **didn't** see **anybody** (*or* **anyone**).
- Are you doing **anything** tonight?
- Where's Sue? Has **anybody** seen her?

a and **some** → Unit 68 **somebody/anything** etc. → Unit 79

76.1 Write some or any.

1 I bought ...some... cheese, but I didn't buy ...any... bread.
2 I'm going to the post office. I need .... stamps.
3 There aren't .... shops in this part of town.
4 Gary and Alice haven't got .... children.
5 Have you got .... brothers or sisters?
6 There are .... beautiful flowers in the garden.
7 Do you know .... good hotels in London?
8 'Would you like .... tea?' 'Yes, please.'
9 When we were on holiday, we visited .... very interesting places.
10 Don't buy .... rice. We don't need ....
11 I went out to buy .... oranges, but they didn't have .... in the shop.
12 I'm thirsty. Can I have .... water, please?

76.2 Complete the sentences. Use some or any + the words in the box.

air	cheese	help	milk	questions
batteries	friends	languages	photographs	~~shampoo~~

1 I want to wash my hair. Is there ...any shampoo... ?
2 The police want to talk to you. They want to ask you ....
3 I haven't got my camera, so I can't take ....
4 Do you speak .... foreign .... ?
5 Yesterday evening I went to a restaurant with .... of mine.
6 Can I have .... in my coffee, please?
7 The radio isn't working. There aren't .... in it.
8 It's hot in this office. I'm going out for .... fresh ....
9 A: Would you like .... ?
B: No, thank you. I've had enough to eat.
10 I can do this job alone. I don't need ....

76.3 Complete the sentences. Use some or any.

1 Jane didn't take any photographs, but ...I took some... . (I/take)
2 'Where's your luggage?' '...I haven't got any... .' (I/not/have)
3 'Do you need any money?' 'No, thank you. ....' (I/have)
4 'Can you lend me some money?' 'I'm sorry, but ....' (I/not/have)
5 The tomatoes in the shop didn't look very good, so .... (I/not/buy)
6 There were some nice oranges in the shop, so .... (I/buy)
7 'How many phone calls did you make yesterday?' '........ .' (I/not/make)

76.4 Write something/somebody or anything/anybody.

1 A woman stopped me and said ...something... , but I didn't understand.
2 'What's wrong?' 'There's .... in my eye.'
3 Do you know .... about politics?
4 I went to the shop, but I didn't buy ....
5 .... has broken the window. I don't know who.
6 There isn't .... in the bag. It's empty.
7 I'm looking for my keys. Has .... seen them?
8 Would you like .... to drink?
9 I didn't eat .... because I wasn't hungry.
10 This is a secret. Please don't tell ....

Unit 77

not + any   no   none

A

The car park is empty.

There are**n't any** cars } in the car park.
There are **no** cars }

How many cars are there in the car park?
None.

not (**-n't**) + **any**

- There are**n't any** cars in the car park.
- Tracey and Jeff have**n't** got **any** children.
- You can have some coffee, but I do**n't** want **any**.

no + *noun* (**no cars** / **no garden** etc.)

no ... = **not any** *or* **not a**

- There are **no cars** in the car park. (= there are**n't any** cars)
- We've got **no coffee**. (= we have**n't** got **any** coffee)
- It's a nice house, but there's **no garden**. (= there is**n't a** garden)

We use **no** ... especially after **have** (**got**) and **there is**/**are**.

negative verb + **any** = *positive verb* + **no**

- They **haven't** got **any** children. *or* They**'ve** got **no** children.
  (*not* They haven't got no children)
- There **isn't any** sugar in your coffee. *or* There**'s no** sugar in your coffee.

B

no and **none**

Use **no** + *noun* (**no money** / **no children** etc.):

- We've got **no money**.
- Everything was OK. There were **no problems**.

Use **none** alone (*without* a noun):

- 'How much money have you got?' '**None**.' (= no money)
- 'Were there any problems?' 'No, **none**.' (= no problems)

C

none and **no-one**

none = 0 (zero)
no-one = nobody

None is an answer for **How much**? / **How many**? (things or people):

- '**How much** money have you got?' '**None**.' (= no money)
- '**How many** people did you meet?' '**None**.' (= no people)

No-one is an answer for **Who**?:

- '**Who** did you meet?' '**No-one**.' *or* '**Nobody**.'

negatives → Unit 43 some and any → Unit 76 anybody/nobody/nothing etc. → Units 78–79

Exercises

77.1 Write these sentences again with no.

1 We haven't got any money. *We've got no money.*
2 There aren't any shops near here. There are ....
3 Carla hasn't got any free time. ....
4 There isn't a light in this room. ....

Write these sentences again with any.

5 We've got no money. *We haven't got any money.*
6 There's no milk in the fridge. ....
7 There are no buses today. ....
8 Tom has got no brothers or sisters. ....

77.2 Write no or any.

1 There's *no* sugar in your coffee.
2 My brother is married, but he hasn't got .... children.
3 Sue doesn't speak .... foreign languages.
4 I'm afraid there's .... coffee. Would you like some tea?
5 'Look at those birds!' 'Birds? Where? I can't see .... birds.'
6 'Do you know where Jessica is?' 'No, I've got .... idea.'

Write no, any or none.

7 There aren't .... pictures on the wall.
8 The weather was cold, but there was .... wind.
9 I wanted to buy some oranges, but they didn't have .... in the shop.
10 Everything was correct. There were .... mistakes.
11 'How much luggage have you got?' '.......... .'
12 'How much luggage have you got?' 'I haven't got ....'

77.3 Complete the sentences. Use any or no + the words in the box.

answer	difference	friends	furniture	heating
money	~~problems~~	questions	queue	

1 Everything was OK. There were *no problems* .
2 Jack and Emily would like to go on holiday, but they've got ....
3 I'm not going to answer ....
4 He's always alone. He's got ....
5 There is .... between these two machines. They're exactly the same.
6 There wasn't .... in the room. It was completely empty.
7 I tried to phone you yesterday, but there was ....
8 The house is cold because there isn't ....
9 There was .... outside the cinema, so we didn't have to wait to get our tickets.

77.4 Write short answers (one or two words) to these questions. Use none where necessary.

1 How many letters did you write yesterday? *Two.* or *A lot.* or *None.*
2 How many sisters have you got? ....
3 How much coffee did you drink yesterday? ....
4 How many photographs have you taken today? ....
5 How many legs has a snake got? ....

Unit 78 not + anybody/anyone/anything nobody/no-one/nothing

A

not + anybody/anyone
nobody/no-one
(for *people*)

- There **isn't** { **anybody** / **anyone** } in the room.
- There **is** { **nobody** / **no-one** } in the room.
- A: **Who** is in the room?
  B: **Nobody**. / **No-one**.

-body and **-one** are the same:
any**body** = any**one**   no**body** = no-**one**

not + anything
nothing
(for *things*)

- There **isn't anything** in the bag.
- There **is nothing** in the bag.
- A: **What**'s in the bag?
  B: **Nothing**.

B

not + anybody/anyone

- I do**n't** know **anybody** (*or* **anyone**) here.

nobody = not + anybody
no-one = not + anyone

- I'm lonely. I've got **nobody** to talk to. (= I have**n't** got **anybody**)
- The house is empty. There is **no-one** in it. (= There is**n't anyone** in it.)

not + anything

- I ca**n't** remember **anything**.

nothing = not + anything

- She said **nothing**. (= She did**n't** say **anything**.)
- There's **nothing** to eat. (= There is**n't anything** to eat.)

C

You can use **nobody/no-one/nothing** at the beginning of a sentence or alone (to answer a question):

- The house is empty. **Nobody** lives there. (*not* Anybody lives there)
- 'Who did you speak to?' '**No-one**.'
- **Nothing** happened. (*not* Anything happened)
- 'What did you say?' '**Nothing**.'

D

Remember: *negative verb* + **anybody/anyone/anything**
positive verb + **nobody/no-one/nothing**

- He does**n't** know **anything**. (*not* He doesn't know nothing)
- Do**n't** tell **anybody**. (*not* Don't tell nobody)
- There **is nothing** to do in this town. (*not* There isn't nothing)

some and any → Unit 76   any and no → Unit 77   somebody/anything/nowhere etc. → Unit 79

Exercises

78.1 Write these sentences again with nobody/no-one or nothing.

1 There isn't anything in the bag. ...There's nothing in the bag.....
2 There isn't anybody in the office. There's ....
3 I haven't got anything to do. I ....
4 There isn't anything on TV. ....
5 There wasn't anyone at home. ....
6 We didn't find anything. ....

78.2 Write these sentences again with anybody/anyone or anything.

1 There's nothing in the bag. ...There isn't anything in the bag.....
2 There was nobody on the bus. There wasn't ....
3 I've got nothing to read. ....
4 I've got no-one to help me. ....
5 She heard nothing. ....
6 We've got nothing for dinner. ....

78.3 Answer these questions with nobody/no-one or nothing.

1a What did you say? ...Nothing.....
2a Who saw you? ...Nobody.....
3a What do you want? ....
4a Who did you meet? ....
5a Who knows the answer? ....
6a What did you buy? ....
7a What happened? ....
8a Who was late? ....

Now answer the same questions with full sentences.
Use nobody/no-one/nothing or anybody/anyone/anything:

1b ...I didn't say anything.....
2b ...Nobody saw me.....
3b I don't ....
4b I ....
5b .... the answer.
6b ....
7b ....
8b ....

78.4 Complete the sentences. Use:

nobody / no-one / nothing or **anybody / anyone / anything**

1 That house is empty. ...Nobody... lives there.
2 Jack has a bad memory. He can't remember ...anything... .
3 Be quiet! Don't say ....
4 I didn't know about the meeting. .... told me.
5 'What did you have to eat?' '.......... . I wasn't hungry.'
6 I didn't eat .... I wasn't hungry.
7 Helen was sitting alone. She wasn't with ....
8 I'm afraid I can't help you. There's .... I can do.
9 I don't know .... about car engines.
10 The museum is free. It doesn't cost .... to go in.
11 I heard a knock on the door, but when I opened it, there was .... there.
12 The hotel receptionist spoke very fast. I didn't understand ....
13 'What are you doing tonight?' '.......... . Why?'
14 Helen has gone away. .... knows where she is. She didn't tell .... where she was going.

Unit 79

somebody/anything/nowhere etc.

A

Somebody (or **Someone**) has broken the window.

somebody/someone = a person, but we don't know who

She has got **something** in her mouth.

something = a thing, but we don't know what

Tom lives **somewhere** near London.

somewhere = in/to a place, but we don't know where

B

people (**-body** *or* **-one**)

somebody *or* **someone**
anybody *or* **anyone**
nobody *or* **no-one**

- There is **somebody** (*or* **someone**) at the door.
- Is there **anybody** (*or* **anyone**) at the door?
- There isn't **anybody** (*or* **anyone**) at the door.
- There is **nobody** (*or* **no-one**) at the door.

-body and **-one** are the same: **somebody** = **someone**, **nobody** = **no-one** etc.

things (**-thing**)

something
anything
nothing

- Lucy said **something**, but I didn't understand what she said.
- Are you doing **anything** at the weekend?
- I was angry, but I did**n't** say **anything**.
- 'What did you say?' '**Nothing**.'

places (**-where**)

somewhere
anywhere
nowhere

- Ruth's parents live **somewhere** in the south of England.
- Did you go **anywhere** interesting for your holidays?
- I'm staying here. I'm **not** going **anywhere**.
- I don't like this town. There is **nowhere** to go.

C

something/anybody etc. + *adjective* (**big/cheap/interesting** etc.)

- Did you meet **anybody interesting** at the party?
- We always go to the same place. Let's go **somewhere different**.
- 'What's that letter?' 'It's **nothing important**.'

D

something/anybody etc. + **to** ...

- I'm hungry. I want **something to eat**. (= something that I can eat)
- Tony hasn't got **anybody to talk** to. (= anybody that he can talk to)
- There is **nowhere to go** in this town. (= nowhere where people can go)

some and any → Unit 76 any and no → Unit 77 anybody/nothing etc. → Unit 78
everything/-body/-where → Unit 80

Exercises

79.1 Write somebody (or someone) / something / somewhere.

1	Lucy said *something* .	What did she say?
2	I've lost	What have you lost?
3	Sue and Tom went	Where did they go?
4	I'm going to phone	Who are you going to phone?

79.2 Write nobody (or no-one) / nothing / nowhere.

1a	What did you say?	*Nothing.*
2a	Where are you going?	....
3a	What do you want?	....
4a	Who are you looking for?	....

Now answer the same questions with full sentences.
Use not + anybody/anything/anywhere.

1b *I didn't say anything.*
2b I'm not ....
3b ....
4b ....

79.3 Write somebody/anything/nowhere etc.

1 It's dark. I can't see *anything* .
2 Tom lives *somewhere* near London.
3 Do you know .... about computers?
4 'Listen!' 'What? I can't hear ....'
5 'What are you doing here?' 'I'm waiting for ....'
6 We need to talk. There's .... I want to tell you.
7 'Did .... see the accident?' 'No, ...'
8 We weren't hungry, so we didn't eat ....
9 'What's going to happen?' 'I don't know. .... knows.'
10 'Do you know .... in Paris?' 'Yes, a few people.'
11 'What's in that cupboard?' '.......... . It's empty.'
12 I'm looking for my glasses. I can't find them ....
13 I don't like cold weather. I want to live .... warm.
14 Is there .... interesting on television tonight?
15 Have you ever met .... famous?

79.4 Complete the sentences. Choose from the boxes.

something	anything	nothing
something	anywhere	~~nowhere~~
somewhere		nowhere

do	eat	park	sit
drink	~~go~~	read	stay

1 We don't go out very much because there's *nowhere to go* .
2 There isn't any food in the house. We haven't got ....
3 I'm bored. I've got ....
4 'Why are you standing?' 'Because there isn't ....'
5 'Would you like .... ?' 'Yes, please – a glass of water.'
6 If you're going to the city centre, take the bus. Don't drive because there's

....
7 I want .... I'm going to buy a magazine.
8 I need .... in London. Can you recommend a hotel?

Unit 80

every and all

A every

Every house in the street is the same.

every house in the street =
all the houses in the street

We use **every** + *singular noun* (**every house** / **every country** etc.):

- Sarah has been to **every country** in Europe.
- **Every summer** we have a holiday by the sea.
- She looks different **every time** I see her.

Use a *singular verb* after **every** … :

- **Every house** in the street is the same. (*not* are the same)
- **Every country has** a national flag. (*not* have)

Compare **every** and **all**:

- **Every student** in the class passed the exam.
- **Every country has** a national flag.

- **All the students** in the class passed the exam.
- **All countries have** a national flag.

B every day and all day

every day = on all days:

how often?

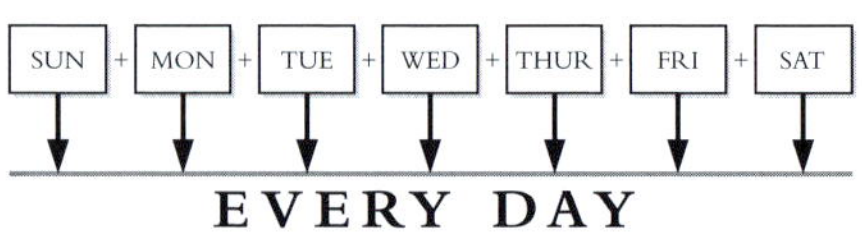

- It rained **every day** last week.
- Bill watches TV for about two hours **every evening**. (= on all evenings)

also **every morning/night/summer** etc.

all day = the complete day:

how long?

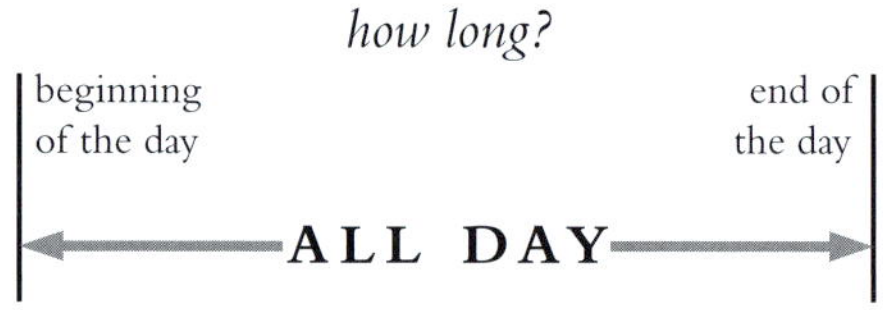

- It rained **all day** yesterday.
- On Monday, I watched TV **all evening**. (= the complete evening)

also **all morning/night/summer** etc.

C everybody (*or* everyone) / everything / everywhere

everybody or **everyone**
(people)
everything
(things)
everywhere
(places)

- **Everybody** (*or* **Everyone**) needs friends. (= all people need friends)
- Have you got **everything** you need? (= all the things you need)
- I lost my watch. I've looked **everywhere** for it. (= I've looked in all places)

Use a *singular verb* after **everybody/everyone/everything**:

- **Everybody has** problems. (*not* Everybody have)

all → Unit 81

Exercises

Unit 80

80.1 Complete the sentences. Use every + these words:

day **room** ~~**student**~~ **time** **word**

1 ...Every student... in the class passed the exam.
2 My job is very boring. .... is the same.
3 Kate is a very good tennis player. When we play, she wins ....
4 .... in the hotel has satellite TV.
5 'Did you understand what she said?' 'Most of it, but not ....'

80.2 Complete the sentences with every day or all day.

1 Yesterday it rained ...all day... .
2 I buy a newspaper ...., but sometimes I don't read it.
3 I'm not going out tomorrow. I'll be at home ....
4 I usually drink about four cups of coffee ....
5 Paula was ill yesterday, so she stayed in bed ....
6 I'm tired now because I've been working hard ....
7 Last year we went to the seaside for a week, and it rained ....

80.3 Write every or all.

1 Bill watches TV for about two hours ...every... evening.
2 Julia gets up at 6.30 .... morning.
3 The weather was nice yesterday, so we sat outside .... afternoon.
4 I'm going away on Monday. I'll be away .... week.
5 'How often do you go skiing?' '.......... year. Usually in March.'
6 A: Were you at home at 10 o'clock yesterday?
B: Yes, I was at home .... morning. I went out after lunch.
7 My sister loves new cars. She buys one .... year.
8 I saw Sam at the party, but he didn't speak to me .... evening.
9 We go away on holiday for two or three weeks .... summer.

80.4 Write everybody/everything/everywhere.

1 ...Everybody... needs friends.
2 Chris knows .... about computers.
3 I like the people here. .... is very friendly.
4 This is a nice hotel. It's comfortable and .... is very clean.
5 Kevin never uses his car. He goes .... by motorcycle.
6 Let's get something to eat. .... is hungry.
7 Sue's house is full of books. There are books ....
8 You are right. .... you say is true.

80.5 Complete the sentences. Use one word only each time.

1 Everybody ...has... problems.
2 Are you ready yet? Everybody .... waiting for you.
3 The house is empty. Everyone .... gone out.
4 Gary is very popular. Everybody .... him.
5 This town is completely different now. Everything .... changed.
6 I got home very late last night. I came in quietly because everyone .... asleep.
7 Everybody .... mistakes!
8 A: ....everything clear? ....everybody know what to do?
B: Yes, we all understand.

all most some any no/none

A

Compare:

children/money/books etc. (in general):

- **Children** like playing. (= children in general)
- **Money** isn't everything. (= money in general)
- I enjoy reading **books**.
- Everybody needs **friends**.

the children / **the** money / **these** books etc :

- Where are **the children**? (= our children)
- I want to buy a car, but I haven't got **the money**. (= the money for a car)
- Have you read **these books**?
- I often go out with **my friends**.

B

most / **most of** ... , **some** / **some of** ... etc.

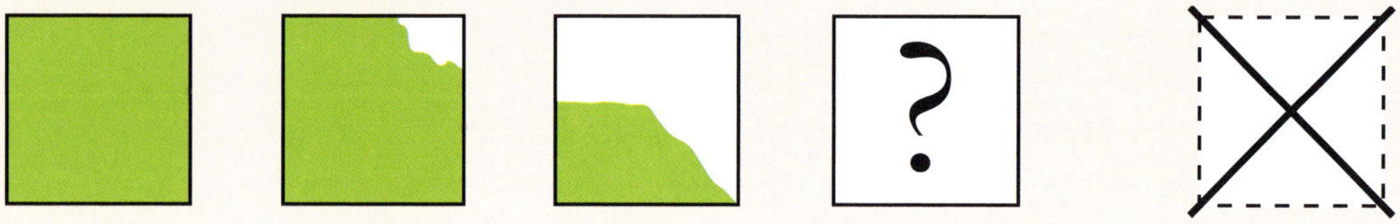

all **most** **some** **any** **no / none / not + any**

most/some etc. + noun

all **most** **some** **any** **no**	~~of~~	**cities** **children** **books** **money**

- **Most children** like playing. (= children in general)
- I don't want **any money**.
- **Some books** are better than others.
- He's got **no friends**.
- **All cities** have the same problems. (= cities in general)

Do not use **of** in these sentences:

- **Most people** drive too fast. (*not* Most of people)
- **Some birds** can't fly. (*not* Some of birds)

most of/some of etc.+ **the/this/my** ... etc.

all	(**of**)	**the** ... **this/that** ... **these/those** ... **my/your** ... etc.
most **some** **any** **none**	**of**	

- **Most of the children at this school** are under 11 years old.
- I don't want **any of this money**.
- **Some of these books** are very old.
- **None of my friends** live near me.

You can say **all the** ... or **all of the** ... (with or without **of**):

- **All the students in our class** passed the exam. (*or* **All of the students** ...)
- Silvia has lived in London **all her life**. (*or* ... **all of her life**.)

C

all of it / **most of them** / **none of us** etc.

all **most** **some** **any** **none**	**of**	**it** **them** **us** **you**

- You can have **some of this cake**, but not **all of it**.
- A: Do you know those people?
B: **Most of them**, but not **all of them**.
- **Some of us** are going out tonight. Why don't you come with us?
- I've got a lot of books, but I haven't read **any of them**.
- 'How many of these books have you read?' '**None of them**.'

the ... (children / the children etc.) → Unit 72 some and any → Unit 76 no/none/any → Unit 77
all and every → Unit 80

81.1 Complete the sentences. Use the word in brackets (some/most etc.). Sometimes you need of (some of / most of etc.).

1 ...Most... children like playing. (**most**)
2 ...Some of... this money is yours. (**some**)
3 .... people never stop talking. (**some**)
4 .... the shops in the city centre close at 6.30. (**most**)
5 You can change your money in .... banks. (**most**)
6 I don't like .... the pictures in the living room. (**any**)
7 He's lost .... his money. (**all**)
8 .... my friends are married. (**none**)
9 Do you know .... the people in this photograph? (**any**)
10 .... birds can fly. (**most**)
11 I enjoyed .... the film, but I didn't like the ending. (**most**)
12 .... sports are very dangerous. (**some**)
13 We can't find anywhere to stay. .... the hotels are full. (**all**)
14 You must have .... this cheese. It's delicious. (**some**)
15 The weather was bad when we were on holiday. It rained .... the time. (**most**)

81.2 Look at the pictures and answer the questions. Use:

all/most/some/none + of them / of it

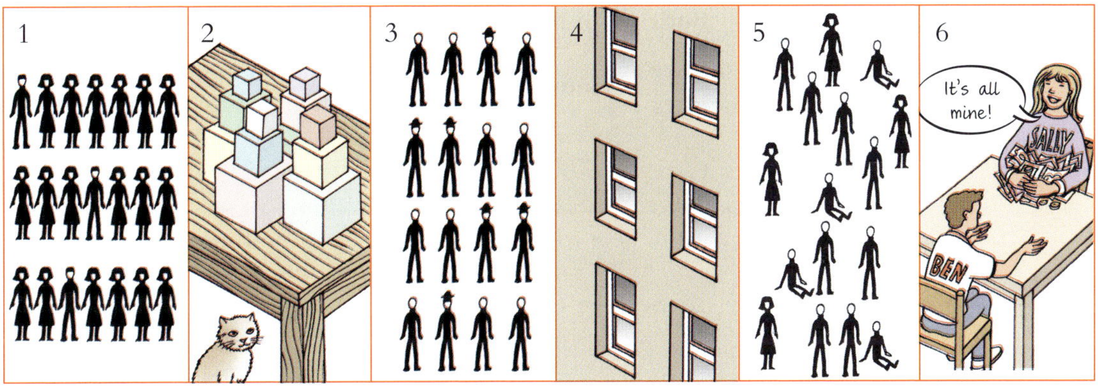

1 How many of the people are women? ...Most of them....
2 How many of the boxes are on the table? ....
3 How many of the men are wearing hats? ....
4 How many of the windows are open? ....
5 How many of the people are standing? ....
6 How much of the money is Ben's? ....

81.3 Are these sentences OK? Correct the sentences that are wrong.

1 Most of children like playing. ...Most children...
2 All the students failed the exam. ...OK...
3 Some of people work too hard. ....
4 Some of questions in the exam were very easy. ....
5 I haven't seen any of those people before. ....
6 All of insects have six legs. ....
7 Have you read all these books? ....
8 Most of students in our class are very nice. ....
9 Most of my friends are going to the party. ....
10 I'm very tired this morning – I was awake most of night. ....

both either neither

A

We use **both/either/neither** to talk about two things or people:

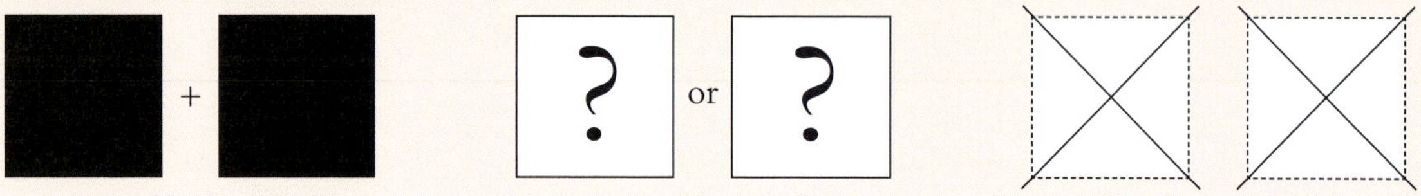

both **either** **neither (not + either)**

- Rebecca has two children. **Both** are married. (**both** = the two children)
- Would you like tea or coffee? You can have **either**. (**either** = tea or coffee)
- A: Do you want to go to the cinema or the theatre?
  B: **Neither**. I want to stay at home. (**neither** = not the cinema or the theatre)

Compare **either** and **neither**:

- 'Would you like **tea** or **coffee**?'
  - '**Either**. I don't mind.' (= tea or coffee)
  - 'I **don't** want **either**.' (*not* I don't want neither)
  - '**Neither**.' (= not tea or coffee)

B

both/either/neither + *noun*

both + *plural*

either / **neither** + *singular*

both	**windows/books/children** etc.
either **neither**	**window/book/child** etc.

- Last year I went to Paris and Rome. I liked **both cities** very much.
- First I worked in an office, and later in a shop. **Neither job** was very interesting.
- There are two ways from here to the station. You can go **either way**.

C

both of ... / either of ... / neither of ...

both	**(of)**	**the ...**
either **neither**	**of**	**these/those ...** **my/your/Paul's** ... etc.

- **Neither of my parents** is British.
- I **haven't** read **either of these books**.

You can say **both of the/those/my** ... or **both the/those/my** ... (with or without **of**):

- I like **both of** those pictures. *or* I like **both** those pictures.
- **Both of** Paul's sisters are married. *or* **Both** Paul's sisters are married.

but **Neither of** Paul's sisters is married. (*not* Neither Paul's sisters)

D

both of them / neither of us

both **either** **neither**	**of**	**them** **us** **you**

- Paul has got two sisters. **Both of them** are married.
- Sue and I didn't eat anything. **Neither of us** was hungry.
- Who are those two people? I **don't** know **either of them**.

I can't either / neither can I → Unit 42

82.1 Write both/either/neither. Use of where necessary.

1 Last year I went to Paris and Rome. I liked ...both... cities very much.
2 There were two pictures on the wall. I didn't like ...either of... them.
3 It was a good football match. .... teams played well.
4 It wasn't a good football match. .... team played well.
5 'Is your friend English or American?' '.................... . She's Australian.'
6 We went away for two days, but the weather wasn't good. It rained .... days.
7 A: I bought two newspapers. Which one do you want?
B: .... It doesn't matter which one.
8 I invited Donna and Mike to the party, but .... them came.
9 'Do you go to work by car or by bus?' '.................... . I always walk.'
10 'Which jacket do you prefer, this one or that one?' 'I don't like .... them.'
11 'Do you work or are you a student?' '.................... . I work and I'm a student too.'
12 Paula and I didn't know the time because .... us had a watch.
13 Helen has got two sisters and a brother. .... sisters are married.
14 Helen has got two sisters and a brother. I've met her brother, but I haven't met .... her sisters.

82.2 Complete the sentences for the pictures. Use Both ... and Neither ... .

1 ...Both cups are... empty.
2 .... are open.
3 .... wearing a hat.
4 .... beards.
5 .... to the airport.
6 .... right.

82.3 A man and a woman answered some questions. Their answers were the same. Write sentences with Both/Neither of them ... .

1	Are you married?	No	No
2	How old are you?	21	21
3	Are you a student?	Yes	Yes
4	Have you got a car?	No	No
5	Where do you live?	London	London
6	Do you like cooking?	Yes	Yes
7	Can you play the piano?	No	No
8	Do you read newspapers?	Yes	Yes
9	Are you interested in sport?	No	No

1 ...Neither of them is married....
2 ...Both of them are 21....
3 .... students.
4 .... a car.
5 ....
6 ....
7 ....
8 ....
9 ....

Unit 83 a lot much many

A

a lot of money

not much money

a lot of books

not many books

We use **much** + *uncountable noun* (**much food** / **much money** etc.):

- ☐ Did you buy **much food**?
- ☐ We haven't got **much luggage**.
- ☐ How **much money** do you want?
- ☐ A: Have you got any **money**?
  B: I've got some, but **not much**.

We use **many** + *plural noun* (**many books** / **many people** etc.):

- ☐ Did you buy **many books**?
- ☐ We don't know **many people**.
- ☐ How **many photos** did you take?
- ☐ A: Did you take any **photos**?
  B: I took some, but **not many**.

We use **a lot of** + *both types of noun*:

- ☐ We bought **a lot of food**.
- ☐ Paula hasn't got **a lot of** free **time**.
- ☐ We bought **a lot of books**.
- ☐ Did they ask **a lot of questions**?

We say:

- ☐ There **is** a lot of **food**/**money**/**water** ... *(singular verb)*
- ☐ There **are** a lot of **trees**/**shops**/**people** ... *(plural verb)*
- ☐ A lot of **people speak** English. (*not* speaks)

B

We use **much** in *questions* and *negative sentences:*

- ☐ Do you drink **much coffee**?
- ☐ I don't drink **much coffee**.

But we do not often use **much** in *positive sentences:*

- ☐ I drink **a lot of coffee**. (*not* I drink much coffee)
- ☐ 'Do you drink much coffee?' 'Yes, **a lot**.' (*not* Yes, much)

We use **many** and **a lot of** in all types of sentences (positive/negative/question):

- ☐ We've got **many** friends / **a lot of** friends.
- ☐ We haven't got **many** friends / **a lot of** friends.
- ☐ Have you got **many** friends / **a lot of** friends?

C

You can use **much** and **a lot** without a noun:

- ☐ Donna spoke to me, but she didn't say **much**.
- ☐ 'Do you watch TV **much**?' 'No, **not much**.' (= not often)
- ☐ We like films, so we go to the cinema **a lot**. (*not* go to the cinema much)
- ☐ I don't like him very **much**.

countable/uncountable → Units 67–68

83.1 Write much or many.

1 Did you buy ....much.... food?
2 There aren't .... hotels in this town.
3 We haven't got .... petrol. We need to stop and get some.
4 Were there .... people on the train?
5 Did .... students fail the exam?
6 Paula hasn't got .... money.
7 I wasn't hungry, so I didn't eat ....
8 I don't know where Gary lives these days. I haven't seen him for .... years.

Write How much or How many.

9 .... people are coming to the party?
10 .... milk do you want in your coffee?
11 .... bread did you buy?
12 .... players are there in a football team?

83.2 Complete the sentences. Use much or many with these words:

~~books~~ **countries** **luggage** **people** **time** **times**

1 I don't read very much. I haven't got ....many books.... .
2 Hurry up! We haven't got ....
3 Do you travel a lot? Have you been to .... ?
4 Tina hasn't lived here very long, so she doesn't know ....
5 'Have you got .... ?' 'No, only this bag.'
6 I know Tokyo well. I've been there ....

83.3 Complete the sentences. Use a lot of + these words:

accidents ~~books~~ **fun** **interesting things** **traffic**

1 I like reading. I have ....a lot of books.... .
2 We enjoyed our visit to the museum. We saw ....
3 This road is very dangerous. There are ....
4 We enjoyed our holiday. We had ....
5 It took me a long time to drive here. There was ....

83.4 In some of these sentences much is not natural. Change the sentences or write *OK*.

1 Do you drink much coffee? ....OK....
2 I drink much tea. ....a lot of tea....
3 It was a cold winter. We had much snow. ....
4 There wasn't much snow last winter. ....
5 It costs much money to travel around the world. ....
6 We had a cheap holiday. It didn't cost much. ....
7 Do you know much about computers? ....
8 'Have you got any luggage?' 'Yes, much.' ....

83.5 Write sentences about these people. Use much and a lot.

1 Jim loves films. (go to the cinema) ....He goes to the cinema a lot....
2 Nicole thinks TV is boring. (watch TV) ....She doesn't watch TV much....
3 Tina is a good tennis player. (play tennis) She ....
4 Martin doesn't like driving. (use his car) He ....
5 Paul spends most of the time at home. (go out) ....
6 Sue has been all over the world. (travel) ....

Unit 84 (a) little (a) few

A

(**a**) **little** + *uncountable noun:*

(a) **little water**
(a) **little time**
(a) **little money**
(a) **little soup**

a little water

(**a**) **few** + *plural noun:*

(a) **few books**
(a) **few questions**
(a) **few people**
(a) **few days**

a few books

B

a little = some but not much

- She didn't eat anything, but she drank **a little water**.
- I speak **a little Spanish**. (= some Spanish but not much)
- A: Can you speak Spanish?
  B: **A little**.

a few = some but not many

- Excuse me, I have to make **a few phone calls**.
- We're going away for **a few days**.
- I speak **a few words** of Spanish.
- A: Are there any shops near here?
  B: Yes, **a few**.

C

~~a~~ **little** (*without* **a**) = nearly no *or* nearly nothing

- There was **little food** in the fridge. It was nearly empty.

You can say **very little**:
- Dan is very thin because he eats **very little**. (= nearly nothing)

~~a~~ **few** (*without* **a**) = nearly no

- There were **few people** in the theatre. It was nearly empty.

You can say **very few**:
- Your English is very good. You make **very few mistakes**.

D

little and **a little**

A little is a *positive* idea:
- They have **a little** money, so they're not poor. (= they have some money)

Little (or **very little**) is a *negative* idea:
- They have **little** money. They are very poor. (= nearly no money)

few and **a few**

A few is a *positive* idea:
- I've got **a few** friends, so I'm not lonely. (= I've got some friends)

Few (or **very few**) is a *negative* idea:
- I'm sad and I'm lonely. I've got **few** friends. (= nearly no friends)

countable/uncountable → Units 67–68

84.1 Answer the questions with *a little* or *a few*.

1 'Have you got any money?' 'Yes, *a little* .'
2 'Have you got any envelopes?' 'Yes, ...'
3 'Do you want sugar in your coffee?' 'Yes, ... , please.'
4 'Did you take any photographs when you were on holiday?' 'Yes, ...'
5 'Does your friend speak English?' 'Yes, ...'
6 'Are there any good restaurants in this town?' 'Yes, ...'

84.2 Write *a little* or *a few* + these words:

chairs **days** **fresh air** **friends** **milk** **Russian** **times** ~~**years**~~

1 Martin speaks Italian well. He lived in Italy for *a few years* .
2 Can I have .... in my coffee, please?
3 'When did Julia go away?' '.................... ago.'
4 'Do you speak any foreign languages?' 'I can speak ....'
5 'Are you going out alone?' 'No, I'm going with ....'
6 'Have you ever been to Mexico?' 'Yes, ...'
7 There wasn't much furniture in the room – just a table and ....
8 I'm going out for a walk. I need ....

84.3 Complete the sentences. Use *very little* or *very few* + these words:

coffee **hotels** ~~**mistakes**~~ **people** **rain** **time** **work**

1 Your English is very good. You make *very few mistakes* .
2 I drink .... I don't like it.
3 The weather here is very dry in summer. There is ....
4 It's difficult to find a place to stay in this town. There are ....
5 Hurry up. We've got ....
6 The town is very quiet at night. .... go out.
7 Some people in the office are very lazy. They do ....

84.4 Write *little* / *a little* or *few* / *a few*.

1 There was *little* food in the fridge. It was nearly empty.
2 'When did Sarah go out?' '.................... minutes ago.'
3 I can't decide now. I need .... time to think about it.
4 There was .... traffic, so we arrived earlier than we expected.
5 The bus service isn't very good at night – there are .... buses after 9 o'clock.
6 'Would you like some soup?' 'Yes, ... , please.'
7 I'd like to practise my English more, but I have .... opportunity.

84.5 Right or wrong? Change the sentences where necessary. Write *OK* if the sentence is correct.

1 We're going away for few days next week. *for a few days*
2 Everybody needs little luck. ....
3 I can't talk to you now – I've got few things to do. ....
4 I eat very little meat – I don't like it very much. ....
5 Excuse me, can I ask you few questions? ....
6 There were little people on the bus – it was nearly empty. ....
7 Martin is a very private person. Few people know him well. ....

old/nice/interesting etc. (adjectives)

A

adjective + *noun* (**nice day** / **blue eyes** etc.)

adjective	+ *noun*
It's a **nice**	**day** today.
Laura has got **brown**	**eyes**.
There's a very **old**	**bridge** in this village.
Do you like **Italian**	**food**?
I don't speak any **foreign**	**languages**.
There are some **beautiful yellow**	**flowers** in the garden.

The adjective is *before* the noun:

- They live in a **modern house**. (*not* a house modern)
- Have you met any **famous people**? (*not* people famous)

The ending of an adjective is always the same:

a **different place** **different** places (*not* differents)

B

be (**am**/**is**/**was** etc.) + *adjective*

- The weather **is nice** today.
- These flowers **are** very **beautiful**.
- **Are** you **cold**? Shall I close the window?
- **I'm hungry**. Can I have something to eat?
- The film **wasn't** very **good**. It **was boring**.
- Please **be quiet**. I'm reading.

C

look/**feel**/**smell**/**taste**/**sound** + *adjective*

- 'You **look tired**.' 'Yes, I **feel tired**.'
- Gary told me about his new job. It **sounds** very **interesting**.
- I'm not going to eat this fish. It doesn't **smell good**.

Compare:

He	**is** **feels** **looks**	**tired**.

They	**are** **look** **sound**	**happy**.

It	**is** **smells** **tastes**	**good**.

get + adjective (**get hungry**/**tired** etc.) → Unit 56 **something**/**anybody** + adjective → Unit 79

85.1 Put the words in the right order.

1 (new / live in / house / they / a) They live in a new house.
2 (like / jacket / I / that / green) I ....
3 (music / like / do / classical / you?) Do ....
4 (had / wonderful / a / I / holiday) ....
5 (went to / restaurant / a / Japanese / we) ....

85.2 The words in the box are adjectives (**black/foreign** etc.) or nouns (**air/job** etc.). Use an adjective and a noun to complete each sentence.

air	clouds	~~foreign~~	holiday	job	~~languages~~	sharp
black	dangerous	fresh	hot	knife	long	water

1 Do you speak any foreign languages ?
2 Look at those .... It's going to rain.
3 Sue works very hard, and she's very tired. She needs a ....
4 I would like to have a shower, but there's no ....
5 Can you open the window? We need some ....
6 I need a .... to cut these onions.
7 Fire-fighting is a ....

85.3 Write sentences for the pictures. Choose from the boxes.

feel(s)	look(s)	~~sound(s)~~
look(s)	smell(s)	taste(s)

\+

~~happy~~	ill	nice
horrible	new	surprised

85.4 A and B don't agree. Complete B's sentences. Use **feel/look** etc.

	A	B	
1	You look tired.	Do I? I don't feel tired .	(feel)
2	This is a new coat.	Is it? It doesn't	(look)
3	I'm American.	Are you? You	(sound)
4	You look cold.	Do I? I	(feel)
5	These bags are heavy.	Are they? They	(look)
6	That soup looks good.	Maybe, but it	(taste)

Unit 86

quickly/badly/suddenly etc. (adverbs)

A

He ate his dinner very **quickly**.

Suddenly the shelf fell down.

Quickly and **suddenly** are adverbs.

adjective + **-ly** → adverb:

adjective	**quick**	**bad**	**sudden**	**careful**	**heavy**	
adverb	**quickly**	**badly**	**suddenly**	**carefully**	**heavily**	etc.

Spelling (→ Appendix 5): easy → eas**ily** heavy → heav**ily**

B

Adverbs tell you *how* something happens or *how* somebody does something:

- The train **stopped suddenly**.
- I **opened** the door **slowly**.
- Please **listen carefully**.
- I **understand** you **perfectly**.

It's **raining heavily**.

Compare:

adjective	*adverb*
Sue is very **quiet**.	Sue **speaks** very **quietly**. (*not* speaks very quiet)
Be careful!	**Listen carefully**! (*not* listen careful)
It was **a bad game**.	Our team **played badly**. (*not* played bad)
I **felt nervous**. (= I was nervous)	I **waited nervously**.

C

hard fast late early

These words are adjectives *and* adverbs:

Sue's job **is** very **hard**.	Sue **works** very **hard**. (*not* hardly)
Ben is **a fast runner**.	Ben can **run fast**.
The bus **was late/early**.	I **went** to bed **late/early**.

D

good *(adjective)* → **well** *(adverb)*

Your English **is** very **good**.	You **speak** English very **well**. (*not* very good)
It was **a good game**.	Our team **played well**.

But **well** is also an *adjective* (= not ill, in good health):

- 'How are you?' '**I'm** very **well**, thank you. And you?'

adjectives → Unit 85

Exercises

86.1 Look at the pictures and complete the sentences with these adverbs:

angrily **badly** **dangerously** **fast** ~~**heavily**~~ **quietly**

1 It's raining heavily.
2 He sings very ....
3 They came in ....
4 She shouted at me ....
5 She can run very ....
6 He was driving ....

86.2 Complete the sentences. Choose from the boxes.

come	know	sleep	win
explain	~~listen~~	think	work

\+

~~carefully~~	clearly	hard	well
carefully	easily	quickly	well

1 I'm going to tell you something very important, so please listen carefully.
2 They .... At the end of the day they're always tired.
3 I'm tired this morning. I didn't .... last night.
4 You play tennis much better than me. When we play, you always ....
5 .... before you answer the question.
6 I've met Alice a few times, but I don't .... her very ....
7 Our teacher doesn't .... things very .... We never understand him.
8 Helen! I need your help. .... !

86.3 Which is right?

1 Don't eat so ~~quick~~/quickly. It's not good for you. (quickly *is right*)
2 Why are you angry/angrily? I haven't done anything.
3 Can you speak slow/slowly, please?
4 Come on, Dave! Why are you always so slow/slowly?
5 Bill is a very careful/carefully driver.
6 Jane is studying hard/hardly for her examinations.
7 'Where's Diane?' 'She was here, but she left sudden/suddenly.'
8 Please be quiet/quietly. I'm studying.
9 Some companies pay their workers very bad/badly.
10 Those oranges look nice/nicely. Can I have one?
11 I don't remember much about the accident. Everything happened quick/quickly.

86.4 Write good or well.

1 Your English is very good. You speak it very well.
2 Jackie did very .... in her exams.
3 The party was very .... I enjoyed it very much.
4 Martin has a difficult job, but he does it ....
5 How are your parents? Are they .... ?
6 Did you have a .... holiday? Was the weather .... ?

old/older expensive / more expensive

A

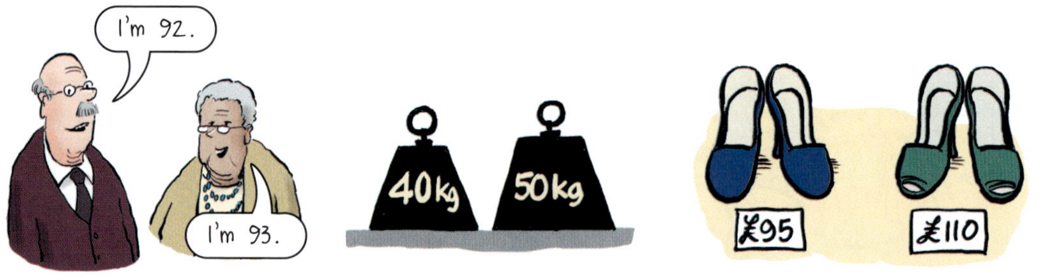

old **older** heavy **heavier** expensive **more expensive**

Older / **heavier** / **more expensive** are *comparative* forms.
The comparative is **-er** (**older**) or **more** ... (**more expensive**).

B

older/heavier etc.

Short words (1 syllable) → **-er**:
old → **older** slow → **slower** cheap → **cheaper**
nice → **nicer** late → **later** big → **bigger**

Spelling (→ Appendix 5): big → bigger hot → hotter thin → thinner

Words ending in **-y** → **-ier**:
easy → **easier** heavy → **heavier** early → **earlier**

- □ Rome is **old**, but Athens is **older**. (*not* more old)
- □ Is it **cheaper** to go by car or by train? (*not* more cheap)
- □ Helen wants a **bigger** car.
- □ This coat is OK, but I think the other one is **nicer**.
- □ Don't take the bus. It's **easier** to take a taxi. (*not* more easy)

far → **further**:
- □ 'How far is it to the station? A mile?' 'No, it's **further**. About two miles.'

C

more ...

Long words (2/3/4 syllables) → **more** ... :
careful → **more careful** polite → **more polite**
expensive → **more expensive** interesting → **more interesting**

- □ You must be **more careful**.
- □ I don't like my job. I want to do something **more interesting**.
- □ Is it **more expensive** to go by car or by train?

D

good/well → **better** **bad** → **worse**

- □ The weather wasn't very **good** yesterday, but it's **better** today.
- □ 'Do you feel **better** today?' 'No, I feel **worse**.'
- □ Which is **worse** – a headache or a toothache?

older than ... / more expensive than ... → Unit 88 the oldest / the most expensive → Unit 90

87.1 Look at the pictures and write the comparative (**older** / **more interesting** etc.).

87.2 Write the comparative.

1 old ... older ...
2 strong ....
3 happy ....
4 modern ....
5 important ....
6 good ....
7 large ....
8 serious ....
9 pretty ....
10 crowded ....

87.3 Write the opposite.

1 younger ... older ...
2 colder ....
3 cheaper ....
4 better ....
5 nearer ....
6 easier ....

87.4 Complete the sentences. Use a comparative.

1 Helen's car isn't very big. She wants a ... bigger ... one.
2 My job isn't very interesting. I want to do something ... more interesting ... .
3 You're not very tall. Your brother is ....
4 David doesn't work very hard. I work ....
5 My chair isn't very comfortable. Yours is ....
6 Your idea isn't very good. My idea is ....
7 These flowers aren't very nice. The blue ones are ....
8 My bag isn't very heavy. Your bag is ....
9 I'm not very interested in art. I'm .... in history.
10 It isn't very warm today. It was .... yesterday.
11 These tomatoes don't taste very good. The other ones tasted ....
12 Britain isn't very big. France is ....
13 London isn't very beautiful. Paris is ....
14 This knife isn't very sharp. Have you got a .... one?
15 People today aren't very polite. In the past they were ....
16 The weather isn't too bad today. Often it is much ....

older than ... more expensive than ...

A

She's **taller than** him.

The Europa Hotel is **more expensive than** the Grand.

We use **than** after comparatives (**older than** ... / **more expensive than** ... etc.):

- Athens is **older than** Rome.
- Are oranges **more expensive than** bananas?
- It's **easier** to take a taxi **than** to take the bus.
- 'How are you today?' 'Not bad. **Better than** yesterday.'
- The restaurant is **more crowded than** usual.

B

We usually say: than **me** / than **him** / than **her** / than **us** / than **them**.
You can say:

- I can run faster **than him**. *or* I can run faster **than he can**.
- You are a better singer **than me**. *or* You are a better singer **than I am**.
- I got up earlier **than her**. *or* I got up earlier **than she did**.

C

more/less than ...

- A: How much did your shoes cost? £50?
  B: No, **more than** that. (= **more than** £50)
- The film was very short – **less than** an hour.
- They've got **more money than** they need.
- You go out **more than** me.

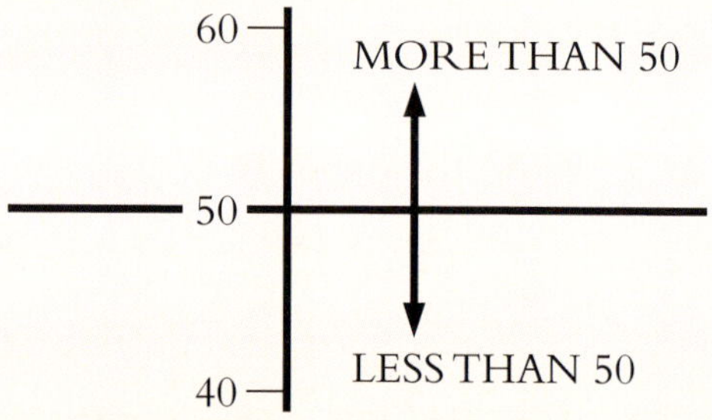

D

a bit older / **much older** etc.

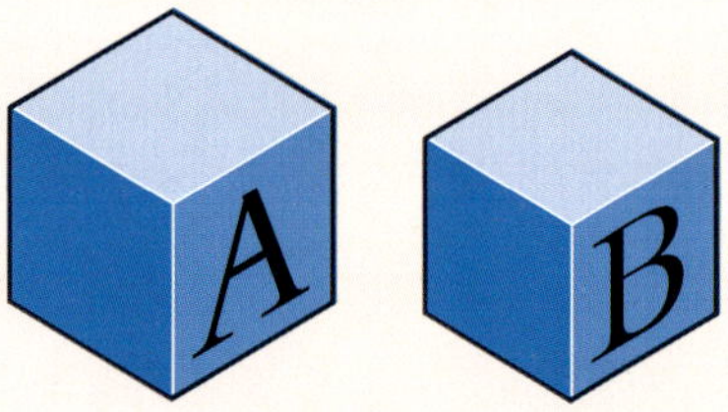

Box A is **a bit bigger** than Box B.

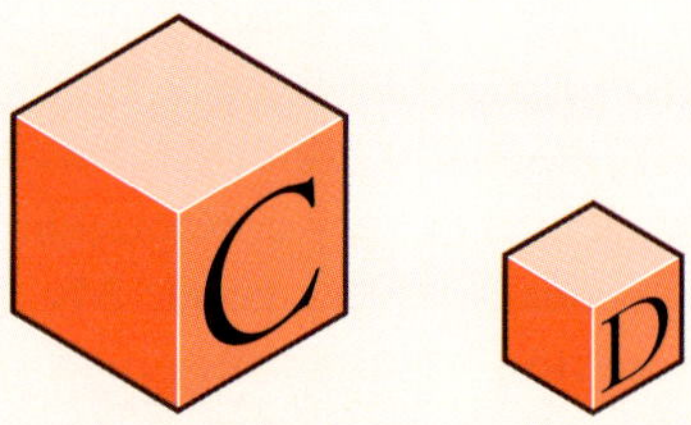

Box C is **much bigger** than Box D.

a bit **much**	bigger older better more difficult more expensive	than ...

- Canada is **much bigger** than France.
- Sue is **a bit older** than Gary – she's 25 and he's 24.
- The hotel was **much more expensive** than I expected.
- You go out **much more** than me.

old → older, expensive → more expensive → Unit 87 not as ... as → Unit 89

Exercises

88.1 Write sentences about Liz and Ben. Use **than**.

Liz

1 I'm 26.
2 I'm not a very good swimmer.
3 I'm 1 metre 68 tall.
4 I start work at 8 o'clock.
5 I don't work very hard.
6 I haven't got much money.
7 I'm a very good driver.
8 I'm not very patient.
9 I'm not a very good dancer.
10 I'm very intelligent.
11 I speak French very well.
12 I don't go to the cinema very much.

Ben

1 I'm 24.
2 I'm a very good swimmer.
3 I'm 1 metre 63 tall.
4 I start work at 8.30.
5 I work very hard.
6 I've got a lot of money.
7 I'm not a very good driver.
8 I'm very patient.
9 I'm a good dancer.
10 I'm not very intelligent.
11 I don't speak French very well.
12 I go to the cinema a lot.

1 Liz *is older than Ben* .
2 Ben *is a better swimmer than Liz* .
3 Liz is ....
4 Liz starts .... Ben.
5 Ben ....
6 Ben has got ....
7 Liz is a ....
8 Ben ....
9 Ben ....
10 Liz ....
11 Liz ....
12 Ben ....

88.2 Complete the sentences. Use **than**.

1 He isn't very tall. You're *taller than him (OR taller than he is)* .
2 She isn't very old. You're ....
3 I don't work very hard. You work ....
4 He doesn't watch TV very much. You ....
5 I'm not a very good cook. You ....
6 We don't know many people. You ....
7 They haven't got much money. You ....
8 I can't run very fast. You can ....
9 She hasn't been here very long. You ....
10 They didn't get up very early. You ....
11 He wasn't very surprised. You ....

88.3 Complete the sentences with **a bit** or **much** + comparative (**older/better** etc.).

1 Emma is 25. Gary is $24\frac{1}{2}$.
Emma *is a bit older than Gary.* .
2 Jack's mother is 52. His father is 69.
Jack's mother ....
3 My camera cost £100. Yours cost £96.
My camera ....
4 Yesterday I felt terrible. Today I feel OK.
I feel ....
5 Today the temperature is 12 degrees. Yesterday it was 10 degrees.
It's ....
6 Sarah is an excellent tennis player. I'm not very good.
Sarah ....

not as ... as

A

not as ... as

She's old, but she's **not as old as** he is.

Box A is**n't as big as** Box B.

- Rome **is not as old as** Athens. (= Athens is **older**)
- The Grand Hotel **isn't as expensive as** the Europa. (= the Europa is **more expensive**)
- I **don't** play tennis **as often as** you. (= you play **more often**)
- The weather is better than it was yesterday. It **isn't as cold**. (= as cold **as it was yesterday**)

B

not as much as ... / not as many as ...

- I haven't got **as much money as** you. (= you've got **more money**)
- I don't know **as many people as** you. (= you know **more people**)
- I don't go out **as much as** you. (= you go out **more**)

C

Compare **not as ... as** and **than**:

- Rome is **not as old as** Athens.
  Athens is **older than** Rome. (*not* older as Rome)
- Tennis **isn't as popular as** football.
  Football is **more popular than** tennis.
- I **don't** go out **as much as** you.
  You go out **more than** me.

D

We usually say: as **me** / as **him** / as **her** etc.
You can say:

- She's not as old **as him**. *or* She's not as old **as he is**.
- You don't work as hard **as me**. *or* You don't work as hard **as I do**.

E

We say **the same as ...** :

- The weather today is **the same as** yesterday.
- My hair is **the same colour as** yours.
- I arrived at **the same time as** Tim.

much/many → Unit 83 older than ... / more expensive than ... → Unit 88

89.1 Look at the pictures and write sentences about A, B and C.

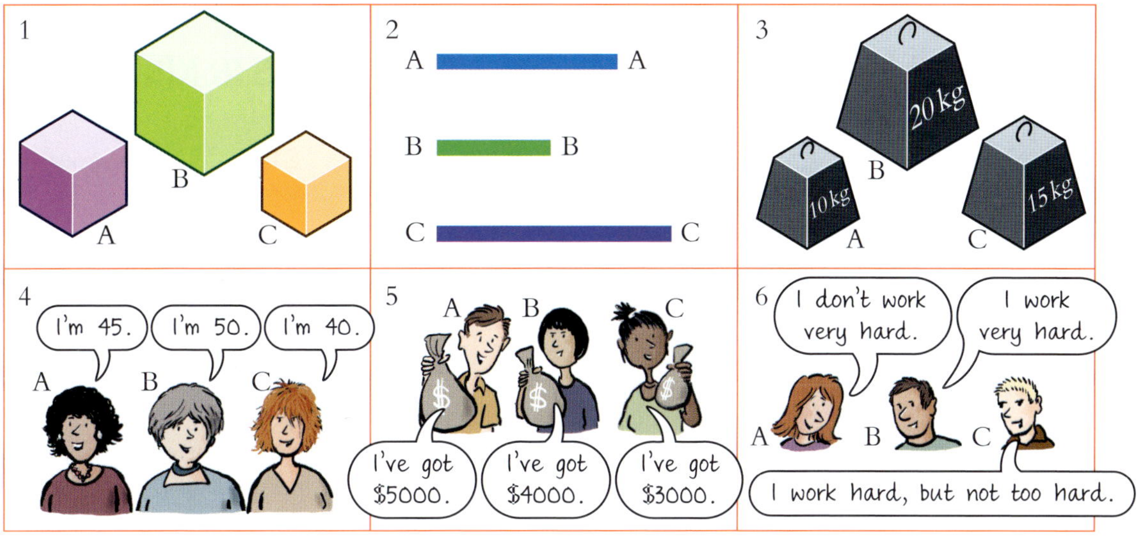

1 A is *bigger than C, but not as big as B* .
2 A is .... B, but not .... C.
3 C is .... A, but ....
4 A is .... , but ....
5 B has got ....
6 C works ....

89.2 Write sentences with as ... as ... .

1 Athens is older than Rome. Rome *isn't as old as Athens* .
2 My room is bigger than yours. Your room isn't ....
3 You got up earlier than me. I didn't ....
4 We played better than them. They ....
5 I've been here longer than you. You ....
6 She's more nervous than him. He ....

89.3 Write as or than.

1 Athens is older *than* Rome.
2 I don't watch TV as much .... you.
3 You eat more .... me.
4 I'm more tired today .... I was yesterday.
5 Joe isn't as intelligent .... he thinks.
6 Belgium is smaller .... Switzerland.
7 Brazil isn't as big .... Canada.
8 I can't wait longer .... an hour.

89.4 Complete the sentences about Julia, Andy and Laura. Use the same age / the same street etc.

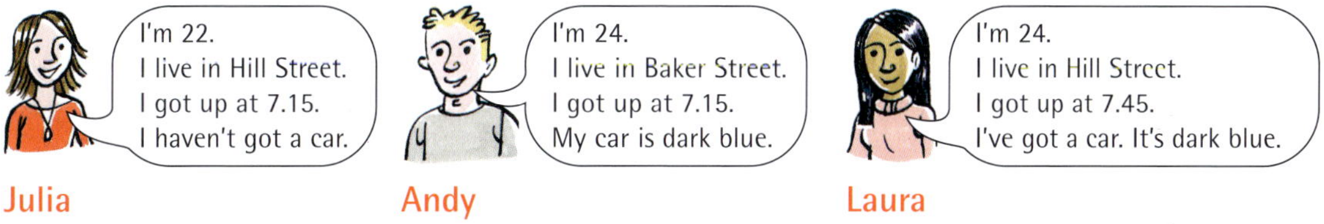

1 (age) *Andy is the same age as Laura* .
2 (street) Julia lives ....
3 (time) Julia got up ....
4 (colour) Andy's ....

the oldest   the most expensive

A

HOTEL PRICES IN KINTON
(Per room per night)

Europa Hotel	£140	Grosvenor	£100
Grand Hotel	£125	Bennets	£90
Royal	£120	Carlton	£85
Astoria	£115	Star	£75
Palace	£110	Station	£75

Box A is **bigger than** Box B.

Box A is **bigger than** all the other boxes.
Box A is **the biggest** box.

The Europa Hotel is **more expensive than** the Grand.
The Europa Hotel is **more expensive than** all the other hotels in the city.
The Europa Hotel is **the most expensive** hotel in the city.

Bigger / **older** / **more expensive** etc. are *comparative* forms (→ Unit 87).
Biggest / **oldest** / **most expensive** etc. are *superlative* forms.

B

The superlative form is **-est** (**oldest**) or **most** … (**most expensive**).

Short words (**old/cheap/nice** etc.) → **the -est**:
old → **the oldest**   cheap → **the cheapest**   nice → **the nicest**
but good → **the best**   bad → **the worst**

Spelling (→ Appendix 5): big → the bi**gg**est   hot → the ho**tt**est

Words ending in **-y** (**easy/heavy** etc.) → **the -iest**:
easy → **the easiest**   heavy → **the heaviest**   pretty → **the prettiest**

Long words (**careful**/**expensive**/**interesting** etc.) → **the most** … :
careful → **the most careful**   interesting → **the most interesting**

C

We say **the** oldest … / **the** most expensive … etc. (with **the**):

- The church is very old. It's **the oldest** building in the town.
  (= it is **older than** all the other buildings)
- What is **the longest** river in the world?
- Money is important, but it isn't **the most important** thing in life.
- Excuse me, where is **the nearest** bank?

D

You can use **the oldest** / **the best** / **the most expensive** etc. without a noun:

- Ken is a good player, but he isn't **the best** in the team.
  (**the best** = the best player)

E

You can use *superlative* + **I've ever** … / **you've ever** … etc. :

- The film was very bad. I think it's **the worst** film **I've ever seen**.
- What is **the most unusual** thing **you've ever done**?

90.1 Write sentences with comparatives (older etc.) and superlatives (the oldest etc.).

1

big/small
(A/D) A is bigger than D.
(A) A is the biggest.
(B) B is the smallest.

2
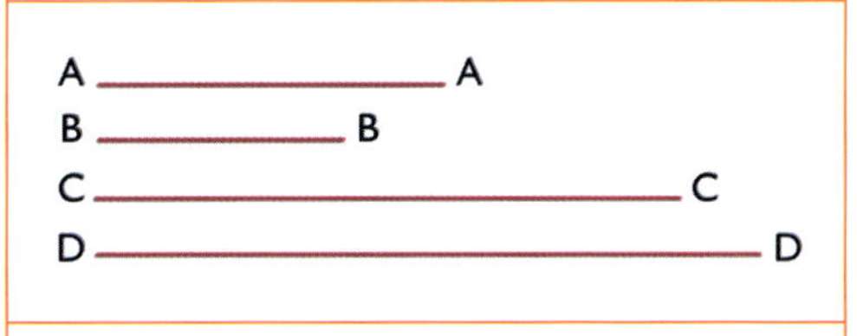

long/short
(C/A) C is .... A.
(D) D is ....
(B) B ....

3

young/old
(D/C) D ....
(B) ....
(C) ....

4

expensive/cheap
(D/A) ....
(C) ....
(A) ....

5

RESTAURANT A *excellent*
RESTAURANT B *not bad*
RESTAURANT C *good but not wonderful*
RESTAURANT D *awful*

good/bad
(A/C) ....
(A) ....
(D) ....

90.2 Complete the sentences. Use a superlative (the oldest etc.).

1 This building is very old. It's the oldest building in the town.
2 It was a very happy day. It was .... of my life.
3 It's a very good film. It's .... I've ever seen.
4 She's a very popular singer. She's .... in the country.
5 It was a very bad mistake. It was .... I've ever made.
6 It's a very pretty village. It's .... I've ever seen.
7 It was a very cold day. It was .... of the year.
8 He's a very boring person. He's .... I've ever met.

90.3 Write sentences with a superlative (the longest etc.). Choose from the boxes.

~~Sydney~~	Alaska
Everest	the Nile
Brazil	Jupiter

high
large
long

country	river
~~city~~	state
mountain	planet

Africa	South America
~~Australia~~	the world
the USA	the solar system

1 Sydney is the largest city in Australia.
2 Everest ....
3 ....
4 ....
5 ....
6 ....

enough

A

She isn't going to take a taxi.
She hasn't got **enough money**.

He can't reach the shelf.
He isn't **tall enough**.

B

enough + *noun* (**enough money** / **enough people** etc.)

- 'Is there **enough milk** in your coffee?' 'Yes, thank you.'
- We wanted to play football, but we didn't have **enough players**.
- Why don't you buy a car? You've got **enough money**. (*not* money enough)

enough *without a noun*

- I've got some money, but not **enough** to buy a car. (= I need more money to buy a car)
- 'Would you like some more to eat?' 'No, thanks. I've had **enough**.'
- You're always at home. You don't go out **enough**.

C

adjective + **enough** (**good enough** / **tall enough** etc.)

- 'Shall we sit outside?' 'No, it isn't **warm enough**.' (*not* enough warm)
- Can you hear the radio? Is it **loud enough** for you?
- Don't buy that coat. It's nice, but it isn't **long enough**. (= it's too short)

Remember:

enough + *noun*	but	*adjective* + **enough**
enough money		tall **enough**
enough time		good **enough**
enough people		old **enough**

D

We say:

enough for somebody/something	This pullover isn't **big enough for me**. I haven't got **enough money for a new car**.
enough to do something	I haven't got **enough money to buy** a new car. (*not* for buy) Is your English **good enough to have** a conversation? (*not* for have)
enough for somebody/something **to do** something	There aren't **enough chairs for everybody to sit** down.

to ... and for ... → Unit 54 too → Unit 92

91.1 Look at the pictures and complete the sentences. Use **enough** + these words:

chairs ~~**money**~~ **paint** **wind**

1 She hasn't got enough money .
2 There aren't ....
3 She hasn't got ....
4 There isn't ....

91.2 Look at the pictures and complete the sentences. Use these adjectives + **enough**:

big **long** **strong** ~~**tall**~~

1 He isn't tall enough .
2 The car ....
3 His legs aren't ....
4 He ....

91.3 Complete the sentences. Use **enough** with these words:

big **eat** ~~**loud**~~ ~~**milk**~~ **old** **practise** **space** **time** **tired**

1 'Is there enough milk in your coffee?' 'Yes, thank you.'
2 Can you hear the radio? Is it loud enough for you?
3 He can leave school if he wants – he's ....
4 When I visited New York last year, I didn't have .... to see all the things I wanted to see.
5 This house isn't .... for a large family.
6 Tina is very thin. She doesn't ....
7 My office is very small. There isn't ....
8 It's late, but I don't want to go to bed now. I'm not ....
9 Lisa isn't a very good tennis player because she doesn't ....

91.4 Complete the sentences. Use **enough** with these words:

1 We haven't got enough money to buy a new car. (money/buy)
2 This knife isn't .... tomatoes. (sharp/cut)
3 The water wasn't .... swimming. (warm/go)
4 Have we got .... sandwiches? (bread/make)
5 We played well, but not .... the game. (well/win)
6 I don't have .... newspapers. (time/read)

Unit 92

too

A

His shoes are **too big** for him.

There is **too much** sugar in it.

B

too + *adjective / adverb* (**too big** / **too hard** etc.)

- Can you turn the radio down?
  It's **too loud**. (= louder than I want)
- I can't work. I'm **too tired.**
- I think you work **too hard**.

C

too much / **too many** = more than you want, more than is good:

- I don't like the weather here. There is **too much rain**. (= more rain than is good)
- Let's go to another restaurant. There are **too many people** here.
- Emily studies all the time. I think she studies **too much**.
- Traffic is a problem in this town. There are **too many cars**.

D

Compare **too** and **not enough**:

too big

- The hat is **too big** for him.
- The radio is **too loud**. Can you turn it down, please?
- There's **too much sugar** in my coffee. (= more sugar than I want)
- I don't feel very well. I ate **too much**.

not big enough

- The hat is**n't big enough** for him. (= it's **too small**)
- The radio is**n't loud enough**. Can you turn it up, please?
- There's **not enough sugar** in my coffee. (= I need more sugar)
- You're very thin. You do**n't** eat **enough**.

E

We say:

too … **for** somebody/something	These shoes are **too big for me**. It's a small house – **too small for a large family**.
too … **to do** something	I'm **too tired to go** out. (*not* for go out) It's **too cold to sit** outside.
too … **for** somebody **to do** something	She speaks **too fast for me to understand**.

to … and for … → Unit 54 much/many → Unit 83 enough → Unit 91

92.1 Look at the pictures and complete the sentences. Use too + these words:

big crowded fast heavy ~~loud~~ low

1 The music is too loud .
2 The box is ....
3 The net is ....
4 She's driving ....
5 The ball is ....
6 The museum is ....

92.2 Write too / too much / too many or enough.

1 You're always at home. You don't go out enough .
2 I don't like the weather here. There's too much rain.
3 I can't wait for them. I haven't got .... time.
4 There was nowhere to sit on the beach. There were .... people.
5 You're always tired. I think you work .... hard.
6 'Did you have .... to eat?' 'Yes, thank you.'
7 You drink .... coffee. It's not good for you.
8 You don't eat .... vegetables. You should eat more.
9 I don't like the weather here. It's .... cold.
10 Our team didn't play well. We made .... mistakes.
11 'Would you like some milk in your tea?' 'Yes, but not ....'

92.3 Complete the sentences. Use too or enough with these words:

1 I couldn't work. I was too tired . (tired)
2 Can you turn the radio up, please? It isn't loud enough . (loud)
3 I don't want to walk home. It's .... (far)
4 Don't buy anything in that shop. It .... (expensive)
5 You can't put all your things in this bag. It .... (big)
6 I couldn't do the exercise. It .... (difficult)
7 Your work needs to be better. It .... (good)
8 I can't talk to you now. I .... (busy)
9 I thought the film was boring. It .... (long)

92.4 Complete the sentences. Use too (+ adjective) + to ... .

1 (I'm not going out / cold) It's too cold to go out .
2 (I'm not going to bed / early) It's ....
3 (they're not getting married / young) They're ....
4 (nobody goes out at night / dangerous)
It's ....
5 (don't phone Sue now / late)
It's ....
6 (I didn't say anything / surprised)
I was ....

Unit 93 He speaks English very well. (word order 1)

A verb + object

Sue **reads** **a newspaper** every day.
subject *verb* *object*

The *verb* (**reads**) and the *object* (**a newspaper**) are usually together. We say:

- Sue **reads a newspaper** every day.
  (*not* Sue reads every day a newspaper)

	verb + object	
He **speaks**	**English** very well.	(*not* He speaks very well English)
I **like**	**Italian food** very much.	(*not* I like very much ...)
Did you **watch**	**television** all evening?	(*not* Did you watch all evening ...)
Paul often **wears**	**a black hat**.	(*not* Paul wears often ...)
We **invited**	**a lot of people** to the party.	
I **opened**	**the door** slowly.	
Why do you always **make**	**the same mistake**?	
I'm going to **borrow**	**some money** from the bank.	

B where and when

We went **to a party** **last night** .
where? *when?*

Place *(where?)* is usually before time *(when?)*. We say:

- We went **to a party last night**. (*not* We went last night to a party)

	place *(where?)* +	time *(when? how long? how often?)*	
Lisa walks	**to work**	**every day**.	(*not* ... every day to work)
Will you be	**at home**	**this evening**?	(*not* ... this evening at home)
I usually go	**to bed**	**early**.	(*not* ... early to bed)
We arrived	**at the airport**	**at 7 o'clock**.	
They've lived	**in the same house**	**for 20 years**.	
Joe's father has been	**in hospital**	**since June**.	

word order in questions → Units 44–46 always/usually/often etc. → Unit 94

Exercises

93.1 Right or wrong? Correct the sentences that are wrong.

1 Did you watch all evening television? ... Did you watch television all evening?
2 Sue reads a newspaper every day. ... OK
3 I like very much this picture. ...
4 Tom started last week his new job. ...
5 I want to speak English fluently. ...
6 Jane bought for her friend a present. ...
7 I drink every day three cups of coffee. ...
8 Don't eat your dinner too quickly! ...
9 I borrowed from my brother fifty pounds. ...

93.2 Put the words in order.

1 (the door / opened / I / slowly) ... I opened the door slowly.
2 (a new computer / I / last week / bought) I ...
3 (finished / Paul / quickly / his work) ...
4 (Emily / very well / French / doesn't speak) ...
5 (a lot of shopping / did / I / yesterday) ...
6 (London / do you know / well?) ...
7 (we / enjoyed / very much / the party) ...
8 (the problem / carefully / I / explained) ...
9 (we / at the airport / some friends / met) ...
10 (did you buy / in England / that jacket?) ...
11 (every day / do / the same thing / we) ...
12 (football / don't like / very much / I) ...

93.3 Put the words in order.

1 (to work / every day / walks / Lisa) ... Lisa walks to work every day.
2 (at the hotel / I / early / arrived) I ...
3 (goes / every year / to Italy / Julia) Julia ...
4 (we / since 1988 / here / have lived) We ...
5 (in London / Sue / in 1980 / was born)
Sue ...
6 (didn't go / yesterday / Paul / to work)
Paul ...
7 (to a wedding / last weekend / went / Helen)
Helen ...
8 (I / in bed / this morning / my breakfast / had)
I ...
9 (in September / Barbara / to university / is going)
Barbara ...
10 (I / a beautiful bird / this morning / in the garden / saw)
I ...
11 (many times / have been / my parents / to the United States)
My ...
12 (my umbrella / I / last night / left / in the restaurant)
I ...
13 (to the cinema / tomorrow evening / are you going?)
Are ...
14 (the children / I / took / this morning / to school)
I ...

Unit 94

always/usually/often etc. (word order 2)

A

These words (**always/never** etc.) are with the verb in the middle of a sentence:

always	**often**	**ever**	**rarely**	**also**	**already**	**all**
usually	**sometimes**	**never**	**seldom**	**just**	**still**	**both**

- My brother **never speaks** to me.
- She**'s always** late.
- Do you **often go** to restaurants?
- I **sometimes eat** too much. (*or* **Sometimes** I eat too much.)
- 'Don't forget to phone Laura.' '**I've already phoned** her.'
- I've got three sisters. They**'re all** married.

B

Always/never etc. are *before* the verb:

	verb
always **often** **never** etc.	**go** **play** **have** etc.

- I **always drink** coffee in the morning. (*not* I drink always coffee)
- Helen **often goes** to London. (*not* Helen goes often)
- You **sometimes look** unhappy.
- They **usually have** dinner at 7 o'clock.
- We **rarely** (*or* **seldom**) **watch** television.
- Richard is a good footballer. He **also plays** tennis and volleyball. (*not* He plays also tennis)
- I've got three sisters. They **all live** in London.

But **always/never** etc. are *after* **am/is/are/was/were**:

am **is** **are** **was** **were**	**always** **often** **never** etc.

- I **am always tired**. (*not* I always am tired)
- They **are never** at home during the day.
- It **is usually** very cold here in winter.
- When I was a child, I **was often** late for school.
- 'Where's Laura?' 'She**'s still** in bed.'
- I've got two brothers. They**'re both** doctors.

C

Always/never etc. are *between* two verbs (**have** … **been** / **can** … **find** etc.):

verb 1		*verb 2*
will **can** **do** etc.	**always** **often** **never** etc.	**go** **find** **remember** etc.
have **has**		**gone** **been** etc.

- I **will always remember** you.
- It **doesn't often rain** here.
- **Do** you **usually go** to work by car?
- I **can never find** my keys.
- **Have** you **ever been** to Egypt?
- A: Where's Laura?
  B: She**'s just gone** out. (She's = She has)
- My friends **have all gone** to the cinema.

always/never + present simple → Unit 5 **just/already** + present perfect → Unit 16 **all** → Units 80–81
both → Unit 82 **still** → Unit 95

94.1 Read Paul's answers to the questions. Write sentences about Paul with **often/never** etc.

Paul

	Question	Paul's answer	
1	Do you ever play tennis?	Yes, often.	*Paul often plays tennis.*
2	Do you get up early?	Yes, always.	He ....
3	Are you ever late for work?	No, never.	He ....
4	Do you ever get angry?	Sometimes.	....
5	Do you ever go swimming?	Rarely.	....
6	Are you at home in the evenings?	Yes, usually.	....

94.2 Write these sentences with **never/always/usually** etc.

1. My brother speaks to me. (never) *My brother never speaks to me.*
2. Susan is polite. (always) Susan ....
3. I finish work at 5 o'clock. (usually) I ....
4. Sarah has started a new job. (just) Sarah ....
5. I go to bed before midnight. (rarely) ....
6. The bus isn't late. (usually) ....
7. I don't eat fish. (often) ....
8. I will forget what you said. (never) ....
9. Have you lost your passport? (ever) ....
10. Do you work in the same place? (still) ....
11. They stay in the same hotel. (always) ....
12. Jane doesn't work on Saturdays. (usually) ....
13. Is Tina here? (already) ....
14. What do you have for breakfast? (usually) ....
15. I can remember his name. (never) ....

94.3 Write sentences with **also**.

1. Do you play football? (tennis) *Yes, and I also play tennis.*
2. Do you speak Italian? (French) Yes, and I ....
3. Are you tired? (hungry) Yes, and ....
4. Have you been to England? (Ireland) Yes, ...
5. Did you buy any clothes? (some books) ....

94.4 Write sentences with **both** and **all**.

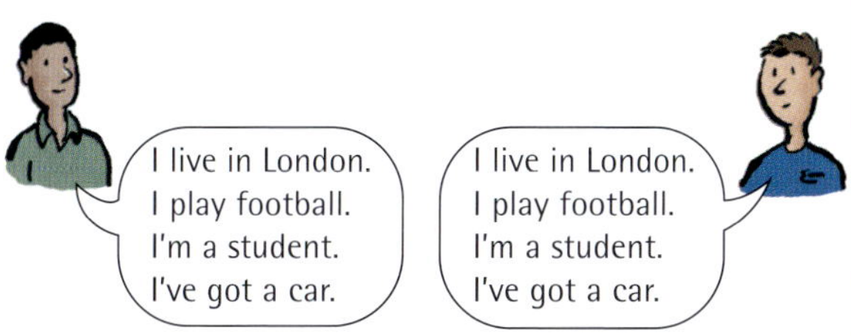

1 *They both live in London.*
They .... football.
.... students.
.... cars.

2 They .... married.
They .... England.
....

still yet already

A still

an hour ago

An hour ago it was raining.

The rain hasn't stopped

now

It is **still** raining now.

still = something is the same as before:

- I had a lot to eat, but I'm **still** hungry. (= I was hungry before, and I'm hungry now)
- 'Did you sell your car?' 'No, I've **still** got it.'
- 'Do you **still** live in Barcelona?' 'No, I live in Madrid now.'

B yet

20 minutes ago

Twenty minutes ago they were waiting for Bill.

now

They are **still** waiting for Bill.
Bill **hasn't come yet**.

yet = until now

We use **yet** in *negative* sentences (He **hasn't** come yet.) and in *questions* (**Has he** come yet?).
Yet is usually at the end of a sentence:

- A: Where's Emma?
  B: She **isn't** here **yet**. (= she will be here, but until now she hasn't come)
- A: What are you doing this evening?
  B: I **don't** know **yet**. (= I will know later, but I don't know at the moment)
- A: Are you ready to go **yet**?
  B: **Not yet**. In a minute. (= I will be ready, but I'm not ready at the moment)
- A: Have you finished with the newspaper **yet**?
  B: No, I'm still reading it.

Compare **yet** and **still**:

- She hasn't gone **yet**. = She's **still** here. (*not* she is yet here)
- I haven't finished eating **yet**. = I'm **still** eating.

C

already = earlier than expected:

- 'What time is Joe coming?' 'He's **already** here.' (= earlier than we expected)
- 'I'm going to tell you what happened.' 'That's not necessary. I **already** know.'
- Sarah isn't coming to the cinema with us. She has **already** seen the film.

already/yet + present perfect → Unit 16 word order (**still/already**) → Unit 94

95.1 You meet Tina. The last time you saw her was two years ago. You ask her some questions with still.

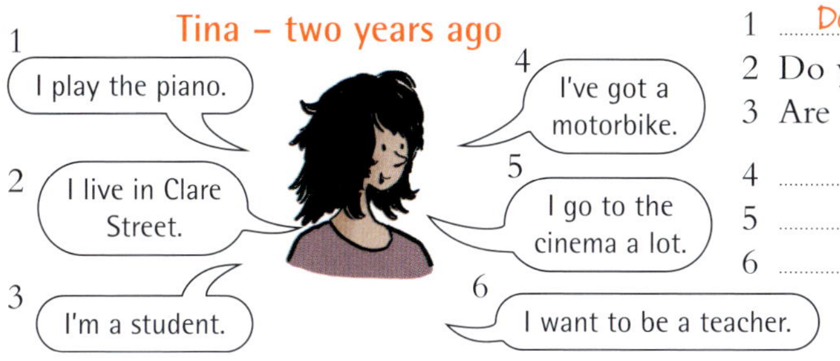

1 Do you still play the piano?
2 Do you ....
3 Are ....
4 ....
5 ....
6 ....

95.2 Write three sentences for each situation. Look at the example carefully.

before → *now*

1

(*before*) They were waiting for the bus.
(still) They are still waiting.
(yet) The bus hasn't come yet.

2

(*before*) He was ....
(still) He ....
(yet) .... yet.

3

(*before*) She .... asleep.
(still) ....
(yet) ....

4

(*before*) They ....
(still) ....
(yet) ....

95.3 Write questions with yet.

1 You and Sue are going out together. You are waiting for her to get ready. Perhaps she is ready now. You ask her: Are you ready yet?
2 You are waiting for Helen to arrive. She wasn't here ten minutes ago. Perhaps she is here now. You ask somebody: .... Helen ....
3 Anna did an exam and is waiting for the results. Perhaps she has her results now. You ask her: .... you ....
4 A few days ago you spoke to Tom. He wasn't sure where to go on holiday. Perhaps he has decided now. You ask him: ....

95.4 Complete the sentences. Use already.

1	What time is Joe coming?	He's already here.
2	Does Sarah want to see the film?	No, she has already seen it.
3	I have to see Julia before she goes.	It's too late. She ....
4	Do you need a pen?	No, thanks. I .... one.
5	Shall I pay the bill?	No, it's OK. I ....
6	Shall I tell Paul about the meeting?	No, he .... I told him.

Unit 96 Give me that book! Give it to me!

A

give **lend** **pass** **send** **show**

After these verbs (**give**/**lend** etc.), there are two possible structures:

give something to somebody

- I gave **the keys to Sarah**.

give somebody something

- I gave **Sarah the keys**.

B

give something to somebody

		something	**to** somebody
That's my book.	**Give**	it	**to** me.
These are Sue's keys. Can you	**give**	them	**to** her?
Can you	**give**	these flowers	**to** your mother?
I	**lent**	my car	**to** a friend of mine.
Did you	**send**	a postcard	**to** Kate?
We've seen these photos. You	**showed**	them	**to** us.

C

give somebody something

		somebody	something
	Give	me	that book. It's mine.
Tom	**gave**	his mother	some flowers.
I	**lent**	Joe	some money.
How much money did you	**lend**	him?	
I	**sent**	you	an email. Did you get it?
Nicole	**showed**	us	her holiday photos.
Can you	**pass**	me	the salt, please?

You can also say '**buy**/**get** somebody something':

- I **bought** my mother some flowers. (= I bought some flowers **for** my mother.)
- Can you **get** me a newspaper when you go out? (= get a newspaper **for** me)

D

You can say:

- I **gave** the keys **to Sarah**.

and I **gave Sarah** the keys.
(*but not* I gave to Sarah the keys)

- That's my book. Can you **give** it **to me**?

and Can you **give me** that book?
(*but not* Can you give to me that book?)

We prefer the first structure (**give** something **to** somebody) with **it** or **them**:

- I gave **it to her**. (*not* I gave her it)
- Here are the keys. Give **them to your father**. (*not* Give your father them)

it/him/them etc. → Unit 59

96.1 Mark had some things that he didn't want. He gave them to different people.

Write sentences beginning **He gave ...** .

1 What did Mark do with the armchair? *He gave it to his brother.*
2 What did he do with the tennis racket? He gave ……
3 What happened to the books? He ……
4 What about the lamp? ……
5 What did he do with the pictures? ……
6 And the ladder? ……

96.2 You gave presents to your friends. You decided to give them the things in the pictures. Write a sentence for each person.

1 *I gave Paul a book.*
2 I gave ……
3 I ……
4 ……
5 ……
6 ……

96.3 Write questions beginning Can you give me ... ? / Can you pass me ... ? etc.

1 (you want the salt) (pass) *Can you pass me the salt?*
2 (you need an umbrella) (lend) Can you ……
3 (you want my address) (give) Can …… your ……
4 (you need twenty pounds) (lend) ……
5 (you want some information) (send) ……
6 (you want to see the letter) (show) ……
7 (you want some stamps) (get) ……

96.4 Which is right?

1 ~~I gave to Sarah the keys.~~ / I gave Sarah the keys. (I gave Sarah the keys *is right*)
2 I'll lend to you some money if you want. / I'll lend you some money if you want.
3 Did you send the letter me? / Did you send the letter to me?
4 I want to buy for you a present. / I want to buy you a present.
5 Can you pass to me the sugar, please? / Can you pass me the sugar, please?
6 This is Lisa's bag. Can you give it to her? / Can you give her it?
7 I showed to the policeman my identity card. / I showed the policeman my identity card.

and but or so because

A

and **but** **or** **so** **because**

We use these words *(conjunctions)* to join two sentences. They make one longer sentence from two shorter sentences:

sentence A The car stopped. — The driver got out. *sentence B*

The car stopped **and** the driver got out.

B

and/but/or

sentence A		*sentence B*
We stayed at home	**and**	(we)* watched television.
My sister is married	**and**	(she)* lives in London.
He doesn't like her,	**and**	she doesn't like him.
I bought a newspaper,	**but**	I didn't read it.
It's a nice house,	**but**	it hasn't got a garden.
Do you want to go out,	**or**	are you too tired?

* It is not necessary to repeat 'we' and 'she'.

In lists, we use commas (**,**). We use **and** before the last thing:

- I got home**,** had something to eat**,** sat down in an armchair **and** fell asleep.
- Karen is at work**,** Sue has gone shopping **and** Chris is playing football.

C

so (the result of something)

sentence A		*sentence B*
It was very hot,	**so**	I opened the window.
Joe does a lot of sport,	**so**	he's very fit.
They don't like travelling,	**so**	they haven't been to many places.

D

because (the reason for something)

sentence A		*sentence B*
I opened the window	**because**	it was very hot.
Joe can't come to the party	**because**	he's going away.
Lisa is hungry	**because**	she didn't have breakfast.

Because is also possible at the beginning:

- **Because it was very hot**, I opened the window.

E

In these examples there is more than one conjunction:

- It was late **and** I was tired, **so** I went to bed.
- I always enjoy visiting London, **but** I wouldn't like to live there **because** it's too big.

when/while/before etc. → Unit 98

Exercises

97.1 Write sentences. Choose from the boxes and use **and/but/or.**

~~I stayed at home.~~	I didn't have your number.
~~I bought a newspaper.~~	Shall I wait here?
I went to the window.	~~I didn't read it.~~
I wanted to phone you.	I went by bus this morning.
I jumped into the river.	~~I watched television.~~
I usually drive to work.	I swam to the other side.
Do you want me to come with you?	I looked out.

1 *I stayed at home and watched television.*
2 *I bought a newspaper, but I didn't read it.*
3 I ....
4 ....
5 ....
6 ....
7 ....

97.2 Look at the pictures and complete the sentences. Use **and/but/so/because.**

1 It was very hot, *so he opened the window.*
2 They couldn't play tennis ....
3 They went to the museum, ...
4 Bill wasn't hungry, ...
5 Helen was late ....
6 Sue said ....

97.3 Write sentences about what you did yesterday. Use **and/but** etc.

1 (and) *In the evening I stayed at home and studied.*
2 (because) *I went to bed very early because I was tired.*
3 (but) ....
4 (and) ....
5 (so) ....
6 (because) ....

Unit 98

When ...

A

When I went out, it was raining.

This sentence has two parts:

when I went out + **it was raining**

You can say:

- **When I went out**, it was raining. *or* **It was raining** when I went out.

We write a comma (**,**) if **When** ... is at the beginning:

- { **When** you're tired, don't drive. / Don't drive **when** you're tired.
- { Helen was 25 **when** she got married. / **When** Helen got married, she was 25.

We do the same in sentences with **before/while/after**:

- { Always look both ways **before** you cross the road. / **Before** you cross the road, always look both ways.
- { **While** I was waiting for the bus, it began to rain. / It began to rain **while** I was waiting for the bus.
- { He never played football again **after** he broke his leg. / **After** he broke his leg, he never played football again.

B

When I am ... / **When I go** ... etc.

Next week Sarah is going to New York.
She has a friend, Lisa, who lives in New York,
but Lisa is also going away – to Mexico.
So they won't see each other in New York.

Lisa **will be** in Mexico **when** Sarah **is** in New York.

The time is *future* (**next week**) but we say:
... **when** Sarah **is** in New York.
(*not* when Sarah will be)

SARAH *LISA*

We use the *present* (**I am** / **I go** etc.) with a *future meaning* after **when**:

- **When** I **get** home this evening, I'm going to have a shower. (*not* When I will get home)
- I can't talk to you now. I'll talk to you later **when** I **have** more time.

We do the same after **before/while/after/until**:

- Please close the window **before** you **go** out. (*not* before you will go)
- Rachel is going to stay in our flat **while** we **are** away. (*not* while we will be)
- I'll wait here **until** you **come** back. (*not* until you will come back)

if and when → Unit 99 until → Unit 104 before/while/after → Unit 105

Exercises

98.1 Write sentences beginning with when. Choose from the boxes.

When +

~~I went out~~ I'm tired I phoned her I go on holiday the programme ended I got to the hotel	+	I turned off the TV I always go to the same place there were no rooms ~~it was raining~~ there was no answer I like to watch TV

1 When I went out, it was raining.
2 ....
3 ....
4 ....
5 ....
6 ....

98.2 Complete the sentences. Choose from the box.

somebody broke into the house ~~before they crossed the road~~ they went to live in New Zealand	before they came here while they were away	when they heard the news they didn't believe me

1 They looked both ways before they crossed the road.
2 They were very surprised ....
3 After they got married, ...
4 Their house was damaged in a storm ....
5 Where did they live ....?
6 While we were asleep, ...
7 When I told them what happened, ...

98.3 Which is right?

1 ~~I stay~~ / I'll stay here until you come / ~~you'll come~~ back. (I'll stay *and* you come *are right*)
2 I'm going to bed when I finish / I'll finish my work.
3 We must do something before it's / it will be too late.
4 Helen is going away soon. I'm / I'll be very sad when she leaves / she'll leave.
5 Don't go out yet. Wait until the rain stops / will stop.
6 We come / We'll come and visit you when we're / we'll be in England again.
7 When I come / I'll come to see you tomorrow, I bring / I'll bring our holiday photos.
8 I'm going to Paris next week. I hope to see some friends of mine while I'm / I'll be there.
9 'I need your address.' 'OK, I give / I'll give it to you before I go / I'll go.'
10 I'm not ready yet. I tell / I'll tell you when I'm / I'll be ready.

98.4 Use your own ideas to complete these sentences.

1 Can you close the window before you go out?
2 What are you going to do when ....?
3 When I have enough money, ...
4 I'll wait for you while ....
5 When I start my new job, ...
6 Will you be here when ....?

If we go ... If you see ... etc.

A

If can be at the beginning of a sentence or in the middle:

If at the beginning

If we go by bus,	it will be cheaper.
If you don't hurry,	you'll miss the train.
If you're hungry,	have something to eat.
If the phone rings,	can you answer it, please?

if in the middle

It will be cheaper	**if** we go by bus.
You'll miss the train	**if** you don't hurry.
I'm going to the concert	**if** I can get a ticket.
Is it OK	**if** I use your phone?

In conversation, we often use the **if**-part of the sentence alone:
- 'Are you going to the concert?' 'Yes, **if I can get a ticket**.'

B

If you see Ann tomorrow ... etc.

After **if**, we use the present (*not* will). We say '**if** you **see** ...' (*not* if you will see):
- **If** you **see** Ann tomorrow, can you ask her to call me?
- **If I'm** late this evening, don't wait for me. (*not* if I will be)
- What shall we do **if** it **rains**? (*not* if it will rain)
- **If** I **don't feel** well tomorrow, I'll stay at home.

C

if and **when**

If I go out = it is possible that I will go out, but I'm not sure:
- A: Are you going out later?
- B: Maybe. **If I go out**, I'll close the windows.

When I go out = I'm going out (for sure):
- A: Are you going out later?
- B: Yes, I am. **When I go out**, I'll close the windows.

Compare **when** and **if**:
- **When** I get home this evening, I'm going to have a shower.
- **If** I'm late this evening, don't wait for me. (*not* When I'm late)
- We're going to play tennis **if** it doesn't rain. (*not* when it doesn't rain)

when → Unit 98 if I had / if we went ... etc. → Unit 100

Exercises

99.1 Write sentences beginning with if. Choose from the boxes.

If +		+	
	~~you don't hurry~~		we can have lunch now
	you pass the exam		you can have them
	you fail the exam		I can lend you some
	you don't want this magazine		you'll get a certificate
	you want those pictures		~~you'll be late~~
	you're busy now		I'll throw it away
	you're hungry		we can talk later
	you need money		you can do it again

1 *If you don't hurry, you'll be late.*
2 If you pass ……
3 If ……
4 ……
5 ……
6 ……
7 ……
8 ……

99.2 Which is right?

1 If I'm / ~~I'll be~~ late this evening, don't wait for me. (*I'm is right*)
2 Will you call me if I give / I'll give you my phone number?
3 If there is / will be a fire, the alarm will ring.
4 If I don't see you tomorrow morning, I call / I'll call you in the evening.
5 I'm / I'll be surprised if Martin and Jane get / will get married.
6 Do you go / Will you go to the party if they invite / they'll invite you?

99.3 Use your own ideas to complete these sentences.

1 I'm going to the concert if *I can get a ticket.*
2 If you don't hurry, *you'll miss the train.*
3 I don't want to disturb you if ……
4 If you go to bed early tonight, ……
5 Turn the television off if ……
6 Tina won't pass her exams if ……
7 If I have time tomorrow, ……
8 We can go to the beach tomorrow if ……
9 I'll be surprised if ……

99.4 Write if or when.

1 *If* I'm late this evening, don't wait for me.
2 I'm going to do some shopping now. …… I come back, we can have lunch.
3 I'm thinking of going to see Tim. …… I go, will you come with me?
4 …… you don't want to go out tonight, we can stay at home.
5 Is it OK …… I close the window?
6 John is still at school. …… he leaves school, he wants to go to college.
7 Shall we have a picnic tomorrow …… the weather is good?
8 We're going to Madrid next week. We haven't got anywhere to stay – we hope to find a hotel …… we get there. I don't know what we'll do …… we don't find a room.

Unit 100 If I had … If we went … etc.

A

Dan likes fast cars, but he doesn't have one. He doesn't have enough money.

If he **had** the money, he **would buy** a fast car.

Usually **had** is *past*, but in this sentence **had** is *not* past. **If** he **had** the money = if he had the money *now* (but he doesn't have it).

If	I you it they etc.	**had** / **knew** / **lived** / **went** (etc.) … , **didn't have** / **didn't know** (etc.) … , **were** … , **could** … ,	I you it they etc.	**would**(**n't**) **could**(**n't**)	buy … be … have … go … etc.

You can say:

- **If he had** the money, he would buy a car.

or He would buy a car **if he had** the money.

I'd / **she'd** / **they'd** etc. = I **would** / she **would** / they **would** etc. :

- I don't know the answer. **If** I **knew** the answer, I**'d tell** you.
- It's raining, so we're not going out. We**'d get** wet **if** we **went** out.
- Jane lives in a city. She likes cities. She **wouldn't be** happy **if** she **lived** in the country.
- **If** you **didn't have** a job, what **would** you **do**? (but you *have* a job)
- I'm sorry I can't help you. **I'd help** you **if** I **could**. (but I *can't*)
- **If** we **had** a car, we **could travel** more. (but we *haven't* got a car, so we *can't* travel much)

B

If (I) **was/were** …

You can say '**if** I/he/she/it **was**' *or* '**if** I/he/she/it **were**':

- It's not a very nice place. I wouldn't go there **if I were you**. (*or* … **if I was** you)
- It would be nice **if the weather was** better. (*or* … **if the weather were** better)
- What would Tom do **if he were** here? (*or* … **if he was** here)

C

Compare:

if I have / **if it is** etc.

- I must go and see Helen.
  If I **have** time, I **will go** today.
  (= maybe I'll have time, so maybe I'll go)
- I like that jacket.
  I'll buy it **if** it **isn't** too expensive.
  (= maybe it will not be too expensive)
- **I'll help** you **if** I **can**. (= maybe I can help)

if I had / **if it was** etc.

- I must go and see Helen.
  If I **had** time, I **would go** today.
  (= I don't have time today, so I will not go)
- I like that jacket, but it's very expensive.
  I'd buy it **if** it **wasn't** so expensive.
  (= it is expensive, so I'm not going to buy it)
- **I'd help** you **if** I **could**, but I can't.

if we go / if I have / if I can etc. → Unit 99

100.1 Complete the sentences.

1 I don't know the answer. If I ....knew.... the answer, I'd tell you.
2 I have a car. I couldn't travel very much if I ....didn't have.... a car.
3 I don't want to go out. If I .... to go out, I'd go.
4 We haven't got a key. If we .... a key, we could get into the house.
5 I'm not hungry. I would have something to eat if I .... hungry.
6 Sue enjoys her work. She wouldn't do it if she .... it.
7 He can't speak any foreign languages. If he .... speak a foreign language, perhaps he would get a better job.
8 You don't try hard enough. If you .... harder, you would have more success.
9 I have a lot to do today. If I .... so much to do, we could go out.

100.2 Put the verb in the correct form.

1 If ....he had.... the money, he would buy a fast car. (he/have)
2 Jane likes living in a city. ....She wouldn't be.... happy if she lived in the country. (she/not/be)
3 If I wanted to learn Italian, ... to Italy. (I/go)
4 I haven't told Helen what happened. She'd be angry if .... (she/know)
5 If .... a map, I could show you where I live. (we/have)
6 What would you do if .... a lot of money? (you/win)
7 It's not a very good hotel. .... there if I were you. (I/not/stay)
8 If .... nearer London, we would go there more often. (we/live)
9 It's a pity you have to go now. .... nice if you had more time. (it/be)
10 I'm not going to take the job. I'd take it if .... better. (the salary/be)
11 I don't know anything about cars. If the car broke down, ... what to do. (I/not/know)
12 If you could change one thing in the world, what .... ? (you/change)

100.3 Complete the sentences. Choose from the box and put the verb in the correct form.

we (have) a bigger house	~~it (be) a bit cheaper~~	I (watch) it
we (buy) a bigger house	every day (be) the same	I (be) bored
we (have) some pictures on the wall	the air (be) cleaner	

1 I'd buy that jacket if ....it was a bit cheaper.... .
2 If there was a good film on TV tonight, ...
3 This room would be nicer if ....
4 If there wasn't so much traffic, ...
5 Life would be boring if ....
6 If I had nothing to do, ...
7 We could invite all our friends to stay if ....
8 If we had more money, ...

100.4 Complete the sentences. Use your own ideas.

1 I'd be happier if ....I could get a better job.... .
2 If I could go anywhere in the world, ...
3 I wouldn't be very happy if ....
4 I'd buy .... if ....
5 If I saw an accident in the street, ...
6 The world would be a better place if ....

Unit 101

a person who ... a thing that/which ... (relative clauses 1)

A

I met a woman. **She** can speak six languages.
2 sentences

she → **who**

1 sentence
I met **a woman who** can speak six languages.

Jack was wearing a hat. **It** was too big for him.
2 sentences

it → **that** *or* **which**

1 sentence
Jack was wearing **a hat that** was too big for him.
or
Jack was wearing **a hat which** was too big for him.

B

who is for people (not things):

A thief is **a person**	**who** steals things.	
Do you know **anybody**	**who** can play the piano?	
The man	**who** phoned	didn't give his name.
The people	**who** work in the office	are very friendly.

C

that is for things or people:

An aeroplane is **a machine**	**that** flies.	
Emma lives in **a house**	**that** is 400 years old.	
The people	**that** work in the office	are very friendly.

You can use **that** for people, but **who** is more usual.

D

which is for things (not people):

An aeroplane is **a machine**	**which** flies. (*not* a machine who …)
Emma lives in **a house**	**which** is 400 years old.

Do not use **which** for people:

- Do you remember **the woman who** was playing the piano at the party? (*not* the woman which …)

who and **which** in questions → Units 45, 47 **the people we met** (relative clauses 2) → Unit 102

101.1 Choose from the boxes and write sentences: A ... is a person who ... . Use a dictionary if necessary.

~~a thief~~	a dentist
a butcher	a fool
a musician	a genius
a patient	a liar

doesn't tell the truth	is ill in hospital
takes care of your teeth	~~steals things~~
is very intelligent	does stupid things
plays a musical instrument	sells meat

1 A thief is a person who steals things.
2 A butcher is a person ……
3 A musician ……
4 ……
5 ……
6 ……
7 ……
8 ……

101.2 Make one sentence from two.

1 (A man phoned. He didn't give his name.)
The man who phoned didn't give his name.

2 (A woman opened the door. She was wearing a yellow dress.)
The woman …… a yellow dress.

3 (Some students took the exam. Most of them passed.)
Most of the students ……

4 (A policeman stopped our car. He wasn't very friendly.)
The ……

101.3 Write who or which.

1 I met a woman who can speak six languages.
2 What's the name of the man …… has just started work in your office?
3 What's the name of the river …… flows through the town?
4 Where is the picture …… was hanging on the wall?
5 Do you know anybody …… wants to buy a car?
6 You always ask questions …… are difficult to answer.
7 I have a friend …… is very good at repairing cars.
8 I think everybody …… went to the party enjoyed it very much.
9 Why does he always wear clothes …… are too small for him?

101.4 Right or wrong? Correct the mistakes.

1 A thief is a person which steals things. — a person who steals
2 An aeroplane is a machine that flies. — OK
3 A coffee maker is a machine who makes coffee. ……
4 Have you seen the money that was on the table? ……
5 I don't like people which never stop talking. ……
6 I know somebody that can help you. ……
7 I know somebody who works in that shop. ……
8 Correct the sentences who are wrong. ……
9 My neighbour bought a car who cost £40,000. ……

Unit 102 the people we met / the hotel you stayed at (relative clauses 2)

A

The man is carrying a bag. It's very heavy. } *2 sentences*
The bag (that) he is carrying is very heavy. — *1 sentence*

KATE

Kate won some money. What is she going to do with it? } *2 sentences*
What is Kate going to do with **the money (that) she won**? — *1 sentence*

You can say:

- The bag **that** he is carrying ... *or* The bag he is carrying ... (with or without **that**)
- ... the money **that** Kate won? *or* ... the money Kate won?

You do not need **that/who/which** when it is the *object:*

subject	*verb*	*object*	
The man	was carrying	a bag	→ **the bag** (that) **the man was carrying**
Kate	won	some money	→ **the money** (that) **Kate won**
You	wanted	some books	→ **the books** (that) **you wanted**
We	met	some people	→ **the people** (who) **we met**

- Did you find **the books you wanted**? (*or* ... the books **that** you wanted?)
- **The people we met** were very friendly. (*or* The people **who** we met ...)
- **Everything I said** was true. (*or* Everything **that** I said ...)

We say:

- The film **we saw** was very good. (*not* The film we saw it was ...)

B

Sometimes there is a *preposition* (**to/in/at** etc.) after the verb:

Eve **is talking to** a man.	→	Do you know **the man Eve is talking to**?
We **stayed at** a hotel.	→	**The hotel we stayed at** was near the station.
I **told** you **about** some books.	→	These are **the books I told you about**.

We say:

... the books **I told you about**. (*not* the books I told you about them)

You can say '(a place) **where** ...':

- **The hotel where** we stayed was near the station. (= The hotel we stayed at ...)

C

You must use **who/that/which** when it is the *subject* (→ Unit 101):

- I met a woman **who can speak** six languages. (**who** is the subject)
- Jack was wearing a hat **that was** too big for him. (**that** is the subject)

a person who ... , a thing that/which ... (relative clauses 1) → Unit 101

Exercises

102.1 Make one sentence from two.

1 (Helen took some photographs. Have you seen them?)
Have you seen the photographs Helen took?
2 (You gave me a pen. I've lost it.)
I've lost the ....
3 (Sue is wearing a jacket. I like it.)
I like the ....
4 (I gave you some flowers. Where are they?)
Where are the .... ?
5 (He told us a story. I didn't believe it.)
I ....
6 (You bought some oranges. How much were they?)
How .... ?

102.2 Make one sentence from two.

1 (I was carrying a bag. It was very heavy.)
The bag I was carrying was very heavy.
2 (You cooked a meal. It was excellent.)
The ....
3 (I'm wearing shoes. They aren't very comfortable.)
The shoes ....
4 (We invited some people to dinner. They didn't come.)
The ....

102.3 You ask your friend some questions. Complete the sentences.

1 Your friend stayed at a hotel. You ask:
What's the name of the hotel you stayed at ?
2 Your friend was talking to some people. You ask:
Who are the people .... ?
3 Your friend was looking for some keys. You ask:
Did you find the .... ?
4 Your friend is going to a party. You ask:
Where is the .... ?
5 Your friend was talking about a film. You ask:
What's the name of .... ?
6 Your friend is listening to some music. You ask:
What's that .... ?
7 Your friend was waiting for a letter. You ask:
Did you get .... ?

102.4 Complete the questions. Use where.

1 John stayed at a hotel. You ask him:
Did you like the hotel where you stayed ?
2 Sue had dinner in a restaurant. You ask her:
What's the name of the restaurant .... ?
3 Sarah lives in a village. You ask her:
How big is the .... ?
4 Richard works in a factory. You ask him:
Where exactly is .... ?

Unit 103 at 8 o'clock on Monday in April

A

at

at	8 o'clock 10.30 midnight etc.

- I start work **at 8 o'clock**.
- The shops close **at 5.30**.

on

on	Sunday(s) / Monday(s) etc. 25 April / 6 June etc. New Year's Day etc.

- Bye! I'll see you **on Friday**.
- What do you usually do **on Sundays**?
- The concert is **on 22 November**.

in

in	April/June etc. 2003/1968 etc. summer/spring etc.

- I'm going on holiday **in October**.
- Emma was born **in 1983**.
- The park is beautiful **in spring**.

B

We say:

at the weekend **at night** **at Christmas / at Easter** **at the end of** ... **at the moment**

- Are you going away **at the weekend**?
- I can't sleep **at night**.
- Where will you be **at Christmas**? (*but* **on** Christmas **Day**)
- I'm going on holiday **at the end of** October.
- Are you busy **at the moment**?

C

in the morning / in the afternoon / in the evening

- I always feel good **in the morning**.
- Do you often go out **in the evening**?

but

on Monday morning / on Tuesday afternoon / on Friday evening / on Saturday night etc. :

- I'm meeting Joanne **on Monday morning**.
- Are you doing anything **on Saturday night**?

D

We do *not* use **at/on/in** before:

this ... (**this morning / this week** etc.) **last** ... (**last August / last week** etc.) **next** ... (**next Monday / next week** etc.) **every** ... (**every day / every week** etc.)

- Are you going out **this evening**?
- We go on holiday **every summer**. **Last summer** we went to Canada.
- I'm leaving **next Monday**. (*not* on next Monday)

E

in five minutes / in a few days / in six weeks / in two years etc.

now **in five minutes**

- Hurry! The train leaves **in five minutes**. (= it leaves five minutes from now)
- Bye! I'll see you **in a few days**. (= a few days from now)

in/at/on (places) → Units 106–107

103.1 Write at/on/in.

1 ...on... 6 June
2 ...in... the evening
3 .... half past two
4 .... Wednesday
5 1997
6 .... September
7 .... 24 September
8 .... Thursday
9 .... 11.45
10 .... Christmas Day
11 .... Christmas
12 .... the morning
13 .... Friday morning
14 .... Saturday night
15 .... night
16 .... the end of the day
17 .... the weekend
18 .... winter

103.2 Write at/on/in.

1 Bye! See you ...on... Friday.
2 Where were you .... 28 February?
3 I got up .... 8 o'clock this morning.
4 I like getting up early .... the morning.
5 My sister got married .... May.
6 Diane and I first met .... 1991.
7 Did you go out .... Tuesday?
8 Did you go out .... Tuesday evening?
9 Do you often go out .... the evening?
10 Let's meet .... 7.30 tomorrow evening.
11 I often go away .... the weekend.
12 I'm starting my new job .... 3 July.
13 We often go to the beach .... summer.
14 George isn't here .... the moment.
15 Jane's birthday is .... December.
16 Do you work .... Saturdays?
17 The company started .... 1989.
18 I like to look at the stars .... night.
19 I'll send you the money .... the end of the month.

103.3 Look at Lisa's diary for next week and complete the sentences.

1 Lisa is going to the cinema ...on Wednesday evening... .
2 She has to phone Chris ....
3 She isn't doing anything special ....
4 She's got a driving lesson ....
5 She's going to a party ....
6 She's meeting Sam ....

103.4 Write sentences with in ... .

1 It's 8.25 now. The train leaves at 8.30. ...The train leaves in five minutes....
2 It's Monday today. I'll call you on Thursday. I'll .... days.
3 Today is 14 June. My exam is on 28 June. My ....
4 It's 3 o'clock now. Tom will be here at 3.30. Tom ....

103.5 Write at/on/in if necessary. Sometimes the sentence is already complete, and no word is necessary.

1 I'm going ...on... Friday.
2 I'm going ...–... next Friday. *(already complete)*
3 I always feel tired .... the evening.
4 Will you be at home .... this evening?
5 We went to France .... last summer.
6 Laura was born .... 1990.
7 What are you doing .... the weekend?
8 I phone Robert .... every Sunday.
9 Shall we play tennis .... next Sunday?
10 I can't go to the party .... Sunday.
11 I'm going out. I'll be back .... an hour.
12 I don't often go out .... night.

Unit 104 from ... to until since for

A from ... to ...

- We lived in Japan **from** 1992 **to** 2001.
- I work **from** Monday **to** Friday.

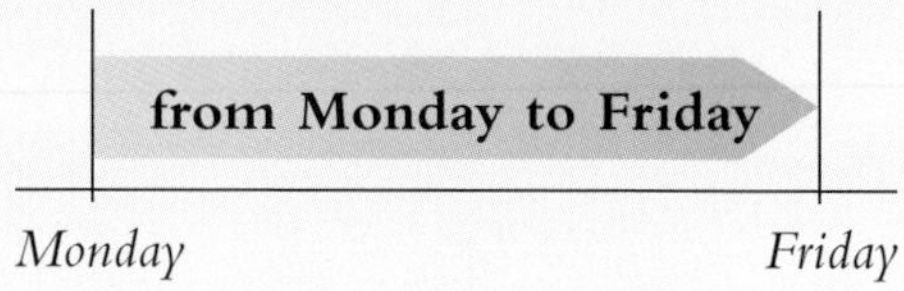

You can also say **from** ... **until** ... :

- We lived in Japan **from** 1992 **until** 2001.

B until ...

until	Friday December 3 o'clock I come back

- They're going away tomorrow. They'll be away **until Friday**.
- I went to bed early, but I wasn't tired. I read a book **until 3 o'clock**.
- Wait here **until I come back**.

You can also say **till** (= **until**):

- Wait here **till** I come back.

Compare:

- '**How long** will you be away?' '**Until** Monday.'
- '**When** are you coming back?' '**On** Monday.'

C since + a time in the past (to now)

We use **since** after the *present perfect* (**have been** / **have done** etc.):

since	Monday 1998 2.30 I arrived

- Joe is in hospital. He has been in hospital **since Monday**. (= from Monday to now)
- Sue and Dave have been married **since 1968**. (= from 1968 to now)
- It has been raining **since I arrived**.

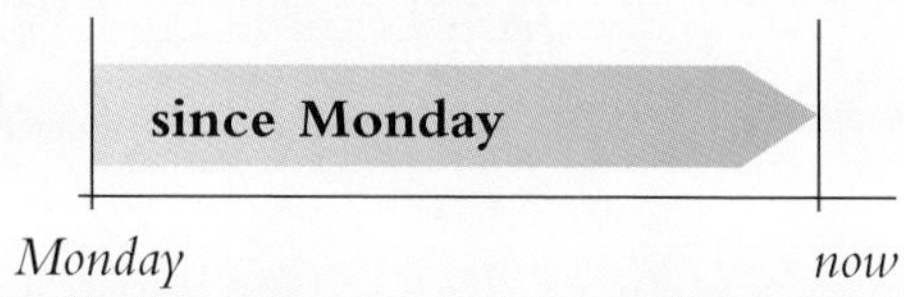

Compare:

- We lived in Japan **from** 1992 **to** 2001.
  We lived in Japan **until** 2001.
- Now we live in Canada. We came to Canada **in** 2001.
  We have lived in Canada **since** 2001. (= from 2001 until now)

We use **for** (*not* **since**) + a period of time (**three days** / **ten years** etc.):

- Joe has been in hospital **for three days**. (*not* since three days)

D for + a period of time

for	three days ten years five minutes a long time

- Gary stayed with us **for three days**.
- I'm going away **for a few weeks**.
- I'm going away **for the weekend**.
- They've been married **for ten years**.

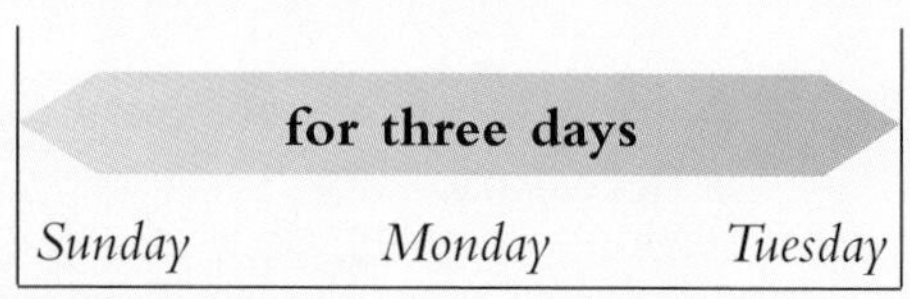

present perfect + **for/since** → Units 18–19 present perfect (**I have lived**) and past simple (**I lived**) → Unit 20

Exercises

104.1 Read the information and complete the sentences. Use from ... to / until / since.

1 (Alex / Canada / 1991 → 1999) Alex lived *in Canada from 1991 to 1999* .
2 (Alex / Canada / → 1999) Alex lived in Canada .... 1999.
3 (Alex / England / 1999 →) Alex has lived in England ....
4 (Karen / France / → 2003) Karen lived in ....
5 (Karen / Switzerland / 2003 →) Karen has lived in ....
6 (Clare / a hotel / 1998–2001) Clare worked .... 1998 ....
7 (Clare / a restaurant / 2001 →) Clare has worked ....
8 (Adam / a teacher / 1992–1998) Adam was a ....
9 (Adam / a journalist / 1998 →) Adam has been ....

Now write sentences with for.

10 (Alex / Canada) *Alex lived in Canada for eight years* .
11 (Alex / England) Alex has lived in England ....
12 (Karen / Switzerland) Karen has ....
13 (Clare / a hotel) Clare worked ....
14 (Clare / restaurant) Clare ....
15 (Adam / a teacher) Adam ....
16 (Adam / a journalist) Adam ....

104.2 Write until/since/for.

1 Sue and Dave have been married *since* 1968.
2 I was tired this morning. I stayed in bed .... 10 o'clock.
3 We waited for Sue .... half an hour, but she didn't come.
4 'Have you just arrived?' 'No, I've been here .... half past seven.'
5 'How long did you stay at the party last night?' '.......... midnight.'
6 Dan and I are good friends. We have known each other .... ten years.
7 I'm tired. I'm going to lie down .... a few minutes.
8 Don't open the door of the train .... the train stops.
9 This is my house. I've lived here .... I was seven years old.
10 Jack has gone away. He'll be away .... Wednesday.
11 Next week I'm going to Paris .... three days.
12 I usually finish work at 5.30, but sometimes I work .... six.
13 'How long have you known Anna?' '.......... we were at school together.'
14 Where have you been? I've been waiting for you .... twenty minutes.

Unit 105 before after during while

A before, during and after

before the film

during the film

after the film

- Everybody feels nervous **before exams**.
- I fell asleep **during the film**.
- We were tired **after our visit** to the museum.

B before, while and after

before we played

while we were playing

after we played

- Don't forget to close the window **before you go out**.
- I often fall asleep **while I'm reading**.
- They went home **after they did the shopping**.

C during, while and for

We use **during** + *noun* (during **the film**). We use **while** + *verb* (while **I'm reading**):

- We didn't speak **during the meal**.

but We didn't speak **while we were eating**. (*not* during we were eating)

Use **for** (*not* during) + *a period of time* (**three days** / **two hours** / **a year** etc.):

- We played tennis **for two hours**. (*not* during two hours)
- I lived in London **for a year**. (*not* during a year)

D

You can use **before/after** + **-ing** (**before going** / **after eating** etc.):

- I always have breakfast **before going** to work. (= before I go to work)
- **After doing** the shopping, they went home. (= after they did)

Remember we say **before going** (*not* before to go), **after doing** (*not* after to do) etc. :

- **Before eating** the apple, I washed it carefully. (*not* before to eat)
- I started work **after reading** the newspaper. (*not* after to read)

past continuous (I was -ing) → Units 13–14 before/after/while/when → Unit 98 for → Unit 104
prepositions + -ing → Unit 112

Exercises

105.1 Complete the sentences. Choose from the boxes.

after	during
before	while

+

lunch	the end	they went to Australia
the concert	~~the exam~~	you're waiting
the course	the night	

1 Everybody was nervous ...before the exam... .
2 I usually work four hours in the morning, and another three hours ....
3 The film was really boring. We left ....
4 Anna went to evening classes to learn German. She learnt a lot ....
5 My aunt and uncle lived in London ....
6 A: Somebody broke a window .... Did you hear anything?
B: No, I was asleep all the time.
7 Would you like to sit down .... ?
8 'Are you going home .... ?' 'Yes, I have to get up early tomorrow.'

105.2 Write **during/while/for.**

1 We didn't speak ...while... we were eating.
2 We didn't speak ...during... the meal.
3 Gary called .... you were out.
4 I stayed in Rome .... five days.
5 Sally didn't read any newspapers .... she was on holiday.
6 The students looked very bored .... the lesson.
7 I fell out of bed .... I was asleep.
8 Last night I watched TV .... three hours.
9 I don't usually watch TV .... the day.
10 Do you ever watch TV .... you are having dinner?

105.3 Complete the sentences. Use **-ing (doing, having** etc.).

1 After ...doing... the shopping, they went home.
2 I felt sick after .... too much chocolate.
3 I'm going to ask you a question. Think carefully before .... it.
4 I felt awful when I got up this morning. I felt better after .... a shower.
5 After .... my work, I left the office and went home.
6 Before .... to a foreign country, you should try and learn a little of the language.

105.4 Write sentences with **before + -ing** and **after + -ing.**

1 They did the shopping. Then they went home.
After ...doing the shopping, they went home.

2 John left school. Then he worked in a bookshop for two years.
John worked ....

3 I read for a few minutes. Then I went to sleep.
Before ....

4 We walked for three hours. We were very tired.
After ....

5 Let's have a cup of coffee. Then we'll go out.
Let's ....

in at on (places 1)

A in

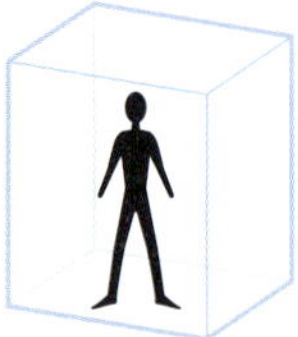

in a room
in a shop
in a car
in the water

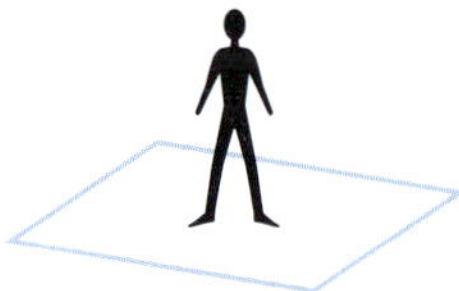

in a garden
in a town
in the city centre
in Brazil

- 'Where's David?' '**In the kitchen.** / **In the garden.** / **In London.**'
- What's **in that box** / **in that bag** / **in that cupboard**?
- Rachel works **in a shop** / **in a bank** / **in a factory**.
- I went for a swim **in the river** / **in the pool** / **in the sea**.
- Milan is **in the north of Italy**. Naples is **in the south**.
- I live **in a big city**, but I'd like to live in the country.

B at

at the bus stop

at the door

at the traffic lights

at her desk

- There's somebody **at the bus stop** / **at the door**.
- The car is waiting **at the traffic lights**.
- Jane is working **at her desk**.

at the top / **at the bottom** / **at the end** (of ...):

- Write your name **at the top of the page**.
- My house is **at the end of the street**.

at the top (of the page)

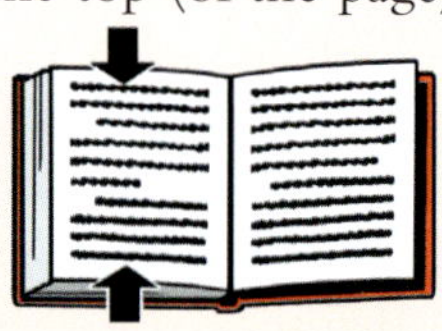

at the bottom (of the page)

C on

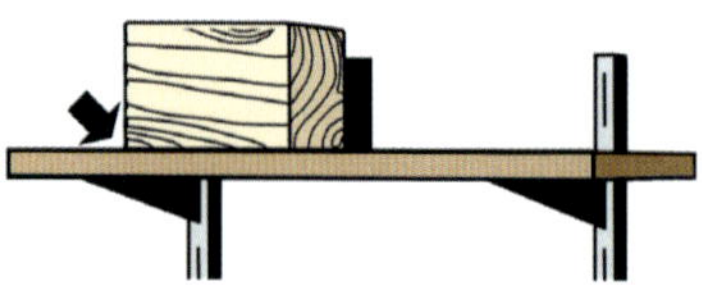

on a shelf
on a plate
on a balcony
on the floor
etc.

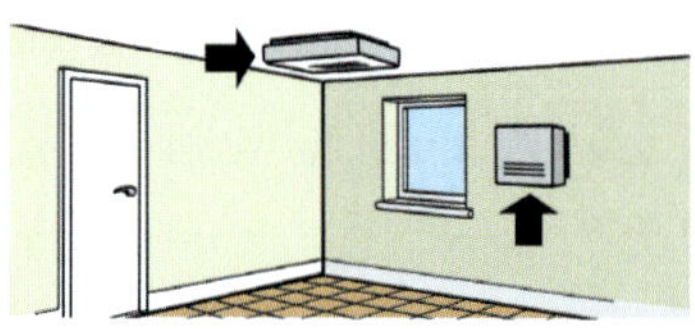

on a wall
on a door
on the ceiling
etc.

- There are some books **on the shelf** and some pictures **on the wall**.
- There are a lot of apples **on those trees**.
- Don't sit **on the grass**. It's wet.
- There is a stamp **on the envelope**.

on a horse / **on a bicycle** / **on a motorbike**:

- Who is that man **on the motorbike**?

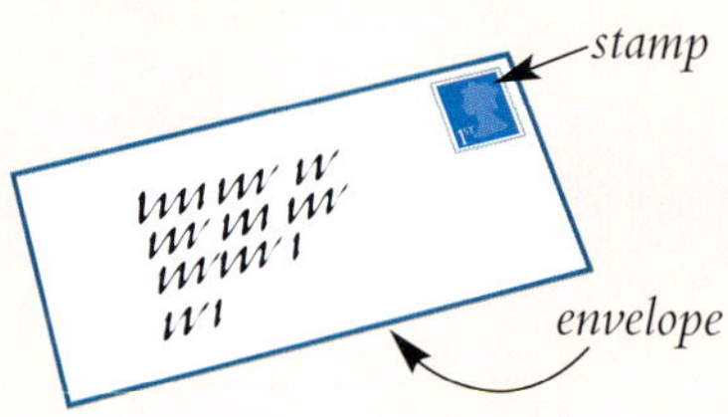

the top / **the bottom** etc. → Unit 70 **at/on/in** (time) → Unit 103 **in/at/on** (places 2) → Unit 107

106.1 Look at the pictures and answer the questions. Use in/at/on.

1 (the kitchen)

2 (the box)

3 (the box)

4 (the wall)

5 (the bus stop)

6 (the field)

7 (the balcony)

8 (the pool)

9 (the window)

10 (the ceiling)

11 (the table)

12 (the table)

1 Where is he? *In the kitchen.*
2 Where are the shoes? ....
3 Where is the pen? ....
4 Where is the clock? ....
5 Where is the bus? ....
6 Where are the horses? ....
7 Where are they standing? ....
8 Where is she swimming? ....
9 Where is he standing? ....
10 Where is the spider? ....
11 Where is he sitting? ....
12 Where is she sitting? ....

106.2 Write in/at/on.

1 Don't sit *on* the grass. It's wet.
2 What have you got .... your bag?
3 Look! There's a man .... the roof. What's he doing?
4 There are a lot of fish .... this river.
5 Our house is number 45 – the number is .... the door.
6 'Is the post office near here?' 'Yes, turn left .... the traffic lights.'
7 It's difficult to park .... the centre of town. It's better to take the bus.
8 My sister lives .... Brussels.
9 There's a small park .... the top of the hill.
10 I think I heard the doorbell. There's somebody .... the door.
11 Munich is a large city .... the south of Germany.
12 There are a few shops .... the end of the street.
13 It's difficult to carry a lot of things .... a bicycle.
14 I looked at the list of names. My name was .... the bottom.
15 There is a mirror .... the wall .... the living room.

in at on (places 2)

A in

- **in** bed
- **in** hospital
- **in** the sky
- **in** the world
- **in** a newspaper / **in** a book
- **in** a photograph / **in** a picture
- **in** a car / **in** a taxi
- **in** the middle (of ...)

□ 'Where's Kate?' 'She's **in bed**.'
□ David's father is ill. He's **in hospital**.
□ I like to look at the stars **in the sky** at night.
□ What's the largest city **in the world**?
□ I read about the accident **in the newspaper**.
□ You look sad **in this photograph**.
□ Did you come here **in your car**?
□ There's a big tree **in the middle** of the garden.

B at

- **at** home
- **at** work / **at** school
- **at** university / **at** college
- **at** the station / **at** the airport
- **at** Jane's (house) / **at** my sister's (house) / **at** the doctor's / **at** the hairdresser's etc.
- **at** a concert / **at** a party / **at** a football match etc.

□ Will you be **at home** this evening?
□ 'Where's Kate?' 'She's **at work**.'
□ Helen is studying law **at university**.
□ I'll meet you **at the station**, OK?
□ A: Where were you yesterday?
B: **At my sister's**.
□ I saw Tom **at the doctor's**.
□ There weren't many people **at the party**.

Often it is possible to use **in** or **at** for buildings (hotels, restaurants etc.):
□ We stayed **at** a nice hotel. *or* We stayed **in** a nice hotel.

C on

on a bus

on the first floor

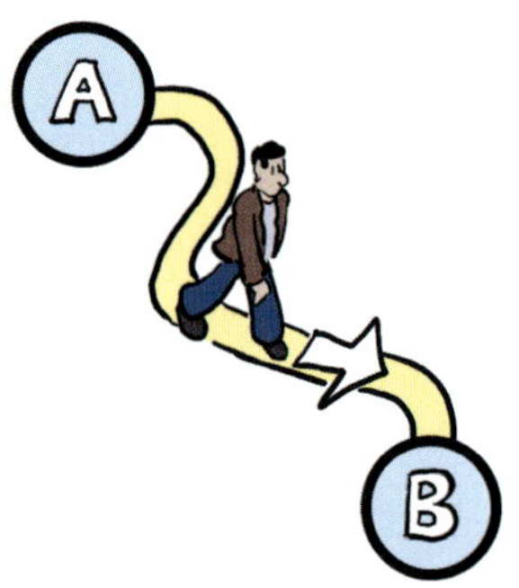

on the way from A to B

- **on** a bus / **on** a train / **on** a plane / **on** a ship
- **on** the ground floor / **on** the first floor etc.
- **on** the way (to ...) / **on** the way home

□ Did you come here **on the bus**?
□ The office is **on the first floor**.
(*not* in the first floor)
□ I met Ann **on the way** to work / **on the way** home.

in/at/on (places 1) → Unit 106 to/in/at → Unit 108 on the left/right → Unit 109

107.1 Look at the pictures and answer the questions. Use in/at/on.

1 (hospital)

2 (the airport)

3 (bed)

4 (a ship)

5 (the sky)

6 (a party)

7 (the doctor's)

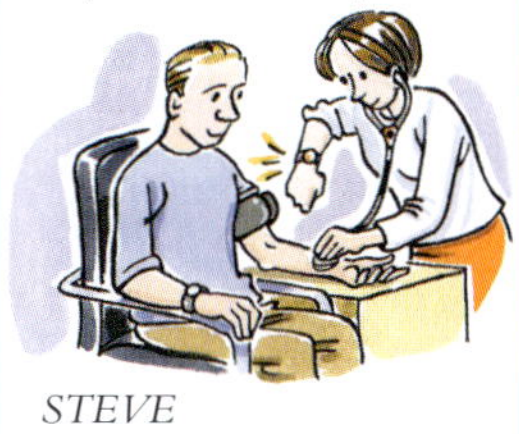

8 (the second floor)

9 (work)

10 (a plane)

11 (a taxi)

12 (a wedding)

1 Where is she? In hospital.
2 Where are they? ....
3 Where is he? ....
4 Where are they? ....
5 Where are the stars? ....
6 Where are they? ....
7 Where is Steve? ....
8 Where is the restaurant? ....
9 Where is she? ....
10 Where are they? ....
11 Where are they? ....
12 Where are they? ....

107.2 Write in/at/on.

1 Helen is studying law at university.
2 There was a big table .... the middle of the room.
3 What is the longest river .... the world?
4 Were there many people .... the concert last night?
5 Will you be .... home tomorrow afternoon?
6 Who is the man .... this photograph? Do you know him?
7 Where are your children? Are they .... school?
8 Gary is coming by train. I'm going to meet him .... the station.
9 Charlie is .... hospital. He had an operation yesterday.
10 How many pages are there .... this book?
11 'Are you hungry after your journey?' 'No, I had something to eat .... the train.'
12 I'm sorry I'm late. My car broke down .... the way here.
13 'Is Tom here?' 'No, he's .... his brother's.'
14 Don't believe everything you see .... the newspaper!
15 I walked to work, but I came home .... the bus.

to in at (places 3)

A

to

go/come/return/walk (etc.) **to** …

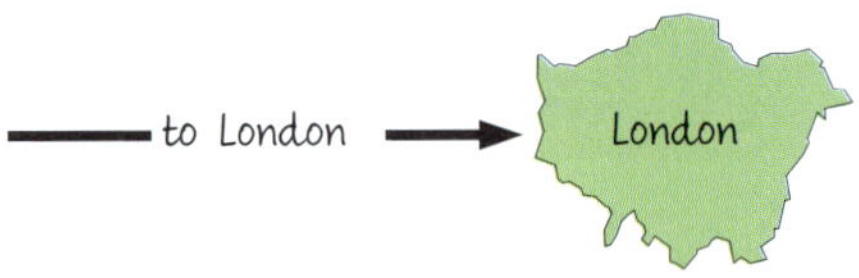

- We're **going to London** on Sunday.
- I want to **go to Italy** next year.
- We **walked** from my house **to the centre of town**.
- What time do you **go to bed**?

- The bus is **going to the airport**.
- Karen didn't **go to work** yesterday.
- I **went to a party** last night.
- You must **come to our house**.

in/at (→ Units 106–107)

be/stay/do something (etc.) **in** …

- Piccadilly Circus **is in London**.
- My brother **lives in Italy**.
- The main shops **are in the centre of town**.
- I like **reading in bed**.

be/stay/do something (etc.) **at** …

- The bus **is at the airport**.
- Sarah **wasn't at work** yesterday.
- I **met a lot of people at the party**.
- Helen **stayed at her brother's house**.

B

home

go/come/walk (etc.) **home** (*without* **to**):

- I'm tired. I'm **going home**.
  (*not* to home)
- Did you **walk home**?

be/stay/do something (etc.) **at home**:

- I'm **staying at home** tonight.
- Dan doesn't go to an office. He **works at home**.

C

arrive and **get**

arrive in a country or town (**arrive in Italy** / **arrive in Paris** etc.):

- They **arrived in England** last week. (*not* arrived to England)

arrive at other places (**arrive at the station** / **arrive at work** etc.):

- What time did you **arrive at the hotel**? (*not* arrive to the hotel)

get to (**a place**):

- What time did you **get to the hotel**?
- What time did you **get to Paris**?

get home / **arrive home** (no preposition):

- I was tired when **I got home**. *or* I was tired when I **arrived home**.

been to → Unit 17 get (to …) → Unit 56 in/at → Units 106–107

Exercises

108.1 Write to or in.

1 I like reading ..*in*.. bed.
2 We're going .... Italy next month.
3 Sue is on holiday .... Italy at the moment.
4 I have to go .... the bank today.
5 I was tired, so I stayed .... bed late.
6 What time do you usually go .... bed?
7 Does this bus go .... the centre?
8 Would you like to live .... another country?

108.2 Write to or at if necessary. One sentence is already complete, and no word is necessary.

1 Paula didn't go ..*to*.. work yesterday.
2 I'm tired. I'm going ..*–*.. home. *(already complete)*
3 Tina is not very well. She has gone .... the doctor.
4 Would you like to come .... a party on Saturday?
5 'Is Liz .... home?' 'No, she's gone .... work.'
6 There were 20,000 people .... the football match.
7 Why did you go .... home early last night?
8 A boy jumped into the river and swam .... the other side.
9 There were a lot of people waiting .... the bus stop.
10 We had a good meal .... a restaurant, and then we went back .... the hotel.

108.3 Write to, at or in if necessary. One sentence is already complete, and no word is necessary.

1 I'm not going out this afternoon. I'm staying ..*at*.. home.
2 We're going .... a concert tomorrow evening.
3 I went .... New York last year.
4 How long did you stay .... New York?
5 Next year we hope to go .... Canada to visit some friends.
6 Do you want to go .... the cinema this evening?
7 Did you park your car .... the station?
8 After the accident three people were taken .... hospital.
9 How often do you go .... the dentist?
10 'Is Sarah here?' 'No, she's .... Helen's.'
11 My house is .... the end of the street on the left.
12 I went .... Maria's house, but she wasn't .... home.
13 There were no taxis, so we had to walk .... home.
14 'Who did you meet .... the party?' 'I didn't go .... the party.'

108.4 Write to, at or in if necessary. Sometimes the sentence is already complete, and no word is necessary.

1 What time do you usually get .... work?
2 What time do you usually get .... home?
3 What time did you arrive .... the party?
4 When did you arrive .... London?
5 What time does the train get .... Paris?
6 We arrived .... home very late.

108.5 Complete these sentences about yourself. Use to/in/at.

1 At three o'clock this morning I was ..*in bed*.......... .
2 Yesterday I went ....
3 At 11 o'clock yesterday morning I was ....
4 One day I'd like to go ....
5 I don't like going ....
6 At 9 o'clock yesterday evening I was ....

Unit 109 under, behind, opposite etc.

A next to / beside / between / in front of / behind

A is **next to** B. *or* A is **beside** B.
B is **between** A and C.
D is **in front of** B.
E is **behind** B.

also
A is **on the left**.
C is **on the right**.
B is **in the middle** (of the group).

B opposite / in front of

A is sitting **in front of** B.
A is sitting **opposite** C.
C is sitting **opposite** A.

C by (= next to / beside)

by the window

- Our house is **by the sea**. (= beside the sea)
- Who is that man standing **by the window**?
- If you feel cold, why don't you sit **by the fire**?

D under

under the table

under a tree

- The cat is **under the table**.
- The girl is standing **under a tree**.
- I'm wearing a jacket **under my coat**.

E above and below

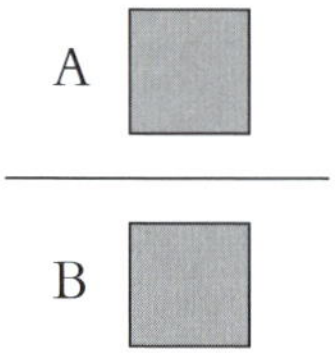

A is **above the line**.
(= higher than the line)

B is **below the line**.
(= lower than the line)

The pictures are **above the shelves**.

The shelves are **below the pictures**.

up/over/through etc. → Unit 110 by → Unit 111

109.1 Where are the people in the picture? Complete the sentences.

1 Colin is standing ....behind.... Frank.
2 Frank is sitting .... Emma.
3 Emma is sitting .... Barbara.
4 Emma is sitting .... Donna and Frank.
5 Donna is sitting .... Emma.
6 Frank is sitting .... Colin.
7 Alan is standing .... Donna.
8 Alan is standing .... left.
9 Barbara is standing .... middle.

109.2 Look at the pictures and complete the sentences.

1 The cat is ....under.... the table.
2 There is a big tree .... the house.
3 The plane is flying .... the clouds.
4 She is standing .... the piano.
5 The cinema is .... the right.
6 She's sitting .... the phone.
7 The switch is .... the window.
8 The cupboard is .... the sink.
9 There are some shoes .... the bed.
10 The plant is .... the piano.
11 Paul is sitting .... Fiona.
12 In Britain people drive .... the left.

109.3 Write sentences about the picture.

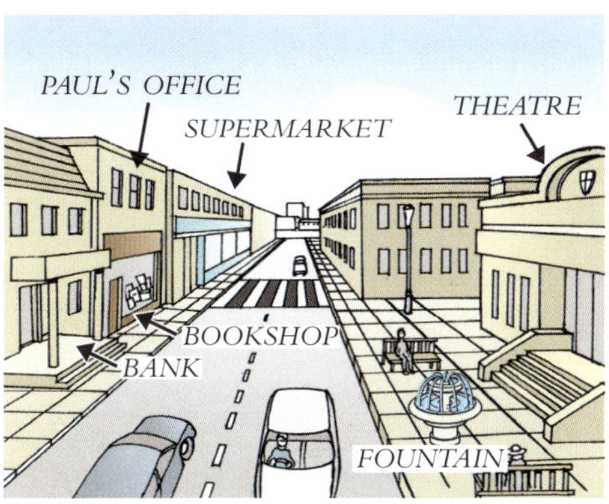

1 (next to) ....The bank is next to the bookshop.
2 (in front of) The .... in front of ....
3 (opposite) ....
4 (next to) ....
5 (above) ....
6 (between) ....

Unit 110

up, over, through etc.

- Jane is going **to** France next week.
- We walked **from** the hotel **to** the station.
- A lot of English words come **from** Latin.

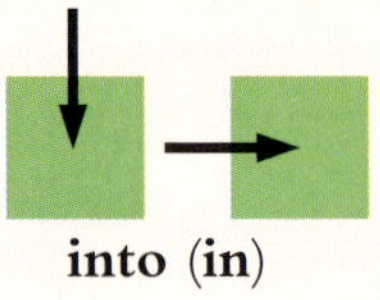

- We jumped **into** the water.
- A man came **out of** the house and got **into** a car.
- Why are you looking **out of** the window?
- I took the old batteries **out of** the radio.

We say **put** something **in** ... (*not usually* into):
- I **put** new batteries **in** the radio.

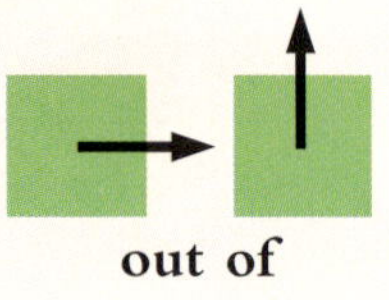

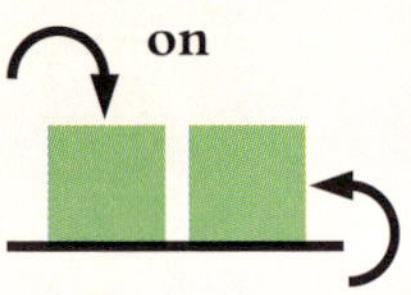

- Don't put your feet **on** the table.
- Please take your feet **off** the table.
- I'm going to hang some pictures **on** the wall.
- Be careful! Don't fall **off** your bicycle.
- We got **on** the bus in Princes Street.

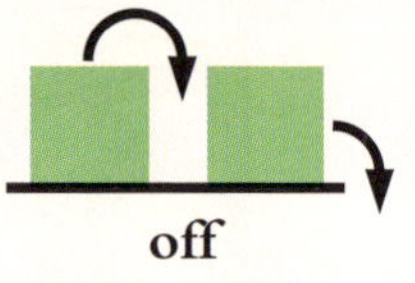

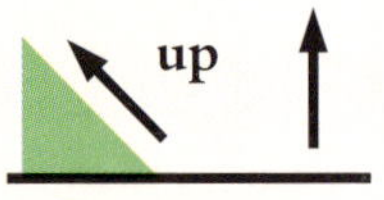

- We walked **up** the hill to the house.
- Be careful! Don't fall **down** the stairs.

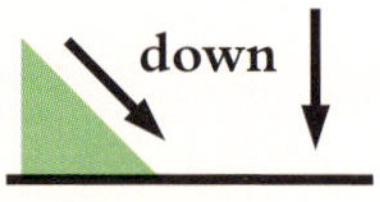

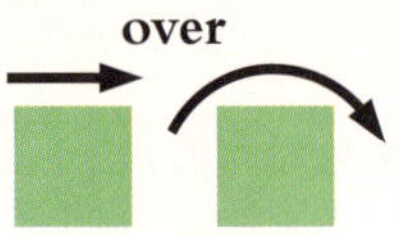

- The plane flew **over** the mountains.
- I jumped **over** the wall into the garden.
- Some people say it is unlucky to walk **under** a ladder.

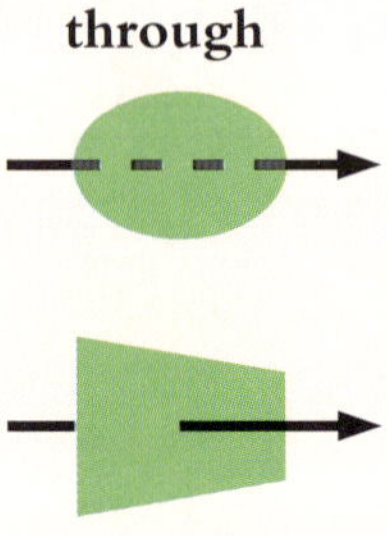

- A bird flew into the room **through** a window.
- The old road goes **through** the village.
- The new road goes **round** the village.
- The bus stop is just **round** the corner.
- I walked **round** the town and took some photographs.

You can also use **around** (= round):
- We walked **around** the town.

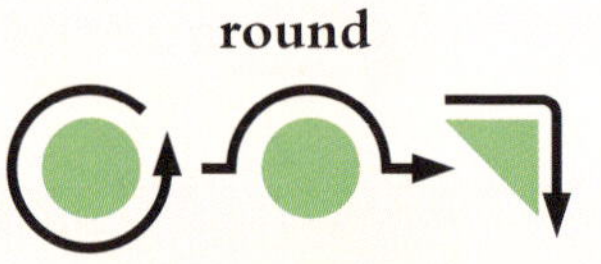

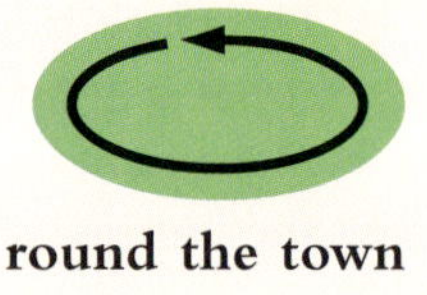

- I was walking **along** the road with my dog.
- Let's go for a walk **along** the river.
- The dog swam **across** the river.

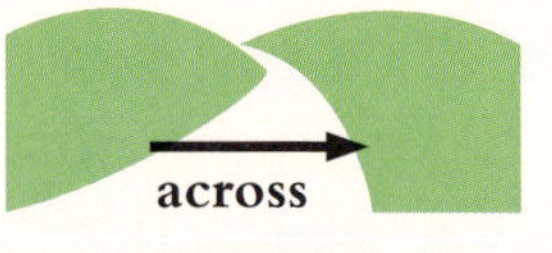

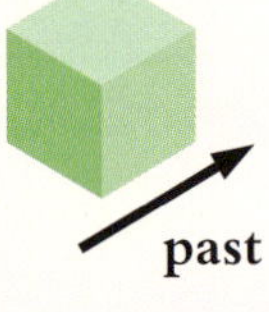

- They walked **past** me without speaking.
- A: Excuse me, how do I get to the hospital?
  B: Go along this road, **past** the cinema, under the bridge and the hospital is on the left.

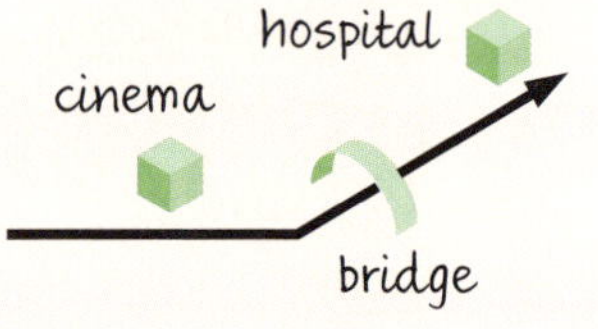

get in/on etc. → Unit 56 in/on → Units 106–107 to → Unit 108 fall off / run away etc. → Unit 114

110.1 Somebody asks you how to get to a place. You say which way to go. Look at the pictures and write sentences beginning **Go ...** .

110.2 Look at the pictures and complete the sentences.

1 The dog swam *across* the river.
2 A book fell ...... the shelf.
3 A plane flew ...... the village.
4 A woman got ...... the car.
5 A girl ran ...... the road.
6 Suddenly a car came ...... the corner.
7 They drove ...... the village.
8 They got ...... the train.
9 The moon travels ...... the earth.
10 They got ...... the house ...... a window.

110.3 Complete the sentences. Use **over/from/into** etc.

1 I looked ...... the window and watched the people in the street.
2 My house is very near here. It's just ...... the corner.
3 'Where's my phone?' 'You put it ...... your bag.'
4 How far is it ...... here ...... the airport?
5 We walked ...... the museum for an hour and saw a lot of interesting things.
6 You can put your coat ...... the back of the chair.
7 In tennis, you have to hit the ball ...... the net.
8 Silvia took a key ...... her bag and opened the door.

on at by with about

A on

on holiday
on television
on the radio
on the phone
on fire
on time (= not late)

- □ Jane isn't at work this week. She's **on holiday**.
- □ We watched the news **on television**.
- □ We listened to the news **on the radio**.
- □ I spoke to Rachel **on the phone** last night.
- □ The house is **on fire**! Call the fire brigade.
- □ 'Was the train late?' 'No, it was **on time**.'

B at

at (**the age of**) **21** / **at 50 kilometres an hour** / **at 100 degrees** etc. :

- □ Lisa got married **at 21**. (*or* … **at the age of 21**.)
- □ A car uses more petrol **at 120 kilometres an hour** than **at 90**.
- □ Water boils **at 100 degrees Celsius**.

C by

by bus

by car / **by bus** / **by plane** / **by bike** etc. :

- □ Do you like travelling **by train**?
- □ Jane usually goes to work **by bike**.

but **on foot**:

- □ You can't get there **by car**. You have to go **on foot**. (= you have to walk)

a book **by** … / a painting **by** … / a piece of music **by** … etc. :

- □ Have you read any books **by Charles Dickens**?
- □ **Who** is that painting **by**? Picasso?

the title
by
the writer

by after the passive (→ Unit 21):

- □ I was bitten **by a dog**.

D with/without

- □ Did you stay at a hotel or **with friends**?
- □ Wait for me. Please don't go **without me**.
- □ Do you like your coffee **with** or **without milk**?
- □ I cut the paper **with a pair of scissors**.

a man **with** a beard / a woman **with** glasses etc. :

- □ Do you know that man **with the beard**?
- □ I'd like to have a house **with a big garden**.

a man **with** a beard

a woman **with** glasses

E about

talk/speak/think/hear/know about … :

- □ Some people **talk about their work** all the time.
- □ I don't **know** much **about cars**.

a book / **a question** / **a programme** / **information** (etc.) **about** … :

- □ There was **a programme about** volcanoes on TV last night. Did you see it?

by → Units 21, 63, 109 at/on → Units 103, 106–107 preposition + -ing → Unit 112

Exercises

111.1 Complete the sentences. Use on + these words:

holiday **the phone** ~~**the radio**~~ **television** **time**

1 We heard the news ....on the radio.... .
2 Please don't be late. Try to be here ....
3 I won't be here next week. I'm going ....
4 'Did you see Linda?' 'No, but I talked to her ....'
5 'What's .... this evening?' 'Nothing that I want to watch.'

111.2 Look at the pictures. Complete the sentences with at/by/with etc.

1 I cut the paper ....with.... a pair of scissors.
2 She usually goes to work .... car.
3 Who is the woman .... short hair?
4 They are talking .... the weather.
5 The car is .... fire.
6 She's listening to some music .... Mozart.
7 The plane is flying .... 600 miles an hour.
8 They're .... holiday.
9 Do you know the man .... sunglasses?
10 He's reading a book .... grammar .... Vera P. Bull.

111.3 Complete the sentences. Use at/by/with etc.

1 In tennis, you hit the ball .... a racket.
2 It's cold today. Don't go out .... a coat.
3 *Hamlet*, *Othello* and *Macbeth* are plays .... William Shakespeare.
4 Do you know anything .... computers?
5 My grandmother died .... the age of 98.
6 How long does it take from New York to Los Angeles .... plane?
7 I didn't go to the football match, but I watched it .... television.
8 My house is the one .... the red door on the right.
9 These trains are very fast. They can travel .... very high speeds.
10 I don't use my car very often. I prefer to go .... bike.
11 Can you give me some information .... hotels in this town?
12 I was arrested .... two policemen and taken to the police station.
13 The buses here are very good. They're nearly always .... time.
14 What would you like to drink .... your meal?
15 We travelled from Paris to Moscow .... train.
16 The museum has some paintings .... Rembrandt.

Unit 112 afraid of ... , good at ... etc. of/at/for etc. (prepositions) + -ing

A

afraid of ... / **good at** ... etc. *(adjective + preposition)*

afraid of ...	□ Are you **afraid of** dogs?
angry with somebody	□ Why are you **angry with** me? What have I done?
angry about something	□ Are you **angry about** last night? (= something that happened last night)
different from ... *or* **different to** ...	□ Lisa is very **different from** (*or* **to**) her sister.
fed up with ...	□ I'm **fed up with** my job. I want to do something different. (= I've had enough of my job)
full of ...	□ The room was **full of people**.
good at ...	□ Are you **good at** maths?
interested in ...	□ I'm not **interested in** sport.
married to ...	□ Sue is **married to** a dentist. (= her husband is a dentist)
nice/**kind of** somebody to ...	□ It was **kind of** you to help us. Thank you very much.
be **nice**/**kind to** somebody	□ David is very friendly. He's always very **nice to** me.
sorry about a situation	□ I'm afraid I can't help you. I'm **sorry about** that.
sorry for/**about** doing something	□ I'm **sorry for**/**about** not phoning you yesterday. (*or* I'm sorry I didn't phone you)
be/feel **sorry for** somebody	□ I feel **sorry for** them. They are in a very difficult situation.

B

of/**at**/**for** (etc.) + **-ing**

After a preposition (**of**/**at**/**for** etc.), a verb ends in **-ing**:

I'm not very good **at**	**telling**	stories.
Are you fed up **with**	**doing**	the same thing every day?
I'm sorry **for**	not **phoning**	you yesterday.
Thank you **for**	**helping**	me.
Mark is thinking **of**	**buying**	a new car.
Tom left **without**	**saying**	goodbye. (= he didn't say goodbye)
After	**doing**	the shopping, they went home.

before/after -ing → Unit 105 think about/of → Unit 113

Exercises

112.1 Look at the pictures and complete the sentences with **of/with/in** etc.

1 He's afraid ......of...... dogs.
2 She's interested .... science.
3 She's married .... a footballer.
4 She's very good .... languages.
5 He's fed up .... the weather.
6 A: Can I help you?
B: Thanks, that's very kind .... you.

112.2 Complete the sentences with **in/of/with** etc.

1 I'm not interested ......in...... sport.
2 I'm not very good .... sport.
3 I like Sarah. She's always very kind .... me.
4 I'm sorry .... your broken window. It was an accident.
5 He's very brave. He isn't afraid .... anything.
6 It was very nice .... Jane to let us stay in her apartment.
7 Life today is very different .... life 50 years ago.
8 Are you interested .... politics?
9 I feel sorry .... her, but I can't help her.
10 Chris was angry .... what happened.
11 These boxes are very heavy. They are full .... books.
12 I'm sorry .... getting angry .... you yesterday.

112.3 Complete the sentences.

1 I'm not very ......good at telling...... stories. (good/tell)
2 I wanted to go to the cinema, but Paula wasn't .... (interested/go)
3 Sue isn't very .... up in the morning. (good/get)
4 Let's go! I'm .... (fed up / wait)
5 I'm .... you up in the middle of the night. (sorry/wake)
6 Sorry I'm late! .... (thank you / wait)

112.4 Complete the sentences. Use **without -ing**.

1 (Tom left / he didn't say goodbye) ......Tom left without saying goodbye......
2 (Sue walked past me / she didn't speak)
Sue walked ....
3 (don't do anything / ask me first)
Don't ....
4 (I went out / I didn't lock the door)
I ....

112.5 Write sentences about yourself.

1 (interested) ......I'm interested in sport......
2 (afraid) I'm ....
3 (not very good) I'm not ....
4 (not interested) ....
5 (fed up) ....

Unit 113

listen to ... , look at ... etc. (verb + preposition)

A

ask (somebody) **for** ...	□ A man stopped me and **asked** me **for** money.
belong to ...	□ Does this book **belong to** you? (= Is this your book?)
happen to ...	□ I can't find my pen. What's **happened to** it?
listen to ...	□ **Listen to** this music. It's great.
speak/talk to somebody **about** something	□ Did you **talk to** Paul **about** the problem? □ *(on the phone)* Can I **speak to** Chris, please?
thank somebody **for** ...	□ **Thank** you very much **for** your help.
think about ... *or* **think of** ...	□ He never **thinks about** (*or* **of**) other people. □ Mark is **thinking of** (*or* **about**) buying a new computer.
wait for ...	□ **Wait for** me. I'm nearly ready.
write to somebody	□ I couldn't contact the company by phone. I had to **write to** them.
but **phone/call** somebody (*without* to)	□ I'm going to **phone** my parents this evening. (*not* phone to my parents)

B

look at / look for / look after

look at ...

□ He's **looking at** his watch.
□ **Look at** these flowers! They're beautiful.
□ Why are you **looking at** me like that?

look for ...
(= try to find)

□ She's lost her key. She's **looking for** it.
□ I'm **looking for** Sarah. Have you seen her?

look after ...
(= take care of, keep safe)

□ When Emily is at work, a friend of hers **looks after** her children.
□ Don't lose this book. **Look after** it. (= Keep it safe.)

C

depend

We say **depend on** ... :

□ A: Do you like eating in restaurants?
B: Sometimes. It **depends on** the restaurant. (*not* it depends of)

You can say **it depends what/where/how** (etc.) with or without **on**:

□ A: Do you want to come out with us?
B: It **depends where** you're going. *or* It **depends on where** you're going.

wait → Unit 54 preposition + -ing → Unit 112

113.1 Look at the pictures and complete the sentences with to/for/at etc.

1 She's looking ....at.... her watch.
2 He's listening .... the radio.
3 They're waiting .... a taxi.
4 Paul is talking .... Jane.
5 They're looking .... a picture.
6 Sue is looking .... Tom.

113.2 Complete the sentences with to/for/about etc. One sentence is already complete, and no word is necessary.

1 Thank you very much ....for.... your help.
2 This isn't my umbrella. It belongs .... a friend of mine.
3 *(on the phone)* Can I speak .... Steven Davis, please?
4 *(on the phone)* Thank you .... calling. Goodbye.
5 What happened .... Ella last night? Why didn't she come to the party?
6 We're thinking .... going to Australia next year.
7 We asked the waiter .... coffee, but he brought us tea.
8 'Do you like reading books?' 'It depends .... the book.'
9 John was talking, but nobody was listening .... what he was saying.
10 We waited .... Karen until 2 o'clock, but she didn't come.
11 If you want to contact me, you can write .... me at this address.
12 Don't forget to phone .... your mother tonight.
13 He's alone all day. He never talks .... anybody.
14 'How much does it cost to stay at this hotel?' 'It depends .... the type of room.'
15 Catherine is thinking .... changing her job.

113.3 Complete these sentences. Use at/for/after.

1 I looked .... the newspaper, but I didn't read it carefully.
2 When you are ill, you need somebody to look .... you.
3 Excuse me, I'm looking .... Hill Street. Can you tell me where it is?
4 Goodbye! Have a great holiday and look .... yourself.
5 I want to take a photograph of you. Please look .... the camera and smile.
6 Barry is looking .... a job. He wants to work in a hotel.

113.4 Answer these questions with It depends ... .

1 Do you want to go out with us? — It depends where you're going.
2 Do you like eating in restaurants? — It depends on the restaurant.
3 Do you enjoy watching TV? — It depends ....
4 Can you do something for me? — It ....
5 Are you going away this weekend? — ....
6 Can you lend me some money? — ....

go in, fall off, run away etc. (phrasal verbs 1)

A *phrasal verb* is a verb (**go/look/be** etc.) + **in/out/up/down** etc.

in

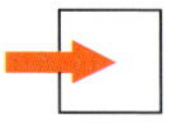

- I waited outside the shop. I didn't **go in**.
- Sarah opened the door of the car and **got in**. (= **into** the car)

out

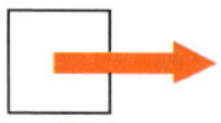

- I went to the window and **looked out**.
- The car stopped and a woman **got out**. (= **out of** the car)

on

- The bus came, and I **got on**.

off

- Be careful! Don't **fall off**.

up

- He **stood up** and left the room.
- I usually **get up** early. (= get out of bed)
- We **looked up** at the stars in the sky.

down

- The picture **fell down**.
- Would you like to **sit down**?
- **Lie down** on the floor.

away *or* **off**

- The thief **ran away**. (*or* … **ran off**)
- Emma got into the car and **drove away**. (*or* … **drove off**)

be/go away (= in/to another place)

- Tim has **gone away** for a few days.

back

- Go away and don't **come back**!
- We went out for dinner and then **went back** to our hotel.

be back

- Tim is away. He'll **be back** on Monday.

over

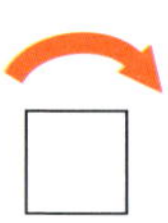

- The wall wasn't very high, so we **climbed over**.
- **Turn over** and look at the next page.

round (*or* **around**)

- Somebody shouted my name, so I **looked round** (*or* **around**).
- We went for a long walk. After an hour we **turned round** (*or* **around**) and went back.

get → Unit 56 **put on** / **take off** etc. (phrasal verbs 2) → Unit 115 more phrasal verbs → Appendix 6

Exercises

114.1 Look at the pictures and complete the sentences. Use these verbs + in/out/up etc.

got got ~~looked~~ looked rode sat turned went

1 I went to the window and *looked out* .
2 The door was open, so we ....
3 He heard a plane, so he ....
4 She got on her bike and ....
5 I said hello, and he ....
6 The bus stopped, and she ....
7 There was a free seat, so she ....
8 A car stopped, and two men ....

114.2 Complete the sentences. Use out/away/back etc.

1 'What happened to the picture on the wall?' 'It fell *down* .'
2 Wait a minute. Don't go .... I want to ask you something.
3 Lisa heard a noise behind her, so she looked .... to see what it was.
4 I'm going .... now to do some shopping. I'll be .... at 5 o'clock.
5 I'm feeling very tired. I'm going to lie .... on the sofa.
6 When you have read this page, turn .... and read the other side.
7 Mark is from Canada. He lives in London now, but he wants to go .... to Canada.
8 We haven't got a key to the house, so we can't get ....
9 I was very tired this morning. I couldn't get ....
10 A: 'When are you going .... ?'
B: 'On the 5th. And I'm coming .... on the 24th.'

114.3 Before you do this exercise, study the verbs in Appendix 6 (page 250). Complete the sentences. Choose a verb from the box + on/off/up etc. If necessary, put the verb into the correct form.

break	fall	give	hold	speak	~~wake~~
carry	get	go	slow	take	

\+ **on/off/up/down/over**

1 I went to sleep at 10 o'clock and *woke up* at 8 o'clock the next morning.
2 'It's time to go.' '............ a minute. I'm not ready yet.'
3 The train .... and finally stopped.
4 I like flying, but I'm always nervous when the plane ....
5 How are your children? How are they .... at school?
6 It's difficult to hear you. Can you .... a little?
7 This car isn't very good. It has .... many times.
8 When babies try to walk, they sometimes ....
9 The hotel isn't far from here. If you .... along this road, you'll see it on the left.
10 I tried to find a job, but I .... It was impossible.
11 The fire alarm .... and everyone had to leave the building.

Unit 115

put on your shoes put your shoes on (phrasal verbs 2)

A

Sometimes a phrasal verb (**put on** / **take off** etc.) has an *object*. For example:

verb	*object*
put on	your coat
take off	your shoes

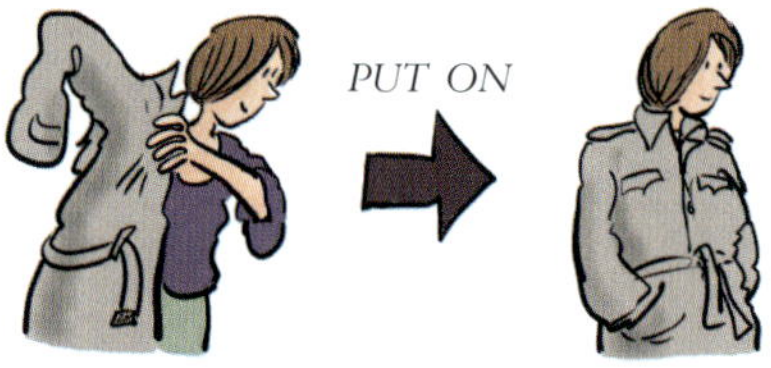

You can say:
  put on your coat
or **put** your coat **on**

You can say:
  take off your shoes
or **take** your shoes **off**

But **it**/**them** *(pronouns)* always go before **on**/**off** etc. :
  put **it on** (*not* put on it) take **them off** (*not* take off them)

- It was cold, so I **put on** my coat. (*or* I **put** my coat **on**)
- Here's your coat. **Put it on.**
- I'm going to **take off** my shoes. (*or* **take** my shoes **off**)
- Your shoes are dirty. **Take them off.**

B

Some more phrasal verbs + *object*:

turn on / **turn off** (lights, machines, taps etc.):

- It was dark, so I **turned on** the light. (*or* I **turned** the light **on**)
- I don't want to watch this programme. You can **turn it off.**

also **switch on** / **switch off** (lights, machines etc.):

- I **switched on** the light and **switched off** the television.

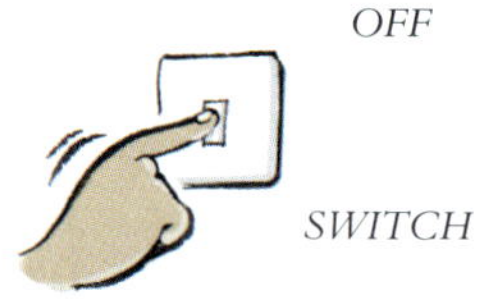

pick up / **put down**:

- Those are my keys on the floor. Can you **pick them up** for me?
- I stopped reading and **put** my book **down**. (*or* **put down** my book)

bring back / **take back** / **give back** / **put back**:

- You can take my umbrella, but please **bring it back**.
- I **took** my new sweater **back** to the shop. It was too small for me.
- I've got Rachel's keys. I have to **give them back** to her.
- I read the letter and then **put it back** in the envelope.

go in / fall off etc. (phrasal verbs 1) → Unit 114 more phrasal verbs + object → Appendix 7

Exercises

115.1 Look at the pictures. What did these people do?

1 He turned on the light .
2 She ....
3 He ....
4 She ....
5 He ....
6 She ....

115.2 You can write these sentences in three different ways. Complete the table.

1	I turned on the radio.	I turned the radio on.	I turned it on.
2	He put on his jacket.	He	He ....
3	She	She took her glasses off.	....
4	I picked up the phone.	....	....
5	They gave back the key.	....	....
6	....	We turned the lights off.	....

115.3 Complete the sentences. Use these verbs with *it* or *them*.

bring back **pick up** **switch off** **take back** **~~turn on~~**

1 I wanted to watch something on television, so I turned it on .
2 My new lamp doesn't work. I'm going to .... to the shop.
3 There were some gloves on the floor, so I .... and put them on the table.
4 The heating was on but it was too warm, so I ....
5 Thank you for lending me these books. I won't forget to ....

115.4 Before you do this exercise, study the verbs in Appendix 7 (page 251). Complete the sentences. Use a verb from the box. Sometimes you will also need to use *it/them/me*.

fill in	~~knock down~~	look up	show round	~~turn down~~
give up	knock over	put out	throw away	try on

1 They knocked a lot of houses down when they built the new road.
2 That music is very loud. Can you turn it down ?
3 I .... a glass and broke it.
4 'What does this word mean?' 'Here's a dictionary. You can ....'
5 I want to keep these magazines. Please don't ....
6 I .... a pair of shoes in the shop, but I didn't buy them.
7 I visited a school last week. One of the teachers ....
8 'Do you play the piano?' 'No, I started to learn, but I .... after a month.'
9 Somebody gave me a form and told me to ....
10 Smoking isn't allowed here. Please .... your cigarette ....

Appendix 1
Active and passive

1.1 Present and past

	active	*passive*
present simple	□ We **make** butter from milk. □ Somebody **cleans** these rooms every day. □ People never **invite** me to parties. □ How **do** they **make** butter?	□ Butter **is made** from milk. □ These rooms **are cleaned** every day. □ I **am** never **invited** to parties. □ How **is** butter **made**?
past simple	□ Somebody **stole** my car last week. □ Somebody **stole** my keys yesterday. □ They **didn't invite** me to the party. □ When **did** they **build** these houses?	□ My car **was stolen** last week. □ My keys **were stolen** yesterday. □ I **wasn't invited** to the party. □ When **were** these houses **built**?

present continuous	□ They **are building** a new airport at the moment. (= it isn't finished) □ They **are building** some new houses near the river.	□ A new airport **is being built** at the moment. □ Some new houses **are being built** near the river.
past continuous	□ When I was here a few years ago, they **were building** a new airport. (= it wasn't finished at that time)	□ When I was here a few years ago, a new airport **was being built**.

present perfect	□ Look! They **have painted** the door. □ These shirts are clean. Somebody **has washed** them. □ Somebody **has stolen** my car.	□ Look! The door **has been painted**. □ These shirts are clean. They **have been washed**. □ My car **has been stolen**.
past perfect	□ Tina said that somebody **had stolen** her car.	□ Tina said that her car **had been stolen**.

1.2 **will** / **can** / **must** / **have to** etc.

active	*passive*
□ Somebody **will clean** the office tomorrow. □ Somebody **must clean** the office. □ I think they**'ll invite** you to the party. □ They **can't repair** my watch. □ You **should wash** this sweater by hand.	□ The office **will be cleaned** tomorrow. □ The office **must be cleaned**. □ I think you**'ll be invited** to the party. □ My watch **can't be repaired**. □ This sweater **should be washed** by hand.
□ They **are going to build** a new airport. □ Somebody **has to wash** these clothes. □ They **had to take** the injured man to hospital.	□ A new airport **is going to be built**. □ These clothes **have to be washed**. □ The injured man **had to be taken** to hospital.

Appendix 2
List of irregular verbs (→ Unit 24)

infinitive	*past simple*	*past participle*
be	**was/were**	**been**
beat	**beat**	**beaten**
become	**became**	**become**
begin	**began**	**begun**
bite	**bit**	**bitten**
blow	**blew**	**blown**
break	**broke**	**broken**
bring	**brought**	**brought**
build	**built**	**built**
buy	**bought**	**bought**
catch	**caught**	**caught**
choose	**chose**	**chosen**
come	**came**	**come**
cost	**cost**	**cost**
cut	**cut**	**cut**
do	**did**	**done**
draw	**drew**	**drawn**
drink	**drank**	**drunk**
drive	**drove**	**driven**
eat	**ate**	**eaten**
fall	**fell**	**fallen**
feel	**felt**	**felt**
fight	**fought**	**fought**
find	**found**	**found**
fly	**flew**	**flown**
forget	**forgot**	**forgotten**
get	**got**	**got**
give	**gave**	**given**
go	**went**	**gone**
grow	**grew**	**grown**
hang	**hung**	**hung**
have	**had**	**had**
hear	**heard**	**heard**
hide	**hid**	**hidden**
hit	**hit**	**hit**
hold	**held**	**held**
hurt	**hurt**	**hurt**
keep	**kept**	**kept**
know	**knew**	**known**
leave	**left**	**left**
lend	**lent**	**lent**

infinitive	*past simple*	*past participle*
let	**let**	**let**
lie	**lay**	**lain**
light	**lit**	**lit**
lose	**lost**	**lost**
make	**made**	**made**
mean	**meant**	**meant**
meet	**met**	**met**
pay	**paid**	**paid**
put	**put**	**put**
read (reed)*	**read** (red)*	**read** (red)*
ride	**rode**	**ridden**
ring	**rang**	**rung**
rise	**rose**	**risen**
run	**ran**	**run**
say	**said**	**said**
see	**saw**	**seen**
sell	**sold**	**sold**
send	**sent**	**sent**
shine	**shone**	**shone**
shoot	**shot**	**shot**
show	**showed**	**shown**
shut	**shut**	**shut**
sing	**sang**	**sung**
sit	**sat**	**sat**
sleep	**slept**	**slept**
speak	**spoke**	**spoken**
spend	**spent**	**spent**
stand	**stood**	**stood**
steal	**stole**	**stolen**
swim	**swam**	**swum**
take	**took**	**taken**
teach	**taught**	**taught**
tear	**tore**	**torn**
tell	**told**	**told**
think	**thought**	**thought**
throw	**threw**	**thrown**
understand	**understood**	**understood**
wake	**woke**	**woken**
wear	**wore**	**worn**
win	**won**	**won**
write	**wrote**	**written**

* *pronunciation*

The following verbs can be regular (**-ed**) *or* irregular (**-t**):

infinitive	*past simple / past participle*
burn	**burned** *or* **burnt**
dream	**dreamed** *or* **dreamt**

infinitive	*past simple / past participle*
learn	**learned** *or* **learnt**
smell	**smelled** *or* **smelt**

Appendix 3
Irregular verbs in groups

The past simple and past participle are the same:

1

cost	→	**cost**
cut	→	**cut**
hit	→	**hit**
hurt	→	**hurt**

let	→	**let**
put	→	**put**
shut	→	**shut**

2

lend	→	**lent**
send	→	**sent**
spend	→	**spent**
build	→	**built**

lose	→	**lost**
shoot	→	**shot**
get	→	**got**
light	→	**lit**
sit	→	**sat**

burn	→	**burnt**
learn	→	**learnt**
smell	→	**smelt**

keep	→	**kept**
sleep	→	**slept**

feel	→	**felt**
leave	→	**left**
meet	→	**met**
dream	→	**dreamt** (dremt)*
mean	→	**meant** (ment)*

3

bring	→	**brought** (brort)*
buy	→	**bought** (bort)*
fight	→	**fought** (fort)*
think	→	**thought** (thort)*
catch	→	**caught** (kort)*
teach	→	**taught** (tort)*

4

sell	→	**sold**
tell	→	**told**

find	→	**found**
have	→	**had**
hear	→	**heard**
hold	→	**held**
read	→	**read** (red)*
say	→	**said** (sed)*

pay	→	**paid**
make	→	**made**

stand	→	**stood**
understand	→	**understood**

* *pronunciation*

The past simple and past participle are different:

1

break	→	**broke**	**broken**
choose	→	**chose**	**chosen**
speak	→	**spoke**	**spoken**
steal	→	**stole**	**stolen**
wake	→	**woke**	**woken**

2

drive	→	**drove**	**driven**
ride	→	**rode**	**ridden**
rise	→	**rose**	**risen**
write	→	**wrote**	**written**

beat	→	**beat**	**beaten**
bite	→	**bit**	**bitten**
hide	→	**hid**	**hidden**

3

eat	→	**ate**	**eaten**
fall	→	**fell**	**fallen**
forget	→	**forgot**	**forgotten**
give	→	**gave**	**given**
see	→	**saw**	**seen**
take	→	**took**	**taken**

4

blow	→	**blew**	**blown**
grow	→	**grew**	**grown**
know	→	**knew**	**known**
throw	→	**threw**	**thrown**
fly	→	**flew**	**flown**
draw	→	**drew**	**drawn**
show	→	**showed**	**shown**

5

begin	→	**began**	**begun**
drink	→	**drank**	**drunk**
swim	→	**swam**	**swum**
ring	→	**rang**	**rung**
sing	→	**sang**	**sung**
run	→	**ran**	**run**

6

come	→	**came**	**come**
become	→	**became**	**become**

Appendix 4
Short forms (he's / I'd / don't etc.)

4.1 In spoken English we usually pronounce '**I am**' as one word. The short form (**I'm**) is a way of writing this:

I am → **I'm**	☐ **I'm** feeling tired this morning.
it is → **it's**	☐ 'Do you like this jacket?' 'Yes, **it's** nice.'
they have → **they've**	☐ 'Where are your friends?' '**They've** gone home.'
etc.	

When we write short forms, we use ' *(an apostrophe)*:

I ~~a~~m → I**'m** he ~~i~~s → he**'s** you ~~ha~~ve → you**'ve** she ~~wi~~ll → she**'ll**

4.2 We use these forms with **I**/**he**/**she** etc. :

am → **'m**	**I'm**							
is → **'s**		**he's**	**she's**	**it's**				
are → **'re**					**we're**	**you're**	**they're**
have → **'ve**	**I've**				**we've**	**you've**	**they've**
has → **'s**		**he's**	**she's**	**it's**			
had → **'d**	**I'd**	**he'd**	**she'd**		**we'd**	**you'd**	**they'd**
will → **'ll**	**I'll**	**he'll**	**she'll**		**we'll**	**you'll**	**they'll**
would → **'d**	**I'd**	**he'd**	**she'd**		**we'd**	**you'd**	**they'd**

☐ I**'ve** got some new shoes.
☐ We**'ll** probably go out this evening.
☐ It**'s** 10 o'clock. You**'re** late again.

's = **is** *or* **has**:

☐ She**'s** going out this evening. (she**'s** going = she **is** going)
☐ She**'s** gone out. (she**'s** gone = she **has** gone)

'd = **would** *or* **had**:

☐ A: What would you like to eat?
B: I**'d** like a salad, please. (I**'d** like = I **would** like)
☐ I told the police that I**'d** lost my passport. (I**'d** lost = I **had** lost)

Do not use **'m**/**'s**/**'d** etc. at the end of a sentence (→ Unit 40):

☐ 'Are you tired?' 'Yes, I **am**.' (*not* Yes, I'm.)
☐ She isn't tired, but he **is**. (*not* he's)

4.3 We use short forms with **I**/**you**/**he**/**she** etc., but you can use short forms (especially **'s**) with other words too:

☐ **Who's** your favourite singer? (= who **is**)
☐ **What's** the time? (= what **is**)
☐ **There's** a big tree in the garden. (= there **is**)
☐ **My sister's** working in London. (= my sister **is** working)
☐ **Paul's** gone out. (= Paul **has** gone out)
☐ **What colour's** your car? (= What colour **is** your car?)

Appendix 4
Short forms (he's / I'd / don't etc.)

4.4 Negative short forms (→ Unit 43):

isn't (= is not)	**don't** (= do not)	**can't** (= cannot)
aren't (= are not)	**doesn't** (= does not)	**couldn't** (= could not)
wasn't (= was not)	**didn't** (= did not)	**won't** (= will not)
weren't (= were not)		**wouldn't** (= would not)
hasn't (= has not)		**shouldn't** (= should not)
haven't (= have not)		**mustn't** (= must not)
hadn't (= had not)		

- We went to her house, but she **wasn't** at home.
- 'Where's David?' 'I **don't** know. I **haven't** seen him.'
- You work all the time. You **shouldn't** work so hard.
- I **won't** be here tomorrow. (= I will not)

4.5 **'s** (*apostrophe* + **s**)

's can mean different things:

(1) **'s** = **is** *or* **has** (→ section 4.2 of this appendix)

(2) **let's** = let **us** (→ Units 35, 53)
- It's a lovely day. **Let's** go out. (= Let **us** go out.)

(3) Kate**'s** camera = her camera
my brother**'s** car = his car
the manager**'s** office = his/her office etc.
(→ Unit 64)

Compare:
- **Kate's** camera was very expensive. (**Kate's** camera = **her** camera)
- **Kate's** a very good photographer. (**Kate's** = Kate **is**)
- **Kate's** got a new camera. (Kate**'s** got = Kate **has** got)

Appendix 5
Spelling

5.1 Words + **-s** and **-es** (bird**s**/watch**es** etc.)

noun + **s** (plural) (→ Unit 66)
bird → bird**s** | mistake → mistake**s** | hotel → hotel**s**

verb + **s** (he/she/it **-s**) (→ Unit 5)
think → think**s** | live → live**s** | remember → remember**s**

but

\+ **es** after **-s** / **-sh** / **-ch** / **-x**

bu**s** → bus**es**	pa**ss** → pass**es**	addre**ss** → address**es**
di**sh** → dish**es**	wa**sh** → wash**es**	fini**sh** → finish**es**
wat**ch** → watch**es**	tea**ch** → teach**es**	sandwi**ch** → sandwich**es**
bo**x** → box**es**		

also

potato → potato**es**	tomato → tomato**es**
do → do**es**	go → go**es**

-f / **-fe** → **-ves**
shel**f** → shel**ves** | kni**fe** → kni**ves** | *but* roo**f** → roo**fs**

5.2 Words ending in **-y** (bab**y** → bab**ies** / stud**y** → stud**ied** etc.)

-y → **-ies**

stud**y** → stud**ies** (*not* studys)		famil**y** → famil**ies** (*not* familys)
stor**y** → stor**ies**	cit**y** → cit**ies**	bab**y** → bab**ies**
tr**y** → tr**ies**	marr**y** → marr**ies**	fl**y** → fl**ies**

-y → **-ied** (→ Unit 11)

stud**y** → stud**ied** (*not* studyed)		
tr**y** → tr**ied**	marr**y** → marr**ied**	cop**y** → cop**ied**

-y → **-ier**/**-iest** (→ Units 87, 90)

eas**y** → eas**ier**/eas**iest** (*not* easyer/easyest)	
happ**y** → happ**ier**/happ**iest**	luck**y** → luck**ier**/luck**iest**
heav**y** → heav**ier**/heav**iest**	funn**y** → funn**ier**/funn**iest**

-y → **-ily** (→ Unit 86)

eas**y** → eas**ily** (*not* easyly)		
happ**y** → happ**ily**	heav**y** → heav**ily**	luck**y** → luck**ily**

y does not change to **i** if the ending is **-ay**/**-ey**/**-oy**/**-uy**:
holid**ay** → holid**ays** (*not* holidaies)
enj**oy** → enj**oys**/enj**oyed** | st**ay** → st**ays**/st**ayed** | b**uy** → b**uys** | k**ey** → k**eys**

but
say → **said** | **pay** → **paid** | *(irregular verbs)*

Appendix 5
Spelling

5.3 -ing

Verbs that end in **-e** (mak**e**/writ**e**/driv**e** etc.) → -~~e~~**ing**:
mak**e** → mak**ing** writ**e** → writ**ing** com**e** → com**ing** danc**e** → danc**ing**

Verbs that end in **-ie** → **-ying**:
l**ie** → l**ying** d**ie** → d**ying** t**ie** → t**ying**

5.4 sto**p** → sto**pp**ed, bi**g** → bi**gg**er etc.

Vowels and consonants:

Vowel letters: a e i o u
Consonant letters: b c d f g k l m n p r s t w y

Sometimes a word ends in a *vowel* + a *consonant*. For example: st**op**, b**ig**, g**et**.
Before **-ing**/**-ed**/**-er**/**-est**, **p**/**g**/**t** etc. become **pp**/**gg**/**tt** etc.
For example:

	V+C			
stop	ST **O P**	p → **pp**	sto**pp**ing	sto**pp**ed
run	R **U N**	n → **nn**	ru**nn**ing	
get	G **E T**	t → **tt**	ge**tt**ing	
swim	SW **I M**	m → **mm**	swi**mm**ing	
big	B **I G**	g → **gg**	bi**gg**er	bi**gg**est
hot	H **O T**	t → **tt**	ho**tt**er	ho**tt**est
thin	TH **I N**	n → **nn**	thi**nn**er	thi**nn**est

V = *vowel*
C = *consonant*

This does *not* happen
(1) if the word ends in *two* consonant letters (C + C):

	C+C		
help	HE **L P**	he**lp**ing	he**lp**ed
work	WO **R K**	wo**rk**ing	wo**rk**ed
fast	FA **S T**	fa**st**er	fa**st**est

(2) if the word ends in two vowel letters + a consonant letter (V + V + C):

	V+V+C		
need	N **E E D**	nee**d**ing	nee**d**ed
wait	W **A I T**	wai**t**ing	wai**t**ed
cheap	CH **E A P**	chea**p**er	chea**p**est

(3) in longer words (two syllables or more) if the last part of the word is *not* stressed:

	stress		
happen	**HAP**-pen	→	happe**n**ing/happe**n**ed (*not* happenned)
visit	**VIS**-it	→	visi**t**ing/visi**t**ed
remember	re-**MEM**-ber	→	remembe**r**ing/remembe**r**ed

but

prefer	pre-**FER**	(*stress at the end*)	→	prefe**rr**ing/prefe**rr**ed
begin	be-**GIN**	(*stress at the end*)	→	begi**nn**ing

(4) if the word ends in **-y** or **-w**. (At the end of words, **y** and **w** are not consonants.)
enjo**y** → enjo**y**ing/enjo**y**ed sno**w** → sno**w**ing/sno**w**ed fe**w** → fe**w**er/fe**w**est

Appendix 6
Phrasal verbs (take off / give up etc.)

This is a list of some important phrasal verbs (→ Unit 114).

on

carry on = *continue*

- Don't stop working. **Carry on.** (= continue working)
- A: Excuse me, where is the station?
  B: **Carry on** along this road and turn right at the lights. (= Continue along ...)

also **go on** / **walk on** / **drive on** etc. = *continue going/walking/driving* etc.

- Don't stop here. **Drive on.**

come on = *be quick*

- **Come on!** Everybody is waiting for you.

get on = *manage (in a job, at school, in an exam etc.)*

- How was your exam? How did you **get on**? (= how did you do?)

hold on = *wait*

- Can you **hold on** a minute? (= can you wait?)

off

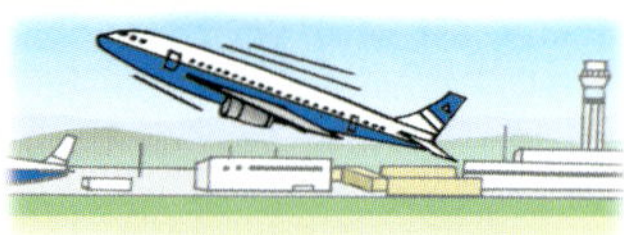
TAKE OFF

take off = *leave the ground (for planes)*

- The plane **took off** 20 minutes late, but arrived on time.

go off = *explode (a bomb etc.) or ring (an alarm, an alarm clock etc.)*

- A bomb **went off** and caused a lot of damage.
- A car alarm **goes off** if somebody tries to break into the car.

GO OFF

up

give up = *stop trying*

- I know it's difficult, but don't **give up**. (= don't stop trying)

GROW UP

grow up = *become an adult*

- What does your son want to do when he **grows up**?

hurry up = *do something more quickly*

- **Hurry up!** We haven't got much time.

WAKE UP

speak up = *speak more loudly*

- I can't hear you. Can you **speak up**, please?

wake up = *stop sleeping*

- I often **wake up** in the middle of the night.

wash up = *wash the plates etc. after a meal*

- Do you want me to **wash up**? (*or* ... to do the washing-up?)

WASH UP

down

slow down = *go more slowly*

- You're driving too fast. **Slow down!**

BREAK DOWN

break down = *stop working (for cars, machines etc.)*

- Sue was very late because her car **broke down**.

over

fall over = *lose your balance*

- I **fell over** because my shoes were too big for me.

FALL OVER

Appendix 7 Phrasal verbs + object (put out a fire / give up your job etc.)

This is a list of some important phrasal verbs + object (→ Unit 115).

in/out

fill in / **fill out** a form = *complete a form*

- ☐ Can you **fill in this form**, please? *or*
  Can you **fill out this form**, please?

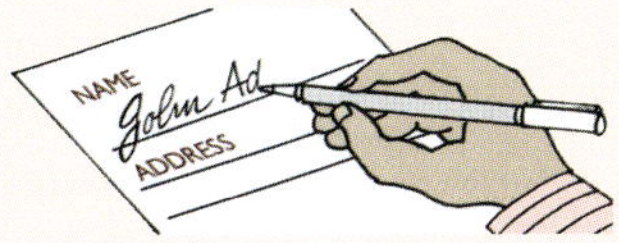

out

put out a fire, a cigarette etc.

- ☐ The fire brigade arrived and **put the fire out**.

cross out a mistake, a word etc.

- ☐ If you make a mistake, **cross it out**.

PUT OUT

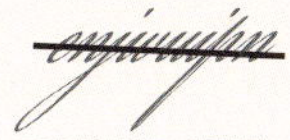

CROSS OUT

on

try on clothes = *put on clothes to see if they fit you*

- ☐ *(in a shop)* This is a nice jacket. Shall I **try it on**?

up

give up something = *stop doing it*

- ☐ Sue **gave up her job** when her baby was born. (= she stopped working)
- ☐ 'Are you still learning Italian?' 'No, I **gave it up**.'

look up a word in a dictionary etc.

- ☐ I didn't know the meaning of the word, so I **looked it up** in a dictionary.

turn up the TV, radio, music, heating etc. = *make it louder or warmer*

- ☐ Can you **turn the radio up**? I can't hear it.

wake up somebody who is sleeping

- ☐ I have to get up early tomorrow. Can you **wake me up** at 6.30?

down

knock down a building = *demolish it*

- ☐ They are going to **knock down** the school and build a new one.

turn down the TV, radio, music, heating etc. = *make it more quiet or less warm*

- ☐ The music is too loud. Can you **turn it down**?

KNOCK DOWN

over

knock over a cup, a glass, a person etc.

- ☐ Be careful. Don't **knock your cup over**.
- ☐ There was an accident at the end of the road. A man was **knocked over** by a car. (*or* A man was **knocked down** by a car.)

KNOCK OVER

KNOCK OVER or KNOCK DOWN

away

throw away rubbish, things you don't want

- ☐ These apples are bad. Shall I **throw them away**?
- ☐ Don't **throw away that picture**. I want it.

put something **away** = *put it in the place where you usually keep it*

- ☐ After they finished playing, the children **put their toys away**.

THROW AWAY

back

pay somebody **back** = *give back money that you borrowed*

- ☐ Thank you for lending me the money. I'll **pay you back** next week.

round/around

show somebody **round/around** = *take somebody on a tour of a place*

- ☐ We visited a factory last week. The manager **showed us round**.

Additional exercises

List of exercises:

1–2	**am/is/are**	Units 1–2
3	present continuous	Units 3–4
4	present simple	Units 5–7
5–7	present simple, **am/is/are** and **have** (**got**)	Units 1–2, 5–7, 9
8–9	present continuous and present simple	Units 3–8
10–13	**was/were** and past simple	Units 10–12
14	past simple and past continuous	Units 11–14
15	present and past	Units 3–14
16–18	present perfect	Units 15–19
19–22	present perfect and past simple	Units 18–20
23	present, past and present perfect	Units 3–20
24–27	passive	Units 21–22
28	future	Units 25–28
29	past, present and future	Units 3–20, 25–28
30–31	past, present and future	Units 3–22, 25–28, 52, 54, 98, 105
32	**-ing** and **to …**	Units 51–55, 105, 112
33–34	**a** and **the**	Units 65, 69–73
35	prepositions	Units 103–108, 111

am/is/are

Units 1–2

1 Write sentences for the pictures. Use the words in the boxes + is/isn't/are/aren't.

~~The windows~~	on the table
~~Lisa~~	hungry
Kate	asleep
The children	~~open~~
Gary	full
The books	near the station
The hotel	a doctor
The bus	~~happy~~

1 *The windows are open.*
2 *Lisa isn't happy.*
3 Kate ……
4 ……
5 ……
6 ……
7 ……
8 ……

2 Complete the sentences.

1 'Are you hungry?' 'No, but *I'm* thirsty.'
2 '*How are* your parents?' 'They're fine.'
3 'Is Anna at home?' 'No, ... at work.'
4 '.......... my keys?' 'On your desk.'
5 Where is Paul from? .... American or British?
6 .... very hot today. The temperature is 38 degrees.
7 'Are you a teacher?' 'No, ... a student.'
8 '.......... your umbrella?' 'Green.'
9 Where's your car? .... in the car park?
10 '.......... tired?' 'No, I'm fine.'
11 'These shoes are nice. How .... ?' 'Fifty pounds.'

present continuous (I'm working / are you working? etc.) — Units 3–4

3 Use the words in brackets to write sentences.

1 A: Where are your parents?
B: *They're watching TV.* (they / watch / TV)
2 A: Paula is going out.
B: *Where's she going?* (where / she / go?)
3 A: Where's David?
B: .... (he / have / a shower)
4 A: .... ? (the children / play?)
B: No, they're asleep.
5 A: .... ? (it / rain?)
B: No, not at the moment.
6 A: Where are Sue and Steve?
B: .... (they / come / now)
7 A: .... ? (why / you / stand / here?)
B: .... (I / wait / for somebody)

present simple (I work / she doesn't work / do you work? etc.) — Units 5–7

4 Complete the sentences. Use the present simple.

1 *Sue always gets* to work early. (Sue / always / get)
2 *We don't watch* TV very often. (we / not / watch)
3 How often *do you wash* your hair? (you / wash)
4 I want to go to the cinema, but .... to go. (Sam / not / want)
5 .... to go out tonight? (you / want)
6 .... near here? (Helen / live)
7 .... a lot of people. (Sarah / know)
8 I enjoy travelling, but .... very much. (I / not / travel)
9 What time .... in the morning? (you / usually / get up)
10 My parents are usually at home in the evening.
.... very often. (they / not / go out)
11 .... work at five o'clock. (Tom / always / finish)
12 A: What .... ? (Julia / do)
B: .... in a hotel. (she / work)

present simple, am/is/are and have (got)

Units 1–2, 5–7, 9

5 Read the questions and Clare's answers. Then write sentences about Clare.

	Question	Clare		Sentence
1	Are you married?	No.	1	She isn't married.
2	Do you live in London?	Yes.	2	She lives in London.
3	Are you a student?	Yes.	3	
4	Have you got a car?	No.	4	
5	Do you go out a lot?	Yes.	5	
6	Have you got a lot of friends?	Yes.	6	
7	Do you like London?	No.	7	
8	Do you like dancing?	Yes.	8	
9	Are you interested in sport?	No.	9	

Clare

6 Complete the questions.

1
What's your name ?
.... married?
Where .... ?
.... any children?
How .... ?

Brian.
Yes, I am.
In Barton Road.
Yes, a daughter.
She's three.

2
.... ?
.... ?
.... your job?
.... a car?
.... to work by car?

I'm 29.
I work in a supermarket.
No, I hate it.
Yes, I have.
No, I usually go by bus.

3
Who is this man ?
.... ?
.... ?
.... in London?

That's my brother.
Michael.
He's a travel agent.
No, in Manchester.

7 Write sentences from these words. All the sentences are present.

1. Sarah often / tennis — Sarah often plays tennis.
2. my parents / a new car — My parents have got a new car.
3. my shoes / dirty — My shoes are dirty.
4. Sonia / 32 years old — Sonia ....
5. I / two sisters — ....
6. we often / TV in the evening — ....
7. Jane never / a hat — ....
8. a bicycle / two wheels — ....
9. these flowers / beautiful — ....
10. Mary / German very well — ....

present continuous (I'm working) and present simple (I work)

Units 3–8

8 Complete the sentences.

1

2

3

4

5

6

7

8

9

9 Which is right?

1 '~~Are you speaking~~ / Do you speak English?' 'Yes, a little.' (Do you speak *is right*)
2 Sometimes we're going / we go away at weekends.
3 It's a nice day today. The sun is shining / shines.
4 *(You meet Kate in the street.)* Hello, Kate. Where are you going / do you go?
5 How often are you going / do you go on holiday?
6 Emily is a writer. She's writing / She writes books for children.
7 I'm never reading / I never read newspapers.
8 'Where are Michael and Jane?' 'They're watching / They watch TV in the living room.'
9 Helen is in her office. She's talking / She talks to somebody.
10 What time are you usually having / do you usually have dinner?
11 John isn't at home at the moment. He's visiting / He visits some friends.
12 'Would you like some tea?' 'No, thank you. I'm not drinking / I don't drink tea.'

was/were and past simple (I worked / did you work? etc.)

Units 10–12

10 Complete the sentences. Use one word only.

1 I got up early and ...*had*... a shower.
2 Tom was tired last night, so he .... to bed early.
3 I .... this pen on the floor. Is it yours?
4 Kate got married when she .... 23.
5 Helen is learning to drive. She .... her first lesson yesterday.
6 'I've got a new job.' 'Yes, I know. David .... me.'
7 'Where did you buy that book?' 'It was a present. Jane .... it to me.'
8 We .... hungry, so we had something to eat.
9 'Did you enjoy the film?' 'Yes, I .... it was very good.'
10 'Did Andy come to your party?' 'No, we .... him, but he didn't come.'

11 Look at the questions and Kevin's answers. Write sentences about Kevin when he was a child.

Kevin

When you were a child …

Were you tall?	No.	1 ...*He wasn't tall.*...
Did you like school?	Yes.	2 ...*He liked school.*...
Were you good at sport?	Yes.	3 He ....
Did you play football?	Yes.	4 ....
Did you work hard at school?	No.	5 ....
Did you have a lot of friends?	Yes.	6 ....
Did you have a bicycle?	No.	7 ....
Were you a quiet child?	No.	8 ....

12 Complete the questions.

	Question	Answer
1	...*Did you have*... a nice holiday?	Yes, it was great, thanks.
2	...*Where did you go*... ?	To Amsterdam.
3	.... there?	Five days.
4	.... Amsterdam?	Yes, very much.
5	.... ?	I have friends in Amsterdam, so I stayed with them.
6	.... good?	Yes, it was warm and sunny.
7	.... back?	Yesterday.

13 Put the verb in the right form (positive, negative or question).

1 It was a good party. ...*I enjoyed*... it. (I / enjoy)
2 '...*Did you do*... the shopping?' (you / do) 'No, I ...*didn't have*... time.' (I / have)
3 'Did you phone Adam?' 'No, I'm afraid ....' (I / forget)
4 I like your new watch. Where .... it? (you / get)
5 I saw Lucy at the party, but .... to her. (I / speak)
6 A: .... a nice weekend? (you / have)
B: Yes, I went to stay with some friends of mine.
7 Paul wasn't well yesterday, so .... to work. (he / go)
8 'Is Mary here?' 'Yes, ... five minutes ago.' (she / arrive)
9 Where .... before he moved here? (Robert / live)
10 The restaurant wasn't expensive. .... very much. (the meal / cost)

past simple (I worked) and past continuous (I was working) — Units 11–14

14 Complete the sentences. Use the past simple or past continuous.

1

It ..*was raining*.. (rain) when we ..*went*.. (go) out.

2

When I arrived at the office, Jane and Paul .... (work) at their desks.

3

I .... (open) the window because it was hot.

4

The phone .... (ring) when Sue .... (cook) the dinner.

5

I .... (hear) a noise outside, so I .... (look) out of the window.

6

Tom .... (look) out of the window when the accident .... (happen).

7

Richard had a book in his hand, but he .... (not/read) it. He .... (watch) TV.

8

Catherine bought a magazine, but she .... (not/read) it. She didn't have time.

9

I .... (finish) my meal, ... (pay) the bill and .... (leave) the restaurant.

10

I .... (see) Kate this morning. I .... (walk) along the street and she .... (wait) for the bus.

present and past

Units 3–14

15 Complete the sentences. Use one of these forms:

present simple (**I work/drive** etc.) present continuous (**I am working/driving** etc.)
past simple (**I worked/drove** etc.) past continuous (**I was working/driving** etc.)

1. You can turn off the television. I 'm not watching (not/watch) it.
2. Last night Jenny fell (fall) asleep while she was reading (read).
3. Listen! Somebody .... (play) the piano.
4. 'Have you got my key?' 'No, I .... (give) it back to you.'
5. David is very lazy. He .... (not/like) hard work.
6. Where .... (your parents / go) for their holidays last year?
7. I .... (see) Diane yesterday. She .... (drive) her new car.
8. A: .... (you/watch) television very much?
   B: No, I haven't got a television set.
9. A: What .... (you/do) at 6 o'clock last Sunday morning?
   B: I was in bed asleep.
10. Andy isn't at home very much. He .... (go) away a lot.
11. I .... (try) to find a job at the moment. It's very difficult.
12. I'm tired this morning. I .... (not/sleep) very well last night.

present perfect (I have done / she has been etc.)

Units 15–19

16 Look at the pictures and complete the sentences. Use the present perfect.

5
Is this a good book?
BOOKS
I don't know.
I .... it.
6
I'm looking for Julia.
.... her?
Yes, she was here a few minutes ago.
7
More coffee?
No, thanks.
I .... enough.
8
.... to Sweden?
SWEDEN
Yes, I went there a few years ago.
9
Hi. We ....
to the cinema.
later
NEMA
10
Enjoy the party!
later
Where are Steve and Jane?
....
to a party.
JANE
STEVE
11
Paul was asleep in the armchair. He ....
.... up.
ZZZZ
12
How long
.... here?
Since 2002.
13
Do you know Alan?
ALAN
Yes, we ....
each other for a long time.
14
The weather is horrible here. It ....
all day.

17 Complete the sentences (1, 2 or 3 words).

1 Mark and Liz are married. They *have been* married for five years.
2 David has been watching TV *since* 5 o'clock.
3 Martin is at work. He .... at work since 8.30.
4 'Have you just arrived in London?' 'No, I've been here .... five days.'
5 I've known Helen .... we were at school together.
6 'My brother lives in Los Angeles.' 'Really? How long .... there?'
7 George has had the same job .... 20 years.
8 Some friends of ours are staying with us at the moment. They .... here since Monday.

18 Complete the sentences. Write about yourself.

1 I've never *ridden a horse.*
2 I've *been to London* many times.
3 I've just ....
4 I've .... (once / twice / a few times / many times)
5 I haven't .... yet.
6 I've never ....
7 I've .... since ....
8 I've .... for ....

present perfect (I have done etc.) and past simple (I did etc.) — Units 18–20

19 Present perfect or past simple? Complete the sentences (positive or negative).

1 A: Do you like London?
B: I don't know. I *haven't been* there.
2 A: Have you seen Kate?
B: Yes, I *saw* her five minutes ago.
3 A: That's a nice sweater. Is it new?
B: Yes, I .... it last week.
4 A: Are you tired this morning?
B: Yes, I .... to bed late last night.
5 A: Do you want this newspaper, or can I have it?
B: You can have it. I .... it.
6 A: Are you enjoying your new job?
B: I .... yet. My first day is next Monday.
7 A: The weather isn't very nice today, is it?
B: No, but it .... nice yesterday.
8 A: Was Helen at the party on Saturday?
B: I don't think so. I .... her there.
9 A: Is your son still at school?
B: No, he .... school two years ago.
10 A: Is Silvia married?
B: Yes, she .... married for five years.
11 A: Have you heard of George Washington?
B: Of course. He .... the first President of the United States.
12 A: How long does it take to make a pizza?
B: I don't know. I .... a pizza.

20 Write sentences with the present perfect or past simple.

1 A: Have you been to Thailand?
B: Yes, I went there last year. (I / go / there / last year)

2 A: Do you like London?
B: I don't know. I've never been there. (I / never / there)

3 A: What time is Paul going out?
B: .... (he / already / go)

4 A: Has Catherine gone home?
B: Yes, ... (she / leave / at 4 o'clock)

5 A: New York is my favourite city.
B: Is it? .... ? (how many times / you / there?)

6 A: What are you doing this weekend?
B: I don't know. .... (I / not / decide / yet)

7 A: I can't find my address book. Have you seen it?
B: .... (it / on the table / last night)

8 A: Do you know the Japanese restaurant in Leeson Street?
B: Yes, ... (I / eat / there a few times)

9 A: Paula and Sue are here.
B: Are they? .... ? (what time / they / arrive?)

21 Present perfect or past simple? Complete the sentences.

1 A: Have you been to France?
B: Yes, many times.
A: When .... the last time?
B: Two years ago.

2 A: Is this your car?
B: Yes, it is.
A: How long .... it?
B: It's new. I .... it yesterday.

3 A: Where do you live?
B: In Harold Street.
A: How long .... there?
B: Five years. Before that .... in Mill Road.
A: How long .... in Mill Road?
B: About three years.

4 A: What do you do?
B: I work in a shop.
A: How long .... there?
B: Nearly two years.
A: What .... before that?
B: I .... a taxi driver.

22 Write sentences about yourself.

1 (yesterday morning) ...I was late for work yesterday morning....
2 (last night) ...
3 (yesterday afternoon) ...
4 (… days ago) ...
5 (last week) ...
6 (last year) ...

present, past and present perfect — Units 3–20

23 Which is right?

1 '...Is Sue working? (C)...' 'No, she's on holiday.'
A Does Sue work? B Is working Sue? C Is Sue working? D Does work Sue?

2 'Where ... ?' 'In a village near London.'
A lives your uncle B does your uncle live C your uncle lives
D does live your uncle

3 I speak Italian, but ... French.
A I speak not B I'm not speaking C I doesn't speak D I don't speak

4 'Where's Tom?' '... a shower at the moment.'
A He's having B He have C He has D He has had

5 Why ... angry with me yesterday?
A were you B was you C you were D have you been

6 My favourite film is *Cleo's Dream*. ... it four times.
A I'm seeing B I see C I was seeing D I've seen

7 I ... out last night. I was too tired.
A don't go B didn't went C didn't go D haven't gone

8 Liz is from Chicago. She ... there all her life.
A is living B has lived C lives D lived

9 My friend ... for me when I arrived.
A waited B has waited C was waiting D has been waiting

10 'How long ... English?' 'Six months.'
A do you learn B are you learning C you are learning
D have you been learning

11 Paul is Canadian, but he lives in France. He has been there ... .
A for three years B since three years C three years ago D during three years

12 'What time ... ?' 'About an hour ago.'
A has Lisa phoned B Lisa has phoned C did Lisa phone D is Lisa phoning

13 What ... when you saw her?
A did Sue wear B was Sue wearing C has Sue worn D was wearing Sue

14 'Can you drive?' 'No, ... a car, but I want to learn.'
A I never drive B I'm never driving C I've never driven
D I was never driving

15 I saw Helen at the station when I was going to work this morning, but she ... me.
A didn't see B don't see C hasn't seen D didn't saw

passive **Units 21–22, Appendix 1**

24 Complete the sentences.

1

These houses were built (build) 20 years ago. Before that there was a cinema here, but the building .... (damage) in a fire and had to .... (knock down).

2

This bridge .... (build) in 1955. It .... (use) by hundreds of people every day. At the moment the bridge .... (paint).

3

This street .... (call) Wilton Street. It used to .... (call) James Street, but the name .... (change) a few years ago.

4

This is a bicycle factory. Bicycles .... (make) here since 1961. It's the largest bicycle factory in the country. Thousands of bicycles .... (produce) here every year.

25 Complete the sentences.

1 We were invited (invite) to the party, but we didn't go.
2 The museum is very popular. Every year it .... (visit) by thousands of people.
3 Many buildings .... (damage) in the storm last week.
4 A new road is going to .... (build) next year.
5 'Where's your jacket?' 'It .... (clean). It will be ready tomorrow.'
6 She's famous now, but in a few years her name will .... (forget).
7 'Shall I do the washing-up?' 'No, it .... (already/do).'
8 Milk should .... (keep) in a fridge.
9 .... (you/ever/bite) by a snake?
10 My bag .... (steal) from my car yesterday afternoon.

26 Write a new sentence with the same meaning.

1 Somebody has stolen my keys. My keys have been stolen.
2 Somebody stole my car last week. My car ....
3 Somebody wants you on the phone. You ....
4 Somebody has eaten all the bananas. All the ....
5 Somebody will repair the machine. The ....
6 Somebody is watching us. We ....
7 Somebody has to do the housework. The ....

27 Active or passive? Complete the sentences.

1 They ....are building........ (build) a new airport at the moment.
2 These shirts are clean now. They ....have been washed........ (wash).
3 'How did you fall?' 'Somebody .... (push) me.'
4 'How did you fall?' 'I .... (push).'
5 I can't find my bag. Somebody .... (take) it!
6 My watch is broken. It .... (repair) at the moment.
7 Who .... (invent) the camera?
8 When .... (the camera/invent)?
9 These shirts are clean now. They .... (wash).
10 These shirts are clean now. I .... (wash) them.
11 The letter was for me, so why .... (they/send) it to you?
12 The information will .... (send) to you as soon as possible.

---

future **Units 25–28**

28 Which is the best alternative?

1 ....We're having (B)........ a party next Sunday. I hope you can come.
A We have B We're having C We'll have

2 Do you know about Karen? .... her job. She told me last week.
A She leaves B She's going to leave C She'll leave

3 There's a programme on television that I want to watch. .... in five minutes.
A It starts B It's starting C It will start

4 The weather is nice now, but I think .... later.
A it rains B it's raining C it will rain

5 'What .... next weekend?' 'Nothing. I've got no plans.'
A do you do B are you doing C will you do

6 'When you see Tina, can you ask her to phone me?' 'OK, ... her.'
A I ask B I'm going to ask C I'll ask

7 'What would you like to drink, tea or coffee?' '................................ tea, please.'
A I have B I'm going to have C I'll have

8 Don't take that newspaper away. .... it.
A I read B I'm going to read C I'll read

9 Rachel is ill, so .... to the party tomorrow night.
A she doesn't come B she isn't coming C she won't come

10 I want to meet Sarah at the station. What time .... ?
A does her train arrive B is her train going to arrive C is her train arriving

11 'Will you be at home tomorrow evening?' 'No. ....'
A I go out B I'm going out C I'll go out

12 .... you tomorrow?' 'Yes, OK.'
A Do I phone B Am I going to phone C Shall I phone

past, present and future

Units 3–20, 25–28

29 Complete the sentences.

1 A: Did you go (you/go) out last night?
B: No, ... (I/stay) at home.
A: What .... (you/do)?
B: .... (I/watch) television.
A: .... (you/go) out tomorrow night?
B: Yes, ... (I/go) to the cinema.
A: Which film .... (you/see)?
B: .... (I/not/know). .... (I/not/decide) yet.

2 A: Are you on holiday here?
B: Yes, we are.
A How long .... (you/be) here?
B: .... (we/arrive) yesterday.
A: And how long .... (you/stay)?
B: Until the end of next week.
A: And .... (you/like) it here?
B: Yes, ... (we/have) a wonderful time.

3 A: Oh, ... (I/just/remember) – .... (Karen/phone) while you were out.
B: .... (she/always/phone) when I'm not here. .... (she/leave) a message?
A: No, but .... (she/want) you to call her back as soon as possible.
B: OK, ... (I/phone) her now. .... (you/know) her number?
A: It's in my address book. .... (I/get) it for you.

4 A: .... (I/go) out with Chris and Steve this evening. .... (you/want) to come with us?
B: Yes, where .... (you/go)?
A: To the Italian restaurant in North Street. .... (you/ever/eat) there?
B: Yes, ... (I/be) there two or three times. In fact I .... (go) there last night, but I'd love to go again!

5 A: .... (I/lose) my glasses again. .... (you/see) them?
B: .... (you/wear) them when .... (I/come) in.
A: Well, ... (I/not/wear) them now, so where are they?
B: .... (you/look) in the kitchen?
A: No, ... (I/go) and look now.

past, present and future — Units 3–22, 25–28, 52, 54, 98, 105

30 Rachel is talking about her best friend, Carolyn. Put the verbs in the correct form.

Rachel

Carolyn is my best friend. I remember very well the first time (1) .... (we/meet). It was our first day at secondary school, and (2) .... (we/sit) next to each other for the first lesson. (3) .... (we/not/know) any other students in our class, and so (4) .... (we/become) friends. We found that (5) .... (we/like) the same things, especially music and sport, and so (6) .... (we/spend) a lot of time together.

(7) .... (we/leave) school five years ago, but (8) .... (we/meet) as often as we can. For the last six months Carolyn (9) .... (be) in Mexico – at the moment (10) .... (she/work) in a school as a teaching assistant. (11) .... (she/come) back to England next month, and when (12) .... (she/come) back, (13) .... (we/have) lots of things to talk about. (14) .... (it/be) really nice to see her again.

31 Nick and his friend Jon are travelling round the world. Read the emails between Nick and his parents, and put the verbs in the correct form.

Dear Mum and Dad

We're in Los Angeles, the first stop on our round-the-world trip! (1) *We arrived* (we/arrive) here yesterday, and now (2) .... (we/stay) at a hotel near the airport. The flight was twelve hours, but (3) .... (we/enjoy) it. (4) .... (we/watch) some films and (5) .... (sleep) a few hours, which is unusual for me – usually (6) .... (I/not/sleep) well on planes.

Today is a rest day for us and (7) .... (we/not/do) anything special, but tomorrow (8) .... (we/go) to Hollywood (9) .... (see) the film studios. (10) .... (we/not/decide) yet what to do after Los Angeles. Jon (11) .... (want) to drive up the coast to San Francisco, but I'd prefer (12) .... (go) south to San Diego.

I hope all is well with you – (13) .... (I/send) you another email next week.

Love

Nick

Nick

Dear Nick

Thanks for your mail. It's good to hear that (14) .... (you/have) a good time. We're fine – Ellie and Jo (15) .... (work) hard for their exams next month. Dad has been busy at work and last week (16) .... (he/have) a lot of important meetings. He's a little tired – I think (17) .... (he/need) a good holiday.

Keep in touch!

Love

Mum

A month later …

Hi Mum and Dad

(18) .... (we/be) in California for a month now. (19) .... (we/get) back to Los Angeles yesterday after (20) .... (see) many wonderful places. I think the place (21) .... (I/like) most was Yosemite National Park – it's beautiful there and (22) .... (we/go) cycling a lot. The day before (23) .... (we/leave), Jon (24) .... (have) an accident on his bike. Luckily (25) .... (he/not/injure), but the bike (26) .... (damage).

(27) .... (we/change) our travel plans since my last message: now (28) .... (we/leave) for Hawaii on Monday (not Tuesday). (29) .... (we/stay) there for a week before (30) .... (fly) to New Zealand. (31) .... (that/be) different, I'm sure! All the best to Ellie and Jo for their exams.

Love

Nick

Hi Nick

Have a good time in Hawaii! Ellie and Jo (32) .... (finish) their exams yesterday – (33) .... (I/let) you know when (34) .... (we/get) the results.

We're all OK. Dad and I (35) .... (look) forward to our holiday next month. (36) .... (we/go) to Italy for two weeks – (37) .... (we/send) you an email from there.

Take care!

Love

Mum

-ing and to ...

Units 51–55, 105, 112

32 Which is correct?

1 Don't forget to switch (B) off the light before you go out.
A switch B to switch C switching

2 It's late. I must .... now.
A go B to go C going

3 I'm sorry, but I haven't got time .... to you now.
A for talking B to talk C talking

4 Gary is always in the kitchen. He enjoys ....
A cook B to cook C cooking

5 We've decided .... away for a few days.
A go B to go C going

6 You're making too much noise. Can you please stop .... ?
A shout B to shout C shouting

7 Would you like .... to dinner on Sunday?
A come B to come C coming

8 That bag is too heavy for you. Let me .... you.
A help B to help C helping

9 There's a swimming pool near my house. I go .... every day.
A to swim B to swimming C swimming

10 Did you use a dictionary .... the letter?
A to translate B for translating C for translate

11 I'd love .... a car like yours.
A have B to have C having

12 Could you .... me with this bag, please?
A help B to help C helping

13 I don't mind .... here, but I'd prefer to sit by the window.
A sit B to sit C sitting

14 Do you want .... you?
A that I help B me to help C me helping

15 I usually read the newspaper before .... work.
A start B to start C starting

16 I wasn't feeling very well, but the medicine made me .... better.
A feel B to feel C feeling

17 Shall I phone the restaurant .... a table?
A for reserve B for reserving C to reserve

18 Tom looked at me without .... anything.
A say B saying C to say

a and the

Units 65, 69–73

33 Complete the sentences.

34 Write a/an or the if necessary. If a/an/the are not necessary, leave an empty space (–).

1 Who is ...the... best player in your team?
2 I don't watch ...–... television very often.
3 'Is there ...a... bank near here?' 'Yes, at ...the... end of this street.'
4 I can't ride .... horse.
5 .... sky is very clear tonight.
6 Do you live here, or are you .... tourist?
7 What did you have for .... lunch?
8 Who was .... first President of .... United States?
9 'What time is it? 'I don't know. I haven't got .... watch.'
10 I'm sorry, but I've forgotten your name. I can never remember .... names.
11 What time is .... next train to London?
12 Kate never sends .... emails. She prefers to phone people.
13 'Where's Sue?' 'She's in .... garden.'
14 Excuse me, I'm looking for .... Majestic Hotel. Is it near here?
15 Gary was ill .... last week, so he didn't go to .... work.
16 Everest is .... highest mountain in .... world.
17 I usually listen to .... radio while I'm having .... breakfast.
18 I like .... sport. My favourite sport is .... basketball.
19 Julia is .... doctor. Her husband is .... art teacher.
20 My apartment is on .... second floor. Turn left at .... top of .... stairs, and it's on .... right.
21 After .... dinner, we watched .... television.
22 Last year we had .... wonderful holiday in .... south of .... France.

---

prepositions Units 103–108, 111

35 Write a preposition (in/for/by etc.).

1 Helen is studying law ...at... university.
2 What is the longest river .... Europe?
3 Is there anything .... television this evening?
4 We arrived .... the hotel after midnight.
5 'Where's Mike?' 'He's .... holiday.'
6 Tom hasn't got up yet. He's still .... bed.
7 Lisa is away. She's been away .... Monday.
8 The next meeting is .... 15 April.
9 I usually go to work .... car.
10 There's too much sugar .... my coffee.
11 Kevin lived in London .... six months. He didn't like it very much.
12 Were there a lot of people .... the party?
13 What are you doing .... the moment? Are you working?
14 I don't know any of the people .... this photograph.
15 The train was very slow. It stopped .... every station.
16 I like this room. I like the pictures .... the walls.
17 'Did you buy that picture?' 'No, it was given to me .... a friend of mine.'
18 I'm going away .... a few days. I'll be back .... Thursday.
19 Silvia has gone .... Italy. She's .... Milan at the moment.
20 Emma left school .... fifteen and got a job .... a shop.

Study guide

If you are not sure which units you need to study, use this study guide.

You have to decide which alternative (A, B, C etc.) is right. SOMETIMES MORE THAN ONE ALTERNATIVE IS CORRECT.

If you don't know (or if you are not sure) which alternatives are correct, study the unit (or units) on the right. You will find the correct sentence in the unit.

The key to this study guide is on page 314.

IF YOU ARE NOT SURE WHICH IS RIGHT	STUDY UNIT
Present	
1.1 ………… . Can you close the window, please? **A** I cold **B** I'm cold **C** I have cold **D** It has cold	1
1.2 Tom ………… in politics. **A** isn't interested **B** not interested **C** doesn't interested **D** doesn't interest	1
1.3 '…………?' 'No, she's out.' **A** Is at home your mother **B** Does your mother at home **C** Is your mother at home **D** Are your mother at home	2
1.4 These postcards are nice. ………… **A** How much are they? **B** How many are they? **C** How much they are? **D** How much is they?	2
1.5 Look, there's Sarah. ………… a brown coat. **A** She wearing **B** She has wearing **C** She is wearing **D** She's wearing	3, 23
1.6 You can turn off the television. ………… it. **A** I'm not watch **B** I'm not watching **C** I not watching **D** I don't watching	3, 23
1.7 '………… today?' 'No, he's at home.' **A** Is working Paul **B** Is work Paul **C** Is Paul work **D** Is Paul working	4, 23
1.8 Look, there's Emily! ………… **A** Where she is going? **B** Where she go? **C** Where's she going? **D** Where she going?	4, 23
1.9 The earth ………… round the sun. **A** going **B** go **C** goes **D** does go **E** is go	5, 23
1.10 We ………… away at weekends. **A** often go **B** go often **C** often going **D** are often go	5, 23, 94
1.11 We ………… television very often. **A** not watch **B** doesn't watch **C** don't watch **D** don't watching **E** watch not	6, 23
1.12 '………… on Sundays?' 'No, not usually.' **A** Do you work **B** Are you work **C** Does you work **D** Do you working **E** Work you	7, 23
1.13 I don't understand this sentence. What …………? **A** mean this word **B** means this word **C** does mean this word **D** does this word mean **E** this word means	7, 23

IF YOU ARE NOT SURE WHICH IS RIGHT	STUDY UNIT
1.14 Please be quiet. .... **A** I working. **B** I work. **C** I'm working. **D** I'm work.	8, 23
1.15 Tom .... a shower every morning. **A** has **B** having **C** is having **D** have	8, 58
1.16 What .... at the weekend? **A** do you usually **B** are you usually doing **C** are you usually do **D** do you usually do **E** you do usually	8, 23
1.17 Sarah isn't feeling well. .... a headache. **A** She have **B** She have got **C** She has **D** She's got	9, 58
1.18 Tracey and Jeff .... any children. **A** don't have **B** doesn't have **C** no have **D** haven't got **E** hasn't got	9, 58
Past	
2.1 The weather .... last week. **A** is good **B** was good **C** were good **D** good **E** had good	10
2.2 Why .... late this morning? **A** you was **B** did you **C** was you **D** you were **E** were you	10
2.3 Terry .... in a bank from 1996 to 2003. **A** work **B** working **C** works **D** worked **E** was work	11
2.4 Caroline .... to the cinema three times last week. **A** go **B** went **C** goes **D** got **E** was	11
2.5 I .... television yesterday. **A** didn't watch **B** didn't watched **C** wasn't watched **D** don't watch **E** didn't watching	12, 23
2.6 'How .... ?' 'I don't know. I didn't see it.' **A** happened the accident **B** did happen the accident **C** does the accident happen **D** did the accident happen **E** the accident happened	12
2.7 What .... at 11.30 yesterday? **A** were you doing **B** was you doing **C** you were doing **D** were you do **E** you was doing	13
2.8 Jack was reading a book when the phone .... **A** ringing **B** ring **C** rang **D** was ringing **E** was ring	14
2.9 I saw Lucy and Steve this morning. They .... at the bus stop. **A** waiting **B** waited **C** were waiting **D** was waiting **E** were waited	14
Present perfect	
3.1 'Where's Rebecca?' '.................. to bed.' **A** She is gone **B** She has gone **C** She goes **D** She have gone **E** She's gone	15
3.2 'Are Diane and Paul here?' 'No, they ....' **A** don't arrive yet **B** have already arrived **C** haven't already arrived **D** haven't arrived yet	16

IF YOU ARE NOT SURE WHICH IS RIGHT	STUDY UNIT
3.3 My sister .... by plane. **A** has never travel **B** has never travelled **C** is never travelled **D** has never been travelled **E** have never travelled	17, 23
3.4 .... that woman before, but I can't remember where. **A** I see **B** I seen **C** I've saw **D** I've seen **E** I've seeing	17, 23
3.5 'How long .... married?' 'Since 1998.' **A** you are **B** you have been **C** has you been **D** are you **E** have you been	18
3.6 'Do you know Lisa?' 'Yes, ... her for a long time.' **A** I knew **B** I've known **C** I know **D** I am knowing	18
3.7 Richard has been in Canada .... **A** for six months **B** since six months **C** six months ago **D** in six months	19, 104
3.8 'When did Tom go out?' '........................' **A** For ten minutes. **B** Since ten minutes. **C** Ten minutes ago. **D** In ten minutes.	19
3.9 We .... a holiday last year. **A** don't have **B** haven't had **C** hasn't had **D** didn't have **E** didn't had	20
3.10 Where .... on Sunday afternoon? I couldn't find you. **A** you were **B** you have been **C** was you **D** have you been **E** were you	20
Passive	
4.1 This house .... 100 years ago. **A** is built **B** is building **C** was building **D** was built **E** built	21, 23
4.2 We .... to the party last week. **A** didn't invite **B** didn't invited **C** weren't invited **D** wasn't invited **E** haven't been invited	21, 23
4.3 'Where .... born?' 'In Cairo.' **A** you are **B** you were **C** was you **D** are you **E** were you	21
4.4 My car is at the garage. It .... **A** is being repaired **B** is repairing **C** have been repaired **D** repaired **E** repairs	22
4.5 I can't find my keys. I think .... **A** they've been stolen **B** they are stolen **C** they've stolen **D** they're being stolen	22
Verb forms	
5.1 It ...., so we didn't need an umbrella. **A** wasn't rained **B** wasn't rain **C** didn't raining **D** wasn't raining	23
5.2 Somebody .... this window. **A** has broke **B** has broken **C** has breaked **D** has break	24

IF YOU ARE NOT SURE WHICH IS RIGHT	STUDY UNIT
Future	
6.1 Andrew .... tennis tomorrow. **A** is playing **B** play **C** plays **D** is play	25
6.2 .... out tonight? **A** Are you going **B** Are you go **C** Do you go **D** Go you **E** Do you going	25
6.3 'What time is the concert tonight?' 'It .... at 7.30.' **A** is start **B** is starting **C** starts **D** start **E** starting	25
6.4 What .... to the wedding next week? **A** are you wearing **B** are you going to wear **C** do you wear **D** you are going to wear	26
6.5 I think Kelly .... the exam. **A** passes **B** will pass **C** will be pass **D** will passing	27
6.6 .... to the cinema on Saturday. Do you want to come with us? **A** We go **B** We'll go **C** We're going **D** We will going	27
6.7 '.................... you tomorrow, OK?' 'OK, bye.' **A** I phone **B** I phoning **C** I'm phoning **D** I'll phone	28
6.8 There's a good film on TV tonight. .... it. **A** I watch **B** I'll watch **C** I'm going to watch **D** I'll watching	28
6.9 It's a nice day. .... for a walk? **A** Do we go **B** Shall we go **C** Are we go **D** We go **E** Go we	28
Modals, imperative etc.	
7.1 .... to the cinema this evening, but I'm not sure. **A** I'll go **B** I'm going **C** I may go **D** I might go	29
7.2 '.................... here?' 'Yes, of course.' **A** Can I sit **B** Do I sit **C** May I sit **D** Can I to sit	29, 30
7.3 I'm having a party next week, but Paul and Rachel .... **A** can't come **B** can't to come **C** can't coming **D** couldn't come	30
7.4 Before Maria came to Britain, she .... understand much English. **A** can **B** can't **C** not **D** couldn't **E** doesn't	30
7.5 We .... walk home last night. There were no buses. **A** have to **B** had to **C** must **D** must to **E** must have	31, 33
7.6 I .... go yet. I can stay a little longer. **A** must **B** mustn't **C** must not **D** don't need **E** don't need to	31
7.7 It's a good film. You .... go and see it. **A** should to **B** ought to **C** ought **D** should **E** need	32
7.8 What time .... go to the dentist tomorrow? **A** you must **B** you have to **C** have you to **D** do you have to	33
7.9 We .... wait long for the bus – it came in a few minutes. **A** don't have to **B** hadn't to **C** didn't have to **D** didn't had to **E** mustn't	33

IF YOU ARE NOT SURE WHICH IS RIGHT	STUDY UNIT
7.10 '.................... some coffee?' 'No, thank you.' **A** Are you liking **B** You like **C** Would you like **D** Do you like	34
7.11 Please .... Stay here with me. **A** don't go **B** you no go **C** go not **D** you don't go	35
7.12 Dave .... in a factory. Now he works in a supermarket. **A** working **B** works **C** worked **D** use to work **E** used to work	36

There and it

8.1 Excuse me, ... a hotel near here? **A** has there **B** is there **C** there is **D** is it	37
8.2 .... a lot of accidents on this road. It's very dangerous. **A** Have **B** It has **C** There have **D** They are **E** There are	37
8.3 I was hungry when I got home, but .... anything to eat. **A** there wasn't **B** there weren't **C** it wasn't **D** there hasn't been	38
8.4 .... three kilometres from our house to the city centre. **A** It's **B** It has **C** There is **D** There are	39
8.5 .... true that you're going away? **A** Is there **B** Is it **C** Is **D** Are you	39

Auxiliary verbs

9.1 I haven't got a car, but my sister .... **A** have **B** is **C** has **D** hasn't **E** has got	40
9.2 I don't like hot weather, but Sue .... **A** does **B** doesn't **C** do **D** does like **E** likes	40
9.3 'Nicole got married last week.' '.................... Really?' **A** Is she? **B** Got she? **C** Did she? **D** Has she?	41
9.4 You haven't met my mother, ... ? **A** haven't you **B** have you **C** did you **D** you have **E** you haven't	41
9.5 Bill doesn't watch TV. He doesn't read newspapers .... **A** too **B** either **C** neither **D** never	42
9.6 'I'd like to go to Australia.' '....................' **A** So do I. **B** So am I. **C** So would I. **D** Neither do I. **E** So I would.	42
9.7 Sue .... much at weekends. **A** don't **B** doesn't **C** don't do **D** doesn't do	43

Questions

10.1 'When .... ?' 'I'm not sure. More than 100 years ago.' **A** did the telephone invent **B** has the telephone invented **C** was invented the telephone **D** was the telephone invented **E** the telephone was invented	44
10.2 'I broke my finger last week.' 'How .... that?' **A** did you **B** you did **C** you did do **D** did you do	44

IF YOU ARE NOT SURE WHICH IS RIGHT — STUDY UNIT

10.3 Why .... me last night? I was waiting for you to phone. — **44**
A didn't you phone **B** you not phone **C** you don't phone
D you didn't phone

10.4 'Who .... in this house?' 'I don't know.' — **45**
A lives **B** does live **C** does lives **D** living

10.5 What .... when you told him the story? — **45**
A said Paul **B** did Paul say **C** Paul said **D** did Paul said

10.6 'Tom's father is in hospital.' '....................................' — **46**
A In which hospital he is? **B** In which hospital he is in?
C Which hospital he is in? **D** Which hospital is he in?

10.7 Did you have a good holiday? .... — **46**
A How was the weather like? **B** What was the weather like?
C What the weather was like? **D** Was the weather like?

10.8 .... taller – Joe or Gary? — **47**
A Who is **B** What is **C** Which is **D** Who has

10.9 There are four umbrellas here. .... is yours? — **47, 75**
A What **B** Who **C** Which **D** How **E** Which one

10.10 How long .... to cross the Atlantic by ship? — **48**
A is it **B** does it need **C** does it take **D** does it want

10.11 I don't remember what .... at the party. — **49**
A Kate was wearing **B** was wearing Kate **C** was Kate wearing

10.12 'Do you know .... ?' 'Yes, I think so.' — **49**
A if Jack is at home **B** is Jack at home **C** whether Jack is at home
D that Jack is at home

Reported speech

11.1 I saw Steve a week ago. He said that .... me, but he didn't. — **50**
A he phone **B** he phones **C** he'll phone **D** he's going to phone
E he would phone

11.2 'Why did Tim go to bed so early?' 'He ....' — **50**
A said he was tired **B** said that he was tired **C** said me he was tired
D told me he was tired **E** told that he was tired

-ing and to ...

12.1 You shouldn't .... so hard. — **51**
A working **B** work **C** to work **D** worked

12.2 It's late. I .... now. — **51**
A must to go **B** have go **C** have to going **D** have to go

12.3 Tina has decided .... her car. — **52**
A sell **B** to sell **C** selling **D** to selling

12.4 I don't mind .... early. — **52**
A get up **B** to get up **C** getting up **D** to getting up

IF YOU ARE NOT SURE WHICH IS RIGHT	STUDY UNIT
12.5 Do you like .... early? **A** get up **B** to get up **C** getting up **D** to getting up	52
12.6 Do you want .... you some money? **A** me lend **B** me lending **C** me to lend **D** that I lend	53
12.7 He's very funny. He makes .... **A** me laugh **B** me laughing **C** me to laugh **D** that I laugh	53
12.8 Paula went to the shop .... a newspaper. **A** for get **B** for to get **C** for getting **D** to get **E** get	54
Go, get, do, make and have	
13.1 It's a nice day. Let's go .... **A** for a swim **B** on a swim **C** to swimming **D** swimming	55
13.2 I'm sorry your mother is ill. I hope she .... better soon. **A** has **B** makes **C** gets **D** goes	56
13.3 Kate .... the car and drove away. **A** went into **B** went in **C** got in **D** got into	56
13.4 'Shall I open the window?' 'No, it's OK. I'll .... it.' **A** do **B** make **C** get **D** open	57
13.5 I'm sorry, I .... a mistake. **A** did **B** made **C** got **D** had	57
13.6 '.......... a good time in London?' 'Yes, I really enjoyed it.' **A** Have you **B** Had you **C** Do you have **D** Did you have	58
Pronouns and possessives	
14.1 I don't want this book. You can have .... **A** it **B** them **C** her **D** him	59, 62
14.2 Sue and Kevin are going to the cinema. Do you want to go with .... ? **A** her **B** they **C** them **D** him	59, 62
14.3 I know Donna, but I don't know .... husband. **A** their **B** his **C** she **D** her	60, 62
14.4 Oxford is famous for .... university. **A** his **B** its **C** it's **D** their	60
14.5 I didn't have an umbrella, so Helen gave me .... **A** her **B** hers **C** her umbrella **D** she's	61, 62
14.6 I went out to meet a friend of .... **A** mine **B** my **C** me **D** I **E** myself	61, 62
14.7 We had a good holiday. We enjoyed .... **A** us **B** our **C** ours **D** ourself **E** ourselves	63
14.8 Kate and Helen are good friends. They know .... well. **A** each other **B** them **C** themselves **D** theirselves	63

IF YOU ARE NOT SURE WHICH IS RIGHT	STUDY UNIT
14.9 Have you met .... ? **A** the wife of Mr Black **B** Mr Black wife **C** the wife Mr Black **D** Mr Black's wife **E** the Mr Black's wife	64
14.10 Have you seen .... ? **A** the car of my parents **B** my parent's car **C** my parents' car **D** my parents car	64

A and the

15.1 I'm going to buy .... **A** hat and umbrella **B** a hat and a umbrella **C** a hat and an umbrella **D** an hat and an umbrella	65, 67
15.2 'What's your job?' '..........' **A** I dentist. **B** I'm a dentist. **C** I'm dentist. **D** I do dentist.	65
15.3 I'm going shopping. I need .... **A** some new jeans **B** a new jeans **C** a new pair of jeans **D** a new pair jeans	66
15.4 I like the people here. .... very friendly. **A** She is **B** They are **C** They is **D** It is **E** He is	66
15.5 We can't get into the house without .... **A** some key **B** a key **C** key	67
15.6 I'd like .... about hotels in London. **A** some information **B** some informations **C** an information	68
15.7 We enjoyed our holiday. .... was very nice. **A** Hotel **B** A hotel **C** An hotel **D** The hotel	69, 70
15.8 My house is at .... **A** end of street **B** end of the street **C** the end of the street **D** the end of street	70
15.9 What did you have for .... ? **A** the breakfast **B** breakfast **C** a breakfast	70
15.10 I finish .... at 5 o'clock every day. **A** the work **B** work **C** a work	71
15.11 I'm tired. I'm going .... **A** in bed **B** in the bed **C** to a bed **D** to the bed **E** to bed	71
15.12 We don't eat .... very often. **A** the meat **B** some meat **C** a meat **D** meat	72
15.13 .... is in New York. **A** The Times Square **B** Times Square	73
15.14 My friends are staying at .... **A** the Regent Hotel **B** Regent Hotel	73

IF YOU ARE NOT SURE WHICH IS RIGHT — STUDY UNIT

Determiners and pronouns

16.1 'I'm going on holiday next week.' 'Oh, ... nice.' — 74
A it's B this is C that's

16.2 'Is there a bank near here?' 'Yes, there's .... at the end of this street.' — 75
A some B it C one D a one

16.3 This cup is dirty. Can I have .... ? — 75
A clean one B a clean one C clean D a clean

16.4 I'm going shopping. I'm going to buy .... clothes. — 76
A any B some

16.5 'Where's your luggage?' 'I haven't got ....' — 76
A one B some C any

16.6 Tracey and Jeff .... — 77, 78
A have got no children B haven't got no children C haven't got any children
D have got any children

16.7 'How much money have you got?' '....................' — 77
A No. B No-one. C Any. D None.

16.8 There is .... in the room. It's empty. — 78, 79
A anybody B nobody C anyone D no-one

16.9 'What did you say?' '....................' — 78, 79
A Nothing. B Nobody. C Anything. D Not anything.

16.10 I'm hungry. I want .... — 79
A something for eat B something to eat C something for eating

16.11 Bill watches TV for about two hours .... — 80
A all evening B all evenings C all the evenings D every evenings
E every evening

16.12 .... friends. — 80
A Everybody need B Everybody needs C Everyone need D Everyone needs

16.13 .... children like playing. — 81
A Most B The most C Most of D The most of

16.14 I like .... those pictures. — 82
A both B both of C either D either of

16.15 I haven't read .... these books. — 82
A neither B neither of C either D either of

16.16 Have you got .... friends? — 83
A a lot of B much C many D much of E many of

16.17 We like films, so we go to the cinema .... — 83
A a lot of B much C many D a lot

16.18 There were .... people in the theatre. It was nearly empty. — 84
A a little B few C little D a few of

16.19 They have .... money, so they're not poor. — 84
A a little B a few C few D little E little of

IF YOU ARE NOT SURE WHICH IS RIGHT	STUDY UNIT

Adjectives and adverbs

17.1 I don't speak any ....
A foreign languages B languages foreign C languages foreigns — 85

17.2 He ate his dinner very ....
A quick B quicker C quickly — 86

17.3 You speak English very ....
A good B fluent C well D slow — 86

17.4 Helen wants ....
A a more big car B a car more big C a car bigger D a bigger car — 87

17.5 'Do you feel better today?' 'No, I feel ....'
A good B worse C more bad D more worse — 87

17.6 Athens is older .... Rome.
A as B than C that D of — 88

17.7 I can run faster ....
A than him B that he can C than he can D as he can E as he — 88

17.8 Tennis isn't .... football.
A popular as B popular than C as popular than D so popular that
E as popular as — 89

17.9 The weather today is the same .... yesterday.
A as B that C than D like — 89

17.10 The Europa Hotel is .... in the city.
A the more expensive hotel B the most expensive hotel
C the hotel most expensive D the hotel the more expensive
E the hotel more expensive — 90

17.11 The film was very bad. I think it's the .... film I've ever seen.
A worse B baddest C most bad D worst E more worse — 90

17.12 Why don't you buy a car? You've got ....
A enough money B money enough C enough of money — 91

17.13 Is your English .... a conversation?
A enough good to have B good enough for have C enough good for
D good enough to have — 91

17.14 I'm .... out.
A too tired for go B too much tired for going C too tired to go
D too much tired to go — 92

Word order

18.1 Sue is interested in the news. She ....
A reads every day a newspaper B reads a newspaper every day
C every day reads a newspaper — 93

18.2 .... coffee in the morning.
A I drink always B Always I drink C I always drink — 94

IF YOU ARE NOT SURE WHICH IS RIGHT	STUDY UNIT
18.3 .... during the day. **A** They are at home never **B** They are never at home **C** They never are at home **D** Never they are at home	94
18.4 'Where's Emma?' 'She ....' **A** isn't here yet **B** isn't here already **C** isn't here still	95
18.5 I locked the door and I gave .... **A** Sarah the keys **B** to Sarah the keys **C** the keys Sarah **D** the keys to Sarah	96
Conjunctions and clauses	
19.1 I can't talk to you now. I'll talk to you later when .... more time. **A** I'll have **B** I had **C** I have **D** I'm going to have	98
19.2 .... late this evening, don't wait for me. **A** If I'm **B** If I'll be **C** When I'm **D** When I'll be	99
19.3 I don't know the answer. If I .... the answer, I'd tell you. **A** know **B** would know **C** have known **D** knew	100
19.4 I like this jacket. .... it if it wasn't so expensive. **A** I buy **B** I'll buy **C** I bought **D** I'd bought **E** I'd buy	100
19.5 Emma lives in a house .... is 400 years old. **A** who **B** that **C** which **D** it **E** what	101
19.6 The people .... work in the office are very friendly. **A** who **B** that **C** they **D** which **E** what	101
19.7 Did you find the book .... ? **A** who you wanted **B** that you wanted **C** what you wanted **D** you wanted **E** you wanted it	102
19.8 I met .... can speak six languages. **A** a woman who **B** a woman which **C** a woman **D** a woman she	102
Prepositions	
20.1 Bye! I'll see you .... **A** until Friday **B** at Friday **C** in Friday **D** on Friday	103
20.2 Hurry! The train leaves .... five minutes. **A** at **B** on **C** from **D** after **E** in	103
20.3 'How long will you be away?' '.................... Monday.' **A** On **B** To **C** Until **D** Till **E** Since	104
20.4 We played tennis yesterday. We played .... two hours. **A** in **B** for **C** since **D** during	105
20.5 I always have breakfast before .... to work. **A** I go **B** go **C** to go **D** going	105
20.6 Write your name .... the top of the page. **A** at **B** on **C** in **D** to	106

IF YOU ARE NOT SURE WHICH IS RIGHT	STUDY UNIT
20.7 There are a lot of apples .... those trees. **A** at **B** on **C** in **D** to	106
20.8 What's the largest city .... the world? **A** at **B** on **C** in **D** of	107
20.9 The office is .... the first floor. **A** at **B** on **C** in **D** to	107
20.10 I met a lot of people .... the party. **A** on **B** to **C** in **D** at	108
20.11 I want to go .... Italy next year. **A** at **B** on **C** in **D** to	108
20.12 What time did you arrive .... the hotel? **A** at **B** on **C** in **D** to	108
20.13 'Where is David in this picture?' 'He's .... Barbara.' **A** at front of **B** in the front of **C** in front of **D** in front from	109
20.14 I jumped .... the wall into the garden. **A** on **B** through **C** across **D** over **E** above	110
20.15 Jane isn't at work this week. She's .... holiday. **A** on **B** in **C** for **D** to **E** at	111
20.16 Do you like travelling .... ? **A** with train **B** with the train **C** in train **D** on train **E** by train	111
20.17 I'm not very good .... telling stories. **A** on **B** with **C** at **D** in **E** for	112
20.18 Tom left without .... goodbye. **A** say **B** saying **C** to say **D** that he said	112
20.19 I'm going to phone .... this evening. **A** with my parents **B** to my parents **C** at my parents **D** my parents	113
20.20 'Do you like eating in restaurants?' 'It depends .... the restaurant.' **A** in **B** at **C** of **D** on **E** over	113
Phrasal verbs	
21.1 The car stopped and a woman got .... **A** off **B** down **C** out **D** out of	114
21.2 It was cold, so I .... **A** put on my coat **B** put my coat on **C** put the coat on me **D** put me the coat on	115
21.3 I've got Rachel's keys. I have to .... to her. **A** give back **B** give them back **C** give back them **D** give it back	115

Key to Exercises

UNIT 1

1
2 they're
3 it isn't / it's not
4 that's
5 I'm not
6 you aren't / you're not

1.2
2 'm/am
3 is
4 are
5 's/is
6 are
7 is … are
8 'm/am … is

1.3
2 I'm / I am
3 He's / He is
4 they're / they are
5 It's / It is
6 You're / You are
7 She's / She is
8 Here's / Here is

1.4
Example answers:
1 My name is Robert.
2 I'm from Australia.
3 I'm 25.
4 I'm a gardener.
5 My favourite colours are black and white.
6 I'm interested in plants.

1.5
2 They're / They are cold.
3 He's / He is hot.
4 He's / He is afraid.
5 They're / They are hungry.
6 She's / She is angry.

1.6
2 It's/It is windy today. *or* It isn't/It's not windy today.
3 My hands are cold. *or* My hands aren't/are not cold.
4 Brazil is a very big country.
5 Diamonds aren't/are not cheap.
6 Toronto isn't/is not in the US.
8 I'm/I am hungry. *or* I'm not/I am not hungry.
9 I'm/I am a good swimmer. *or* I'm not/I am not a good swimmer.
10 I'm/I am interested in football. *or* I'm not/I am not interested in football.

UNIT 2

2.1
2 F
3 H
4 C
5 A
6 E
7 B
8 I
9 D

2.2
3 Is your job interesting?
4 Are the shops open today?
5 Where are you from?
6 Are you interested in sport?
7 Is the post office near here?
8 Are your children at school?
9 Why are you late?

2.3
2 Where's / Where is
3 How old are
4 How much are
5 What's / What is
6 Who's / Who is
7 What colour are

2.4
2 Are you American?
3 How old are you?
4 Are you a teacher?
5 Are you married?
6 Is your wife a lawyer?
7 Where's/Where is she from?
8 What's/What is her name?
9 How old is she?

2.5
2 Yes, I am. *or* No, I'm not.
3 Yes, it is. *or* No, it isn't. / No, it's not.
4 Yes, they are. *or* No, they aren't. / No, they're not.
5 Yes, it is. *or* No, it isn't. / No, it's not.
6 Yes, I am. *or* No, I'm not.

UNIT 3

3.1
2 's/is waiting
3 're/are playing
4 He's/He is lying
5 They're/They are having
6 She's/She is sitting

3.2
2 's/is cooking
3 're/are standing
4 's/is swimming
5 're/are staying
6 's/is having
7 're/are building
8 'm/am going

3.3
3 She's/She is sitting on the floor.
4 She isn't/She's not reading a book.
5 She isn't/She's not playing the piano.
6 She's/She is laughing.
7 She's/She is wearing a hat.
8 She isn't/She's not writing a letter.

3.4
3 I'm sitting on a chair. *or* I'm not sitting on a chair.
4 I'm eating. *or* I'm not eating.
5 It's raining. *or* It isn't raining. / It's not raining.
6 I'm learning English.
7 I'm listening to music. *or* I'm not listening to music.
8 The sun is shining. *or* The sun isn't shining.
9 I'm wearing shoes. *or* I'm not wearing shoes.
10 I'm not reading a newspaper.

UNIT 4

4.1
2 Are you going now?
3 Is it raining?
4 Are you enjoying the film?
5 Is that clock working?
6 Are you waiting for a bus?

4.2
2 Where is she going?
3 What are you eating?
4 Why are you crying?
5 What are they looking at?
6 Why is he laughing?

4.3
3 Are you listening to me?
4 Where are your friends going?
5 Are your parents watching television?
6 What is Jessica cooking?
7 Why are you looking at me?
8 Is the bus coming?

4.4
2 Yes, I am. *or* No, I'm not.
3 Yes, I am. *or* No, I'm not.
4 Yes, it is. *or* No, it isn't. / No, it's not.
5 Yes, I am. *or* No, I'm not.
6 Yes, I am. *or* No, I'm not.

UNIT 5

5.1
2 thinks
3 flies
4 dances
5 has
6 finishes

5.2
2 live
3 She eats
4 He plays
5 They go
6 He sleeps

5.3
2 open
3 closes
4 teaches
5 meet
6 washes
7 costs
8 cost
9 boils
10 like … likes

5.4
2 I never go to the cinema.
3 Martina always works hard.
4 Children usually like chocolate.
5 Julia always enjoys parties.
6 I often forget people's names.
7 Tim never watches television.
8 We usually have dinner at 7.30.
9 Jenny always wears nice clothes.

5.5
Example answers:
2 I sometimes read in bed.
3 I often get up before 7 o'clock.
4 I never go to work by bus.
5 I usually drink two cups of coffee in the morning.

UNIT 6

6.1
2 Jane doesn't play the piano very well.
3 They don't know my phone number.
4 We don't work very hard.
5 He doesn't have a bath every day.
6 You don't do the same thing every day.

6.2
2 Kate doesn't like classical music.
I like (*or* I don't like) classical music.
3 Ben and Sophie don't like boxing.
Kate likes boxing.
I like (*or* I don't like) boxing.
4 Ben and Sophie like horror films.
Kate doesn't like horror films.
I like (*or* I don't like) horror films.

6.3
Example answers:
2 I never go to the theatre.
3 I don't ride a bicycle very often.
4 I never eat in restaurants.
5 I often travel by train.

6.4
2 doesn't use
3 don't go
4 doesn't wear
5 don't know
6 doesn't cost
7 don't see

6.5
3 don't know
4 doesn't talk
5 drinks
6 don't believe
7 like
8 doesn't eat

UNIT 7

7.1
2 Do you play tennis?
3 Does Lucy live near here?
4 Do Tom's friends play tennis? / Do they play tennis?
5 Does your brother speak English? / Does he speak English?
6 Do you do yoga every morning?
7 Does Paul often go away? / Does he often go away?
8 Do you want to be famous?
9 Does Anna work hard? / Does she work hard?

7.2
3 How often do you watch TV?
4 What do you want for dinner?
5 Do you like football?
6 Does your brother like football?
7 What do you do in your free time?
8 Where does your sister work?
9 Do you often go to the cinema?
10 What does this word mean?
11 Does it often snow here?
12 What time do you usually go to bed?
13 How much does it cost to phone New York?
14 What do you usually have for breakfast?

7.3
2 Do you enjoy / Do you like
3 do you start
4 Do you work
5 do you go
6 does he do
7 does he teach
8 Does he enjoy / Does he like

7.4
2 Yes, I do. *or* No, I don't.
3 Yes, I do. *or* No, I don't.
4 Yes, it does. *or* No, it doesn't.
5 Yes, I do. *or* No, I don't.

UNIT 8

8.1
2 No, she isn't.
Yes, she does.
She's playing the piano.
3 Yes, he does.
Yes, he is.
He's cleaning a window.
4 No, they aren't.
Yes, they do.
They teach.

8.2
2 don't
3 are
4 does
5 's/is … don't
6 do
7 does
8 doesn't

8.3
4 is singing
5 She wants
6 do you read
7 you're sitting
8 I don't understand
9 I'm going … Are you coming
10 does your father finish
11 I'm not listening
12 He's/He is cooking
13 doesn't usually drive … usually walks
14 doesn't like … She prefers

UNIT 9

9.1
2 he's got
3 they've got
4 she hasn't got
5 it's got
6 I haven't got

9.2
2 He's got a computer. *or*
He has a computer.
3 He hasn't got a dog. *or*
He doesn't have a dog.
4 He hasn't got a mobile phone. *or*
He doesn't have a mobile phone.
5 He's got a watch. *or*
He has a watch.
6 He's got two brothers and a sister. *or*
He has two brothers and a sister.
7 I've got a computer. / I have a computer. *or*
I haven't got a computer. / I don't have a computer.
8 I've got a dog. / I have a dog. *or*
I haven't got a dog. / I don't have a dog.
9 I've got a bike. / I have a bike. *or*
I haven't got a bike. / I don't have a bike.
10 *(Example answer)* I've got a brother and a sister.

9.3
3 He's got a new job.
4 They haven't got much money.
5 Have you got an umbrella?
6 We've got a lot of work to do.
7 I haven't got your phone number.
8 Has your father got a car?
9 How much money have we got?

9.4
3 's got / has got (*or* has)
4 haven't got (*or* don't have)
5 've got / have got (*or* have)
6 haven't got (*or* don't have)
7 hasn't got (*or* doesn't have)

9.5
3 have got four wheels *or*
have four wheels
4 's got / has got a lot of friends *or*
has a lot of friends
5 haven't got a key *or*
don't have a key
6 has got six legs *or*
has six legs
7 haven't got much time *or*
don't have much time

UNIT 10

10.1
2 Jack and Kate were at/in the cinema.
3 Sue was at the station.
4 Mr and Mrs Hall were in/at a restaurant.
5 Ben was on the beach / on a beach / at the beach / at the seaside.
6 *(Example answer)* I was at work.

10.2
2 is … was
3 'm/am
4 was
5 were
6 're/are
7 Was
8 was
9 are … were

10.3
2 wasn't … was
3 was … were
4 '**Were** Kate and Bill at the party?' 'Kate **was** there, but Bill **wasn't**.' *or*
'Kate **wasn't** there, but Bill **was**.'
5 were
6 weren't … were

10.4
2 Was your exam difficult?
3 Where were Sue and Chris last week?
4 How much was your new camera?
5 Why were you angry yesterday?
6 Was the weather nice last week?

UNIT 11

11.1
2 opened
3 started … finished
4 wanted
5 happened
6 rained
7 enjoyed … stayed
8 died

11.2
2 saw
3 played
4 paid
5 visited
6 bought
7 went
8 thought
9 copied
10 knew
11 put
12 spoke

11.3
2 got
3 had
4 left
5 drove
6 got
7 parked
8 walked
9 checked
10 had
11 waited
12 departed
13 arrived
14 took

11.4
2 lost her keys
3 met her friends
4 bought two newspapers
5 went to the cinema
6 ate an orange
7 had a shower
8 came (to see us)

11.5
Example answers:
2 I got up late yesterday.
3 I met some friends at lunchtime.
4 I went to the supermarket.
5 I phoned a lot of people.
6 I lost my keys.

UNIT 12

12.1
2 didn't work 4 didn't have
3 didn't go 5 didn't do

12.2
2 Did you enjoy the party?
3 Did you have a good holiday?
4 Did you finish work early?
5 Did you sleep well last night?

12.3
2 I got up before 7 o'clock. *or* I didn't get up before 7 o'clock.
3 I had a shower. *or* I didn't have a shower.
4 I bought a magazine. *or* I didn't buy a magazine.
5 I ate meat. *or* I didn't eat meat.
6 I went to bed before 10.30. *or* I didn't go to bed before 10.30.

12.4
2 did you arrive
3 Did you win
4 did you go
5 did it cost
6 Did you go to bed late
7 Did you have a nice time
8 did it happen / did that happen

12.5
2 bought 6 didn't have
3 Did it rain 7 did you do
4 didn't stay 8 didn't know
5 opened

UNIT 13

13.1
2 Jack and Kate were at the cinema. They were watching a film.
3 Tim was in his car. He was driving.
4 Tracey was at the station. She was waiting for a train.
5 Mr and Mrs Hall were in the park. They were walking.
6 *(Example answer)* I was in a café. I was having a drink with some friends.

13.2
2 she was playing tennis
3 she was reading a/the newspaper
4 she was cooking (lunch)
5 she was having breakfast
6 she was cleaning the kitchen

13.3
2 What were you doing
3 Was it raining
4 Why was Sue driving
5 Was Tim wearing

13.4
2 He was carrying a bag.
3 He wasn't going to the dentist.
4 He was eating an ice-cream.
5 He wasn't carrying an umbrella.
6 He wasn't going home.
7 He was wearing a hat.
8 He wasn't riding a bicycle.

UNIT 14

14.1
1 happened … was painting … fell
2 arrived … got … were waiting
3 was walking … met … was going … was carrying … stopped

14.2
2 was studying
3 did the post arrive … came … was having
4 didn't go
5 were you driving … stopped … wasn't driving
6 Did your team win … didn't play
7 did you break … were playing … kicked … hit
8 Did you see … was wearing
9 were you doing
10 lost … did you get … climbed

UNIT 15

15.1
2 She has/She's closed the door.
3 They have/They've gone to bed.
4 It has/It's stopped raining.
5 He has/He's had a shower.
6 The picture has fallen down.

15.2
2 've bought / have bought
3 's gone / has gone
4 Have you seen
5 has broken
6 've told / have told
7 has taken
8 haven't seen
9 has she gone
10 've forgotten / have forgotten
11 's invited / has invited
12 Have you decided
13 haven't told
14 've read / have read

UNIT 16

16.1
2 He's/He has just got up.
3 They've/They have just bought a car.
4 The race has just started.

16.2
2 they've/they have already seen it.
3 I've/I have already phoned him.
4 He's/He has already gone (away).
5 I've/I have already read it.
6 She's/She has already started (it).

16.3
2 The bus has just gone.
3 The train hasn't left yet.
4 He hasn't opened it yet.

5 They've/They have just finished their dinner.
6 It hasn't stopped raining yet.

16.4
2 Have you met your new neighbours yet?
3 Have you paid your phone bill yet?
4 Has Tom/he sold his car yet?

UNIT 17

17.1
3 Have you ever been to Australia?
4 Have you ever lost your passport?
5 Have you ever flown in a helicopter?
6 Have you ever won a race?
7 Have you ever been to New York?
8 Have you ever driven a bus?
9 Have you ever broken your leg?

17.2
Helen:
2 She's/She has been to Australia once.
3 She's/She has never won a race.
4 She's/She has flown in a helicopter a few times.
You (example answers):
5 I've/I have never been to New York.
6 I've/I have played tennis many times.
7 I've/I have never driven a lorry.
8 I've/have been late for work a few times.

17.3
2–6
She's/She has done a lot of interesting things.
She's/She has travelled all over the world. *or*
She's/She has been all over the world.
She's/She has been married three times.
She's/She has written ten books.
She's/She has met a lot of interesting people.

17.4
2 gone
3 been … been
4 been
5 gone
6 been
7 been
8 gone

UNIT 18

18.1
3 have been
4 has been
5 have lived / have been living
6 has worked / has been working
7 has had
8 have been learning

18.2
2 How long have they been there? *or* … been in Brazil?
3 How long have you known her? *or* … known Amy?
4 How long has she been learning Italian?
5 How long has he lived in Canada? / How long has he been living … ?
6 How long have you been a teacher?
7 How long has it been raining?

18.3
2 She has lived in Wales all her life.
3 They have been on holiday since Sunday.
4 The sun has been shining all day.
5 She has been waiting for ten minutes.
6 He has had a beard since he was 20.

18.4
2 I know
3 I've known
4 have you been waiting
5 works
6 She has been reading
7 have you lived
8 I've had
9 is … He has been

UNIT 19

19.1
3 for
4 since
5 since
6 for
7 for
8 for … since

19.2
Example answers:
2 A year ago.
3 A few weeks ago.
4 Two hours ago.
5 Six months ago.

19.3
3 for 20 years
4 20 years ago
5 an hour ago
6 a few days ago
7 for six months
8 for a long time

19.4
2 Jack has been here since Tuesday.
3 It's been raining for an hour.
4 I've known Sue since 2002.
5 Claire and Matthew have been married for six months.
6 Liz has been studying medicine (at university) for three years.
7 David has played / David has been playing the piano since he was seven years old.

19.5
Example answers:
1 I've lived in … all my life.
2 I've been in the same job for ten years.
3 I've been learning English for six months.
4 I've known Chris for a long time.
5 I've had a headache since I got up this morning.

UNIT 20

20.1
2 I started (it)
3 they arrived
4 she went (away)
5 I wore it

20.2
3 I finished
4 *OK*
5 did you finish
6 *OK*
7 (Steve's grandmother) died
8 Where were you / Where did you go

20.3
3 played
4 did you go
5 Have you ever met
6 wasn't
7 's/has visited
8 switched
9 lived
10 haven't been

20.4
1 Did you have
was
2 Have you seen
went
haven't seen
3 has worked / has been working
was
worked
didn't enjoy
4 've/have seen
've/have never spoken
Have you ever spoken
met

UNIT 21

21.1
3 Glass is made from sand.
4 Stamps are sold in a post office.
5 This room isn't used very often.
6 Are we allowed to park here?
7 How is this word pronounced?
9 The house was painted last month.
10 My phone was stolen a few days ago.
11 Three people were injured in the accident.
12 When was this bridge built?
13 I wasn't woken up by the noise.
14 How were these windows broken?
15 Were you invited to Jon's party last week?

21.2
2 Football **is played** in most …
3 Why **was the letter sent** to … ?
4 … where cars **are repaired**.
5 Where **were** you born?
6 How many languages **are spoken** … ?
7 … but nothing **was** stolen.
8 When **was** the bicycle **invented**?

21.3
3 is made
4 were damaged
5 was given
6 are shown
7 were invited
8 was made
9 was stolen … was found

21.4
2 Sally was born in Manchester.
3 Her parents were born in Ireland.
4 I was born in …
5 My mother was born in …

UNIT 22

22.1
2 A bridge is being built.
3 The windows are being cleaned.
4 The grass is being cut.

22.2
3 The window **has been** broken.
4 The roof **is being** repaired.
5 The car **has been** damaged.
6 The houses **are being** knocked down.
7 The trees **have been** cut down.
8 They **have been** invited to a party.

22.3
3 has been repaired
4 was repaired
5 are made
6 were they built
7 Is the computer being used (*or* Is anybody using the computer)
8 are they called
9 were stolen
10 was damaged … hasn't been repaired

UNIT 23

23.1
3 are
4 Does
5 Do
6 Is
7 do
8 Is
9 does
10 Are

23.2
2 don't
3 'm/am not
4 isn't
5 don't
6 doesn't
7 'm/am not
8 aren't / 're not

23.3
2 Did
3 were
4 was
5 Has
6 did
7 were
8 Has
9 did
10 have

23.4
2 was
3 Have
4 are
5 were
6 've/have
7 is
8 was
9 has

23.5
3 eaten
4 enjoying
5 damaged
6 use
7 gone
8 understand
9 listening
10 pronounced
11 open

UNIT 24

24.1
3 got
4 brought
5 paid
6 enjoyed
7 bought
8 sat
9 left
10 happened
11 heard
12 put
13 caught
14 watched
15 understood

24.2
2 began begun
3 ate eaten
4 drank drunk
5 drove driven
6 spoke spoken
7 wrote written
8 came come
9 knew known
10 took taken

11 went gone
12 gave given
13 threw thrown
14 forgot forgotten

24.3
3 slept
4 saw
5 rained
6 lost … seen
7 stolen
8 went
9 finished
10 built
11 learnt/learned
12 ridden
13 known
14 fell … hurt
15 ran … run

24.4
2 told
3 won
4 met
5 woken up
6 swam
7 thought
8 spoken
9 cost
10 driven
11 sold
12 flew

UNIT 25

25.1
2 Richard is going to the cinema.
3 Rachel is meeting Dave.
4 Karen is having lunch with Ken.
5 Tom and Sue are going to a party.

25.2
2 Are you working next week?
3 What are you doing tomorrow evening?
4 What time are your friends coming?
5 When is Liz going on holiday?

25.3
Example answers:
3 I'm going away at the weekend.
4 I'm playing basketball tomorrow.
5 I'm meeting a friend this evening.
6 I'm going to the cinema on Thursday evening.

25.4
3 She's getting
4 are going … are they going
5 finishes
6 I'm not going
7 I'm going … We're meeting
8 are you getting … leaves
9 does the film begin
10 are you doing … I'm working

UNIT 26

26.1
2 I'm going to have a bath.
3 I'm going to buy a car.
4 We're going to play football.

26.2
3 'm/am going to walk
4 's/is going to stay
5 'm/am going to eat
6 're/are going to give
7 's/is going to lie down
8 Are you going to watch
9 is Rachel going to do

26.3
2 The shelf is going to fall (down).
3 The car is going to turn (right).
4 He's / He is going to kick the ball.

26.4
Example answers:
1 I'm going to phone Maria this evening.
2 I'm going to get up early tomorrow.
3 I'm going to buy some shoes tomorrow.

UNIT 27

27.1
2 she'll be
3 she was
4 she'll be
5 she's
6 she was
7 she'll be

27.2
Example answers:
2 I'll be at home.
3 I'll probably be in bed.
4 I'll be at work.
5 I don't know where I'll be.

27.3
2 'll/will
3 won't
4 won't
5 'll/will
6 'll/will
7 won't

27.4
3 I think we'll win the game.
4 I don't think I'll be here tomorrow.
5 I think Sue will like her present.
6 I don't think they'll get married.
7 I don't think you'll enjoy the film.

27.5
2 are you doing
3 They're going
4 will lend
5 I'm going
6 will phone
7 He's working
8 Will you
9 are coming

UNIT 28

28.1
2 I'll send
3 I'll eat
4 I'll sit
5 I'll do
6 I'll stay
7 I'll show

28.2
2 I think I'll have
3 I don't think I'll play
4 I think I'll buy
5 I don't think I'll buy

28.3
2 I'll do
3 I watch
4 I'll go
5 is going to buy
6 I'll give
7 Are you doing … I'm going
8 I'm working

28.4
2 Shall I turn off the television?
3 Shall I make some sandwiches?
4 Shall I turn on the light?

28.5
2 where shall we go?
3 what shall we buy?
4 who shall we invite?

UNIT 29

29.1
2 I might see you tomorrow.
3 Sarah might forget to phone.
4 It might snow today.
5 I might be late tonight.
6 Mark might not be here next week.
7 I might not have time to go out.

29.2
2 I might go away.
3 I might see her on Monday.
4 I might have fish.
5 I might get/take a taxi. *or* … go by taxi.
6 I might buy a new car.

29.3
3 He might get up early.
4 He isn't/He's not working tomorrow.
5 He might be at home tomorrow morning.
6 He might watch television.
7 He's going out in the afternoon.
8 He might go shopping.

29.4
Example answers:
1 I might read a newspaper.
2 I might go out with some friends in the evening.
3 I might have an egg for breakfast.

UNIT 30

30.1
2 Can you ski?
3 Can you play chess?
4 Can you run ten kilometres?
5 Can you drive (a car)?
6 Can you ride (a horse)?
7 I can/can't swim.
8 I can/can't ski.
9 I can/can't play chess.
10 I can/can't run ten kilometres.
11 I can/can't drive (a car).
12 I can/can't ride (a horse).

30.2
2 can see
3 can't hear
4 can't find
5 can speak

30.3
2 couldn't eat
3 can't decide
4 couldn't find
5 can't go
6 couldn't go

30.4
2 Can/Could you pass the salt (please)?
3 Can/Could you turn off the radio (please)?
4 Can/Could I have your phone number (please)?
5 Can/Could I look at your newspaper (please)? *or* Can/Could I have a look at your newspaper (please)?
6 Can/Could I use your pen (please)?

UNIT 31

31.1
2 must meet
3 must wash
4 must learn
5 must go
6 must win
7 must be

31.2
2 I must
3 I had to
4 I must
5 I had to
6 I had to
7 I must

31.3
2 don't need to hurry
3 mustn't lose
4 don't need to wait
5 mustn't forget
6 don't need to phone

31.4
2 C
3 A
4 B
5 D

31.5
3 don't need to
4 had to
5 must
6 mustn't
7 must
8 had to
9 don't need to
10 mustn't

UNIT 32

32.1
2 You should go
3 You should eat
4 you should visit
5 you should wear
6 You should take

32.2
2 He shouldn't eat so much.
3 She shouldn't work so hard.
4 He shouldn't drive so fast.

32.3
2 Do you think I should learn (to drive)?
3 Do you think I should get another job?
4 Do you think I should invite Gary (to the party)?

32.4
3 I think you should sell it.
4 I think she should have a holiday.
5 I don't think they should get married.
6 I don't think you should go to work.
7 I think he should go to the doctor.
8 I don't think we should stay there.

32.5
Example answers:
2 I think everybody should have enough food.
3 I think people should drive more carefully.
4 I don't think the police should carry guns.
5 I think I should take more exercise.

UNIT 33

33.1
2 have to do
3 has to read
4 have to speak
5 has to travel
6 have to hit

33.2
2 have to go
3 had to buy
4 have to change
5 had to answer

33.3
2 did he have to wait
3 does she have to go
4 did you have to pay
5 do you have to do

33.4
2 doesn't have to wait.
3 didn't have to get up early.
4 doesn't have to work (so) hard.
5 don't have to leave now.

33.5
3 have to pay
4 had to borrow
5 must stop *or* have to stop *(both are correct)*
6 has to meet
7 must tell *or* have to tell *(both are correct)*

33.6
2 I have to go to work every day.
3 I had to go to the dentist yesterday.
4 I have to go shopping tomorrow.

UNIT 34

34.1
2 Would you like an apple?
3 Would you like some coffee? / … a cup of coffee?
4 Would you like some cheese? / … a piece of cheese?
5 Would you like a sandwich?
6 Would you like some cake? /… a piece of cake?

34.2
2 Would you like to play tennis tomorrow?
3 Would you like to come to a concert next week?
4 Would you like to borrow my umbrella?

34.3
2 Do you like
3 Would you like
4 would you like
5 Would you like
6 I like
7 would you like
8 Would you like
9 Do you like
10 I'd like
11 I'd like
12 do you like

UNIT 35

35.1
3 Don't buy
4 Smile
5 Don't sit
6 Have
7 Don't forget
8 Sleep
9 Be … Don't drop

35.2
2 let's take a taxi
3 let's watch TV
4 let's go to a restaurant
5 let's wait a little

35.3
3 No, let's not go out. *or* No, don't let's go out.
4 No, don't close the window.
5 No, don't phone me (tonight).
6 No, let's not wait for Andy. *or* No, don't let's wait for Andy.
7 No, don't turn on the light.
8 No, let's not go by bus. *or* No, don't let's go by bus.

UNIT 36

36.1
2 He used to play football.
3 She used to be a taxi driver.
4 They used to live in the country.
5 He used to wear glasses.
6 This building used to be a hotel.

36.2
2–6
She used to play volleyball.
She used to go out most evenings. / She used to go out a lot.
She used to play the guitar.
She used to read a lot. / She used to like reading.
She used to go away two or three times a year. / She used to travel a lot.

36.3
3 used to have
4 used to be
5 go / travel
6 used to eat
7 watches
8 used to live
9 get
10 did you use to play

UNIT 37

37.1
3 There's/There is a hospital.
4 There isn't a swimming pool.
5 There are two cinemas.
6 There isn't a university.
7 There aren't any big hotels.

37.2
Example answers:
3 There is a university in …
4 There are a lot of big shops.
5 There isn't an airport.
6 There aren't many factories.

37.3
2 There's/There is
3 is there
4 There are
5 are there
6 There isn't
7 Is there
8 Are there
9 There's / There is … There aren't

37.4
2–6
There are eight planets in the solar system.
There are fifteen players in a rugby team.
There are twenty-six letters in the English alphabet.
There are thirty days in September.
There are fifty states in the USA.

37.5
2 It's
3 There's
4 There's … Is it
5 Is there … there's
6 It's
7 Is there

UNIT 38

38.1
2 There was a carpet
3 There were three pictures
4 There was a small table
5 There were some flowers
6 There were some books
7 There was an armchair
8 There was a sofa

38.2
3 There was
4 Was there
5 there weren't
6 There wasn't
7 Were there
8 There wasn't
9 There was
10 there weren't

38.3
2 There are
3 There was
4 There's/There is
5 There's been/There has been *or* There was
6 there was
7 there will be
8 there were … there are
9 There have been
10 there will be *or* there are

UNIT 39

39.1
2 It's cold.
3 It's windy.
4 It's sunny/fine. *or* It's a nice day.
5 It's snowing.
6 It's cloudy.

39.2
2 It's / It is
3 Is it
4 is it … it's / it is
5 It's / It is
6 Is it
7 is it
8 It's / It is
9 It's / It is

39.3
2 How far is it from the hotel to the beach?
3 How far is it from New York to Washington?
4 How far is it from your house to the airport?

39.4
3 It
4 It … It
5 There
6 it
7 It … there
8 It

39.5
2 It's nice to see you again.
3 It's impossible to work in this office.
4 It's easy to make friends.
5 It's interesting to visit different places.
6 It's dangerous to go out alone

UNIT 40

40.1
2 is
3 can
4 has
5 will
6 was

40.2
2 'm not
3 weren't
4 haven't
5 isn't
6 hasn't

40.3
3 doesn't
4 do
5 did
6 does
7 don't
8 didn't

40.4
Example answers:
2 I like sport, but my sister doesn't.
3 I don't eat meat, but Jenny does.
4 I'm American, but my husband isn't.
5 I haven't been to Japan, but Jenny has.

40.5
2 wasn't
3 are
4 has
5 can't
6 did
7 has
8 do
9 hasn't
10 will
11 might

40.6
2 Yes, I have. *or* No, I haven't.
3 Yes, I do. *or* No, I don't.
4 Yes, it is. *or* No, it isn't.
5 Yes, I am. *or* No, I'm not.
6 Yes, I do. *or* No, I don't.
7 Yes, I will. *or* No, I won't.
8 Yes, I have. *or* No, I haven't.
9 Yes, I did. *or* No, I didn't.
10 Yes, I was. *or* No, I wasn't.

UNIT 41

41.1
2 Do you?
3 Didn't you?
4 Doesn't she?
5 Do I?
6 Did she?

41.2
3 Have you?
4 Can't she?
5 Were you?
6 Didn't you?
7 Is there?
8 Aren't you?
9 Did you?
10 Does she?
11 Won't you?
12 Isn't it?

41.3
2 aren't they
3 wasn't she
4 haven't you
5 don't you
6 doesn't he
7 won't you

41.4
2 are you
3 isn't she
4 can't you
5 do you
6 didn't she
7 was it
8 doesn't she
9 will you

UNIT 42

42.1
2 either
3 too
4 too
5 either
6 either
7 too

42.2
2 So am I.
3 So have I.
4 So do I.
5 So will I.
6 So was I.
7 Neither can I.
8 Neither did I.
9 Neither have I.
10 Neither am I.
11 Neither do I.

42.3
1 So am I.
2 So can I. *or* I can't.
3 Neither am I. *or* I am.
4 So do I. *or* I don't.
5 Neither do I. *or* I do.
6 So did I. *or* I didn't.
7 Neither have I. *or* I have.
8 Neither do I. *or* I do.
9 So am I. *or* I'm not.
10 Neither have I. *or* I have.
11 Neither did I. *or* I did.
12 So do I. *or* I don't.

UNIT 43

43.1
2 They aren't / They're not married.
3 I haven't had dinner.
4 It isn't cold today.
5 We won't be late.
6 You shouldn't go.

43.2
2 I don't like cheese.
3 They didn't understand.
4 He doesn't live here.
5 Don't go away!
6 I didn't do the shopping.

43.3
2 They haven't arrived.
3 I didn't go to the bank.
4 He doesn't speak German.
5 We weren't angry.
6 He won't be pleased.
7 Don't phone me tonight.
8 It didn't rain yesterday.
9 I couldn't hear them.
10 I don't believe you.

43.4
2 'm not / am not
3 can't
4 doesn't
5 isn't / 's not
6 don't … haven't
7 Don't
8 didn't
9 haven't
10 won't
11 didn't
12 weren't
13 hasn't
14 shouldn't / mustn't

43.5
3 He wasn't born in London.
4 He doesn't like London.
5 He'd like to live in the country.
6 He can drive.
7 He hasn't got a car.
8 He doesn't read newspapers.
9 He isn't interested in politics.
10 He watches TV most evenings.
11 He didn't watch TV last night.
12 He went out last night.

UNIT 44

44.1
3 Were you late this morning?
4 Has Kate got a key?
5 Will you be here tomorrow?
6 Is Paul going out this evening?
7 Do you like your job?
8 Does Nicole live near here?
9 Did you enjoy the film?
10 Did you have a good holiday?

44.2
2 Do you use it a lot?
3 Did you use it yesterday?
4 Do you enjoy driving?
5 Are you a good driver?
6 Have you ever had an accident?

44.3
3 What are the children doing?
4 How is cheese made?
5 Is your sister coming to the party?
6 Why don't you tell the truth?
7 Have your guests arrived yet?
8 What time does your train leave?
9 Why didn't Emily go to work?
10 Was your car damaged in the accident?

44.4
3 What are you reading?
4 What time did she go (to bed)?
5 When are they going (on holiday)?
6 Where did you see him?
7 Why can't you come (to the party)?
8 Where has she gone?
9 How much (money) do you need?
10 Why doesn't she like you?
11 How often does it rain?
12 When did you do it? / … the shopping?

UNIT 45

45.1
2 What fell off the shelf?
3 Who wants to see me?
4 Who took your umbrella? / Who took it?
5 What made you ill?
6 Who is / Who's coming?

45.2
3 Who did you phone?
4 What happened last night?
5 Who knows the answer?
6 Who did the washing-up?
7 What did Jane do? / What did she do?
8 What woke you up?
9 Who saw the accident?
10 Who did you see?
11 Who has got your pen? / Who has got it? *or* Who's got … ?
12 What does this word mean? / What does it mean?

45.3
2 Who phoned you ?
What did she want?
3 Who did you ask?
What did he say?
4 Who got married?
Who told you?
5 Who did you meet?
What did she tell you?
6 Who won?
What did you do (after the game)?
7 Who gave you a/the book?
What did Catherine give you?

UNIT 46

46.1
2 What are you looking for?
3 Who did you go to the cinema with?
4 What/Who was the film about?
5 Who did you give the money to?
6 Who was the book written by?

46.2
2 What are they looking at?
3 Which restaurant is he going to?
4 What are they talking about?
5 What is she listening to?
6 Which bus are they waiting for?

46.3
2 Which hotel did you stay at?
3 Which (football) team does he play for?
4 Which school did you go to?

46.4
2 What is the food like?
3 What are the people like?
4 What is the weather like?

46.5
2 What was the film like?
3 What were the lessons like?
4 What was the hotel like?

UNIT 47

47.1
3 What colour is it?
4 What time did you get up?
5 What type of music do you like?
6 What kind of car do you want (to buy)?

47.2
2 Which coat
3 Which film/movie
4 Which bus

47.3
3 Which
4 What
5 Which
6 What
7 Which
8 Who
9 What
10 Which
11 What

47.4
2 How far
3 How old
4 How often
5 How deep
6 How long

47.5
2 How heavy is this box?
3 How old are you?
4 How much did you spend?
5 How often do you watch TV?
6 How far is it from Paris to Moscow?

UNIT 48

48.1
2 How long does it take by car from Milan to Rome?
3 How long does it take by train from Paris to Geneva?
4 How long does it take by bus from the city centre to the airport?

48.2
Example answers:
2 It takes … hours to fly from … to New York.
3 It takes … years to study to be a doctor in … .
4 It takes … to walk from my home to the nearest shop.
5 It takes … to get from my home to the nearest airport.

48.3
2 How long did it take you to walk to the station?
3 How long did it take him to paint the bathroom?
4 How long did it take you to learn to ski?
5 How long did it take them to repair the computer?

48.4
2 It took us 20 minutes to walk home. / … to get home.
3 It took me six months to learn to drive.
4 It took Mark/him three hours to drive to London. / … to get to London.
5 It took Lisa/her a long time to find a job. / … to get a job.
6 It took me … to …

UNIT 49

49.1
2 I don't know where she is.
3 I don't know how old it is.
4 I don't know when he'll be here.
5 I don't know why he was angry.
6 I don't know how long she has lived here.

49.2
2 where Susan works
3 what Peter said
4 why he went home early
5 what time the meeting begins
6 how the accident happened

49.3
2 are you
3 they are
4 the museum is
5 do you want
6 elephants eat
7 it is

49.4
2 Do you know if/whether they are married?
3 Do you know if/whether Sue knows Bill?
4 Do you know if/whether Gary will be here tomorrow?
5 Do you know if/whether he passed his exam?

49.5
2 Do you know where Paula is?
3 Do you know if/whether she is working today? / … she's working today?
4 Do you know what time she starts work?
5 Do you know if/whether the shops are open tomorrow?
6 Do you know where Sarah and Tim live?
7 Do you know if/whether they went to Jane's party?

49.6
Example answers:
2 Do you know what time the bus leaves?
3 Excuse me, can you tell me where the station is?
4 I don't know what I'm going to do this evening.
5 Do you know if there's a restaurant near here?
6 Do you know how much it costs to rent a car?

UNIT 50

50.1
2 She said (that) she was very busy.
3 She said (that) she couldn't go to the party.
4 He said (that) he had to go out.
5 He said (that) he was learning Russian.
6 She said (that) she didn't feel very well.
7 They said (that) they would be home late. / … they'd be …
8 She said (that) she had just come back from holiday. / … she'd just come back …
9 She said (that) she was going to buy a new computer.
10 They said (that) they hadn't got a key. / They said (that) they didn't have a key.

50.2
2 She said (that) she wasn't hungry.
3 he said (that) he needed it.
4 she said (that) she didn't want to go.
5 She said (that) I could have it.
6 He said (that) he would send me a postcard. / … he'd send …
7 Nicole said (that) he had gone home. / … he'd gone home.
8 He said (that) he wanted to watch TV.
9 She said (that) she was going to the cinema.

50.3
3 said
4 told
5 tell
6 say
7 said
8 told
9 tell
10 say

UNIT 51

51.1
3 phone
4 phone Paul
5 to phone Paul
6 to phone Paul
7 phone Paul
8 to phone Paul
9 phone Paul
10 phone Paul

51.2
3 get
4 going
5 watch
6 flying
7 listening
8 eat
9 waiting
10 wear
11 doing … staying

51.3
4 to go
5 rain
6 to leave
7 help
8 studying
9 to go
10 wearing
11 to stay
12 have
13 having
14 to have
15 hear
16 go
17 listening
18 to make
19 to know … tell
20 use

UNIT 52

52.1
3 to see
4 to swim
5 cleaning
6 to ask
7 visiting
8 going
9 to be
10 waiting
11 to do
12 to speak
13 to go
14 crying / to cry
15 to work … talking

52.2
2 to help
3 to see
4 reading
5 to lose
6 to send
7 raining
8 to go
9 watching / to watch
10 to wait

52.3
2 going to museums
3 to go
4 writing / to write letters
5 to go (there)
6 travelling by train
7 walking

52.4
Example answers:
1 I enjoy cooking.
2 I don't like driving.
3 If it's a nice day tomorrow, I'd like to have a picnic by the lake.
4 When I'm on holiday, I like to do very little.
5 I don't mind travelling alone, but I prefer to travel with somebody.
6 I wouldn't like to live in a big city.

UNIT 53

53.1
2 I want you to listen carefully.
3 I don't want you to be angry.
4 Do you want me to wait for you?
5 I don't want you to phone me tonight.
6 I want you to meet Sarah.

53.2
2 A woman told me to turn left after the bridge.
3 I advised him to go to the doctor.
4 She asked me to help her.
5 I told him to come back in ten minutes.
6 Paul let me use his phone.
7 I told her not to phone before 8 o'clock.
8 Ann's mother taught her to play the piano.

53.3
2 to repeat
3 wait
4 to arrive
5 to get
6 go
7 borrow
8 to tell
9 to make (*or* to get)
10 think

UNIT 54

54.1
2–4
I went to the café to meet a friend.
I went to the chemist to get some medicine.
I went to the supermarket to buy some food.

54.2
2 to read the newspaper
3 to open this door
4 to get some fresh air
5 to wake him up
6 to see who it was

54.3
Example answers:
2 to talk to you now
3 to tell her about the party
4 to do some shopping
5 to buy a car

54.4

2 to	7 to
3 to	8 to
4 for	9 for
5 to	10 for
6 for	11 to … for

54.5
2 for the film to begin
3 for it to arrive
4 for you to tell me

UNIT 55

55.1
3 to
4 to
5 – *(no preposition)*
6 for
7 to
8 on … to
9 for
10 on
11 to
12 – *(no preposition)*
13 on
14 for
15 on

55.2
2 went fishing
3 goes swimming
4 going skiing
5 go shopping
6 went jogging

55.3
2 to university
3 shopping
4 to sleep
5 home
6 skiing
7 riding
8 for a walk
9 on holiday … to Portugal

UNIT 56

56.1
2 get your jacket
3 get a doctor
4 get a taxi
5 gets the job
6 get some milk
7 get a ticket
8 gets a good salary
9 get a lot of rain
10 get a new computer

56.2
2 getting dark
3 getting married
4 getting ready
5 getting late

56.3
2 get wet
3 got married
4 gets angry
5 got lost
6 get old
7 got better

56.4
2 got to Bristol at 11.45.
3 I left the party at 11.15 and got home at midnight.
4 *(Example answer)* I left home at 8.30 and got to the airport at 10 o'clock.

56.5
2 got off
3 got out of
4 got on

UNIT 57

57.1

2 do	7 done
3 make	8 make
4 made	9 making
5 did	10 do
6 do	11 doing

57.2
2 They're/They are doing (their) homework.
3 He's/He is doing the shopping. *or* He is shopping.
4 She's/She is making a jacket.
5 They're/They are doing an exam. (*or* … taking an exam.)
6 He's/He is making the/his bed.
7 She's/She is doing the washing-up. *or* She is washing up. / She is doing the dishes. / She is washing the dishes.
8 He's/He is making a (shopping) list.
9 They're/They are making a film.
10 He's/He is taking a photograph.

57.3

2 make	8 make
3 do	9 do
4 done	10 making
5 made	11 made
6 doing	12 make … do
7 did	

UNIT 58

58.1
3 He hasn't got / He doesn't have
4 Gary had
5 Have you got / Do you have
6 we didn't have
7 She hasn't got / She doesn't have
8 Did you have

58.2
2 She's/She is having a cup of tea.
3 He's/He is having a rest.
4 They're/They are having a good time.
5 They're/They are having dinner.
6 He's/He is having a bath.

58.3
3 Have a nice/good trip!
4 Did you have a nice/good weekend?
5 Did you have a nice/good game (of tennis)?
6 Have a nice/good time! *or* Have a nice/good evening! *or* Have fun!
7 Did you have a nice/good holiday?

58.4
2 have something to eat
3 had a glass of water
4 have a walk
5 had an accident
6 have a look

UNIT 59

59.1
2 him
3 them
4 her
5 him
6 them
7 her

59.2
2 I … them
3 he … her
4 they … us
5 we … him
6 she … them
7 they … me
8 she … you

59.3
2 I like him.
3 I don't like it.
4 Do you like it?
5 I don't like her.
6 Do you like them?

59.4
2 him
3 them
4 they
5 us
6 it
7 She
8 them
9 me
10 her
11 them
12 he … it

59.5
2 Can you give it to him?
3 Can you give them to her?
4 Can you give it to me?
5 Can you give it to them?
6 Can you give them to us?

UNIT 60

60.1
2 her hands
3 our hands
4 his hands
5 their hands
6 your hands

60.2
2 They live with their parents.
3 We live with our parents.
4 Jane lives with her parents.
5 I live with my parents.
6 John lives with his parents.
7 Do you live with your parents?
8 Most children live with their parents.

60.3
2 their
3 his
4 his
5 her
6 their
7 her
8 their

60.4
2 his
3 Their
4 our
5 her
6 my
7 your
8 her
9 their
10 my
11 Its
12 His … his

60.5
2 my key
3 Her husband
4 your coat
5 their homework
6 his name
7 Our house

UNIT 61

61.1
2 mine
3 ours
4 hers
5 theirs
6 yours
7 mine
8 his

61.2
2 yours
3 my … Mine
4 Yours … mine
5 her
6 My … hers
7 their
8 Ours

61.3
3 of hers
4 friends of ours
5 friend of mine
6 friend of his
7 friends of yours

61.4
2 Whose camera is this? It's hers.
3 Whose gloves are these? They're mine.
4 Whose hat is this? It's his.
5 Whose money is this? It's yours.
6 Whose books are these? They're ours.

UNIT 62

62.1
2 Yes, I know **her**, but I can't remember **her name**.
3 Yes, I **know them**, but I **can't remember their** names.
4 Yes, I **know you**, but **I can't remember your name**.

62.2
2 He invited us to stay with **him** at his house.
3 They invited me to stay with **them at their** house.
4 I invited them to stay **with me at my** house.
5 She invited us to stay **with her at her** house.
6 Did you invite him **to stay with you at your** house?

62.3
2 I gave her my address, and she gave me **hers**.
3 He gave me his address, and I gave **him mine**.
4 We gave them **our** address, and they gave **us theirs**.
5 She gave him **her** address, and he gave **her his**.
6 You gave us **your** address, and we gave **you ours**.
7 They gave you **their** address, and you gave **them yours**.

62.4
2 them
3 him
4 our
5 yours
6 us
7 her
8 their
9 mine

UNIT 63

63.1
2 myself
3 herself
4 themselves
5 myself
6 himself
7 yourself
8 yourselves

63.2
2 When I saw him, he **was by himself**.
3 Don't **go out by yourself**.
4 **I went to the cinema by myself**.
5 My sister **lives by herself**.
6 Many people **live by themselves**.

63.3
2 They can't see each other.
3 They phone each other a lot.
4 They don't know each other.
5 They're/They are sitting next to each other.
6 They gave each other presents / a present.

63.4
3 each other
4 yourselves
5 us
6 ourselves
7 each other
8 each other
9 them
10 themselves

UNIT 64

64.1
3 Helen is **Brian's** wife.
4 James is Sarah's **brother**.
5 James is **Daniel's** uncle.
6 Sarah is **Paul's** wife.
7 Helen is Daniel's **grandmother**.
8 Sarah is James's **sister**.
9 Paul is **Sarah's** husband.
10 Paul is Daniel's **father**.
11 Daniel is **James's** nephew.

64.2
2 Andy's
3 Dave's
4 Jane's
5 Diane's
6 Alice's

64.3
3 *OK*
4 Simon's phone number
5 My brother's job
6 *OK*
7 *OK*
8 Paula's favourite colour
9 your mother's birthday
10 My parents' house
11 *OK*
12 *OK*
13 Silvia's party
14 *OK*

UNIT 65

65.1
2 a
3 a
4 an
5 a
6 an
7 a
8 an
9 an

65.2
2 a vegetable
3 a game
4 a tool
5 a mountain
6 a planet
7 a fruit
8 a river
9 a flower
10 a musical instrument

65.3
2 He's a shop assistant.
3 She's an architect.
4 He's a taxi driver.
5 He's an electrician.
6 She's a photographer.
7 She's a nurse.
8 I'm a/an …

65.4
2–8
Tom never wears **a** hat.
I can't ride **a** bicycle.
My brother is **an** artist.
Rebecca works in **a** bookshop.
Jane wants to learn **a** foreign language.
Mike lives in **an** old house.
This evening I'm going to **a** party.

UNIT 66

66.1
2 boats
3 women
4 cities
5 umbrellas
6 addresses
7 knives
8 sandwiches
9 families
10 feet
11 holidays
12 potatoes

66.2
2 teeth
3 people
4 children
5 fish
6 leaves

66.3
3 … with a lot of beautiful **trees**.
4 … with two **men**.
5 *OK*
6 … three **children**.
7 Most of my **friends** are **students**.
8 He put on his **pyjamas** …
9 *OK*
10 Do you know many **people** …
11 I like your **trousers**. Where did you get **them**?
12 … full of **tourists**.
13 *OK*
14 **These scissors aren't** …

66.4
2 are
3 don't
4 watch
5 were
6 live
7 Do
8 are
9 them
10 some

UNIT 67

67.1
3 a jug
4 water
5 toothpaste
6 a toothbrush
7 an egg
8 money
9 a wallet
10 sand
11 a bucket
12 an envelope

67.2
3 … **a** hat.
4 … **a** job?
5 *OK*
6 … **an** apple …
7 … **a** party …
8 … **a** wonderful thing.
9 … **an** island.
10 … **a** key.
11 *OK*
12 … **a** good idea.
13 … **a** car?
14 … **a** cup of coffee?
15 *OK*
16 … **an** umbrella.

67.3
2 a piece of wood
3 a glass of water
4 a bar of chocolate
5 a cup of tea
6 a piece of paper
7 a bowl of soup
8 a loaf of bread
9 a jar of honey

UNIT 68

68.1
2 I bought a newspaper (*or* a paper), some flowers (*or* a bunch of flowers) and a pen.
3 I bought some stamps, some postcards and some bread (*or* a loaf of bread).

4 I bought some toothpaste, some soap (*or* a bar of soap) and a comb.

68.2
2 Would you like some coffee? (*or* … a cup of coffee?)
3 Would you like a biscuit?
4 Would you like some bread? (*or* … a piece of bread? / a slice of bread?)
5 Would you like a chocolate?
6 Would you like some cake? (*or* … a piece of cake?)

68.3
2 some … some
3 some
4 a … some
5 an … some
6 a … a … some
7 some
8 some
9 some … a

68.4
2 eyes
3 hair
4 information
5 chairs
6 furniture
7 job
8 wonderful weather

UNIT 69

69.1
3 a
4 the
5 an
6 the … the
7 a … a
8 a … a
9 … **a** student … **a** journalist … **an** apartment near **the** college … **The** apartment is …
10 … two children, **a** boy and **a** girl. **The** boy is seven years old, and **the** girl is three … in **a** factory … hasn't got **a** job …

69.2
2 **the** airport
3 **a** cup
4 **a** nice picture
5 **the** dictionary
6 **the** floor

69.3
2 … send me **a** postcard.
3 What is **the** name of …
4 … **a** very big country.
5 What is **the** largest …
6 … **the** colour of **the** carpet.
7 … **a** headache.
8 … **an** old house near **the** station.
9 … **the** name of **the** director of **the** film …

UNIT 70

70.1
3 … **the** second floor.
4 … **the** moon?
5 … **the** best hotel in this town?
6 *OK*
7 … **the** city centre.
8 … **the** end of May.
9 *OK*
10 … **the** first time I met her.
11 *OK*
12 **The** Internet is a good way of getting information.
13 *OK*
14 … on **the** top shelf on **the** right.
15 … in **the** country about ten miles from **the** nearest town.

70.2
2 the same time
3 the same age
4 the same colour
5 the same problem

70.3
2 **the** guitar
3 breakfast
4 television/TV
5 **the** sea
6 **the** bottom

70.4
2 **the** name
3 **The** sky
4 television
5 **the** police
6 **the** capital
7 lunch
8 **the** middle

UNIT 71

71.1
2 **the** cinema
3 hospital
4 **the** airport
5 home
6 prison

71.2
3 school
4 **the** station
5 home
6 bed
7 **the** post office

71.3
2 **the** cinema
3 go to bed
4 go to prison
5 go to **the** dentist
6 go to university/college
7 go to hospital / are taken to hospital

71.4
3 **the** doctor
4 *OK*
5 *OK*
6 *OK*
7 **the** bank
8 *OK*
9 *OK*
10 **the** city centre
11 **the** station
12 *OK*
13 *OK*
14 *OK*
15 **the** theatre

UNIT 72

72.1
Example answers:
2 I don't like dogs.
3 I hate museums.
4 I love big cities.
5 Tennis is all right.
6 I love chocolate.
7 I don't like computer games.
8 I hate parties.

72.2
Example answers:
2 I'm not interested in politics.
3 I'm interested in sport.
4 I don't know much about art.
5 I don't know anything about astronomy.
6 I know a little about economics.

72.3

3 friends
4 parties
5 **The** shops
6 **the** milk
7 milk
8 basketball
9 computers
10 **The** water
11 cold water
12 **the** salt
13 **the** people
14 Vegetables
15 **The** houses
16 **the** words
17 photographs
18 **the** photographs
19 English ... international business
20 Money ... happiness

UNIT 73

73.1

3 Sweden
4 **The** Amazon
5 Asia
6 **The** Pacific
7 **The** Rhine
8 Kenya
9 **The** United States
10 **The** Andes
11 Bangkok
12 **The** Alps
13 **The** Red Sea
14 Jamaica
15 **The** Bahamas

73.2

3 *OK*
4 **the** Philippines
5 **the** south of France
6 **the** Regal Cinema
7 *OK*
8 **the** Museum of Art
9 *OK*
10 Belgium is smaller than **the** Netherlands.
11 **the** Mississippi ... **the** Nile
12 **the** National Gallery
13 **the** Park Hotel in Hudson Road
14 *OK*
15 **The** Rocky Mountains are in North America.
16 *OK*
17 **the** United States
18 **the** west of Ireland
19 *OK*
20 **The** Panama Canal joins **the** Atlantic Ocean and **the** Pacific Ocean.

UNIT 74

74.1

2 that house
3 these postcards
4 those birds
5 this seat
6 These plates

74.2

2 Is that your umbrella?
3 Is this your book?
4 Are those your books?
5 Is that your bicycle/bike?
6 Are these your keys?
7 Are those your keys?
8 Is this your watch?
9 Are those your glasses?
10 Are these your gloves?

74.3

2 that's
3 This is
4 That's
5 that
6 this is
7 That's
8 that's

UNIT 75

75.1

2 I don't need one
3 I'm going to get one
4 I haven't got one
5 I've just had one
6 there's one in Mill Road

75.2

2 a new one
3 a better one
4 an old one
5 a big one
6 a different one

75.3

2 Which ones? The green ones.
3 Which one? The one with a/the red door.
4 Which ones? The ones on the top shelf.
5 Which one? The black one.
6 Which one? The one on the wall.
7 Which one? The tall one with long hair.
8 Which ones? The yellow ones.
9 Which one? The one with a/the moustache and glasses.
10 Which ones? The ones I took at the party last week.

UNIT 76

76.1

2 some
3 any
4 any
5 any
6 some
7 any
8 some
9 some
10 any ... any
11 some ... any
12 some

76.2

2 some questions
3 any photographs
4 any foreign languages
5 some friends
6 some milk
7 any batteries
8 some fresh air
9 some cheese
10 any help

76.3

3 I've got some / I have some
4 I haven't got any / I haven't any / I don't have any
5 I didn't buy any
6 I bought some
7 I didn't make any

76.4

2 something
3 anything
4 anything
5 Somebody/Someone
6 anything
7 anybody/anyone
8 something
9 anything
10 anybody/anyone

UNIT 77

77.1

2 There are no shops near here.
3 Carla has got no free time.
4 There is no light in this room.
6 There isn't any milk in the fridge.
7 There aren't any buses today.
8 Tom hasn't got any brothers or sisters.

77.2

2 any	8 no
3 any	9 any
4 no	10 no
5 any	11 None
6 no	12 any
7 any	

77.3
2 no money
3 any questions
4 no friends
5 no difference
6 any furniture
7 no answer
8 any heating
9 no queue

77.4
Example answers:
2 Three.
3 Two cups.
4 None.
5 None.

UNIT 78

78.1
2 There's nobody in the office.
3 I've got nothing to do.
4 There's nothing on TV.
5 There was no-one at home.
6 We found nothing.

78.2
2 There wasn't anybody on the bus.
3 I haven't got anything to read.
4 I haven't got anyone to help me.
5 She didn't hear anything.
6 We haven't got anything for dinner.

78.3
3a Nothing.
4a Nobody./No-one.
5a Nobody./No-one.
6a Nothing.
7a Nothing.
8a Nobody./No-one.
3b I don't want anything.
4b I didn't meet anybody/anyone.
5b Nobody/No-one knows the answer.
6b I didn't buy anything.
7b Nothing happened.
8b Nobody/No-one was late.

78.4
3 anything
4 Nobody/No-one
5 Nothing
6 anything
7 anybody/anyone
8 nothing
9 anything
10 anything
11 nobody/no-one
12 anything
13 Nothing
14 Nobody/No-one … anybody/anyone

UNIT 79

79.1
2 something
3 somewhere
4 somebody/someone

79.2
2a Nowhere.
3a Nothing.
4a Nobody./No-one.
2b I'm not going anywhere.
3b I don't want anything.
4b I'm not looking for anybody/anyone.

79.3
3 anything
4 anything
5 somebody/someone
6 something
7 anybody/anyone … nobody/ no-one
8 anything
9 Nobody/No-one
10 anybody/anyone
11 Nothing
12 anywhere
13 somewhere
14 anything
15 anybody/anyone

79.4
2 anything to eat
3 nothing to do
4 anywhere to sit
5 something to drink
6 nowhere to park
7 something to read
8 somewhere to stay

UNIT 80

80.1
2 Every day
3 every time
4 Every room
5 every word

80.2
2 every day
3 all day
4 every day
5 all day
6 all day
7 every day

80.3

2 every	6 all
3 all	7 every
4 all	8 all
5 Every	9 every

80.4
2 everything
3 Everybody/Everyone
4 everything
5 everywhere
6 Everybody/Everyone
7 everywhere
8 Everything

80.5

2 is	6 was
3 has	7 makes
4 likes	8 Is … Does
5 has	

UNIT 81

81.1

3 Some	10 Most
4 Most of	11 most of
5 most	12 Some
6 any of	13 All *or* All of
7 all *or* all of	14 some of
8 None of	15 most of
9 any of	

81.2
2 All of them.
3 Some of them.
4 None of them.
5 Most of them.
6 None of it.

81.3
3 Some people …
4 Some of **the** questions … *or* Some questions …
5 *OK*
6 All insects …
7 *OK* (*or* … all **of** these books)

8 Most of **the** students ... *or* Most students ...
9 *OK*
10 ... most of **the** night

UNIT 82

82.1

3 Both
4 Neither
5 Neither
6 both
7 Either
8 neither of
9 Neither
10 either of
11 Both
12 neither of
13 Both
14 either of

82.2

2 Both windows are open.
3 Neither man is wearing a hat. *or* Neither of them is wearing ...
4 Both men have (got) beards. *or* Both of them have ...
5 Both buses go to the airport. *or* ... are going to the airport.
6 Neither answer is right.

82.3

3 Both of them are students.
4 Neither of them has (got) a car.
5 Both of them live in London.
6 Both of them like cooking.
7 Neither of them can play the piano.
8 Both of them read newspapers.
9 Neither of them is interested in sport.

UNIT 83

83.1

2 many
3 much
4 many
5 many
6 much
7 much
8 many
9 How many
10 How much
11 How much
12 How many

83.2

2 much time
3 many countries
4 many people
5 much luggage
6 many times

83.3

2 a lot of interesting things
3 a lot of accidents
4 a lot of fun
5 a lot of traffic

83.4

3 a lot of snow
4 *OK*
5 a lot of money
6 *OK*
7 *OK*
8 a lot

83.5

3 She plays tennis a lot.
4 He doesn't use his car much. (*or* ... a lot.)
5 He doesn't go out much. (*or* ... a lot.)
6 She travels a lot.

UNIT 84

84.1

2 a few
3 a little
4 a few
5 a little
6 a few

84.2

2 a little milk
3 A few days
4 a little Russian
5 a few friends
6 a few times
7 a few chairs
8 a little fresh air

84.3

2 very little coffee
3 very little rain
4 very few hotels
5 very little time
6 Very few people
7 very little work

84.4

2 A few
3 a little
4 little
5 few
6 a little
7 little

84.5

2 ... **a** little luck
3 ... **a** few things
4 *OK*
5 ... **a** few questions
6 ... **few** people
7 *OK*

UNIT 85

85.1

2 I like that green jacket.
3 Do you like classical music?
4 I had a wonderful holiday.
5 We went to a Japanese restaurant.

85.2

2 black clouds
3 long holiday
4 hot water
5 fresh air
6 sharp knife
7 dangerous job

85.3

2 It looks new.
3 I feel ill.
4 You look surprised.
5 They smell nice.
6 It tastes horrible.

85.4

2 It doesn't look new.
3 You don't sound American.
4 I don't feel cold.
5 They don't look heavy.
6 Maybe, but it doesn't taste good.

UNIT 86

86.1

2 badly
3 quietly
4 angrily
5 fast
6 dangerously

86.2

2 work hard
3 sleep well
4 win easily
5 Think carefully
6 know her very well
7 explain things very clearly/well
8 Come quickly

86.3

2 angry
3 slowly
4 slow
5 careful
6 hard
7 suddenly
8 quiet
9 badly
10 nice *(See Unit 85C.)*
11 quickly

86.4

2 well
3 good
4 well
5 well
6 good ... good

UNIT 87

87.1
2 bigger
3 slower
4 more expensive
5 higher
6 more dangerous

87.2
2 stronger
3 happier
4 more modern
5 more important
6 better
7 larger
8 more serious
9 prettier
10 more crowded

87.3
2 hotter/warmer
3 more expensive
4 worse
5 further
6 more difficult *or* harder

87.4
3 taller
4 harder
5 more comfortable
6 better
7 nicer
8 heavier
9 more interested
10 warmer
11 better
12 bigger
13 more beautiful
14 sharper
15 more polite
16 worse

UNIT 88

88.1
3 Liz is taller than Ben.
4 Liz starts work earlier than Ben.
5 Ben works harder than Liz.
6 Ben has got more money than Liz.
7 Liz is a better driver than Ben.
8 Ben is more patient than Liz.
9 Ben is a better dancer than Liz. / Ben dances better than Liz.
10 Liz is more intelligent than Ben.
11 Liz speaks French better than Ben. / Liz speaks better French than Ben. / Liz's French is better than Ben's.
12 Ben goes to the cinema more than Liz. / … more often than Liz.

88.2
2 You're older than her. / … than she is.
3 You work harder than me. / … than I do.
4 You watch TV more than him. / … than he does.
5 You're a better cook than me. / … than I am. *or* You cook better than me. / … than I do.
6 You know more people than us. / … than we do.
7 You've got more money than them. / … than they have.
8 You can run faster than me. / … than I can.
9 You've been here longer than her. / … than she has.
10 You got up earlier than them. / … than they did.
11 You were more surprised than him. / … than he was.

88.3
2 Jack's mother is much younger than his father.
3 My camera cost a bit more than yours. / … than your camera. *or* My camera was a bit more expensive than …
4 I feel much better today than yesterday. /… than I did yesterday. /… than I felt yesterday.
5 It's a bit warmer today than yesterday. /… than it was yesterday.
6 Sarah is a much better tennis player than me / … than I am. *or* Sarah is much better at tennis than me / … than I am. *or* Sarah plays tennis much better than me / … than I do.

UNIT 89

89.1
2 A is longer than B, but not as long as C.
3 C is heavier than A, but not as heavy as B.
4 A is older than C, but not as old as B.
5 B has got more money than C, but not as much as A. *or* … but less (money) than A.
6 C works harder than A, but not as hard as B.

89.2
2 Your room isn't as big as mine. / … as my room.
3 I didn't get up as early as you. / … as you did.
4 They didn't play as well as us. / … as we did.
5 You haven't been here as long as me. / … as I have.
6 He isn't as nervous as her. / … as she is.

89.3
2 as
3 than
4 than
5 as
6 than
7 as
8 than

89.4
2 Julia lives in the same street as Laura.
3 Julia got up at the same time as Andy.
4 Andy's car is the same colour as Laura's.

UNIT 90

90.1
2 C is longer than A.
D is the longest.
B is the shortest.
3 D is younger than C.
B is the youngest.
C is the oldest.
4 D is more expensive than A.
C is the most expensive.
A is the cheapest.
5 A is better than C.
A is the best.
D is the worst.

90.2
2 the happiest day
3 the best film
4 the most popular singer
5 the worst mistake
6 the prettiest village
7 the coldest day
8 the most boring person

90.3
2 Everest is the highest mountain in the world.
3–6
Brazil is the largest country in South America.
Alaska is the largest state in the USA.
The Nile is the longest river in Africa. / … in the world.
Jupiter is the largest planet in the solar system.

UNIT 91

91.1
2 enough chairs
3 enough paint
4 enough wind

91.2
2 The car isn't big enough.
3 His legs aren't long enough.
4 He isn't strong enough.

91.3
3 old enough
4 enough time
5 big enough
6 eat enough
7 enough space
8 tired enough
9 practise enough

91.4
2 sharp enough to cut
3 warm enough to go
4 enough bread to make
5 well enough to win
6 enough time to read

UNIT 92

92.1
2 too heavy
3 too low
4 too fast
5 too big
6 too crowded

92.2
3 enough
4 too many
5 too
6 enough
7 too much
8 enough
9 too
10 too many
11 too much

92.3
3 It's too far.
4 It's too expensive.
5 It isn't/It's not big enough.
6 It was too difficult.
7 It isn't good enough.
8 I'm too busy.
9 It was too long.

92.4
2 too early to go to bed
3 too young to get married
4 too dangerous to go out at night
5 too late to phone Sue (now)
6 too surprised to say anything

UNIT 93

93.1
3 I like this picture very much.
4 Tom started his new job last week.
5 *OK*
6 Jane bought a present for her friend. *or* Jane bought her friend a present.
7 I drink three cups of coffee every day.
8 *OK*
9 I borrowed fifty pounds from my brother.

93.2
2 I bought a new computer last week.
3 Paul finished his work quickly.
4 Emily doesn't speak French very well.
5 I did a lot of shopping yesterday.
6 Do you know London well?
7 We enjoyed the party very much.
8 I explained the problem carefully.
9 We met some friends at the airport.
10 Did you buy that jacket in England?
11 We do the same thing every day.
12 I don't like football very much.

93.3
2 I arrived at the hotel early.
3 Julia goes to Italy every year.
4 We have lived here since 1988.
5 Sue was born in London in 1980.
6 Paul didn't go to work yesterday.
7 Helen went to a wedding last weekend.
8 I had my breakfast in bed this morning.
9 Barbara is going to university in September.
10 I saw a beautiful bird in the garden this morning.
11 My parents have been to the United States many times.
12 I left my umbrella in the restaurant last night.
13 Are you going to the cinema tomorrow evening?
14 I took the children to school this morning.

UNIT 94

94.1
2 He always gets up early.
3 He's/He is never late for work.
4 He sometimes gets angry.
5 He rarely goes swimming.
6 He's/He is usually at home in the evenings.

94.2
2 Susan is always polite.
3 I usually finish work at 5 o'clock.
4 Sarah has just started a new job.
5 I rarely go to bed before midnight.
6 The bus isn't usually late.
7 I don't often eat fish.
8 I will never forget what you said.
9 Have you ever lost your passport?

10 Do you still work in the same place?
11 They always stay in the same hotel.
12 Jane doesn't usually work on Saturdays.
13 Is Tina already here?
14 What do you usually have for breakfast?
15 I can never remember his name.

94.3
2 Yes, and I also speak French.
3 Yes, and I'm also hungry.
4 Yes, and I've also been to Ireland.
5 Yes, and I also bought some books.

94.4
1 They both play football.
They're/They are both students.
They've both got cars. / They both have cars.
2 They're/They are all married.
They were all born in England.
They all live in New York.

UNIT 95

95.1
2 Do you still live in Clare Street?
3 Are you still a student?
4 Have you still got a motorbike? / Do you still have …
5 Do you still go to the cinema a lot?
6 Do you still want to be a teacher?

95.2
2 He was looking for a job.
He's/He is still looking (for a job).
He hasn't found a job yet.
3 She was asleep.
She's/She is still asleep.
She hasn't woken up yet. / She isn't awake yet. *or* She hasn't got up yet. / She isn't up yet.
4 They were having dinner. / They were eating.
They're/They are still having dinner. / … still eating.
They haven't finished (dinner) yet. / They haven't finished eating yet.

95.3
2 Is Helen here yet? *or* Has Helen arrived/come yet?
3 Have you got your (exam) results yet? / Have you had your … / Have you received your …
4 Have you decided where to go yet? / Do you know where you're going yet?

95.4
3 She's/She has already gone/left.
4 I've already got one. / I already have one.
5 I've/I have already paid (it).
6 he already knows.

UNIT 96

96.1
2 He gave it to Gary.
3 He gave them to Sarah.
4 He gave it to his sister.
5 He gave them to Robert.
6 He gave it to a neighbour.

96.2
2 I gave Joanna a plant.
3 I gave Richard a tie.
4 I gave Emma some chocolates / a box of chocolates.
5 I gave Rachel some flowers / a bunch of flowers.
6 I gave Kevin a pen.

96.3
2 Can you lend me an umbrella?
3 Can you give me your address?
4 Can you lend me twenty pounds?
5 Can you send me some information?
6 Can you show me the letter?
7 Can you get me some stamps?

96.4
2 lend you some money
3 send the letter to me
4 buy you a present
5 pass me the sugar
6 give it to her
7 showed the policeman my identity card

UNIT 97

97.1
3 I went to the window and (I) looked out.
4 I wanted to phone you, but I didn't have your number.
5 I jumped into the river and (I) swam to the other side.
6 I usually drive to work, but I went by bus this morning.
7 Do you want me to come with you, or shall I wait here?

97.2
Example answers:
2 because it was raining. / because the weather was bad.
3 but it was closed.
4 so he didn't eat anything. / so he didn't want anything to eat.
5 because there was a lot of traffic. / because the traffic was bad.
6 Sue said goodbye, got into her car and drove off/away.

97.3
Example answers:
3 I went to the cinema, **but** the film wasn't very good.
4 I went to a café **and** met some friends of mine.
5 There was a film on television, **so** I watched it.
6 I got up in the middle of the night **because** I couldn't sleep.

UNIT 98

98.1
2 When I'm tired, I like to watch TV.
3 When I phoned her, there was no answer.

4 When I go on holiday, I always go to the same place.
5 When the programme ended, I turned off the TV.
6 When I got to the hotel, there were no rooms.

98.2
2 when they heard the news
3 they went to live in New Zealand
4 while they were away
5 before they came here
6 somebody broke into the house
7 they didn't believe me

98.3
2 I finish
3 it's
4 I'll be … she leaves
5 stops
6 We'll come … we're
7 I come … I'll bring
8 I'm
9 I'll give … I go
10 I'll tell … I'm

98.4
Example answers:
2 you finish your work
3 I'm going to buy a motorbike
4 you get ready
5 I won't have much free time
6 I come back

UNIT 99

99.1
2 If you pass the exam, you'll get a certificate.
3 If you fail the exam, you can do it again.
4 If you don't want this magazine, I'll throw it away.
5 If you want those pictures, you can have them.
6 If you're busy now, we can talk later.
7 If you're hungry, we can have lunch now.
8 If you need money, I can lend you some.

99.2
2 I give
3 is
4 I'll call
5 I'll be … get
6 Will you go … they invite

99.3
Example answers:
3 … you're busy.
4 … you'll feel better in the morning.
5 … you're not watching it.
6 … she doesn't study.
7 … I'll go and see Chris.
8 … the weather is good.
9 … it rains today.

99.4
2 When
3 If
4 If
5 if
6 When
7 if
8 when … if

UNIT 100

100.1
3 wanted
4 had
5 were/was
6 didn't enjoy
7 could
8 tried
9 didn't have

100.2
3 I'd go / I would go
4 she knew
5 we had
6 you won
7 I wouldn't stay
8 we lived
9 It would be
10 the salary was/were
11 I wouldn't know
12 would you change

100.3
2 I'd watch it / I would watch it
3 we had some pictures on the wall
4 the air would be cleaner
5 every day was/were the same
6 I'd be bored / I would be bored
7 we had a bigger house / we bought a bigger house
8 we would/could buy a bigger house

100.4
Example answers:
2 I'd go to Antarctica
3 I didn't have any friends
4 I'd buy a house if I had enough money.
5 I'd try and help
6 there were no guns

UNIT 101

101.1
2 A butcher is a person who sells meat.
3 A musician is a person who plays a musical instrument.
4 A patient is a person who is ill in hospital.
5 A dentist is a person who takes care of your teeth.
6 A fool is a person who does stupid things.
7 A genius is a person who is very intelligent.
8 A liar is a person who doesn't tell the truth.

101.2
2 The woman who opened the door was wearing a yellow dress.
3 Most of the students who took the exam passed (it).
4 The policeman who stopped our car wasn't very friendly.

101.3
2 who	6 which
3 which	7 who
4 which	8 who
5 who	9 which

that *is also correct in all these sentences.*

101.4
3 … a machine **that/which** makes coffee.
4 *OK* (**which** *is also correct*)
5 … people **who/that** never stop talking.
6 *OK* (**who** *is also correct*)
7 *OK* (**that** *is also correct*)
8 … the sentences **that/which** are wrong.
9 … a car **that/which** cost £40,000.

UNIT 102

102.1
2 I've lost the pen you gave me.
3 I like the jacket Sue is wearing.
4 Where are the flowers I gave you?
5 I didn't believe the story he told us.
6 How much were the oranges you bought?

102.2
2 The meal you cooked was excellent.
3 The shoes I'm wearing aren't very comfortable.
4 The people we invited to dinner didn't come.

102.3
2 Who are the people you were talking to?
3 Did you find the keys you were looking for?
4 Where is the party you're going to?
5 What's the name of the film you were talking about?
6 What's that music you're listening to?
7 Did you get the letter you were waiting for?

102.4
2 What's the name of the restaurant where you had dinner?
3 How big is the village where you live?
4 Where exactly is the factory where you work?

UNIT 103

103.1
3 at	11 at
4 on	12 in
5 in	13 on
6 in	14 on
7 on	15 at
8 on	16 at
9 at	17 at
10 on	18 in

103.2
2 on	11 at
3 at	12 on
4 in	13 in
5 in	14 at
6 in	15 in
7 on	16 on
8 on	17 in
9 in	18 at
10 at	19 at

103.3
2 on Friday
3 on Monday
4 at 4 o'clock on Thursday / on Thursday at 4 o'clock
5 on Saturday evening
6 at 2.30 on Tuesday (afternoon) / on Tuesday (afternoon) at 2.30

103.4
2 I'll call you in three days.
3 My exam is in two weeks.
4 Tom will be here in half an hour. / … in 30 minutes.

103.5
3 in
4 – *(already complete)*
5 – *(already complete)*
6 in
7 at
8 – *(already complete)*
9 – *(already complete)*
10 on
11 in
12 at

UNIT 104

104.1
2 Alex lived in Canada **until** 1999.
3 Alex has lived in England **since** 1999.
4 Karen lived in France **until** 2003.
5 Karen has lived in Switzerland **since** 2003.
6 Clare worked in a hotel **from** 1998 **to** 2001.
7 Clare has worked in a restaurant **since** 2001.
8 Adam was a teacher **from** 1992 **to** 1998.
9 Adam has been a journalist **since** 1998.
11 Alex has lived in England for ...... years.
12 Karen has lived in Switzerland for ...... years.
13 Clare worked in a hotel for three years.
14 Clare has worked in a restaurant for ...... years.
15 Adam was a teacher for six years.
16 Adam has been a journalist for ...... years.

104.2
2 until	9 since
3 for	10 until
4 since	11 for
5 Until	12 until
6 for	13 Since
7 for	14 for
8 until	

UNIT 105

105.1
2 after lunch
3 before the end
4 during the course
5 before they went to Australia
6 during the night
7 while you are waiting
8 after the concert

105.2
3 while
4 for
5 while
6 during
7 while
8 for
9 during
10 while

105.3
2 eating
3 answering
4 having/taking
5 finishing/doing
6 going/travelling

105.4
2 John worked in a bookshop for two years after leaving school.
3 Before going to sleep, I read for a few minutes.
4 After walking for three hours, we were very tired.
5 Let's have a cup of coffee before going out.

UNIT 106

106.1
2 **In** the box.
3 **On** the box.
4 **On** the wall.
5 **At** the bus stop.
6 **In** the field.
7 **On** the balcony.

8 **In** the pool.
9 **At** the window.
10 **On** the ceiling.
11 **On** the table.
12 **At** the table.

106.2
2 in
3 on
4 in
5 on
6 at
7 in
8 in
9 at
10 at
11 in
12 at
13 on
14 at
15 **on** the wall **in** the living room

UNIT 107

107.1
2 **At** the airport.
3 **In** bed.
4 **On** a ship.
5 **In** the sky.
6 **At** a party.
7 **At** the doctor's.
8 **On** the second floor.
9 **At** work.
10 **On** a plane.
11 **In** a taxi.
12 **At** a wedding.

107.2
2 in
3 in
4 at
5 at
6 in
7 at
8 at
9 in
10 in
11 on
12 on
13 at
14 in
15 on

UNIT 108

108.1
2 to
3 in
4 to
5 in
6 to
7 to
8 in

108.2
3 to
4 to
5 **at** home … **to** work
6 at
7 – *(already complete)*
8 to
9 at
10 **at** a restaurant … **to** the hotel

108.3
2 to
3 to
4 in
5 to
6 to
7 at
8 to
9 to
10 at
11 at
12 **to** Maria's house … **at** home
13 – *(already complete)*
14 meet **at** the party… go **to** the party

108.4
1 to
2 – *(already complete)*
3 at
4 in
5 to
6 – *(already complete)*

108.5
Example answers:
2 to work
3 at work
4 to Canada
5 to parties
6 at a friend's house

UNIT 109

109.1
2 next to / beside / by
3 in front of
4 between
5 next to / beside / by
6 in front of
7 behind
8 on the left
9 in the middle

109.2
2 behind
3 above
4 in front of
5 on
6 by / next to / beside
7 below / under
8 above
9 under
10 by / next to / beside
11 opposite
12 on

109.3
2 The fountain is in front of the theatre.
3 The bank/bookshop is opposite the theatre. *or*
Paul's office is opposite the theatre. *or*
The theatre is opposite …
4 The bank/bookshop/supermarket is next to …
5 Paul's office is above the bookshop.
6 The bookshop is between the bank and the supermarket.

UNIT 110

110.1
2 Go under the bridge.
3 Go up the hill.
4 Go down the steps.
5 Go along this street.
6 Go into the hotel.
7 Go past the hotel.
8 Go out of the hotel.
9 Go over the bridge.
10 Go through the park.

110.2
2 off
3 over
4 out of
5 across
6 round/around
7 through
8 on
9 round/around
10 **into** the house **through** a window

110.3
1 out of
2 round/around
3 in
4 **from** here **to** the airport
5 round/around
6 on/over
7 over
8 out of

UNIT 111

111.1
2 on time
3 on holiday
4 on the phone
5 on television

111.2
2 by
3 with
4 about
5 on
6 by
7 at
8 on
9 with
10 **about** grammar **by** Vera P. Bull

111.3

1 with	9 at
2 without	10 by
3 by	11 about
4 about	12 by
5 at	13 on
6 by	14 with
7 on	15 by
8 with	16 by

UNIT 112

112.1
2 in
3 to
4 at
5 with
6 of

112.2
2 at
3 to
4 about
5 of
6 of
7 from/to (*You can also say* different than ...)
8 in
9 for
10 about
11 of
12 **for/about** getting angry **with** you

112.3
2 interested in going
3 good at getting
4 fed up with waiting
5 sorry for/about waking
6 Thank you for waiting.

112.4
2 Sue walked past me without speaking.
3 Don't do anything without asking me first.
4 I went out without locking the door.

112.5
Example answers:
2 I'm afraid of the dark.
3 I'm not very good at drawing.
4 I'm not interested in cars.
5 I'm fed up with living here.

UNIT 113

113.1

2 to	5 at
3 for	6 for
4 to	

113.2
2 to
3 to
4 for
5 to
6 of/about
7 for
8 on
9 to
10 for
11 to
12 – *(already complete)*
13 to
14 on
15 of/about

113.3

1 at	4 after
2 after	5 at
3 for	6 for

113.4
Example answers:
3 It depends on the programme.
4 It depends (on) what it is.
5 It depends on the weather.
6 It depends (on) how much you want.

UNIT 114

114.1
2 went in
3 looked up
4 rode off/away
5 turned round/around
6 got off
7 sat down
8 got out

114.2
2 away
3 round/around
4 going **out** ... be **back**
5 down
6 over
7 back
8 in
9 up
10 going **away** ... coming **back**

114.3
2 Hold on
3 slowed down
4 takes off
5 getting on
6 speak up
7 broken down
8 fall over / fall down
9 carry on
10 gave up
11 went off

UNIT 115

115.1
2 She took off her hat. *or* She took her hat off.
3 He put down his bag. *or* He put his bag down.
4 She picked up the magazine. *or* She picked the magazine up.
5 He put on his sunglasses. *or* He put his sunglasses on.
6 She turned off the tap. *or* She turned the tap off.

115.2
2 He put his jacket on. He put it on.
3 She took off her glasses. She took them off.
4 I picked the phone up. I picked it up.
5 They gave the key back. They gave it back.
6 We turned off the lights. We turned them off.

115.3
2 take it back
3 picked them up
4 switched it off
5 bring them back

115.4
3 knocked over
4 look it up
5 throw them away
6 tried on
7 showed me round
8 gave it up *or* gave up (*without* it)
9 fill it in
10 put your cigarette out

Key to Additional exercises

1
3 Kate is a doctor.
4 The children are asleep.
5 Gary isn't hungry.
6 The books aren't on the table.
7 The hotel is near the station.
8 The bus isn't full.

2
3 she's / she is
4 Where are
5 Is he
6 It's / It is
7 I'm/I am *or* No, I'm not. I'm a student.
8 What colour is
9 Is it
10 Are you
11 How much are they?

3
3 He's/He is having a shower.
4 Are the children playing?
5 Is it raining?
6 They're/They are coming now.
7 Why are you standing here? I'm/I am waiting for somebody.

4
4 Sam doesn't want
5 Do you want
6 Does Helen live
7 Sarah knows
8 I don't travel
9 do you usually get up
10 They don't go out
11 Tom always finishes
12 does Julia do … She works

5
3 She's/She is a student.
4 She hasn't got a car.
5 She goes out a lot.
6 She's got/She has got a lot of friends.
7 She doesn't like London.
8 She likes dancing.
9 She isn't/She's not interested in sport.

6
1 Are you married? Where do you live? Have you got / Do you have any children? How old is she?
2 How old are you? What do you do? / Where do you work? / What's your job? Do you like/enjoy your job? Have you got / Do you have a car? Do you (usually) go to work by car?
3 What's his name? / What's he called? What does he do? / What's his job? Does he live/work in London?

7
4 Sonia is 32 years old.
5 I've got / I have two sisters.
6 We often watch TV in the evening.
7 Jane never wears a hat.
8 A bicycle has got two wheels. / … has two wheels.
9 These flowers are beautiful.
10 Mary speaks German very well.

8
3 are you cooking
4 plays
5 I'm going
6 It's raining
7 I don't watch
8 we're looking
9 do you pronounce

9
2 we go
3 is shining
4 are you going
5 do you go
6 She writes
7 I never read
8 They're watching
9 She's talking
10 do you usually have
11 He's visiting
12 I don't drink

10
2 went
3 found
4 was
5 had
6 told
7 gave
8 were
9 thought
10 invited/asked

11
3 He was good at sport.
4 He played football.
5 He didn't work hard at school.
6 He had a lot of friends.
7 He didn't have a bicycle.
8 He wasn't a quiet child.

12
3 How long were you there? / How long did you stay there?
4 Did you like/enjoy Amsterdam?
5 Where did you stay?
6 Was the weather good?
7 When did you get/come back?

13
3 I forgot
4 did you get
5 I didn't speak
6 Did you have
7 he didn't go
8 she arrived
9 did Robert live
10 The meal didn't cost

14
2 were working
3 opened
4 rang … was cooking
5 heard … looked
6 was looking … happened
7 wasn't reading … was watching
8 didn't read
9 finished … paid … left
10 saw … was walking … was waiting

15
3 is playing
4 gave
5 doesn't like
6 did your parents go
7 saw … was driving
8 Do you watch
9 were you doing
10 goes
11 'm/am trying
12 didn't sleep

16
3 it's/it has just finished/ended.
4 I've/I have found them. *or* I've got them.
5 I haven't read it.
6 Have you seen her?
7 I've/I have had enough.
8 Have you (ever) been to Sweden?
9 We've/We have (just) been to the cinema.
10 They've/They have gone to a party.
11 He's/He has (just) woken up.
12 How long have you lived here? *or* … have you been living here?
13 we've/we have known each other for a long time.
14 It's/It has been raining all day. *or* It has rained all day. *or* It has been horrible/bad all day.

17
3 's/has been
4 for
5 since
6 has he lived / has he been / has he been living
7 for
8 've been/have been

18
Example answers:
3 I've just started this exercise.
4 I've met Julia a few times.
5 I haven't had dinner yet.
6 I've never been to Australia.
7 I've lived here since I was born.
8 I've lived here for three years.

19
3 bought/got
4 went
5 've/have read *or* read *or* 've/have finished with
6 haven't started (it) *or* haven't begun (it)
7 was
8 didn't see
9 left
10 's/has been
11 was
12 've/have never made

20
3 He's/He has already gone.
4 she left at 4 o'clock.
5 How many times have you been there?
6 I haven't decided yet.
7 It was on the table last night.
8 I've eaten there a few times.
9 What time did they arrive?

21
1 When was the last time? *or* When did you go the last time?
2 How long have you had it?
I bought/got it yesterday.
3 How long have you lived there / have you been there / have you been living here?
Before that we lived in Mill Road.
How long did you live in Mill Road?
4 How long have you worked there / have you been working there?
What did you do before that?
I was a taxi driver. *or* I worked as a taxi driver.

22
Example answers:
2 I didn't go out last night.
3 I was at work yesterday afternoon.
4 I went to a party a few days ago.
5 It was my birthday last week.
6 I went to America last year.

23
2 B
3 D
4 A
5 A
6 D
7 C
8 B
9 C
10 D
11 A
12 C
13 B
14 C
15 A

24
1 was damaged … be knocked down
2 was built … is used … is being painted
3 is called … be called … was changed
4 have been made … are produced

25
2 is visited
3 were damaged
4 be built
5 is being cleaned
6 be forgotten
7 has already been done
8 be kept
9 Have you ever been bitten
10 was stolen

26
2 My car was stolen last week.
3 You're/You are wanted on the phone.
4 All the bananas have been eaten.
5 The machine will be repaired.
6 We're/We are being watched.
7 The housework has to be done.

27
3 pushed
4 was pushed
5 has taken
6 is being repaired
7 invented
8 was the camera invented
9 have been washed *or* were washed
10 I've/I have washed them. *or* I washed them.
11 did they send *or* have they sent
12 be sent

28
2 B
3 A
4 C
5 B
6 C
7 C
8 B
9 B
10 A
11 B
12 C

29
1 I stayed
did you do
I watched
Are you going
I'm going
are you going to see
I don't know. I haven't decided
2 have you been
We arrived
are you staying / are you going to stay
do you like
we're having
3 I've just remembered – Karen phoned
She always phones … Did she leave
she wants
I'll phone … Do you know
I'll get
4 I'm going … Do you want
are you going
Have you ever eaten
I've been … I went
5 I've lost … Have you seen
You were wearing … I came
I'm not wearing
Have you looked / Did you look
I'll go

30
1 we met
2 we sat / we were sitting
3 We didn't know
4 we became
5 we liked
6 we spent
7 We left
8 we meet
9 has been
10 she's working
11 She's coming
12 she comes
13 we'll have / we're going to have
14 It will be

31
2 we're staying
3 we enjoyed
4 We watched
5 slept
6 I don't sleep
7 we're not doing / we're not going to do
8 we're going
9 to see
10 We haven't decided
11 wants
12 to go
13 I'll send
14 you're having
15 are working / have been working
16 he had
17 he needs
18 We've been
19 We got
20 seeing
21 I liked
22 we went
23 we left
24 had
25 he wasn't injured
26 was damaged
27 We've changed / We changed
28 we're leaving
29 We're staying / We're going to stay / We'll stay
30 flying
31 That will be / That's going to be
32 finished
33 I'll let
34 we get
35 are looking
36 We're going
37 we'll send

32
2 A
3 B
4 C
5 B
6 C
7 B
8 A
9 C
10 A
11 B
12 A
13 C
14 B
15 C
16 A
17 C
18 B

33
2 a car
3 the fridge
4 a teacher
5 school
6 the cinema
7 a taxi
8 the piano
9 computers
10 the same

34
4 **a** horse
5 **The** sky
6 **a** tourist
7 for lunch (–)
8 **the** first President of **the** United States
9 **a** watch
10 remember names (–)
11 **the** next train
12 sends emails (–)
13 **the** garden
14 **the** Majestic Hotel
15 ill last week (–) … to work (–)
16 **the** highest mountain in **the** world
17 to **the** radio … having breakfast (–)
18 like sport (–) … is basketball (–)
19 **a** doctor … **an** art teacher
20 **the** second floor … **the** top of **the** stairs … on **the** right
21 After dinner (–) … watched television (–)
22 **a** wonderful holiday in **the** south of France (–)

35
2 in
3 on
4 at
5 on
6 in
7 since
8 on
9 by
10 in
11 for
12 at
13 at
14 in
15 at
16 on
17 by
18 for … on
19 to … in
20 at … in

Key to Study guide

Present

1.1	B
1.2	A
1.3	C
1.4	A
1.5	C, D
1.6	B
1.7	D
1.8	C
1.9	C
1.10	A
1.11	C
1.12	A
1.13	D
1.14	C
1.15	A
1.16	D
1.17	C, D
1.18	A, D

Past

2.1	B
2.2	E
2.3	D
2.4	B
2.5	A
2.6	D
2.7	A
2.8	C
2.9	C

Present perfect

3.1	B, E
3.2	D
3.3	B
3.4	D
3.5	E
3.6	B
3.7	A
3.8	C
3.9	D
3.10	E

Passive

4.1	D
4.2	C
4.3	E
4.4	A
4.5	A

Verb forms

5.1	D
5.2	B

Future

6.1	A
6.2	A
6.3	C
6.4	A, B
6.5	B
6.6	C
6.7	D
6.8	C
6.9	B

Modals, imperative etc.

7.1	C, D
7.2	A, C
7.3	A
7.4	D
7.5	B
7.6	E
7.7	B, D
7.8	D
7.9	C
7.10	C
7.11	A
7.12	E

There and it

8.1	B
8.2	E
8.3	A
8.4	A
8.5	B

Auxiliary verbs

9.1	C
9.2	A
9.3	C
9.4	B
9.5	B
9.6	C
9.7	D

Questions

10.1	D
10.2	D
10.3	A
10.4	A
10.5	B
10.6	D
10.7	B
10.8	A
10.9	C, E
10.10	C
10.11	A
10.12	A, C

Reported speech

11.1	E
11.2	A, B, D

-ing and to ...

12.1	B
12.2	D
12.3	B
12.4	C
12.5	B, C
12.6	C
12.7	A
12.8	D

Go, get, do, make and have

13.1	A, D
13.2	C
13.3	C, D
13.4	A, D
13.5	B
13.6	D

Pronouns and possessives

14.1	A
14.2	C
14.3	D
14.4	B
14.5	B, C
14.6	A
14.7	E
14.8	A
14.9	D
14.10	C

A and the

15.1	C
15.2	B
15.3	A, C
15.4	B
15.5	B
15.6	A
15.7	D
15.8	C
15.9	B
15.10	B
15.11	E
15.12	D
15.13	B
15.14	A

Determiners and pronouns

16.1	C
16.2	C
16.3	B
16.4	B
16.5	C
16.6	A, C
16.7	D
16.8	B, D
16.9	A
16.10	B
16.11	E
16.12	B, D
16.13	A
16.14	A, B
16.15	D
16.16	A, C
16.17	D
16.18	B
16.19	A

Adjectives and adverbs
17.1 A
17.2 C
17.3 C
17.4 D
17.5 B
17.6 B
17.7 A, C
17.8 E
17.9 A
17.10 B
17.11 D
17.12 A
17.13 D
17.14 C

Word order
18.1 B
18.2 C
18.3 B
18.4 A
18.5 A, D

Conjunctions and clauses
19.1 C
19.2 A
19.3 D
19.4 E
19.5 B, C
19.6 A, B
19.7 B, D
19.8 A

Prepositions
20.1 D
20.2 E
20.3 C, D
20.4 B
20.5 A, D
20.6 A
20.7 B
20.8 C
20.9 B
20.10 D
20.11 D
20.12 A
20.13 C
20.14 D
20.15 A
20.16 E
20.17 C
20.18 B
20.19 D
20.20 D

Phrasal verbs
21.1 C
21.2 A, B
21.3 B

Index

The numbers are unit numbers (not page numbers).

under, behind, between etc. (prepositions)

next to / beside / between / in front of / behind

A is **next to** B. *or* A is **beside** B.
B is **between** A and C.
D is **in front of** B.
E is **behind** B.

also
A is **on the left**.
C is **on the right**.
B is **in the middle** (of the group).

up, over, under etc. (prepositions)

- Jane is going **to** France next week.
- We walked **from** the hotel **to** the station.
- A lot of English words come **from** Latin.

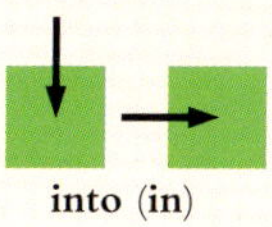

- We jumped **into** the water.
- A man came **out of** the house and got **into** a car.
- Why are you looking **out of** the window?
- I took the old batteries **out of** the radio.

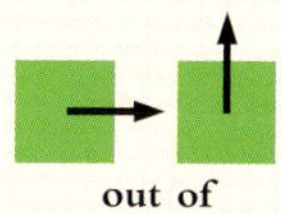

We say **put** something **in** ... (*not usually* into):
- I **put** new batteries **in** the radio.

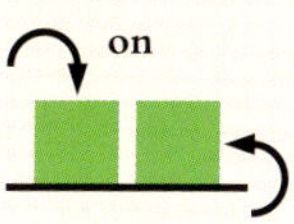

- Don't put your feet **on** the table.
- Please take your feet **off** the table.
- I'm going to hang some pictures **on** the wall.
- Be careful! Don't fall **off** your bicycle.
- We got **on** the bus in Princes Street.

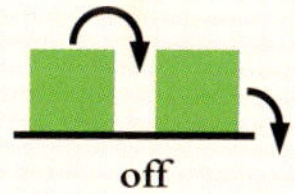

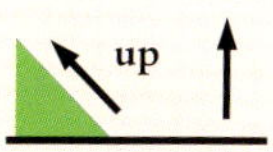

- We walked **up** the hill to the house.
- Be careful! Don't fall **down** the stairs.

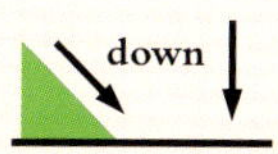

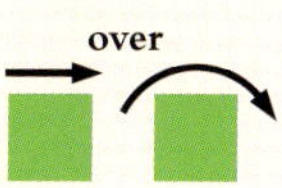

- The plane flew **over** the mountains.
- I jumped **over** the wall into the garden.
- Some people say it is unlucky to walk **under** a ladder.

am/is/are

positive

I	**am**	(I**'m**)
he she it	**is**	(he**'s**) (she**'s**) (it**'s**)
we you they	**are**	(we**'re**) (you**'re**) (they**'re**)

short form

negative

I	**am not**	(I**'m not**)
he she it	**is not**	(he**'s not** *or* he **isn't**) (she**'s not** *or* she **isn't**) (it**'s not** *or* it **isn't**)
we you they	**are not**	(we**'re not** *or* we **aren't**) (you**'re not** *or* you **aren't**) (they**'re not** *or* they **aren't**)

short forms

positive

I	**am**
he she it	**is**
we you they	**are**

question

am	I?
is	he? she? they?
are	we? you? they?

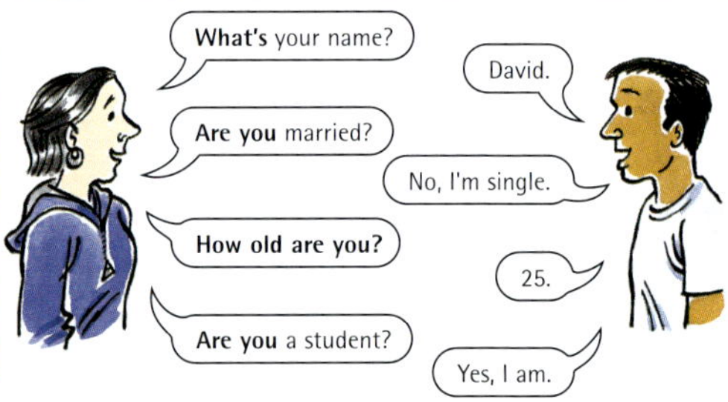

- 'Am I late?' 'No, **you're** on time.'
- '**Is your mother** at home?' 'No, **she's** out.'
- '**Are your parents** at home?' 'No, **they're** out.'
- '**Is it** cold in your room?' 'Yes, a little.'
- **Your shoes are** nice. **Are they** new?

I/me he/him they/them etc.

People

subject	**I**	**we**	**you**	**he**	**she**	**they**
object	**me**	**us**	**you**	**him**	**her**	**them**

subject	
I	**I** know Tom.
we	**We** know Tom.
you	**You** know Tom.
he	**He** knows Tom.
she	**She** knows Tom.
they	**They** know Tom.

	object
Tom knows **me**.	**me**
Tom knows **us**.	**us**
Tom knows **you**.	**you**
Tom knows **him**.	**him**
Tom knows **her**.	**her**
Tom knows **them**.	**them**

Things

subject	**it**	**they**
object	**it**	**them**

Whose is this? It's mine/yours/hers etc.

I	→	**my**	→	**mine**
we	→	**our**	→	**ours**
you	→	**your**	→	**yours**
he	→	**his**	→	**his**
she	→	**her**	→	**hers**
they	→	**their**	→	**theirs**

It's **my** money.	It's **mine**.
It's **our** money.	It's **ours**.
It's **your** money.	It's **yours**.
It's **his** money.	It's **his**.
It's **her** money.	It's **hers**.
It's **their** money.	It's **theirs**.

can

He **can play** the piano.

can + *infinitive* (**can do** / **can play** / **can come** etc.):

I/we/you/they he/she/it	**can** **can't** (**cannot**)	**do** **play** **see** **come** etc.

can	I/we/you/they he/she/it	**do?** **play?** **see?** **come?** etc.

I can do something = I *know how* to do it, or *it is possible* for me to do it:

- I **can play** the piano. My brother **can play** the piano too.
- Sarah **can speak** Italian, but she **can't speak** Spanish.
- '**Can** you **swim**?' 'Yes, but I'm not a very good swimmer.'
- '**Can** you **change** twenty pounds?' 'I'm sorry, I **can't**.'
- I'm having a party next week, but Paul and Rachel **can't come**.

a/an and the

a/an

There are *three* windows here.
a window = window 1 or 2 or 3

- I've got **a car**. (there are many cars and I've got one)
- Can I ask **a question**? (there are many questions – can I ask one?)
- Is there **a hotel** near here? (there are many hotels – is there one near here?)
- Paris is **an interesting city**. (there are many interesting cities and Paris is one)

the

There is only *one* window here – **the** window.

- I'm going to clean **the car** tomorrow. (= my car)
- Can you repeat **the question**, please? (= the question that you asked)
- We enjoyed our holiday. **The hotel** was very nice. (= our hotel)
- Paris is **the capital of France**. (there is only one capital of France)

trains(s) bus(es) (singular and plural)

The plural of a noun is usually **-s**:

singular (= one)		*plural* (= two or more)
a flower	→	some **flowers**
a train	→	two **trains**
one week	→	a few **weeks**
a nice place	→	some nice **places**
this student	→	these **students**

a flower

some **flowers**

Some plurals do *not* end in **-s**:

this **man** → these **men**	one **foot** → two **feet**	that **sheep** → those **sheep**
a **woman** → some **women**	a **tooth** → all my **teeth**	a **fish** → a lot of **fish**
a **child** → many **children**	a **mouse** → some **mice**	

old/nice/interesting etc. (adjectives)

adjective + *noun* (**nice day** / **blue eyes** etc.)

adjective	+ *noun*
It's a **nice**	**day** today.
Laura has got **brown**	**eyes**.
There's a very **old**	**bridge** in this village.
Do you like **Italian**	**food**?
I don't speak any **foreign**	**languages**.
There are some **beautiful yellow**	**flowers** in the garden.

be (**am**/**is**/**was** etc.) + *adjective*

- The weather **is nice** today.
- These flowers **are** very **beautiful**.
- **Are** you **cold**? Shall I close the window?
- **I'm hungry**. Can I have something to eat?
- The film **wasn't** very **good**. It **was boring**.
- Please **be quiet**. I'm reading.

look/**feel**/**smell**/**taste**/**sound** + *adjective*

the oldest the most expensive

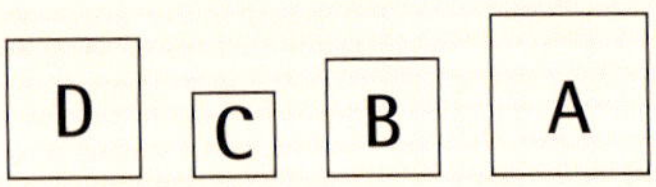

Box A is **bigger than** Box B.

Box A is **bigger than** all the other boxes.
Box A is **the biggest** box.

Bigger / **older** / **more expensive** etc. are *comparative* forms.
Biggest / **oldest** / **most expensive** etc. are *superlative* forms.

I do/work/like etc. (present simple)

positive

I we you they	**work** **like** **do** **have**
he she it	**works** **likes** **does** **has**

negative

<table>
<tr><td>I
we
you
they</td><td>don't
(do not)</td><td rowspan="2">work
like
do
have</td></tr>
<tr><td>he
she
it</td><td>doesn't
(does not)</td></tr>
</table>

We use the present simple for things that are true in general, or for things that happen sometimes or all the time:

- I **like** big cities.
- Your English is good. You **speak** very well.
- Tim **works** very hard. He **starts** at 7.30 and **finishes** at 8 o'clock in the evening.
- The earth **goes** round the sun.
- We **do** a lot of different things in our free time.
- It **costs** a lot of money to build a hospital.
- I **drink** coffee, but I **don't drink** tea.
- Sue **drinks tea**, but she **doesn't drink** coffee.
- You **don't work** very hard.
- We **don't watch** television very often.
- The weather is usually nice. It **doesn't rain** very often.
- Gary and Nicole **don't know** many people.

Questions **do/does** + *subject* + *infinitive*

	Do	you	**work**	on Sundays?
	Do	your friends	**live**	near here?
	Does	Chris	**play**	tennis?
Where	**do**	your parents	**live?**	
How often	**do**	you	**wash**	your hair?
What	**does**	this word	**mean?**	
How much	**does**	it	**cost**	to fly to Rome?

I am doing (present continuous)

am/is/are + **-ing** = something is happening *now:*

I'm working
she**'s wearing** a hat
they**'re playing** football
I'm not watching television

past — *now* — *future*

- Please be quiet. **I'm working**. (= I'm working now)
- Look, there's Sarah. She**'s wearing** a brown coat. (= she is wearing it now)
- The weather is nice. It**'s not raining**.
- 'Where are the children?' 'They**'re playing** in the park.'
- *(on the phone)* We**'re having** dinner now. Can I phone you later?
- You can turn off the television. **I'm not watching** it.

I'm going to ...

I'm going to do something

She **is going to watch** TV this evening.

We use **am/is/are going to** ... for the *future:*

I	**am**	(not) **going to**	do ...
he/she/it	**is**		drink ...
we/you/they	**are**		watch ...

am	I	**going to**	buy ... ?
is	he/she/it		eat ... ?
are	we/you/they		wear ... ?

worked/got/went etc. (past simple)

They **watch** television every evening. *(present simple)*

They **watched** television yesterday evening. *(past simple)*

watched is the *past simple:*

I/we/you/they he/she/it	**watched**

We use **did** in past simple negatives and questions:

infinitive

play
start
watch
have
see
do
go

positive

I	**played**
we	**started**
you	**watched**
they	**had**
he	**saw**
she	**did**
it	**went**

negative

I		play
we		start
you		watch
they	**did not (didn't)**	have
he		see
she		do
it		go

question

	I	play?
	we	start?
	you	watch?
did	they	have?
	he	see?
	she	do?
	it	go?

- I **played** tennis yesterday, but I **didn't win**.
- '**Did** you **do** the shopping?' 'No, I **didn't have** time.'
- We **went** to the cinema, but we **didn't enjoy** the film.

Questions

	did +	*subject* +	*infinitive*	
	Did	your sister	**phone**	you?
What	**did**	you	**do**	last night?
How	**did**	the accident	**happen**?	
Where	**did**	your parents	**go**	for their holiday?

Short answers

Yes,	I/we/you/they he/she/it	**did**.

No,	I/we/you/they he/she/it	**didn't**.

- '**Did you** see Joe yesterday?' 'No, **I didn't.**'
- '**Did it** rain on Sunday?' 'Yes, **it did.**'
- '**Did Helen** come to the party?' 'No, **she didn't.**'
- '**Did your parents** have a good holiday?' 'Yes, **they did.**'

a bottle / some water (countable/uncountable)

A noun can be *countable* or *uncountable*.

Countable nouns

For example: (a) **car** (a) **man** (a) **bottle** (a) **house** (a) **key** (an) **idea** (an) **accident**

You can use **one**/**two**/**three** (etc.) + *countable nouns* (you can count them):

one **bottle**

two **bottles**

three **men**

four **houses**

Countable nouns can be *singular* (= one) or *plural* (= two or more):

singular	**a car**	**the car**	**my car** etc.		
plural	**cars**	**two cars**	**the cars**	**some cars**	**many cars** etc.

Uncountable nouns

For example: **water** **air** **rice** **salt** **plastic** **money** **music** **tennis**

water

salt

money

music

You can't say **one**/**two**/**three** (etc.) + these things: ~~one water~~ ~~two musics~~

Uncountable nouns have only *one* form:
money the **money** my **money** some **money** much **money** etc.

I have ... and I've got ...

You can say **I have** or **I've got**, **he has** or **he's got**:

I we you they	**have**	*or*	I we you they	**have got**	(I**'ve got**) (we**'ve got**) (you**'ve got**) (they**'ve got**)
he she it	**has**	*or*	he she it	**has got**	(he**'s got**) (she**'s got**) (it**'s got**)

short form

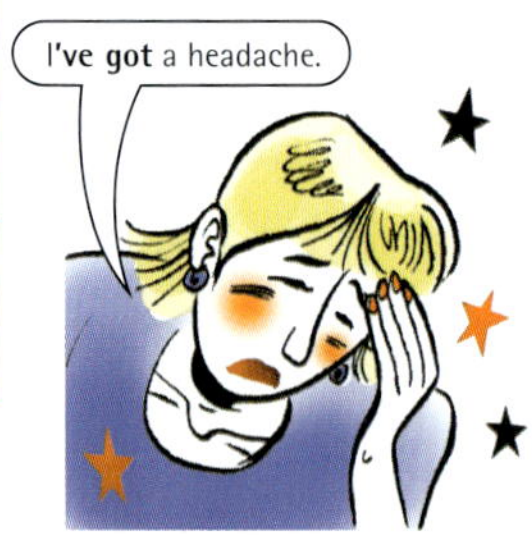

List of irregular verbs

infinitive	*past simple*	*past participle*
be	**was/were**	**been**
beat	**beat**	**beaten**
become	**became**	**become**
begin	**began**	**begun**
bite	**bit**	**bitten**
blow	**blew**	**blown**
break	**broke**	**broken**
bring	**brought**	**brought**
build	**built**	**built**
buy	**bought**	**bought**
catch	**caught**	**caught**
choose	**chose**	**chosen**
come	**came**	**come**
cost	**cost**	**cost**
cut	**cut**	**cut**
do	**did**	**done**
draw	**drew**	**drawn**
drink	**drank**	**drunk**
drive	**drove**	**driven**
eat	**ate**	**eaten**
fall	**fell**	**fallen**
feel	**felt**	**felt**
fight	**fought**	**fought**
find	**found**	**found**
fly	**flew**	**flown**
forget	**forgot**	**forgotten**
get	**got**	**got**
give	**gave**	**given**
go	**went**	**gone**
grow	**grew**	**grown**
hang	**hung**	**hung**
have	**had**	**had**
hear	**heard**	**heard**
hide	**hid**	**hidden**
hit	**hit**	**hit**
hold	**held**	**held**
hurt	**hurt**	**hurt**
keep	**kept**	**kept**
know	**knew**	**known**
leave	**left**	**left**
lend	**lent**	**lent**

infinitive	*past simple*	*past participle*
let	**let**	**let**
lie	**lay**	**lain**
light	**lit**	**lit**
lose	**lost**	**lost**
make	**made**	**made**
mean	**meant**	**meant**
meet	**met**	**met**
pay	**paid**	**paid**
put	**put**	**put**
read (reed)*	**read** (red)*	**read** (red)*
ride	**rode**	**ridden**
ring	**rang**	**rung**
rise	**rose**	**risen**
run	**ran**	**run**
say	**said**	**said**
see	**saw**	**seen**
sell	**sold**	**sold**
send	**sent**	**sent**
shine	**shone**	**shone**
shoot	**shot**	**shot**
show	**showed**	**shown**
shut	**shut**	**shut**
sing	**sang**	**sung**
sit	**sat**	**sat**
sleep	**slept**	**slept**
speak	**spoke**	**spoken**
spend	**spent**	**spent**
stand	**stood**	**stood**
steal	**stole**	**stolen**
swim	**swam**	**swum**
take	**took**	**taken**
teach	**taught**	**taught**
tear	**tore**	**torn**
tell	**told**	**told**
think	**thought**	**thought**
throw	**threw**	**thrown**
understand	**understood**	**understood**
wake	**woke**	**woken**
wear	**wore**	**worn**
win	**won**	**won**
write	**wrote**	**written**

* *pronunciation*

Essential Grammar in Use
Grammar Reference

Raymond Murphy

Contents

For further practice:
Essential Grammar in Use Supplementary Exercises
Helen Naylor with Raymond Murphy

Essential Grammar in Use CD ROM
Helen Naylor with Raymond Murphy